…with the fist-
…sts. He was

Francis Beckett … …t his fine jour-
nalist's pen nor cloud his judgement and integrity; but the pain
shines through. He writes with compelling candour about his
father. It is as moving for the reader as it must have been painful
for the author.

Alastair Stewart OBE, *ITV News*

The youngest Labour MP in 1925, by 1940 John Beckett was in
prison as a danger to the war effort. His son has written a coura-
geously honest, moving and sensitive account of a socialist who
ended up despising the workers, a Jew who ended up hating Jews,
a democrat who became contemptuous of democracy. It is a pene-
trating analysis of the political times in which he lived, not least
because it illuminates the conditions that can – if freedom is not
strong, vigilant and purposeful – breed bigotry and fascism. It is a
valuable history as well as an instructive biography.

Neil Kinnock, *Leader of the Labour Party 1983–92*

A fascinating insight into the unsavoury practices of the security
services, and a moving portrait of a talented, wayward father who
denied his Jewishness at great cost to himself and all around him.

Paul Routledge, *political biographer and commentator for the*
Daily Mirror *and* Tribune *magazine, UK*

John Beckett was a Labour MP who later took up with fascism. In
Fascist in the Family his son Francis, journalist, historian and playwright, engages in the difficult task of tracing his father's tempestu-
ous and ultimately unfulfilled life. His readable, well-researched,
questioning and honest biography serves as a British equivalent of
My Nazi Legacy.

Colin Holmes, *Emeritus Professor of History,*
University of Sheffield, UK

FASCIST IN THE FAMILY

John Beckett was a rising political star. Elected as Labour's youngest MP in 1924, he was constantly in the news and tipped for greatness. But ten years later he was propaganda chief for Mosley's fascists, and one of Britain's three best-known anti-Semites. Yet his mother, whom he loved, was a Jew. Her ancestors were Solomons, Isaacs and Jacobsons, originally from Prussia. He successfully hid his Jewish ancestry all his life – he said his mother's family were "fisher folk from the east coast". His son, the author of this book, acclaimed political biographer and journalist Francis Beckett, did not discover the truth until John Beckett had been dead for years. John Beckett left Mosley and founded the National Socialist League with William Joyce, later Lord Haw-Haw, and spent the war years in prison, considered a danger to the war effort. For the rest of his life, and all of Francis Beckett's childhood, John Beckett and his family were closely watched by the security services. Their devious machinations, traced in records only recently released, damaged chiefly his young family.

This is a fascinating and brutally honest account of a troubled man in turbulent times.

Francis Beckett is an author, journalist, playwright and contemporary historian. His eighteen books include biographies of four Prime Ministers, the first of which is about his own political hero, Clement Attlee. He has written for several national newspapers, but mostly for the *Guardian*, for which he was a regular feature writer and reviewer for many years. His plays have been performed on radio and at the London Fringe. He is a former president of the National Union of Journalists and a Labour Party and trade union press officer and editor, and is currently editor of *Third Age Matters*, the national magazine published by the University of the Third Age.

Routledge Studies in Fascism and the Far Right
Series editors: Nigel Copsey, *Teesside University*, and
Graham Macklin, *Teesside University*

This book series examines fascist, far right and right-wing politics
within a historical context. Fascism falls within the far right but the
far right also extends to so-called 'radical-right populism'. Boundaries
are not fixed and it is important to recognise points of convergence
and exchange with the mainstream right.

The series will include books with a broad thematic or biographi-
cal focus suitable for students, teachers and general readers. These will
be available in hardback, paperback and e-book. The series will also
include books aimed largely at subject specialists which will appear in
hardback and e-book format only.

Titles include:

FASCIST IN THE FAMILY

The tragedy of
John Beckett MP

Francis Beckett

Routledge
Taylor & Francis Group

LONDON AND NEW YORK

First published 2017
by Routledge
2 Park Square, Milton Park, Abingdon, Oxon OX14 4RN

and by Routledge
711 Third Avenue, New York, NY 10017

Routledge is an imprint of the Taylor & Francis Group, an informa business

British Library Cataloguing in Publication Data
A catalogue record for this book is available from the British
Library

Library of Congress Cataloging in Publication Data
Names: Beckett, Francis, 1945– author.
Title: Fascist in the family : the tragedy of John Beckett M.P. /
Francis Beckett.
Other titles: Rebel who lost his cause
Description: Milton Park, Abingdon, Oxon ; New York, NY :
Routledge, 2017. | Includes bibliographical references.
Identifiers: LCCN 2016012317| ISBN 9781138907669 (hardback) |
ISBN 9781138907874 (paperback) | ISBN 9781315686738 (e-book)
Subjects: LCSH: Beckett, John, 1894–1964. | Great Britain–Politics
and government–1910–1936. | Great Britain–Politics and
government–1936–1945. | Fascism–Great Britain–History–
20th century. | Right-wing extremists–Great Britain–Biography. |
British Union of Fascists–Biography. | Political prisoners–Great
Britain–Biography. | Politicians–Great Britain–Biography. | World
War, 1939–1945–Great Britain.
Classification: LCC DA566.9.B375 B43 2017 | DDC 941.082092
[B] –dc23
LC record available at https://lccn.loc.gov/2016012317

ISBN: 978-1-138-90766-9 (hbk)
ISBN: 978-1-138-90787-4 (pbk)
ISBN: 978-1-315-68673-8 (ebk)

Typeset in Bembo
by Wearset Ltd, Boldon, Tyne and Wear

CONTENTS

INTRODUCTION

John Beckett was just 30 when he became Labour's youngest MP in 1924, and he was seen as one of the Party's brightest rising stars. He was on intimate terms with the greatest political names in the land, as well as the friend and confidant of all those who, two decades later, were to run the 1945 government, especially its Prime Minister, Clement Attlee.

By 1929 he had become the most extreme, most newsworthy left-wing Labour rebel of his day. He was more than once physically thrown out of the House of Commons, and in 1930 he seized the Mace from the Speaker's table and ran off with it, the first person to do so since Cromwell.

In the early 1930s he managed London's Strand Theatre, knew all the leading actors of his day, made money and went bankrupt.

And then he became a fascist. His career, which had looked so promising in 1924, ended in the squalid wastelands of neo-Nazi politics, and in prison for nearly four years, for fascists were interned during the war.

It's the stuff of fiction, and at least two popular novels contain characters based on him. In 1922 Mary Agnes Hamilton modelled one of her political agitators in her novel *Follow My Leader* on the young John Beckett. Nearly a century later, Carmody in Anthony Quinn's 2015 novel *Curtain Call* is based on him.

Which is quite suitable, because the father I knew was a bit of a fantasist, though his image of himself would be rather more heroic than Mr Quinn's Carmody. Perhaps a clean-cut hero from another age taken out of one of his beloved G.A. Henty novels; perhaps a John Buchan hero; perhaps Flambeau, looking for his Father Brown (and eventually, as we shall see, finding him).

And his own life, as he chose to present it, was largely fantasy too. It was not so much that he made things up: he only did that occasionally, and always obeyed his own rule of giving his fiction some characteristics of the truth. It was more that he edited his life. His version, as he wrote it in his memoirs in 1938 and as he told it to me, contained heroic highlights. Researching this book has given me the chance to find out the truth about my father.

The biggest lie, the strangest, the most important and inexplicable lie, was about the fundamental question of who he was. He talked of his "yeoman ancestors", the generations of Cheshire farmers from which he had sprung. In the 1930s he embraced anti-Semitism and complained of "alien control of our country".

But he was a Jew. His mother was a thoroughbred: born Eva Solomon of a union between Mark Solomon and Jessy Isaacs. It has taken me years to find out, for she, and later he, went to great lengths to hide it.

I was born in May 1945, four days after VE day and a little more than a year after the Home Secretary released my father from prison, in the small Berkshire village of Chenies, 21 miles from the centre of London. It was exactly that distance because the dangerous fascist John Beckett was still under a sort of house arrest, not allowed to travel more than five miles from his home or within 20 miles of London.

He died when I was 19, and, in the late 1990s, I wrote a book about his life, *The Rebel Who Lost His Cause*. It wasn't a bad book – several people were kind enough to say it was rather a good one – but I have come to see that it did not nail the man or the history through which he lived, it did not face up to what he did and said and wrote, and it did not tell the end of the story – my part of the story – properly.

It accepted, by and large, what he wrote in 1938 in his unpublished memoirs, and these were as reliable as the man. That is to say, where they misled, they kept in the vague vicinity of the truth, but they contained what he wanted the world to know about himself.

There was no mention – not even a word – of either of his first two wives, even when describing events at which they were not only present, but active participants. He just wrote them out of his history.

But does it matter? I have disinterred it once. Why not let my father rest in peace, even though resting in peace was always the very last thing he ever wished to do?

There are several reasons.

First, my contemporaries, unlike my father's, grew up knowing that racism was something dreadful, for its results were part of our childhood. That memory ensured that most of us managed to avoid blaming people of another race for our troubles. But knowledge decays. The conditions that bred fascism are returning, and we are governed by a generation which knows little of the holocaust.

The historian Richard Griffiths puts it well:

> Most people, when they wake up in the morning, look in the mirror and say to themselves "I am all right; my attitudes and actions are justified." And then some of those people go out and do, or get involved in, dreadful things. My aim, throughout, has been to try and work out such people's reasons for action, or the justifications they make to themselves. Only thereby can we learn how to deal with such people and attitudes in the future.

My father was a racist and an anti-Semite. But – and I apologise to no one for saying this – he was not a bad man. In many ways he was a rather attractive character, as the late Fenner Brockway, among others, confirmed to me. How does such a man do the things he did?

Second, when I wrote the first book, I was not ready to write about my own dysfunctional childhood. My father, without wishing to, damaged the lives of those whom he loved and wanted to protect – his three wives, his four children, his brother. My earlier book did not tell the reader what it was like to grow up with a father who had rendered himself an outcast.

Third, for much of his life, my father was in prison, under house arrest or under constant surveillance by MI5.

Some of this was right and necessary. But if we give the state the right to override our liberties, we should always examine whether the security services and the politicians confine themselves to what is right and necessary; and be ready to nail the moments when they start to misuse their power, to enjoy them, to use them to settle scores.

There are a lot more security files open than there were in the late 1990s. Throughout my early life, long after there was any conceivable security reason for it, the security services were opening all my parents' letters, monitoring and laboriously transcribing their phone calls, following them about. My father knew it. It helped make him mad.

It gives me now the extraordinary experience of seeing my own childhood from the vantage point of the man in a grubby raincoat leaning against the lamp post, the spy opening letters and finding personal secrets. I can see things as Graham Mitchell of MI5 saw them. And Mr Mitchell, as we shall see, was something of a voyeur.

At a time when a new national emergency is leading to demands from the security services for more curtailment of our liberties as the price of our security, we should want to look closely at how they have used these powers in the past. I am in a unique position to shed a little light on that.

Fourth, this book will have been worth the trouble of writing if it helps explain John Beckett's extraordinary political journey, without falling into the trap – which a few readers felt the first book fell into – of becoming his apologia. It makes fascism and racism no less dreadful – in fact, perhaps it makes them worse – to see how they can sometimes come out of abused and distorted idealism.

Which brings me, fifth and finally, to the hardest question of all. Part of that journey led to anti-Semitism. It is a strange enough destination for a man who once genuinely championed the underdog, but almost inexplicable when you have discovered that his mother, whom he loved, was a Jew. He hid his Jewishness all his life, from me and from everyone else. No wonder he was unstable. I cannot explain thoroughly; but I offer here the best answers I can.

Acknowledgements and sources

As before, my greatest debt is to Professor Colin Holmes of Sheffield University, whose books include *Anti-Semitism in British Society* and, most recently, the definitive biography of William Joyce, for his wise advice and generosity with his knowledge and contacts.

Colin has been supportive of this book from the start. He has read and commented on great chunks of it, giving wise counsel and saving me from some errors and superficial conclusions, as well as letting me read his fine new book *Searching for Lord Haw-Haw* before publication.

Other writers, researchers and academics have helped me too. Some of them came to consult me and ended up telling me more than I told them. Dr Graham Macklin, now of Teesside University and the top expert on British fascism post 1945 and author of *Very Deeply Died in Black*, certainly falls into this category.

Richard Griffiths, whose *Patriotism Perverted* I have used extensively, has generously allowed me to make use of parts of his forthcoming book, *What Did You Do in the War?*

I'm grateful to Jonathan Croall and Dr Rose Merkin for their expertise on theatre history, as well as Stephen Dorril, the late David Englander, Simon Fowler, Jeremy Gibson, Professor David Howell, Jeanette Rosenberg, the late Professor Brian Simpson, Alan Slingsby, Peta Steel, Nigel Todd and David Turner.

For the title I have to thank my old American friend, the actor turned publisher Kelly Monaghan (known to his British friends as Ed Monaghan). This is not the first time I have been grateful for his inspired contributions to my literary efforts.

My editors at Routledge, Craig Fowlie and Emma Chappell, have been constantly supportive and helpful, and I have been able to make use of Craig's deep knowledge of the period and the subject.

I always find archivists a pleasure to deal with. They take their role as the guardians of history very seriously, and try hard to help people like me to understand their holdings. This book has benefitted from the kindness and professional expertise of Jacky Hodgson at Sheffield University, which houses the British Union of Fascists archive as well as my father's papers, Lizzie Richmond at Bath University, which holds A.K. Chesterton's papers, and especially the late Monty Kolsky, volunteer archivist at the Board of Deputies of British Jews.

For the original book, back in the 1990s, the Society of Authors gave me a generous grant from one of their funds, without which I could not then have cleared enough time. Without these funds, many important books would not get written, because the economics of publishing means that writers cannot be paid enough to keep their families while they are writing them.

The Board of Deputies of British Jews opened their archives for me and gave me every help, which is quite impressive really, all things considered. The Friends of Oswald Mosley helped me, even though they knew they were not going to like the result of my efforts, and I thank them sincerely for it, especially the late John Warburton and the late Bob Row.

Senior politicians who knew my father helped me, though some of them guarded their secrets. They are all dead now, but I record my gratitude to Fenner Brockway, Barbara Castle, Denis Healey and Michael Foot. Others who knew my father, and talked helpfully to me, but are no longer with us, include Revd Brendan Fox AA, Douglas Hyde and Colin Jordan.

I am enormously grateful to Patric Dickinson (Robert Forgan's grandson), Bob Edmonds (Harry Edmonds's son), Valerie Forgan (Robert Forgan's daughter), Edward Greene (Ben Greene's nephew), Martin Jameson (Sylvia Morris's adopted son), Heather Joyce (William Joyce's daughter), Daphne Stone (who knew Harry Edmonds well), Jeffrey Wallder (for insights into Mosley's organisations) and Lesley von Goetz (Ben Greene's daughter).

Patric Dickinson, as well as discussing his grandfather with me, used his professional expertise to track down my grandmother.

For this new edition I have made much more use of my own family, especially Richard Knowles, my second cousin and the Beckett family's historian, and of Jean Davenport's comprehensive family tree. Peter Holford, on my mother's side, helped with the Holfords and Cutmores.

My late aunt, Mrs Jo Carter, provided several valuable new insights. My sister Clare Beckett has helped enormously, and kindly read and commented upon several drafts. My late half-sister

Lesley Beckett contributed knowledge, understanding and common sense.

The key sources for this book are John Beckett's memoirs, covering the period 1918–38, written in 1938, plus a short account of his first days in prison written soon after the Second World War; and my own memories of what he and my mother Anne Cutmore told me. I have become quite good at knowing which parts of all this are reliable, and which are not. I have also had access to Colin Holmes's John Beckett file.

When information comes from one of these sources, I have not referenced it.

Neither have I referenced sources when they are newspaper cuttings, instead generally naming the publication in the text. And I have not referenced it when the source is an interview – I hope this is generally clear from the text.

At the end of each chapter there is a note on other sources used in that chapter – books, theses, academic articles, letters.

I have deposited John Beckett's memoirs, most of his few remaining books, the small number of papers he left and his bound volumes of some of the publications he edited, in the library of Sheffield University; and together with other papers collected by the university, they constitute the John Beckett collection. With them I have left my own research for this book, including my notes, and copies of documents from the Public Record Office and other places.

1

EVA SOLOMON AND THE YEOMEN OF CHESHIRE

When Shylock's daughter Jessica ran off with a Christian, she took her father's precious jewels. That, says Howard Jacobson in his analysis of *The Merchant of Venice*, was the unforgivable crime. Yes, take the lover of whom your father disapproves; yes, take the lover who despises your family's religion, if that is the lover you want; but don't steal. That is what Jessica did.

I think it is also what my Jewish grandmother did. She was declared dead by her orthodox Jewish family for marrying my grandfather, William Beckett, on 18 September 1893, at St James's Church in Islington, north London, according to the rites of the Established Church. None of her family attended her wedding. So far as anyone knows, she never saw any of them again.

She was born Eva Solomon, but the name in her marriage certificate is Eva Dorothy Salmon. Her father was named as Mark Salmon; his real name was Mark Solomon, and all her brothers and sisters called themselves Solomon. For good measure, she lied about her age too: she was born in 1868, not 1869. This may have been so that she would appear to be a few months younger than her husband, when in fact she was a few months older.

William turned out to be useless with money. But Dorothy, as her husband and sons always referred to her, had a small supply of jewels which she sold or pawned whenever his rash investments or spendthrift ways brought another crisis. They had been her father's – Mark Solomon was a jeweller by trade. Perhaps, like Jessica, she stole them. Perhaps one of her family slipped them to her as a goodbye gift.

I never knew any of this when I was a child. All families have secrets, and the one my family buried deepest was that my grandmother was Jewish.

When I was in my thirties, and my father was long dead, I found a telephone number for my much older half-sister Lesley, the daughter of my father's first wife (my mother was his third wife). I had not seen her since I was a baby, I think now because she knew too many of the family secrets.

"What I could never understand about our father," Lesley told me the first day we met, "was how he could make speeches against the Jews when he loved his mother so much." Then she looked at me and said: "You know she was Jewish, don't you?"

The more I research my father, the more I find that his life, as he told it to me, was full of carefully guarded secrets. There was, I realise, a reason why I almost never, in my father's lifetime, met any of his relatives. They would have told me things he didn't want me to know. Lesley, born in 1920, was around before John started to move in fiercely anti-Semitic circles.

He once told me that cunning Jews would change their names to hide their origins. I am fairly sure he even said: if you meet someone called Salmon, you are probably talking to a Jew whose real name is Solomon or Salaman. Did he intend me to work it out from there?

Well, it took a while. But now, thanks to the generous and clever Patric Dickinson of the College of Arms, I know that Eva was the seventh of nine children born to Mark Solomon and his wife, born Jessy Isaacs, the daughter of Solomon Isaacs.

Eva's older siblings were Isaac, Charles, Bilhah, Hyam, Myer and Phoebe. After her came Edward and Benjamin. And changing her name seems to have been a family tradition, for her father Mark Solomon was born Mark Jacobson, the son of Isaac Jacobson and his wife Eve Solomon. Isaac Jacobson was born in Fordon in the

Prussian province of Posen, now part of Poland. He was naturalised in 1854, when he was a jeweller in Oxford Street. Mark followed him into this trade.

So what about the jewels? Perhaps Lesley heard the story from Eva. Perhaps John himself once felt able to tell it, before he became an anti-Semite and his Jewishness became a shameful secret. My father was quite capable of annexing a romantic fable and attaching it to himself, and he knew *The Merchant of Venice* well.

I knew John's mother died in 1932, because after his death I found a faded photograph of an elderly, dignified lady, on the back of which my father had written: "Daddy's mother, died 1932."

He never stopped loving her. He was, I think, more bereft than he knew after her early death, which helps to explain some of his most incomprehensible decisions, which were taken soon after her death. My own mother's given names were Doris Anne, but he always called her Dorothy Anne. I think she was supposed to be pleased. Whether she was or not, I have no idea.

My father went to a lot of trouble to hide his mother's Jewishness. Her family, he wrote in 1938 in his autobiography, were "fisher folk on the east coast".

One of the pieces of wisdom John picked up in a turbulent life, and passed on to me, was that while it is of course better always to tell the truth, if you have to lie, you should give your lie as many elements of the truth as possible. It helps to keep track of it. And, indeed, census records show that Eva's father Mark Solomon was brought up partly by his mother in Ramsgate, where she seems to have had relatives. Ramsgate is a fishing town on the east coast.

When people started to suspect that she was Jewish, my father blustered. It worked. During his lifetime the truth was suppressed. Three decades after he died, I placed in the public domain my beloved father's most closely guarded secret. I wonder whether he would think I betrayed him. Perhaps I have.

Poor Eva. Whatever she felt about her treatment at the hands of her family, she surely could never in her worst nightmares have imagined that her oldest son, for whom she had scrimped and saved and pawned (perhaps sold) her father's jewels, would one day be

among the three best-known anti-Semites in Britain, alongside
William Joyce and Oswald Mosley.

Eva was tall and slim, with a huge mass of golden hair, and by all
accounts heart-rendingly beautiful. That picture, the only surviving
picture of her, shows a lady of 60 or so, her face already marked by the
pain of the breast cancer that was to kill her at 62, but you can catch a
glimpse of the grace and dignity which was to endure in the minds of
both her sons for as long as they lived. John's love for her was, I think,
almost too great for him to bear. "If a boy really loves his mother, he'll
choose a woman just like her", John would say, though his own
attempts to do this were not marked with conspicuous success.

John's father William had a dark Victorian secret of his own. William
was short, thick-set and emphatic, and John, born on 11 October the
year following their marriage, had little affection for him. William held
Conservative political opinions and prided himself on his Englishness
and his patriotism. He was at one point chairman of the election committee for the Conservative MP for Hammersmith, Sir William Bull.

William was the oldest of the 11 children of a Cheshire farmer,
another John Beckett. My father talked proudly of his "yeoman
ancestry", a phrase which was starting to sound very odd by the
1960s. Ah, the Yeomen of Olde England, as written about by one of
John's favourite poets, G.K. Chesterton. "The Becketts, Billingtons
and Warburtons had lived, farmed and intermarried in that part of
Cheshire for generations", wrote my father.

Well, up to a point, Lord Copper. Richard Knowles, grandson of
William's youngest sister, has been researching his family history, and
he found something quite odd about the farmer and his wife who
were his great grandparents as well as mine.

It was not just that Hannah Beckett, nee Warburton, was just 18 at
the time of her marriage in June 1868, or that she was already seven
months pregnant, though that was a dreadful scandal in rural Victorian
England, or that they were married in Warrington, way outside their
own area, for that was simply explained: the two young people must
have been sent away to get married secretly, because of the bride's
pregnancy, which would have caused a scandal in their own area.

But what made Richard sit up and take notice was that Hannah's
mother was born Hannah Wood, and her husband's mother was born

Jane Wood. Jane and the older Hannah were sisters. So John and the younger Hannah were first cousins. Marriage between first cousins had been actively discouraged by the Synod of the Church of England in 1853, and all the families concerned were devout members of the Church of England.

Hannah's mother Hannah died aged 34 when her daughter was only three, and the younger Hannah was brought up by the third Wood sister, Sarah, and her husband, William Billington. It was in William and Sarah Billington's house, then, that 21-year-old John Beckett met 17-year-old Hannah Warburton and they did the deed that young men and young women like to do together.

When their son was born – my grandfather, William Beckett, the result of this activity – the decision seems to have been made that he, like his mother, would be brought up by William and Sarah Billington, and it is in their house that we find him in the next census.

John and Hannah went on to have ten more children, two of them profoundly deaf, whom they brought up themselves in their own home; but William seems to have been treated differently, to have been left some of William Billington's money and to have been encouraged to go out into the world and try his luck, while the other ten stayed in the farming community their parents knew.

Someone, whether his own parents or the Billingtons, decided that William Beckett should become a draper, which seems to have been their idea of placing him on the first rung of the ladder which led to gentility.

Eva Dorothy's family seems to have thought the same, and William and Dorothy met when they were both being turned into lower-middle-class gentlefolk in a draper's shop. Their older son, my father, John Beckett, was born on 11 October 1894.

William tended to take his enthusiasms too far, a family trait which his son inherited with devastating effect; and William was very enthusiastic about his patriotism. He called his second son, born in 1899 at the start of the Boer War, Cecil Rhodes Beckett, a burden my unfortunate Uncle Cecil had to carry for the next 81 years, alongside the burden of his older brother's fame and then notoriety.

John grew up in an atmosphere of lower-middle-class jingoism, learning his poetry from Rudyard Kipling and his history from G.A.

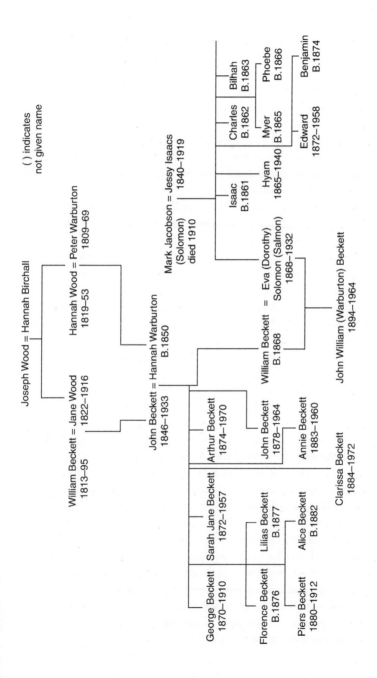

( ) indicates
not given name

Joseph Wood = Hannah Birchall

William Beckett = Jane Wood
1813–95   1822–1916

Hannah Wood = Peter Warburton
1819–53   1809–69

John Beckett = Hannah Warburton
1846–1933   B.1850

Mark Jacobson = Jessy Isaacs
(Solomon)   1840–1919
died 1910

William Beckett = Eva (Dorothy)
B.1868   Solomon (Salmon)
                  1868–1932

Isaac   Hyam
B.1861   1865–1940

Charles   Myer
B.1862   B.1865

Bilhah   Phoebe
B.1863   B.1866

Edward   Benjamin
1872–1958 B.1874

John William (Warburton) Beckett
1894–1964

George Beckett   Sarah Jane Beckett
1870–1910   1872–1957

Arthur Beckett
1874–1970

John Beckett
1878–1964

Annie Beckett
1883–1960

Clarissa Beckett
1884–1972

Florence Beckett   Lilias Beckett
B.1876   B.1877

Alice Beckett
B.1882

Piers Beckett
1880–1912

Henty. Henty was a very popular late Victorian historical novelist. His central character was always a brave, clean-cut Englishman who, after tremendous adventures, always won through, defeated the foreigners and the infidels, and saved the situation for everyone.

John and Hannah farmed Thurlwood Farm, in the village of Rode Heath near Alsager in Cheshire, where most of William's ten brothers and sisters still lived and worked. It might have been less genteel, but it was almost certainly a lot happier and more secure. John was a tenant farmer – his 72 acres could be taken away from him at any moment by the wealthy local landowner Randle Wilbraham, scion of the family which lived in Rode Hall and owned most of the land round there, a total of 2,032 acres. One dreadful day in September 1917, the Wilbrahams took it away.

But there was no hint of that in the pre-war years, and while the Becketts had the land, they could live well, and provide employment for some of their sons.

Each summer, William, Dorothy, John and Cecil decamped to Thurlwood. These long summer holidays were the happiest memories of the boys' childhood.

John saw his grandfather, the farmer John Beckett, as a mountain of a man, big and broad and fat. He lived until he was 80, and from the age of 40 he was unable to see his feet or tie his own shoelaces. "A goose is a fool of a bird," he would say, "too big for one and not big enough for two." His wife was substantial too.

Some of his sons helped him work the farm. One of them became the landlord of the Broughton Arms public house in Rode Heath which was (and still is) owned by Marstons Brewery. He seems to have inherited all the family charm – "handsome, charming, very good looking, lovely blue eyes, marvellous at parties", I heard from his wife's niece Margaret Harrex, though she added that his roving eye was a positive menace.

John and Cecil played, watched the men work the fields and helped a little. In the evenings they sat round the huge kitchen table while their grandfather played host to a good number of his 11 children and some of his grandchildren, as well as his workers, and everyone would eat gargantuan quantities of food which his wife Hannah had spent the whole day preparing. My father's memory was of the enormous amount they ate, and he was himself a formidable trencherman; and Margaret Harrex says they "used to feed like fighting cocks, never stinted themselves – wild duck, wonderful cheeses, you couldn't see their toast for butter. The tables were always groaning, I never knew such people for eating."

It was a rough life on the farm, far removed from the fragile gentility which William and Dorothy knew in the city. The amenities included a vast outside lavatory, designed for two people to sit companionably side by side. The seat was simply a polished plank of wood with two holes cut into it a few inches apart, allowing for easy conversation between the users. It was considered a mark of favour if, after a huge supper washed down with plenty of beer and cider, Uncle George invited you to "have one with me". Dorothy, a nicely brought up Victorian city lady, was permanently terrified that one day she might be in favour with Uncle George.

Yet that, as it turned out, was nothing compared to the troubles that overtook her at home. The family lived in King Street, Hammersmith, West London, above William's draper's shop: William, Dorothy, John and Cecil.

Small shopkeepers in the twilight of Queen Victoria's long reign were an intermediate class somewhere between manual workers and professionals like lawyers, doctors and clergymen. They worked hard, their hours were dreadfully long and they sweated their labour – or, if they could not afford labour, they sweated themselves and their families. They were, as social historian Paul Thompson puts it, "drawn to the standards of respectability of their clients and customers ... yet without the income and security to maintain them".

They lived constantly on the edge. If the business failed there was nothing, and they would join the one-third of the population which lived in real poverty, unable to feed themselves or their children properly, or to rely on a roof over their heads.

Eva had cut herself off forever from her own family, not only "marrying out" but marrying in a Christian church. Perhaps she did not realise how much this made her dependent on the character of the man she married.

Among the Cheshire Becketts, William was considered irresponsible and feckless, and there seems to have been a determination that he should not get his hands on any more of the family money. He was considered to have frittered away a £500 legacy from William Billington, and his father John Beckett Senior's will decreed that the sum should be deducted from his share of the estate (which, as it turned out, meant that he got nothing, John Beckett's estate being a great deal smaller than he had once hoped). It also laid down that two of William's younger brothers, rather than William, the oldest, should be trustees, a pretty clear statement that he did not consider William to be trustworthy. Perhaps also he did not feel close to William, the only one of his children who had not been brought up in his house.

In 1909 William proved them right by speculating all he possessed on the stock exchange, in one of the many schemes proposed by that great politician and confidence trickster Horatio Bottomley, who offered the irresistible combination of the chance to invest in something patriotic and the chance to make loads of money. William, according to my father, lost half of his capital in one wild speculation, and went angrily to Bottomley's shareholders' meeting, from which he emerged having invested everything he had left in another of Bottomley's schemes. That, too, he duly lost.

So at 14, John's childhood came to a sudden end – and Cecil's ended at nine, which, I now realise, is why my uncle wrote so slowly, painstakingly and badly. It was like watching a child write.

There were no more leisurely summer holidays at Thurlwood, and John was forced to leave the Latymer School in Hammersmith at once, and to give up his officer's position with the First Middlesex Territorial Cadet Battalion.

He was heartbroken. He enjoyed school and the cadets and seems to have been doing rather well. The son of a shopkeeper could grow up with expectations of becoming a professional man: but the son of a bankrupt could have no expectations but grinding labour until he was too old and weak to do any more, and then a pauper's grave.

The boy who had become a scout at the age of ten and an officer in the cadets at 12 became, at 14, a draper's errand boy. He was part of the child labour on which London's prosperity was based, working every waking hour and sleeping on the job – "the victim," he wrote, "of the twin horrors of a Welsh draper and the living-in system in

Willesden". It must have been harder to bear than if he had never had any other expectations.

And that is where Eva's father's jewels were put to use. For the rest of her life, she pawned them on the frequent occasions that her husband fell on hard times, and reclaimed them when things improved. By this method she enabled John to gain some qualifications at correspondence courses and night schools. In 1910, aged 16, he got some sort of a job with the *Harrow Observer*, perhaps as a cub reporter, perhaps selling advertising space.

Eva too came from a family which hankered after that elusive quality, gentility. She seems to have defined gentility in a traditional Jewish way; she hoped that her son would be a lawyer. He certainly had dreams of following that profession but, when the chance came, he rather negligently tossed it aside, for that was how he lived his life.

His misfortunes did not change my father's conviction, inherited from his own patriotic father William, that he lived in the finest nation on Earth, and that its values and its prosperity were forever. Few people who reached the age of 20 by 1914 ever quite freed themselves from a secret and unacknowledged wish that the pre-war world might return – even those, like John, who were most loudly to repudiate its values once the earthquake of the First World War had blown their world to pieces.

Half a century later, in the 1950s, he could still sigh, only half humorously, for an age when people did not call you by your Christian name unless they were very close friends indeed. Even in the 1950s he could still mourn that young men no longer seemed inclined to address older men as "Sir".

Still, there was pleasure to be had for a young man in Edwardian London, and for John that pleasure was mostly to be found in the music hall, with its entertainment, laughter and girls to fall in love with. To the end of his life he remembered the songs he heard there. Not just the ones everyone remembers, though he sang those too:

> I'm Burlington Bertie, I rise at 10.30 and saunter along like a toff
> I walk down the Strand with my glove on my hand, and I walk back again with it off

> I'm Bert, Bert, I haven't a shirt
> Though my people are well off, you know...

but also long-forgotten ditties:

> We're Cholly and Dolly
> We're two of the very best.
> We are specimen of the dressy men
> You meet up west.
> And when in the morning down Bond Street we trot
> Every Molly and Polly
> Says "Golly, how jolly.
> It's Cholly and Dolly. What what?"

He also understood what they meant, and I like to think of him sitting in the gods, laughing his loud, cracked laugh at the glorious Edwardian euphemisms in Burlington Bertie:

> I've just had a banana with Lady Diana,
> I'm Burlington Bertie from Bow.

He recalled standing outside the Hammersmith Lyceum, aged perhaps 15, waiting for a chorus girl with whom he had fallen in love. Falling in love in an instant was a habit which he never lost.

Another habit he never shed was that of thinking of something one minute and doing it the next, without pausing to consider the consequences. So on the day war broke out, 4 August 1914, he rushed to enlist, filled with boyish jingoistic enthusiasm – and perhaps, too, filled with boredom, for William seems to have managed to open another shop, and John, now an experienced draper's assistant, was probably required to work in it, for little more than his keep.

Three days later, the night before he was due to put on his uniform, he celebrated with a massive pub crawl. At last his friends left him sleeping on the pavement, to be awoken in the small hours by a policeman. He started his military training with the mother and father of all hangovers, and never got that drunk again.

Notes on sources

Genealogical research by Jean Davenport, Patric Dickinson, Richard Knowles and Jeanette Rosenberg.

Shylock Is My Name by Howard Jacobson (Hogarth, 2016).

The Edwardians: The Remaking of British Society by Paul Thompson (Routledge, 1992).

2

THE LEGACY OF WAR

The First World War left the whole of John's generation scarred for life. Some opposed the war, to be abused and assaulted daily by men, and spat on and handed white feathers by women. Others saw things in the trenches which would haunt them all their lives, and lost nearly all their friends.

Quite what John saw, I do not know, for he never talked about it except to tell funny stories. He did not experience the worst horrors of the war, but for the rest of his life the war was with him, every day, and his dead and horribly maimed friends were with him too. The burning anger that rich men should send poor men to suffer and die in pain and without dignity never left him.

He enlisted in the 9th Middlesex Battalion, but quickly transferred to the King's Shropshire Light Infantry (KSLI) because Shropshire was closer to the ancestral home in Cheshire. There he served with G Company, recruited (apart from himself) entirely from Ludlow in Shropshire.

These early decisions almost certainly saved his life. While others, including most of the KSLI's battalions, were sent to France, to be mown down like flies in the squalor of the trenches, and others to Gallipoli to be killed by Turkish guns amid the sand and the ferocious insects, John's battalion embarked for India in October 1914. The idea was that these raw recruits would take over routine imperial garrison duty, so as to free regular soldiers for the real fighting, in Europe. So the battalion served in Hong Kong, the Andaman Islands, Singapore and Rangoon from 1914–17.

So on 23 January 1915 John found himself in Rangoon. It was by far the safest place to be. And his memories, as he passed them on to me, were not those of the typical First World War soldier – though perhaps, like many others, he suppressed the worst of them. He remembered entering the regimental boxing tournament and reaching the final because all the best boxers were in the other half of the draw. In the final bout he was blasted to the canvas in the first round. He remembered getting lost and separated from his comrades, and walking for hours trying to find them, terrified by footsteps behind him. When he arrived at the camp he found that the footsteps belonged to the native water-carrier, who, possessing no boots, found it less uncomfortable to step in John's footprints. One of his favourite war poems was always Rudyard Kipling's "Gunga Din", about a native Indian water-carrier:

> Of all them blackfaced crew,
> The finest man I knew
> Was our regimental bhisti, Gunga Din

and especially the lines

> Though I've belted you and flayed you,
> By the livin' Gawd that made you,
> You're a better man than I am, Gunga Din!

The stories, so far as it goes, are doubtless true. But as so often with John, the truth about his war, as he afterwards presented it, does not quite hang together. It is not true, as he sometimes claimed, that he lied about his age to get into the army. A young man of 19 did not have to lie in 1914, and his army record gives his age accurately.

Much odder is that he always claimed to have been a thoroughly insubordinate soldier, but the record suggests that he was a very good one, highly thought of by his officers. In the ex-servicemen's movement which he helped found, his two court-martials became the stuff of legend. He told me that every time he was promoted, he did something disorderly and was demoted again. Yet his discharge papers say that his character in the army was "exemplary" and he was swiftly promoted to corporal and became signals instructor to his company, though he must have been demoted because he left as a private.

I think he must indeed have shown insubordination, despite his attested character, because for all his talk of discipline, he was highly undisciplined, and because ever afterwards, among his many hatreds, he had nothing but contempt for army regulations and those who imposed them. Forty years later, as a child in the 1950s, I found it hard to understand the pleasure and gusto with which he sang the First World War song:

> If you want the sergeant major, we know where he is,
> We know where he is,
> We know where he is.
> If you want the sergeant major, we know where he is,
> He's hanging on the old barbed wire.

He told me what the song was about, and why he liked it:

> The barbed wire was between the trenches. When you went over the top, you'd get shot as you tried to climb over it, and then you'd hang there till you were dead. No one liked the sergeant major, that's why they all laughed when they sang the last line.

I think he saw himself, in the first of many fantasies, as a G.A. Henty hero, doing brave and unconventional things on behalf of God and his king; and that it took him rather longer than it should have done to realise, if he ever realised it, that the harsh, cynical, class-ridden British army was no place for swashbuckling.

He was discharged in March 1917 with heart disease. "Dyspepsia on slight exertion. Palpitations with faintness and giddiness, loud systolic murmur, considerable enlargement of heart, result of active service and climate", records his discharge certificate. It would be "permanent and semi-disabling" and he was "no longer physically fit for war service".

He was in hospital for about a year, and a semi-invalid for some time after that. He emerged from hospital without teeth. The war revealed that most working-class people's dental care was rudimentary or non-existent, and by the time they reached the age of 20 their teeth were in such a rotten state that they could only eat pulped-up food. John's teeth must have been a real mess, because they pulled the lot out, and he wore dentures for the rest of his life.

For all that, he was the luckiest of men. In July 1917 his battalion made its long-delayed acquaintance with the Western Front. Later that year, it moved to the Ypres Salient to take part in the great Passchendaele Offensive and suffered 130 casualties on its first real day in action. It fought around Messines during the great German Spring offensive of 1918. It was then moved southwards to support French operations in the Soissons region; its greatest moment came in the capture of Bligny Hill on 6 June 1918, for which feat the battalion – reduced to company strength by then – was awarded the French Croix-de-Guerre avec Palme. August 1918 found it near Bethune before moving to the Somme in October. Not many men survived, and insubordinate soldiers tended to be sent into the most dangerous places. Illness was the best bit of luck John could have had.

I suspect that, perhaps unconsciously, he never quite recovered from a feeling of shame, not only that he survived – most of the survivors felt guilty about that – but that he had a comparatively easy war.

A single man, handsome and fancy-free, entered the army in 1914. A married man emerged from it. On leave one week, he met a tall, beautiful woman named Helen Shaw on Monday, married her on Wednesday and returned to his company on Friday.

Or so he told me, and perhaps he did propose on Wednesday, but the unforgiving marriage certificate I unearthed recently states that the wedding actually took place on 2 April 1920, several months after he left the army. The wedding was in Middlesex, near the homes of both sets of parents, according to the rites of the Presbyterian Church

– almost certainly the first and last time John did anything with the Presbyterians.

I never met Helen, but more than half a century later I met their daughter, and I have seen pictures of her. She seems to have been intelligent, thoughtful, attractive and down-to-earth, and at first they were very happy.

The engaged man who was discharged from the army was very different from the man who had rushed to enlist two years earlier. When the war started, John believed, with all his irresponsible, spontaneous, passionate heart, in the things his father believed: Britain ruling the waves, Conservative government, the moral value of material success. By 1918, "I had completely lost the old views, and thought God and the politicians equally to blame for international strife and inequality of opportunity at home."

Twenty years later, he wrote sadly of the idealism of his generation in 1918: "Proud of having conquered our inherited inhibitions, in our innocence we believed there was little else to conquer."

He had a new name. He often told me that he had been given the middle name Warburton in deference to his yeoman ancestors. This, it appears, is not true. He was christened John William Beckett, and in a family full of John Becketts, he had always been called Jack, and it was Jack William Beckett whose service record begins on 8 August 1914. Soon after he left the army, Jack William Beckett seems to have ceased to exist, and in his place was a clever young man with a brilliant future in front of him, whose name was John Warburton Beckett.

He simply assumed the name, typically without going to the trouble of registering the change. Formalities such as registration never seemed important to him, as at least one of his wives was to discover.

By the time the armistice was signed in November 1918 he had "a reasonably good job" in Sheffield. He never said what it was, but his wedding certificate says he was a draper's manager. He was handsome and fluent, with a loud voice full of absolute certainty which he did not always feel, and was six feet tall – exceptional in those days, when people were not as tall as they are now, and the working class suffered stunted growth from bad diet and malnutrition.

He had also found socialism, after the most intense period of reading of his whole life and a road to Damascus experience on a night in 1918 shortly before the armistice, when the Labour MP for Sheffield Attercliffe, W.C. Anderson, came to speak at the Ethical Society.

Anderson was 41, from a Scottish family of crofters. At the turn of the century he had been a radical and effective trade union organiser, and he was an Independent Labour Party (ILP) MP who was thought of as a future Labour leader. He was, as John was to become, an effective campaigning journalist and platform propagandist.

He had also been a pacifist during the war. "Across the roar of guns, we send sympathy and greetings to the German socialists", he had written in 1914, the year he became an MP. "They are no enemies of ours but faithful friends. In forcing this appalling crime upon the nations, it is the rulers, the diplomats, the militarists who have sealed their doom."

John went to the meeting and badgered the speaker with questions. He carried on after the meeting had closed, until Anderson invited him back to supper at his lodgings. There John blurted out the worst accusation, he thought, that you could hurl at any man – that Anderson lacked patriotism. He waited to be thrown out.

According to the *Dictionary of Labour Biography*, Anderson's "open manner and handsome appearance all served to disarm critics", and it certainly worked wonders on the 24-year-old ex-soldier. Anderson answered quietly and clearly, and

> for the first time I realised that foreign affairs were not so simple as the daily press had led me to believe, and that the war had other origins beside the lunacy of the Kaiser. I left my mentor at dawn and walked across the city to my own lodgings, hardly noticing the tiredness of my body for the turbulence of my mind.

A few days later Anderson sent him a huge pile of pamphlets and a reading list: Marx, Engels, Ruskin, John Stuart Mill. For the next few months John spent all the hours he could spare from work devouring the reading list and attending meetings on politics and economics.

Anderson did not live to see the results of his persuasiveness. He died suddenly and unexpectedly the next year, 1919.

By then, John was back in London, this time in the East End, in Hackney. He had lodgings at 9 St John's Mansions, Clapton Square, a job and a new, raw, exciting religion. He was certain now that only a revolutionary change in the way society was run would be good enough for those who had been ground down and exploited for generations; certain that he must devote his life to making an end to the system that enabled one man to amass huge wealth while another could not earn enough to feed his family.

Liberal Prime Minister David Lloyd George had called a snap election in 1918, the "khaki election", which was a triumph for the Conservatives and produced a coalition government dominated, in a memorable phrase which John used often, by "hard faced men who had done well out of the war".

Britain in 1918 was probably closer to armed revolution than at any other time in its history. The Communist Party was founded in 1920, and on the day of its foundation the editorial in the Labour-supporting *Daily Herald* expressed, not wild optimism, but something like conventional wisdom: "The founders of the new Party believe – as most competent observers are coming to believe – that the capitalist system is collapsing."

The reasons were the same as those that motivated John. The *Herald* reported a commonplace story.

> An ex-serviceman was turned out of a job to make way for a girl, his pension temporarily withheld. One of his three children, owing to the effects of malnutrition, was sent to a poor law institution, and the father received a bill for 24 shillings for four weeks' maintenance in hospital. Then another child was taken ill and in hospital seven weeks, and, with empty pocket and barely a crust in the house, the father received a demand for another 28 shillings.

British socialists, unlike those in Europe, had never taken the army seriously as a possible source of support. Soldiers were, by their nature, considered reactionary. The biggest socialist group – the ILP, led by Ramsay MacDonald – had adopted a pacifist policy, and many ILP leaders had gone to prison for it. "The socialist left in Britain," writes historian David Englander, "in so far as it considered the subject at all, regarded the army with a mixture of fear and contempt."

The ILP, even in 1915, had rejected the idea of military trade unions on the grounds that it might make soldiering into a respectable occupation. Soldiers, as much as pacifists, had bitter grievances against the existing order. In their view, unemployment of former servicemen seemed to show the treachery of the civilian population.

Their disability pensions were niggardly, and were meanly and inefficiently distributed. Fearfully maimed former soldiers begged for their bread on the streets of London, while war profiteers drove past them in splendid motor cars to the best restaurants, throwing up dust and mud from the un-tarmacked streets on to the already filthy war heroes.

John saw what few socialists saw at that time, that ex-soldiers were the best possible source of support for revolutionary change in society. They had not seen their friends killed and maimed in order to come back to the same exploitative, class-ridden society they had left. The Labour Party did not make the same mistake in 1945.

John started by joining the Comrades of the Great War, but quickly decided that this government-encouraged organisation was simply a ruse to trick his old army comrades, to persuade them to take jobs at low wages which they had to subsidise with their war pensions and to try to prevent them from joining trade unions. George Bernard Shaw wrote despondently in September 1918: "Already employers openly ask what pension a man has, and make him an offer accordingly."

So, early in 1919, John Beckett and Ernest Mander founded the National Union of Ex-Servicemen (NUX), to show the former soldier that his interests lay with the Labour movement, and that he should resist efforts by the Comrades of the Great War to persuade him to be a strike-breaker. Mander, a former temporary captain in the army who worked in the Ministry of Munitions, was general secretary, and John became president.

The union stood for a better deal for ex-servicemen and the families of those who had been killed:

> We aim to maintain that spirit of comradeship which existed among us while we were together in the Services. And to reinforce it with that sense of comradeship which should inspire us who are still fighting together, but this time for political and industrial aims at home ... We are ex-Service men, but we are also citizens ... We shall therefore support the Labour Party in its efforts to improve the conditions under which all the people ... must live ... We shall therefore support the trade unions ... We did not fight to save the country for the capitalists, but for the people.

But its spirit was probably better summed up by Mander's article in the *Labour Leader* of November 1920, which talked of "the manner in which the people have been betrayed by lies into fighting for the financial interests of their masters".

It campaigned for better pensions, jobs for ex-servicemen and a root-and-branch reform of the hated court martial system which had summarily condemned so many men to death. It demanded back pay for former soldiers at the much higher rates given to Australian, New Zealand and Canadian troops. This would have meant a huge lump sum for all former soldiers, and the NUX proposed that it should be paid for by a land tax which would hit war profiteers.

Within six months the NUX grew from one branch with 50 members to over 100 branches with almost 100,000 members. The Ministry of Labour was seriously concerned. The British Legion (according to its official history) saw the NUX as "a bitter brooding group of militant Marxists".

The Labour Party supported the NUX and brought its leading members on to its relevant policy committees. But it refused to support its proposals on back pay for soldiers.

When Major Clement Attlee, a prominent Labour Party activist from east London, proposed amendment of the court martial system, John, on behalf of the NUX, submitted a memorandum demanding much more draconian reform than Major Attlee contemplated. John demanded that the Labour Party should reconstruct the army along democratic and classless lines.

The NUX also acted as the ex-serviceman's "trade union", and John represented dozens of men denied their pensions, or shell-shocked men who were being treated as "pauper lunatics". He saw all the human misery created by a country which had won a war and seemed neither to know nor to care about the human cost, and he saw on the other side of the table the men who had taken no risks and reaped all the benefits, and it filled him with rage.

It was a good and holy rage, but it led him to peer into dark places. During this time he almost certainly met and worked with one of the leaders of another ex-servicemen's organisation, Henry Hamilton Beamish of the National Federation of Discharged and Demobilised Soldiers and Sailors.

Beamish was also involved with a nationalist organisation called the Vigilante Society, which folded in 1919 when Beamish was one of the founders of a specifically anti-Semitic organisation called The Britons. He was to become one of Britain's most obsessive anti-Semites, and his path and John's were to cross again.

Mander sold his home to finance the NUX. From the pacifist wing of the ILP, Fenner Brockway and Ramsay MacDonald worked to secure money to supplement the one shilling a month membership subscription. Brockway and MacDonald used their influence to persuade the ILP to underwrite £150 of a £400 over-draft which the NUX ran up, and to donate £50, and Brockway helped to get some private finance. But it was nothing like enough, especially with the NUX now producing a monthly publication, *New World*.

The newly formed Communist Party offered money, but the conditions were onerous. John and Mander both had to join the Communist Party and become paid Party officials. Their executive was to be confined to members approved by the Communist Party, and they were to accept the principle of democratic centralism which would oblige them to obey instructions issued by the Comintern, the Moscow-dominated Third International.

The communists' conditions were put to the two NUX leaders at a meeting with the Communist Party national executive at their headquarters in Maiden Lane, where the union received, so John claimed, "the kind of greeting which the Millionaires' Federation might offer to a deputation of office boys ... We did not trouble these autocratic 'proletarians' with a further visit", he wrote later.

The money, however, was not found from anywhere else: and money was not the only problem. Special Branch reported that the NUX was the seedbed of revolution, and the government gave Lord Haig – Field Marshal Douglas Haig – £2 million profit from the services' wartime canteens so that he could build an organisation which would put all other ex-servicemen's groups out of business.

As a result of the foundation of the British Legion and its own chronic shortage of money, the NUX was forced to wind up and offer its branches the choice of either carrying on independently or throwing in their lot with the ILP, the Labour Party or the Communist Party. Special Branch was distressed to find how many of them chose the Communist Party.

Mander emigrated to New Zealand. John seriously considered going with him, and only his ILP work kept him in Britain. In New Zealand, Mander worked for the Workers Educational Association, published popular books on psychology and moved to Australia in the 1930s.

In 1928 he seems to have been in some way involved with the New Zealand Conservative Party, and Labour Party headquarters asked John if he could provide information to be used against him, but John said he knew nothing to Mander's discredit. Mander was "a loveable man with a fine brain and few things would give me greater pleasure than to hear good news of him". Visceral loyalty always meant everything to John, and Mander was his second political hero, taking over from W.C. Anderson. There were to be many more – charismatic, clever, passionate men who could inspire his fierce loyalty and his fertile fantasy life, the romantic hero to John's swashbuckler, the fellow musketeer, the joint hero of a Henty novel.

Labour leaders Ramsay MacDonald and Clement Attlee, socialist leaders John Wheatley and Jimmy Maxton, fascist leaders Oswald Mosley and William Joyce, all were to have spells in Mander's shoes. Unlike Mander, most of them lacked the good taste to emigrate before their clay feet became so obvious that even John could not avoid seeing them.

In two years, John had found a faith, a loathing of injustice and a wife. Others took decades to accommodate all of that. John did it fast, and in his usual untidy, haphazard way, he took in alongside it some very undesirable baggage.

The meeting at the Communist Party headquarters put in place the last of the trio of prejudices which were to sit and fester in the back of John's mind until, under the pressure of events, they fatally coalesced.

He disliked communists, he said, because they were receiving huge sums of money from Moscow. The Party denied it, but everyone on the political left knew it was true, and documents which have come to light since the fall of the Soviet Union show that the sums were greater even than the Party's enemies dreamed of. He thought communists were rich, showy and trendy, and, worst of all, unpatriotic. "Almost all political Bloomsbury belongs to the Party", he said, and he knew few worse insults.

He disliked pacifists, whom he still considered unpatriotic.

And his third dislike was the most corrosive of them all. Anti-Semitism was as common in John's new home on the political left as it was in his old home on the right. Colin Holmes has pointed out that, in the years before the First World War, it was largely Jewish businessmen who made the City of London pre-eminent in finance, and that anti-Semitism was common on the left because Jews tended to be identified with capitalism.

There was a feeling that war profiteers were mostly Jews, and such profiteers were the class of people towards whom John displayed the most blinding, disabling hatred of which even he was capable.

John claimed all his life, and may have believed, that he was never an anti-Semite; he just opposed the financial power that he believed Jews controlled. In the 1920s that must surely have been true. His mother was very much alive, and still had his ferocious love, admiration and gratitude, and he does not yet seem to have started to consider her Jewishness a state secret. For the moment, prejudice was smothered by the excitement of the times and the dream of creating a better world which he shared with the best of his generation. Pacifists, communists and Jews, all saw in John simply what everyone else saw – a very able, energetic, fluent young man with an acute form of the revolutionary socialist fervour which his generation had brought out of the war; a fine platform performer with a loud voice, a strong personality and massive self-confidence.

Notes on sources

The history of the KSLI at the Shropshire Regimental Museum website.

Anti-Semitism in British Society by Colin Holmes (Edward Arnold, 1979).

Dictionary of Labour Biography (for W.C. Anderson) edited by K. Gildart and D. Howell (Palgrave Macmillan, 2010).

Haters, Baiters and Would-be Dictators by Nick Toczek (Routledge, 2016).

The National Union of Ex-Servicemen and the Labour Movement, 1918–1920, by David Englander (*History*, 76(246), 1991).

3
MAJOR ATTLEE AND CORPORAL BECKETT

John returned to London to work, according to a statement he made years later in court, "as trade union representative for a bookselling news agency". He joined the Hackney branch of the ILP in 1918.

ILP leader Ramsay MacDonald, knowing that he needed the support of ex-soldiers, to whom he was suspect because he was a former pacifist, invited the well-known ex-servicemen's leader to meet him at the ILP head office in Johnson's Court, off Fleet Street. So John, still only in his mid twenties, and just two years out of uniform, found himself moving in elevated political circles.

After the demise of the NUX, all John's energy went into the ILP. It had been founded in 1883 by Keir Hardie in order to get independent parliamentary representation for working men, and its title at first implied independence of the Liberal Party.

In 1900 it came under the umbrella of the newly formed Labour Representation Committee. The LRC was an alliance of trade unions and socialist societies, including the ILP, formed to return Labour MPs who would form an independent party in the House of Commons.

In 1918 the LRC ceased to be a loose federation of trade unions and societies and became a political party with branches in each constituency. It became what we now know as the Labour Party.

Before 1918 you could only join the Labour Party by joining an affiliated society like the ILP, or an affiliated trade union. After 1918 anyone could join the Labour Party directly. In the long term this destroyed the ILP. But no one would have predicted that in 1918, when the ILP seemed to be the inspiration of all Labour's activities, as well as the keeper of its socialist conscience.

For a short time, MacDonald took Mander's place as John's political hero. John wrote:

> The handsome face behind the heavy black moustache, the organ-like voice and the graceful gestures seemed too good to be true. It took me a year to learn the ability behind this God-given exterior, and more than five to discover the vanity and cunning.

MacDonald was favourably impressed, and told the new secretary of the London Labour Party, Herbert Morrison, also a pacifist, to make use of John. So John found himself invited to a vegetarian meal at the home of another important political figure. Here are his first impressions of the man who, 20 years later as Home Secretary, was to hold the keys of his prison cell:

> Herbert Morrison was under 40, a small, unprepossessing looking man with one almost blind eye and a queer expression of furtive pugnacity mainly engendered by a stubborn jaw and an unruly forelock spreading over a low but well developed forehead. Son of a London policeman, he seemed, except for his vegetarian, non-smoking and prosaic manner, a typical smart-alec cockney, and while his businesslike manner and shrewdness suggested sound organising ability, there seemed no sign of any real statesmanlike qualities.

Vegetarians always rather puzzled John, who was, like his Cheshire ancestors, a hearty carnivore, and he worried all evening about how he was supposed to handle "the extraordinary meal I was kindly invited to share".

The political importance of the evening lay in the decision that Labour could win Hackney, even though it had not at that time a single representative on the borough council. John explained the problems of the Hackney branch, and they planned how to overcome them.

There was, he told Morrison, a group of malcontents in the branch led by the Secretary, who would need to be sidelined. He wrote later:

> This man was the type of socialist Bernard Shaw must have had in mind when he declared that "only Socialists have prevented the coming of socialism". Small and inoffensive, with vague features, a wispish gingery moustache and a weak, peevish voice, he and two doctrinaire Jews, who spoke voluble and incoherent English, attempted to dominate the meetings and thought themselves real revolutionaries. They had not strength, kindness or charity, and many promising faces faded out after an evening spent listening to the diatribes of these incorruptible nuisances.

With help and guidance from Morrison, John took the Hackney party in hand. He held three open air meetings every week, generally attracting 600 or 700 people. He ran indoor meetings and lectures. John spoke at least once a week, the ex-servicemen always came out to hear him, and they achieved a sensational victory in the November 1919 borough elections. Labour, which had not previously held a single council seat, obtained a majority of one.

According to John, this spectacular outcome was the result entirely of his organisation and charisma. Allowing for his pardonable exaggeration, he certainly played a major part. Because of what he later became, his contemporaries tended not to dwell on it, but I would like not to lose sight of the fact that, at his best, John was a socialist propagandist of something like genius.

The result was a shock to everyone, especially the newly elected Labour councillors who, suddenly finding themselves expected to run the borough, at once co-opted Herbert Morrison as an alderman, and elected him leader of the council, so that he could tell them what to do.

As council leader, Morrison's policy was ultra-cautious, and Hackney's left-wingers quickly became very restive, none more so than

John Beckett. Two months later there was a by-election for a council seat which Morrison considered unwinnable. When John pushed through a decision that a candidate would be fielded whether Morrison liked it or not, Morrison took his revenge by nominating John as the candidate. John did not want to be a councillor, but in the circumstances he could not refuse without embarrassment, so he put his heart and soul into the fight.

To everyone's surprise except his own, he won. He at once became the leader of a group of five left-wing councillors opposed to Morrison's rule. This group, because of Labour's tiny majority, could hold up the work of the council whenever it chose to do so.

The big issue was unemployment. Morrison, unlike George Lansbury in neighbouring Poplar, refused to commit council money to unemployment relief.

But a much smaller issue brought the conflict to the boil. Some council employees threatened a strike over a fairly modest pay claim. John was for paying, Morrison was against. But many Conservatives also wanted to meet the claim, and Morrison knew he faced defeat in the council chamber. He moved a half-hour adjournment and, in an adjacent room, he raged at his rebel councillors. He was forced to give in.

Neither man ever forgot or forgave. As we shall see, both were still talking about it more than a quarter of a century later, after the Second World War, after the dangerous fascist Beckett had finally been released from prison by Home Secretary Morrison.

And more than half a century later, in the 1970s, Labour councils were still playing out precisely the battle that John Beckett and Herbert Morrison fought in Hackney in 1919. No one has yet found a way of reconciling Labour's ideals with the desire of its leaders to appear moderate and unthreatening.

John summed it up in words that could have been used about almost any Labour council at any time in the last 100 years:

> A Labour majority on a local authority may make a determined effort to implement its lavish election promises, which will mean increased rates and eventually a sharp conflict with the national government; or it may throw aside its promises and

endeavour to prove that Labour majorities are safer, more economical and more efficient than their opponents. The personal beliefs and ambitions of the leaders do not allow the first course, and the rank and file make the second impossible.

The same battle was fought out in neighbouring Poplar but with very different results. There, George Lansbury and his colleagues imposed high rates so as to keep the unemployed from starving, and the government surcharged the borough. The councillors cheerfully went to prison for their refusal to commit the borough to paying the surcharge. While Lansbury was in prison, Morrison attacked him for breaking the law.

John had by then spent more evenings in Lansbury's "comfortable old home in Bow Road" than he ever spent in Morrison's vegetarian household, and sprang to Lansbury's defence, concealing from no one his wish that Hackney had a courageous and committed leader like Lansbury, and his extremely low opinion of its present leader. He organised a conference of London Labour parties which, with Clement Attlee from Limehouse in the chair, passed a unanimous vote of censure on Morrison.

John's heart was in Brixton Prison with Lansbury. The memory must have returned to haunt him when he entered the same prison in 1940. "Only twenty years after did I realise the full weight of the enmity I had incurred", he wrote after the Second World War. He was convinced that Morrison took a terrible revenge for his humiliation in Hackney by keeping him in prison unnecessarily.

The notoriety attached to a rebel left-wing Hackney councillor ensured that John lost his job. And in this way, a fateful decision was made. He had agonised for months about whether to throw up a promising career to become a full-time politician. I am not certain whether at this time he was in advertising or journalism. Whichever it was, his boats were burned, for the first time – he made a career of burning his boats. There was no more agonising to be done. It was the first of four promising careers which he threw away, almost without really meaning to.

At the time it must have looked like a good move. He had the misfortune to sound as though he had all the political skills, while he actually possessed very few of them.

He became one of the small army of full-time ILP speakers who toured the country, from one draughty meeting hall to another, selling the socialist message. He lived by taking modest fees from the local parties whose meetings he addressed.

He loved the hard work, the comradeship, the discovery that he had the ability to lift an audience. If this was politics, give him more of it!

The life greatly enriched his store of anecdotes – he had, as Colin Cross put it, "a schoolboy delight in elaborating an anecdote".

"We've 'eard the greatest socialists in this 'all", enthused one local chairman. "We've 'eard Brother Keir 'ardie in this 'all, we've 'eard Brother Ramsay MacDonald, and tonight we're honoured, brothers, to 'ave with us Brother ... what did you say your name was, Brother?"

An elderly trade unionist, standing for Labour in a mining constituency, faced a young Conservative candidate with a beautiful, patrician wife, and on the eve of the poll he told his audience: "I hear Lady X has told you that tomorrow she will be going away with the Member for this Division. You know old Tom well enough to know that he will defend his honour with his life."

It was important to finish a meeting in good time for the audience to get a pint in the pub afterwards, and sometimes a long-winded chairman would make it impossible. One visiting speaker, after listening to a local chairman's very long introduction, stood up and said: "Well, now, comrades, I think we should all thank our brother chairman for that long and interesting address, and now let's get round the pub, before we all die of thirst."

He loved the people he met, the rough and ready accommodation he stayed in. He wrote:

> In every town there were a number of good comrades who possessed a spare room, or at any rate a spare bed. The same folk put up all speakers who visited their districts, and usually at supper on Sunday evenings, the leading local members were invited to meet the visitor. Such evenings are a source of many happy memories. These men and women on small wages were financing the propaganda for a great movement. Fierce arguments were carried on until the small hours of the morning.

In Maidstone he set up camp with Ernest Hunter, later political editor for the *Daily Herald*, and Seymour Cocks, later an MP, and there the three of them were witnesses to one of the great mysteries of Labour movement politics.

They held an outdoor meeting just outside Maidstone prison in 1920. After John closed the meeting, a tall man approached him and said, "That was a fine speech. I used to give them just the same stuff." He took them to the nearest pub and said that his name was Victor Grayson.

The name meant nothing to them, which showed how little they knew of the history of the movement they served. Victor Grayson, MP for Colne Valley, had been the great romantic hero of socialist politics before the First World War. He had disappeared suddenly, and no one ever saw him again. If this man was really Victor Grayson, they were the only people known to have met him since before the war.

And it is now, I think, certain that the man they met really was Victor Grayson, and that they were the last people known to have seen Grayson alive. For John said this in his account: "He told us some interesting stories of Irish politics, and admitted a connection with the Irish secret service."

He could only have had that from Grayson himself. The research which showed Grayson's involvement with the Irish secret service and the IRA was not done in John's lifetime.

Grayson, unknown to John, was playing a dangerous game. Maundy Gregory, one of MI5's most unattractive spies, was spying on him. Gregory had been told: "We believe this man may have friends among the Irish rebels. Whatever it is, Grayson always spells trouble. He can't keep out of it ... he will either link up with the Sinn Feiners or the Reds." So Gregory became friendly with Grayson, and may have financed a rather more affluent lifestyle than Grayson had known before.

Maundy Gregory kept an eye on the sexual transgressions of politicians, lest he might wish to blackmail them, and he it was who first took evidence of Sir Roger Casement's alleged homosexual activities to MI5 (and who may have invented them and forged the evidence).

During the summer of 1919 Grayson became aware that Gregory was spying on him. He told a friend: "Just as he spied on me, so now

I'm spying on him. One day I shall have enough evidence to nail him, but it's not going to be easy."

At a public meeting in Liverpool he accused David Lloyd George, the Prime Minister, of selling political honours for between £10,000 and £40,000. Grayson said: "This sale of honours is a national scandal. It can be traced right down to 10 Downing Street, and to a monocled dandy with offices in Whitehall. I know this man, and one day I will name him." The monocled dandy was Gregory.

At the beginning of September 1920, a few weeks after that meeting in Maidstone, Victor Grayson was beaten up in the Strand. This was probably an attempt to frighten him but he made further speeches about the selling of honours and threatening to name the man behind this corrupt system. Later that month he visited Gregory's home, and was never seen again. He was probably murdered. His body was never found.

Maundy Gregory continued to work closely with MI5 chiefs in their efforts to stop left-wing politicians from gaining power in Britain, and John Beckett was later to know people like Gregory a very great deal better than he wished. Gregory eventually served a short prison sentence for corruption, and retired to France with a pension which bought his silence on the question of who else might have been involved in cash for honours. He was as nasty a piece of work as has ever graced a nasty profession, though he has some strong competition from some of the men who were later to spy on John. He died in France in 1941.

John specialised, as Grayson had, in a rough, knockabout platform style which was very popular on the ILP circuit. Some full-time speakers lived like that for years, and brought up their families as part of the ILP "family", but John was a young man and seemed to have a brilliant future ahead of him.

A better opportunity swiftly presented itself. Major Clement Attlee, Labour candidate for Limehouse, put it about in the 1917 Club that he required a secretary and election agent.

The club, founded in 1917 by Ramsay MacDonald and some other Labour and Liberal pacifists, was based at 4 Gerrard Street in London's West End, and was where the political and literary left met, dined and talked the excitable radical politics of the time.

Years later, after its descent into sectarian feuding and eventual closure, the Fabian socialist Margaret Cole was to describe it as "a dingy hole in Gerrard Street with some pretty poor food in the basement ... a place of meeting and gossip for those on the left who couldn't afford to join established clubs" but it did not seem so to the excitable and ambitious young politico who was introduced to the club, of which Attlee was a committee member, in 1918, and who often lunched there several times a week.

John had heard a lot about Major Attlee, all of it good: a left-winger, a soldier and a charming and witty man. Attlee, too, had heard of John. While John was waiting to be interviewed by the Limehouse Party Executive, a member came out and told him his appointment had already been settled because "the Major wants you".

Attlee had that precious political asset, an inheritance which gave him a modest income, though not as large as had been rumoured. John told him that he needed real money for propaganda work, not just the pennies you could collect from impoverished members. The only money Attlee could offer was earmarked for John's first year's salary of £6 a week. So John made a proposal.

Attlee had bought a big old house, Norway House, in the constituency. The ground floor was used as a club for the Labour Party. Attlee lived on the first floor, with his former army batman to look after him. There was a flat on the top floor, and John proposed that he and Helen should move into it rent-free, and he would therefore take no salary, raising his own living expenses by part-time work for the ILP, to which he could add some journalism and a few advertising commissions.

Attlee noted in his terse way: "November 1920. Jack Beckett came to act as secretary and agent and subsequently lived at Norway House with his wife and little girl who was born there." Jack had not completely given place to John, but he was on his way out. John and Helen's daughter Lesley was born in Limehouse in May 1923.

There, in Attlee's rambling East End home, John found the first stability and contentment he had known since he was 14, and the last he was to know for many more years. Attlee was 11 years older and had received the university education which John seemed now to crave. The two men spent long, calm evenings puffing on their pipes together and talking about God, politics and the state of the world. They made a complete genealogical tree of the Forsytes some years before it was published in the complete edition. I am sure this project was Attlee's idea, for he loved precise, detailed work, and Galsworthy's *Forsyte Saga* was a favourite of his. John, left to himself, could not have sat still long enough, but he loved the company of his gentle, witty, Oxford-educated friend.

If Attlee provided the learning that John lacked, John liked to think he could give his less outgoing friend some instruction in the ways of the world. Attlee's childhood had been spent with his rather protective family in Putney and at a boys' boarding school. He was painfully shy, and probably knew even less about women than the average unmarried former public schoolboy in 1920. John, on the other hand, was thoroughly extrovert. If he ever suffered from shyness in his life, no one ever noticed, and he had discovered early that he was very attractive to women. He wrote of his friend with amused affection:

> The few occasions when his humour became caustic were in his discussions about feminine methods and their effect on masculine life. Never a young woman came near a friend without his instant realisation that she was "gunning for poor old so-and-so..." It was therefore a great surprise when [Attlee] went off for a continental tour with a man friend, and returned completely absorbed in his friend's sister who, by some strange chance, had been, with her mother, on his line of route. In response to a query whether she had been "gunning", he spent some time telling me how difficult his task was, and how fortunate he hoped to be.

When Attlee married the friend's sister and moved to the suburbs, "I missed our regular talks very much". Attlee's friendship was a deep happiness to John, so much so that it was nearly a decade before he smashed it to pieces.

All John's flair for a phrase, a slogan, a propaganda method, went into selling Attlee to the electors of Limehouse. One of his most successful innovations was a free advice service. He spent each morning listening to people's troubles. If anything could be done he promised to "see the Major about it". If he was sure that nothing could be done, the case never reached Attlee. "I was the Hyde to Clem's Jekyll, and there were many who lamented that if only I had let them go to the Major, things would have been different."

The *East London Pioneer* was another propaganda success, and the first of a series of newspapers which John founded regularly over the next four decades, through which he disseminated his gospel of the moment. It set the pattern for all the rest. John was editor, business manager, despatch clerk – he was the paper. It lasted two years, reached 5,000 people in Limehouse, Mile End, Bow and Poplar, and even paid its way. This was partly because of its success at attracting advertising. Attlee as mayor managed to ensure that some of the borough's advertising went into it, trade union branches took space and some Labour supporters owned shops which they advertised in its columns.

The journalistic style is unmistakably John's, with big headlines and no restraint in the writing, but also with a real news sense. In November 1921 he was writing about the failure of the transport strike of that year, attacking "the noisy and dangerous people who urged all sorts of impossible cures" on the one hand, and the right-wing union leaders on the other: "Those masterly recruiting agents for the Communist Party ... The lesson is: avoid bad leaders." TURN THE WASTERS OUT was the lead headline just before the borough elections in March 1922. Hearing that railway magnate Sir Eric Geddes was being paid huge sums of money to recommend cuts in public expenditure (the so-called Geddes axe) he wrote under the headline BRAZEN IMPUDENCE OF A SHAMELESS PARA-SITE: "Sir Eric is eating up the share of twelve families. So the other eleven families must starve. And Sir Eric has the brass face to be Chairman of a Committee which calls upon the other eleven families to economise."

Attlee and John worked together on a small committee which wrote a new policy for the ILP. It was adopted by the 1922 conference and served the ILP until 1933 – and by then the four men who drafted it were in four different political parties. Attlee wrote in his autobiography:

The membership reads rather curiously today, for in addition to myself, there was Fenner Brockway, who after a long period in the political wilderness has now rejoined the Labour Party; Clifford Allen, who supported MacDonald's "National" government in 1931; and John Beckett, who adhered to Sir Oswald Mosley who founded the new Party which later developed into the British Union of Fascists.

There were two ex-soldiers – Attlee and John – and two ex-"conshies", Fenner Brockway and Clifford Allen. In 1922 the divide between soldiers and "conshies" was still bitter, the wounds still raw. John already knew and liked Brockway, but he instinctively disliked and distrusted Clifford Allen, and the feeling was almost certainly mutual.

Yet in 1922 they must all have felt that they were creating a new world together. None of them could have imagined that by 1933, the Labour Party and the ILP would have split: Attlee would be in the Labour Party, Brockway in the ILP, Allen supporting a Conservative-dominated government and John bringing to fascism the skills which, in 1922, he was using on behalf of Attlee.

It was Brockway who brought the four of them together in a flat in one of those splendid mansion blocks in Prince of Wales Drive, Battersea, which Clifford Allen shared with Bertrand Russell. John, impressed that he was about to meet the great philosopher, seems to have been irrationally but angrily disappointed to find the two flatmates squabbling over some domestic matter.

The final detailed draft was left to John and Attlee, which must have been a relief to John. Never good at being polite to someone he disliked, there was something about Allen which roused all his anger and contempt. He wrote of him: "His gentle 'charm' had gained him great popularity among the wealthy Quakers and pacifists who provided ample means for the lavish anti-war campaign of the No-Conscription Fellowship of which he had been Chairman."

John was a good hater. His hatred of Clifford Allen deepened over the years as the latter linked himself with the treachery of Ramsay MacDonald, until John could write, only half humorously: "I am against war because it is a blind and expensive way of weeding out the population. It takes your Rupert Brookes and leaves your Clifford Aliens, and that is an extremely bad thing."

Three years after they drew up a policy together, we find him at an ILP conference, furiously opposing the minimum wage proposal put forward by "Clifford Allen and his little band of middle class intellectuals ... well known writers and thinkers who could pass Allen's standards of gentility." I think Allen must have seemed, whether intentionally or not, to look down on John's untutored ways and rough style of speaking.

In October 1922, Lloyd George's coalition government was brought down by his Conservative supporters. The new Conservative Prime Minister, Andrew Bonar Law, called a general election the next month.

In Limehouse, Attlee faced a sitting member with a 6,000 majority, yet there was a sense of victory about his campaign from the start. The Liberal split already looked terminal, and the 1918 Representation of the People Act had changed the electorate radically. For the first time, women could vote (though only if they were over 30) and so could many more working men. Attlee engaged an additional agent to handle the detailed work so that John could concentrate on propaganda and publicity. John thought his candidate needed careful handling, writing in 1938:

> Even now he is far from being an orator, and in those days his best friends could not have called him even a tolerably good speaker. His strongest cards were his erudition and wit, both of which were over the heads of a Limehouse audience which needed fireworks and crudity. I was able to supply them with both.

They hired an old two-seater car. "Look out for the little yellow car", said the election literature. Every day, with supporters clinging to it, they drove through the narrow streets. They would pull up in the middle of a street and make as much noise as possible while supporters knocked at the doors, inviting electors to appear at windows and doors and listen to the Major. When an audience had gathered, John would speak for five minutes and introduce Attlee, who would answer questions and exchange friendly greetings before they drove to the next street. John loved it, but sensed that his candidate was never quite comfortable:

> Once we met a number of Conservative canvassers, and as one of our men rang a bell loudly to attract attention, a resident thrust his head out and asked if we were selling muffins. Like lightning a Tory woman replied "No, mate, pups", a retort which the crowd, seeing my shy and miserable companion, were not slow to appreciate.

The election address has John's finger marks all over it. To the end of his life, Attlee was justly proud that his election speeches contained the same policies in every election he fought. That was true, but his later addresses never again had the same fire, the same short, direct sentences, the same bite-size chunks, the same heavy headlines or the same extravagance of abuse. Attlee never again found anyone with the same talent for forceful, over-the-top propaganda.

John produced a tabloid newspaper, *Limehouse Election News*. Half the front page was taken up with a picture of the scene outside the Hotel Cecil when the Conservatives decided to dump Lloyd George and make Bonar Law Prime Minister. In 1922 the idea of taking up half the front page with a picture would have seemed revolutionary. A huge headline went with the picture:

> THE ROLLS ROISTERERS
> Our picture shows the parade of Rolls-Royce cars which blocked up the Strand when the Tories elected Bonar Law as their leader at the Hotel Cecil.
>
> A Rolls-Royce costs about £2,000. This would provide £5 a week for a family of five or six workers for over seven years – Or it could be used to build four decent houses. Yet when the worker asks for a living wage or somewhere to live, the Rolls Roisterers shout: "We can give you nothing; we are crushed by taxation."

Inside was a strip cartoon of an ugly war profiteer clutching his bag of gold, finally despatched by the heroic figure of organised Labour.

The cartoon was accompanied by a rhyme. We do not know who wrote it, but it was almost certainly either Attlee (who was passionate about poetry, wrote a good deal, and even had some talent as a poet) or John (who wrote hearty doggerel). My money is on John, because Attlee's poetry was generally more subtle than this:

> My name is Mr Profiteer
> And talk of taxes makes me queer.
> I made my millions in the war,
> That's why your living costs you more.
> Let homeless heroes starve in ditches,
> But don't make levies on my riches.
> And if the Empire needs a tax
> Well – shove it on the workers' backs.
> The Tory-Libs, they love me so,
> They'll never make me pay, I know.
> But oh! when Labour wins, I fear,
> It's good-bye Mr Profiteer.

They produced a leaflet in Attlee's name:

THE GREAT BETRAYAL

Like many of you I took part in the Great War in the hope of securing lasting peace and a better life for all. We were promised that wars should end, that the men who fought in the War would be cared for and that unemployment, slums and poverty would be abolished.

ALL THESE PROMISES HAVE BEEN BROKEN

In every way the conditions of the workers are worse than before.

Wars and threats of war continue. Your wages are still falling and many of you are unemployed. You pay high rents and live in overcrowded hovels. Ex-soldiers are found lining up for unemployment pay or outdoor relief.

> The wounded and widows have to struggle on a starvation dole. Men made insane in the War are sent to pauper lunatic asylums.

On election night, 15 November 1922, John joined an excited throng at the 1917 Club. It was the turning point, the night Labour replaced the Liberals as the principal opposition to Bonar Law's Conservative government. Attlee won by 9,688 votes to 7,789, a majority of 1,899 – a considerable achievement since the popular sitting Conservative had held the seat for 16 years.

But it seemed to John and his friends even better than that. It was not just Labour which was on the verge of government. Between 1918 and 1922, ILP left-wingers such as John, Attlee, Brockway and Allen had put their heart and soul into efforts to ensure that ILP candidates carried Labour's banner in as many constituencies as possible. It is a bitter and unreported war that goes on in constituencies all over the land to this day, though almost no one notices – the battle between Labour's different factions over who gets to dominate the next Parliamentary Labour Party.

In 1922 the ILP was so successful that the majority of Labour MPs elected in 1922 were its members. John believed this meant that the Parliamentary Labour Party would be dominated, not by conservative trade union officials as before, but by revolutionary socialists.

That night John was sure that they were going to change the world, and that he had better get into Parliament quickly, or he would be too late. Britain would be a socialist society before he had time to play a real part in the transformation.

The ILP triumph was completed a few days later when it secured the election of ILP leader Ramsay MacDonald as Labour leader instead of the trade union nominee J.R. Clynes. MacDonald had been born 56 years earlier in Lossiemouth, the illegitimate son of a farm worker, and John believed in him, writing:

> From the calling of the Conference to form Soviets in 1917 until his own election as Leader of the Opposition in 1922, Ramsay MacDonald, unreported in the press, travelled like a

revolutionary flame from end to end of the country. Even in East London, where the hold of the ILP had never been strong, I could pack halls for MacDonald ... but the so-called moderate leaders could only get either empty halls or crowds of shouting or indignant hecklers.

John was even party to the attempts by MacDonald's friends to cheer him up (MacDonald was a naturally gloomy man). On one occasion John and some others dragged him out to see Harry Lauder in the West End. They arranged to meet at the 1917 Club, where Mac-Donald arrived with a lady whom he introduced as a Polish countess. He whispered at dinner that he had only enough money to pay for his own ticket. John, who was always careless with loose money, found the exact sum required in the lining of his jacket, and slipped it quietly to his leader. MacDonald brooded during the performance but said at the end that Lauder was just like any other Scotsman.

After Attlee's election to Parliament in 1922, John, Helen and Lesley stayed in the house in Limehouse, though Attlee moved with his wife to a new home in suburban Woodford. John acted as Attlee's private secretary; but the sense of being settled had departed with the older man. Attlee surely never knew how those long, comfortable conversations as they smoked their pipes in the evenings in Limehouse impressed themselves on his younger and less educated companion. Neither man ever knew how much John missed them, or how lost he was without them.

They must have made an odd pair. John was brash, noisy and brimming with apparent confidence and superficial worldly knowledge. Attlee was quiet, diffident and shy. But Attlee possessed an absolute inner certainty which John could never have. John must have sensed it even as he twitted his friend for his sexual naivety.

Subconsciously, John was taking notes. In the mid 1990s, I wrote a biography of Attlee. It was a strange experience to become slowly familiar with Attlee's habits of thought, his prejudices, his general approach to life – and to remember my father saying the words, and know for the first time where he had learned them. What Attlee told him stuck, which is one reason why he was such a mass of contradictions, because Attlee's prescriptions were not natural to him.

Clem Attlee ran his life with care and forethought. If he had to leave a job, or abandon a belief, he always made sure that he left a good feeling behind him. When he disowned the religion he had been brought up with, he did it with infinite care and tact so that his family would not be offended. When he found that Toynbee Hall was not all he had hoped for, he gave up his job there so graciously that no one ever took offence, and he was ever afterwards welcome there. That was how he lived, and how he told John that a man ought to live; and John was still solemnly trying to teach his children that lesson 30 years later. Always leave places cleanly, he said. Never leave a mess on the doorstep as you go. Make sure you leave a good reputation behind. Yet no one could have failed to follow this sensible advice so consistently and spectacularly as he did.

John said often, with a perfectly straight face, that he disapproved of inflammatory language, especially for unremarkable policies. He preferred, he said, to couch his radical policies in quiet and reasonable-sounding words. But his speeches were always the most extreme and the most inflammatory of any of his colleagues, as contemporaries like Fenner Brockway have testified. Attlee could make a call for the tumbrels sound like the London telephone directory. John could hardly ask for buttered toast in the morning without sending the shivers up someone's spine. It must have been Attlee who taught him that, to carry through revolutionary ideas, your behaviour has to be disarmingly normal. Attlee's was. John thought his ought to be, but never managed to make it anything short of terrifying.

He even absorbed Attlee's devotion to Oxford University. For the rest of his life John cheered on the Oxford crew in the boat race every year. James Callaghan wrote in his autobiography that Attlee, as Prime Minister, once asked for someone's background, and when given it, said: "Thought so. Cambridge man. All statistics. No sense of history." For the first time, I knew where my father had learned what he thought was the real difference between these two universities, neither of which he knew anything at all about.

His life was one he could not have imagined before the war. Theatres were one diversion in a frantically busy political life. There was the 1917 Club during the week, and weekends at country houses owned by wealthy ILP supporters.

John's social life revolved round the ILP. His friends were politicians like Attlee and Ernest Hunter, then a key ILP figure and MacDonald confidant; left-wing writers such as the novelist Mary Agnes Hamilton, who modelled two of her political agitators in *Follow My Leader* on John and Ernest Hunter (but the main one on Ramsay MacDonald); and left-wing actors and actresses, including Elsa Lanchester. Each weekend saw either a party or a conference. There were whole weeks spent in the frenzied atmosphere of by-elections. The draper's assistant and lance corporal, still only 28 when he propelled Clement Attlee into Parliament, had come a long way in the five years since he left the army.

He was to go a lot further, and he had become very good – perhaps too good – at hiding his insecurities.

But his heart was weak, and he had to put his teeth in a mug full of water every night. His family had sunk from the precarious lower-middle class into which he was born to the dreadfully impecunious working class. He knew that his loud voice and slightly vulgar accent (he was working on it) told that class-conscious world everything it needed to know about him. He had little education and must often have found himself out of depth in conversations.

What he had going for him was good looks, a strong voice, a flair for propaganda, a fluent and sometimes lethal tongue, a quick brain, a strong platform manner and the prestige of a former soldier in a party with too many pacifists for electoral comfort. It had taken him a long way, very fast. How much further could it take him?

Notes on sources

Attlee's unpublished autobiographical notes housed in Churchill College Cambridge.

As It Happened by Clement Attlee (Heinemann, 1954).

Clem Attlee by Francis Beckett (Haus, 2015).

The Fascists in Britain by Colin Cross (Barrie & Rockliffe, 1961).

Time and Chance by James Callaghan (Politicos, 2006).

4

THE THEATRE AND THE
GENERAL ELECTION

The great actor-manager Arthur Bourchier, from an old and wealthy family, was educated at Eton and Christ Church, Oxford, where he founded the Oxford University Dramatic Society (OUDS) in 1882 while still an undergraduate.

He was nearly 60 when John met him, and was the lessee of the Strand Theatre in London's West End, which he had run since 1919 and would run until his death in 1927, and where his portrait still hangs in the foyer. He also owned a large touring theatre business, and he transformed both John's outlook on life and his financial position.

He had played most of the great Shakespeare roles, some of them several times – Shylock, Jaques, Iago, Macbeth. Some critics thought him a little superficial, suggesting that he did not work quite hard enough, though pictures of him look to me like an actor who inhabits his parts. Each Christmas he played Long John Silver in *Treasure Island* and he once said: "I have made more money on one leg than I ever made on two."

The two may have met in the 1917 Club, but it is more likely that Bourchier was looking for a publicist for his theatre, as well as for a political mentor because he was a new convert to socialism; and that someone senior in the Labour Party recommended John for both roles. Either way, this new friendship greatly enhanced John's life, and then, less than a decade later, helped to destroy it.

Bourchier possessed family wealth, he was famous and had a huge income, yet, wrote John:

> He carried a load of debt big enough to overburden a small nation, and lived in the princeliest style. The fact that he was solvent at all he owed to his remarkable talents and to his two devoted managers.
>
> He never handled money, except for a payment of £5 a week which he called his "wad" and which had to be paid to him every Friday. This money he hoarded closely. His credit was good in the restricted circle in which he moved, and either the box office or his friends were called upon to pay taxi fares and other such outgoings. It was almost impossible to get a coin from him, yet he would part with large cheques.

John was impressed by Bourchier's vast frame, his loud and imperious voice and by the fact that when Bourchier walked into the Harcourt Room to dine, everyone turned to look at him, even if the other tables were full of cabinet ministers. He was impressed by the actor manager's frequent visits to Paris: travelling by the Golden Arrow, staying at the best hotels, entertaining lavishly and afterwards marvelling that one could do so well in Paris on the £22 he had spent in cash, while for months afterwards his managers paid a series of huge bills.

John travelled with Bourchier, who told him: "If you must travel, you should travel like a prince, my boy." Bourchier's homilies, like Attlee's, were never forgotten. It was probably Bourchier who taught him that even if you had no money and were in debt up to your eyeballs, it was important to look like a million dollars. "No one ever lends you money if you look as though you need it", my father used to tell me.

And I remember him saying often, to people who obviously thought it was his own idea, that any budding playwright could make a fortune in any age by putting the story of Cinderella in a modern setting. The idea, of course, came from Bourchier.

Bourchier's productions were probably my father's introduction to Shakespeare, and spoiled everyone else's for him, for no one could live up to his friend. Other productions of *Othello* always seemed tame and stagey to him. Bourchier's Iago, he said, "was no smiling villain, but a garrulous boaster whose lie to Othello was the result of vanity and stupidity".

John recalled how Bourchier would introduce himself to every new producer by saying: "Now, my bloody boy, I've got seven bloody tricks, let me do those and I'll do everything else you say." He remembered with awe the great man as director, impressing on young actors the need for stage technique. One of his favourite stories was of Bourchier telling a young actress to bring up a huge stepladder which was standing in the wings. She struggled on stage with it, and was told to climb it. When she was perched precariously on the top, he told her to look around and tell him what she saw. She stammered the names of a few stage props, until the terrible voice from the darkness roared out: "Can't you see the door handle which you never turn?" Like many inexperienced actors, she had neglected to treat the set door as though it were a real door.

Bourchier was almost the last of the great actor managers, who could take with him on a well-arranged provincial tour as expensive a company and production as he could use in the West End. Sometimes criticised by fellow professionals for not working hard enough at his parts, he was famous for "corpsing" his fellow actors – making them laugh out of character. One evening, bored by the same old play, he made the whole company play it in broken English.

Bourchier, on John's urging, joined the ILP and wrote an ILP pamphlet called Art and Culture in Relation to Socialism which attacked the "sordid, money-grubbing state of society" in which art and culture could only be "judged and accounted for by the self same standards that rule in the commercialised part of our commercialised society." It said that the theatre of the time had become "an after dinner resort ... to be enjoyed only by leaving one's brains in the cloakroom".

He campaigned for municipal and state supported theatres, so that the production of good plays should not depend on the occasional whims of philanthropists – the philosophy that, after the Second World War, created the Arts Council and the National Theatre.

He placed the Strand Theatre at the disposal of the ILP on Sunday evenings, when it was illegal to perform plays to paying audiences, and John organised there some of the most influential left-wing political meetings of the time. The two also worked together to found the Actors Association, the first actors' trade union and the predecessor of Equity.

He was already advising Bourchier when, early in 1923, John was taken to lunch at the 1917 Club by one of his most powerful patrons in the ILP establishment, the MP for Central Newcastle, a former Liberal and now Labour front bench politician, Sir Charles Trevelyan. Trevelyan had heard a great deal about John, liked what he heard and made him a proposal. Would John like to fight North Newcastle at the next general election?

The seat was not winnable, but a young candidate with energy and gifts as a campaigner might take the heat off the city's two winnable seats.

The two men travelled north that very afternoon. The next day John was unanimously adopted as a candidate in a city he had never visited before in his life.

Matters came to a head earlier than expected. After only a year in office Prime Minister Stanley Baldwin, who had replaced a sick Bonar Law, took everyone by surprise by calling a general election on 6 December 1923. He wanted, he said, to secure a mandate for reversing his free trade policy and bringing in protection in order to reduce unemployment. Within a few weeks of being selected, John was fighting the seat.

His brash and brilliant campaign boosted his confidence enormously. But Trevelyan's scheme went disastrously wrong. The press concentrated their attention on John, partly to avoid giving any publicity to the two Labour candidates with a chance of winning, Trevelyan himself and Arthur Henderson. "I was 29 years old," he wrote later, "filled with fanaticism, fire and crude dynamics. I seemed to have the gift of tongues, and after my first few meetings was addressing larger audiences than any two of the other candidates in the city put together."

Arthur Henderson had written Labour's constitution and set up its organisation after the war. He it was, together with Sidney Webb, who, for the first time, had ensured that the Labour Party could enrol individual members. Henderson was, in a real sense, the creator of the modern Labour Party.

This was not a Party for which John had any respect or liking at all. He took pride in the fact that he never joined the Labour Party, which he considered a dreary and uninspired machine. He was only a member by virtue of his membership of the ILP.

Henderson was later to be Foreign Secretary and Labour leader. But he was not a good campaigner. Considered by those who knew him to be a man of ability and integrity, he was ponderous, pompous and dull in public.

He and John addressed a joint eve-of-poll rally. John arrived very late. He had spoken at four exciting meetings and been carried shoulder high through a cheering crowd. He was tired, excited and above himself. The hall, where Henderson had just completed a worthy speech, seemed quiet and drab to him after the excitement of the street. So he worked himself up into a wild revolutionary speech which he wrote contritely many years afterwards, "could not have been anything but extremely embarrassing to Mr Henderson".

And then, turning to the stiff, disapproving figure seated beside him, he launched an impassioned appeal to "march forward led by this great revolutionary who sits here with us tonight". He meant it mischievously, but underestimated his audience. Instead of being carried away, a large section of it burst into mocking laughter.

Like a man who has behaved badly when drunk, John was filled with self-loathing the next day. He never quite forgot how ashamed he had felt. Fifteen years later, in 1938, a fascist and an outcast from the Party he had served, he could still write: "It says much for Mr Henderson's fairness of mind that when, in after days, he and I had much to do with one another, I invariably received courtesy and justice." What John did not do was to learn from this experience.

Henderson's temper was not improved by the election result on 6 December. John polled well in a hopeless seat. Henderson lost a winnable one which he had held previously, and blamed John for the loss.

Soon after the election, when MacDonald set about forming Labour's first government, the fact that his most senior lieutenant had no seat in Parliament caused a good deal of embarrassment, and Henderson had rapidly to be found a seat at a by-election so that he could become Home Secretary. But the speech did John nothing but good among local activists. Neighbouring Gateshead was held by the Liberals, and the Labour Party there believed they could win next time, so long as they had a sufficiently exciting and energetic candidate. John looked just right to them, and he won their nomination to contest the next election, whenever that might be.

Ten months after the formation of the minority Labour government, it fell. John's chance had come.

The 1924 election was precipitated by the Campbell case. A communist, Jonny Campbell, was arrested for distributing a leaflet to soldiers calling on them to "let it be known that, neither in the class war nor in a military war, will you turn your guns on your fellow workers".

The decision to prosecute Campbell was reversed by the cabinet because of its great unpopularity in the Party, and the Conservatives seized the chance to level the charge that Labour was soft on communism. The Liberals offered a face-saving formula: a select committee to look into the whole affair. MacDonald, surprisingly, turned down this chance to save his government. It was rumoured that he feared an inquiry might show he had a more direct part in the affair than he admitted.

Gateshead's sitting Liberal MP at that time was a middle-aged, slightly pompous politician, whom John found it easy to score off. On a tiny sum of money, with a devoted band of supporters, he was justifiably proud of sending to every elector an address, as well as a four-page election newspaper which John, of course, edited himself, and a polling card.

In his election newspaper, he claimed that the Campbell affair was an excuse to bring down the government. The real reason was to scupper bills to outlaw profiteering, as well as Labour's budget, which would have moved "the national burdens from the backs of the working and middle classes and transferring them to the shoulders of the wealthy people who pay the Liberal and Tory election expenses".

Helen wrote, or at least signed, an appeal to the women of Gateshead – for women over 30 now had a vote.

> I hail from the North myself and it is a great joy to me that he should be bearing the standard of Labour in this great Northern constituency, whose men and women are keen, kind and straightforward and appreciate honest endeavour ... In nearly every home the wife and mother is the Chancellor of the Exchequer. Her menfolk earn the money, but I think, in these days of high prices and low wages, that the woman has the hardest job.

He and the Conservative candidate agreed to stage a debate in the Town Hall, and when the Liberal challenged both of them to debate, they replied that the issue was between a Conservative government and a Labour government, so could not concern the Liberal.

Meetings such as this, in a northern constituency in 1924, could make or break a campaign. It made John's campaign. The hall was packed, and the police estimated that 15,000 people gathered in the square outside the Town Hall. After it, the Labour contingent bore their candidate home in triumph.

He loved the public platform, the applause, the feeling that he could move audiences. Just how good he was we cannot know for certain. He himself always thought he was magical, but not everyone agreed. Mrs Bertha Elliott was a child at the time, the daughter of a prominent member of the Gateshead Labour Party. She wrote to me:

> He was flamboyant, had very black hair (long in the style of James Maxton) and he kept flinging his head back. He also was very restless when on a public platform, but he did not stride about. He always sat dangerously on the corner of the chairman's table, with his hand in his left trouser pocket, and he wriggled about so much I remember my mother saying that he got on her nerves and his speech was spoiled for her because she was afraid he would fall off.

Gateshead was one of the poorest constituencies in Britain, with a third of the men either unemployed or under-employed. The poor had to be mobilised; but it was not easy. The women in the poorest wards would not come out to vote because they were ashamed of their clothes. Many women could not leave young children in order to go and vote. The men in work got home tired and dirty, and did not care to go anywhere until they had washed and eaten – by which time the polls had closed.

So John detailed helpers to wait outside as the shift finished, and marshal the men straight to the polls. He organised street processions to the polling stations led by some of the Irish women councillors, so that "the women's rags then became the banners of the people's army, and they were not ashamed when there were many of them together to flaunt their poverty".

Four days before polling day came another communist scare which ended any hope of a Labour victory nationally. The *Daily Mail* printed what purported to be a letter from Grigory Zinoviev, general secretary of the Comintern, calling on the British Communist Party to paralyse the army and navy by forming cells inside them. "And Mr MacDonald would lend Russia our money!" screamed the *Mail* head-line. (The paper also pointed out darkly the sinister fact that Zinoviev's real name was Apfelbaum. Anti-Semitism in the 1920s was not confined to the left.) MacDonald foolishly confirmed that the letter was genuine. We now know that it was a forgery.

John's friend Ernest Hunter was responsible for MacDonald's campaign, so Gateshead was favoured with a visit from the leader. It was not a success. MacDonald made a speech devoted, John said afterwards, mostly to his own personal grievances. The next day, just before he departed, MacDonald disappointed a huge crowd waiting for him on a big open space by leaving before anyone had realised he was there.

John's efforts were rewarded, however, in this Liberal-held seat, with a majority of 10,000 over the Conservative, and 500 over Con-servative and Liberal combined. Never again, until 1945, did Gates-head return a clear Labour majority over all other parties; and in 1945, the Gateshead majority followed a winning trend for Labour. In the 1924 election, Gateshead was one of the few successes in an election at which many of the gains of the 1922 and 1923 elections were lost.

John was proud of it all his life, and he had a right to be. Yet there was a certain rootlessness about representing Gateshead. He knew little about it, and he never felt a part of the place. He hankered for London. He was not like Attlee, representing an area he had lived and worked in and come to know and love.

Still, his old friend Attlee wrote him a graceful and flattering letter. There was a lot to congratulate him about. Just seven years earlier, broke, ill and toothless, he was looking for a job. In November 1924, John Beckett, having celebrated his thirtieth birthday the previous month, was Labour's youngest Member of Parliament, after running what may have been the most professional and energetic of any parliamentary campaign in that election year.

He was already known as one of Labour's most formidable campaigners for his work in getting Major Attlee into Parliament. The Gateshead success was down almost entirely to the young, energetic, charismatic, professional campaigner, who understood journalism, advertising and propaganda as few other Labour figures of the time understood them.

He entered the Palace of Westminster in triumph, to the plaudits of his many glittering friends, who included the rising stars of the Labour Party and some of the biggest theatrical celebrities of the day. He had found a use for his loud voice, holding great audiences with his oratory, and he could captivate women with his handsome face and fluent charm. The rage against the world had been turned into an apparently coherent political philosophy, and one which looked to be on the verge of victory.

Some of the rough edges had been removed from his vowels by regular contact with actors and actresses and with the Old Haileyburian Clem Attlee and the Old Etonian Hugh Dalton. He must have felt that he had a magic touch, that he had put behind him forever any doubts or uncertainties about his own judgement or ability. If he could arrive in such style, how could anything ever go wrong?

Like many another young politician, early in 1925 he saw himself as a future Prime Minister. In his case, no one at the time would have called the dream absurd.

And something else went swiftly right for him. Most Labour MPs were quite hard up, and John had a wife and child. Parliament had always been considered a place for wealthy men who did not need paying, and the parliamentary salary was only £400 a year.

For John, a few newspaper articles on how it felt to be elected eased the immediate financial pressure. And very soon after he became an MP, some real money came his way. With Bourchier's guidance and advice, and probably Bourchier's money (for he had none of his own), John invested heavily in touring companies and West End theatre, and quite quickly made himself far richer than the rangy, toothless Jack Beckett of 1917 could ever have dreamed of being.

Perhaps because of his friendship with Bourchier, a few months after his election to Parliament John found himself, rather improbably, sharing a platform at Wyndham's Theatre with George Bernard Shaw, the actress Sybil Thorndike and the Irish author Conal O'Riordan, discussing the real meaning of Shaw's *Major Barbara*.

Somehow the whole thing got on his nerves. He disliked studied theatricality, or thought he did. He was irritated by Shaw, who "having gained a reputation for wit, suffers agonies in his efforts to retain it". He thought his audience "either Hampstead pseudo-intellectual, or the kind of fan which makes itself a pest at theatrical garden parties, and places where there is an opportunity to intrude its petty ego upon hard-working people whom it could not possibly interest". He loathed "the air of genteel sympathy with the working classes".

So he made a speech of violent class hatred, designed to irritate both his audience and his hosts (who, he later admitted, had deserved better treatment) and left.

He was followed out by a tall, handsome young man who introduced himself as Denis Neilson-Terry, a matinee idol of the day and one of the famous theatrical Terrys of whom John Gielgud is the most recent example. Neilson-Terry had loved the speech, and wanted to make contact with the real world outside the privileged theatrical one in which he had been brought up.

He later spent long periods in Gateshead with John, meeting miners and Labour Party activists. For John it was a glittering friendship, and when one day someone saw the two of them together and remarked how alike they were in appearance, his cup of happiness overflowed.

He moved out of Attlee's rooms in Norway House into a fine detached family home at 48 Anson Road, Cricklewood. Throughout his time in Parliament, John was really quite well off, living in considerable style and able to entertain lavishly. Few of his Labour colleagues could do that.

He must have seemed, in the second half of the 1920s, like a young man with a golden touch. He had not yet learned how quickly and suddenly money and reputation can evaporate.

Altogether, John was very happy indeed when he first entered Parliament. He loved the attention bestowed on the youngest MP in his Party, the glittering audiences anxious to hear his views and to pay them flattering attention. Life was pleasant and exciting for a young man on the verge of what looked like a luminous political career.

Note on sources

Cambridge History of British Theatre, Volume 3, edited by Baz Kenshaw (Cambridge University Press, 2015).

5

LABOUR'S YOUNGEST MP

I think it was the very next day after the general election that it all started to go wrong.

That day John walked proudly into the 1917 Club, where he was welcomed like a conquering hero, and sat in triumph with some of his friends, and also a fat man whom Ernest Hunter introduced as Colonel Harry Day, a wealthy variety agent who had won Southwark in South London for Labour. In came Labour's leader, Ramsay MacDonald. John wrote:

> MacDonald ... at once engaged Day in animated conversation. I have rarely seen him so anxious to please. He had not greeted me; and someone reminded him that I had just returned from my constituency. He turned briefly in my direction. "Oh, yes, Beckett," he said, "weren't you fighting somewhere? How did you get on?" Stifling the thought that the leader of the Party should know something of the very few victories gained under his leadership, I could not resist thanking him for the warmth with which he had recommended my candidature to the people of Gateshead a week before. He smiled coldly, and returned to an animated discussion of some antique furniture

he had seen, but could not afford, with which he regaled Mr Day's wealthy and receptive ear.

Although John's fragile self-esteem plays a part in the way he tells the story, there are too many similar MacDonald stories for us to doubt this one. And John was not alone in his interpretation of the relationship between MacDonald and Day. Seven years later, on 25 August 1931, John's friend and the future Chancellor of the Exchequer Hugh Dalton confided to his diary:

> There was for some months after the [1929 Labour] government came in a standing order for a bottle of champagne, with three glasses, to be sent each night to JRM's room. The order was in the name of Harry Day, and he is still without a job!

To Dalton it was a joke with a serious edge. To John it was one of those things which clouded his brain with so much anger that he could not see. Dalton did not add, but John did, that Day's "original name was not Day". Codes for "Jew" were gradually becoming common in his circles. He could have added, but did not, that his own mother's original name was not Salmon.

I think that was the start of the downward path, but no one would have known at the time, for no one could have seen the thinness of the skin that lay beneath the bluff, noisy orator. John seemed to his colleagues to be a model young MP with a brilliant future. He took care to learn the rules and procedures of the House, discovering to his surprise that quite soon he knew them a great deal better than some MPs of long standing, who relied on the whips for the smallest things.

He was introduced informally to the Prince of Wales by a young Conservative MP, and decided on the spot that the monarchy was not such a bad thing after all, and that this "earnest and intelligent young man", once he became King Edward VIII, would change the face of the nation, and make everything much better. He wrote a weekly Westminster Letter for the *Bradford Pioneer*, the ILP's newspaper, based in the town where the Party had been formed and had its headquarters. It was a prestigious task within the ILP and remarkable that it should go to so young an MP. Moreover, it gave him a sort of power over the Party greats.

When one of his early columns praised a speech by Ramsay Mac-Donald, his leader approached him the next day, for the first time since he had entered Parliament, to say how much he appreciated John's political and journalistic work. But a few weeks later John wrote that railwaymen's leader Jimmy Thomas's buffoonery had made him sick. MacDonald complained bitterly, and Thomas stormed up to him in a fury to tell him that he would ensure that the railwaymen drove John out of Gateshead before the next election. John replied that the fact that he was there at all showed that Gateshead's railwaymen had higher standards than those of their leader.

It seemed to John as though he could do anything. If he could so easily provoke the famous Jimmy Thomas to incoherent threats, he must surely have arrived. It was a wonderful feeling. It may have lasted as much as eight weeks. Then he learned the bitter truth about the powerlessness of a backbench MP, and his wonderful new world was in ruins all about him. I think he went at once from the pinnacle of triumph to the depth of despair.

It was his old friend Clem Attlee who inadvertently burst John's bubble. During the short-lived Labour government, Attlee had been Under Secretary of State for War, and had come across a scandal which he wanted to see exposed. "It's the dirtiest business of the whole war", Attlee said to John.

While he was in the government, Attlee simply stored it up in his huge memory. After the general election, when Labour was again in opposition, he handed over the facts as he knew them to John. Attlee was never to be identified as the source of the story. He knew that John had a talent for publicity, and would feel, as Attlee did, that it was the sort of affair that made a mockery of the deaths of his wartime comrades.

The story was this. During the war the Germans discovered a new method of extracting nitrogen from the air, which was much cheaper than the British method. Nitrogen was vital in the manufacture of explosives, and important in peacetime for the production of ferti-liser. The armistice terms gave the Allies the right to investigate German secrets, and a commission of three army officers went to Cologne for several months to investigate this one.

But Attlee could not find a copy of their report in the War Office; nor could anyone tell him where it was; nor was there any trace of the three officers who compiled it.

Where were these officers? The senior officer on the commission was a director of a company called Brunner, Mond, and the other two officers were employed by it.

The British factory making fertiliser, at Billingham-on-Tees, had been sold at a knockdown price of £450,000 to Sir Alfred Mond in 1920, when Sir Alfred was a member of the government – it had cost the country £1,100,000 to establish and run. Sir Alfred had set up Brunner, Mond, to exploit the new method of extracting nitrogen. And now, at Billingham-on-Tees, Sir Alfred's company was making a fortune because it had a monopoly of this German secret. The company was using its monopoly of the secret to keep the price of fertiliser artificially high.

Here if anywhere was the "hard-faced man who has done well out of the war". Here was the corrupt wartime profiteer whom Attlee and John hated so much. In his innocence, John seems to have believed that he had only to make these facts known, and Sir Alfred would be ruined.

He started in March 1925, with the help of two other young MPs, Neil Maclean and Hugh Dalton, just three months into his parliamentary career, by asking questions in the House about the sale of the Billingham factory. On 1 April he used the mechanism of raising the question on the adjournment. Maclean and Dalton rustled up the 40 MPs he needed for a quorum. He wrote a personal note to Sir Alfred informing him that he would mention him in his speech, and to government whips explaining what questions he would ask.

When the great day arrived, however, Sir Alfred did not attend the debate, and the Under Secretary for War said he knew nothing about it: it was a Treasury matter, and no Treasury spokesman was present. There had, of course, been plenty of time for the Treasury to provide a spokesman. John was left empty-handed. As the House rose, he looked up despairingly at the press gallery. They had all gone home, having heard nothing. It had all been useless.

The next month Mond's firm was given £2 million worth of government credits, and John found he was not permitted to raise any questions about this.

He turned to the press. He was one of Labour's most prolific political journalists, writing frequently for such papers as the left-wing *Daily Herald* and the virulently right-wing and pro-war *John Bull*, the paper which during the war had "exposed" the fact that Ramsay MacDonald was born illegitimate. These papers had been delighted to accept his articles on how it felt to be a new MP, but they all turned down his article on Sir Alfred Mond and the fertiliser.

Eventually he managed to place it in George Lansbury's *Labour Weekly*. John and the editor, Raymond Postgate, decided to do everything they could to goad Mond into suing. Postgate gave it a splendid spread and accompanied it with a huge cartoon. John put all his energetic invective into the story:

> The Mond company has secured a monopoly of the way of turning the air we breathe into profit ... Lieut. Colonel Pollitt, who was the Chairman of the Commission, is now a director of Brunner Mond's new company, and this generous firm have also patriotically found well paid employment for every other member of the Commission ... The factory at Billingham which had cost the country £1,100,000 was sold to Messrs Brunner Mond for the paltry sum of £450,000 by a government of which Sir Alfred Mond was himself a member ... In addition they have the valuable secret obtained for the State from Germany, which has not cost them a penny ... To suborn State servants is a grave crime...
>
> I do not, personally, care tuppence about our being prepared for the next war. I wish nobody at all had any explosives more dangerous than Chinese crackers. But ... the gentlemen who are now steadily preparing the next war handed over the national supply of explosives to a private firm. And if the present government get the war they are preparing, they will have to go cap in hand to Sir Alfred and pay what he asks. And capitalists know patriotism is not enough. They like large profits mixed with it.
>
> Big profits have been made by responsible public men out of a deal in which they secretly sold government property to themselves and their friends. And this is hushed up on the plea of the public interest!

John sent a copy of the article to Sir Alfred, with an accompanying note saying he wanted to ensure that it did not appear without Sir Alfred seeing it. Sir Alfred returned a friendly note, thanking him for sending the article, which, he said, he had read with the greatest interest.

And that was that. Except, perhaps, for one small aspect to the whole affair, which is entirely irrelevant to it, but which I am sure that neither John nor his fellow campaigner Hugh Dalton thought was irrelevant.

Two years earlier, at the 1923 general election, Dalton had unsuccessfully contested Cardiff East for Labour. His biographer Ben Pimlott records:

> The Liberal MP for the neighbouring Swansea constituency was a Jewish manufacturer, Sir Alfred Mond. At one meeting Dalton told his audience that his own policy was to carry out the old injunction "feed my lambs". Encouraged by applause, he added: "Mond, of course, doesn't get beyond the Old Testament."

John was not the only young Labour politician with codes for "Jew".

John himself never referred to Mond's Jewishness, so far as I know. But by then he had probably met H.H. Beamish, who ran *The Britons*, a prototype fascist publication, and in 1919 had published *The Protocols of the Learned Elders of Zion*, the forgery which he believed proved the existence of a Jewish conspiracy aimed at world domination. In 1919 Mond had sued Beamish for writing that, as a Jew, his loyalties during the war were suspect, as evidenced by the fact that he had allotted shares in his companies to Germans. Beamish had used the courtroom publicity to claim that Jews were a separate race whose loyalty could not be trusted: "A man can't be both English and Jew."

Mond was awarded £5,000 damages and Beamish travelled to South Africa to avoid paying. There he retrieved his fortunes and produced a book called *The Jews' Who's Who*, a list of influential Jews and their interconnections.

Beamish returned to Britain in 1923 and Mond refrained from pursuing him for the damages, partly no doubt perhaps because the charge of wartime profiteering was true.

John and Hugh Dalton, unlike Beamish, did not attack Mond
because he was a Jew. They attacked him because he was greedy and
corrupt, and his greed and corruption took a form which they found
especially offensive. Dalton's life was overshadowed by the First
World War, even more than John's. His closest friends, including the
poet Rupert Brooke, had been killed. "People have sometimes asked,
since then," he wrote in his autobiography, "why I had so few men
friends of my own age. The answer is the war. Before that I was very
rich in friendships."

In 1925 one of those few friends was John Beckett. They both
believed passionately that a man who could corruptly make a fortune
over the blood of their dead wartime comrades ought to be hounded
from public life.

In 1925, nonetheless, there may have been a part of both John and
Hugh Dalton which saw a connection between the fact that Mond
was corrupt and the fact that he was a Jew. As they both grew older,
Dalton must have started to see that this was dangerous and wicked,
until by 1945 he was considered the firmest Zionist in the Attlee
cabinet.

For John, the supposed connection turned into an obsession that
helped to destroy him. I think the Mond affair was one of the biggest
single steps on John's road from idealism to bigotry.

John was enraged by his own impotence. It was as though the cup
from which he had started so happily to drink when he entered the
House had turned out to contain the bitterest poison. From believing
he could do everything, he was within six months plunged into the
bleakest despair and believed he could do nothing.

To add to his misery, about the same time as he started pursuing
Mond, just three months into his parliamentary career, this practised
and accomplished orator blew his big chance to make a parliamentary
name for himself.

His old patron, Sir Charles Trevelyan, arranged for John to represent the Party in an important and contentious debate on a motion to
place foreign affairs under parliamentary control. He knew nothing
about the subject though it ought to have been close to his heart, for
it was about preventing war. He was briefed heavily by several
research organisations and lobby groups, and had not yet acquired the

skill to abandon what he did not need. Trevelyan, Attlee and Dalton all impressed on him that this was his big chance to secure a glittering parliamentary future, and that he was lucky and very favoured to get it.

When the big night arrived he was in a pitiful condition. "The House roasted me, and the Speaker called me to order for irrelevance several times. They were both right."

Actually, his performance as reported by Hansard does not look quite as dreadful as he supposed. He went over the top, but then he always did, talking of

> the secret diplomatists of all countries who ... flung the youth of this country into the furnace of hate, horribleness and beast-liness ... Before the war many people in Germany thought quite genuinely that we meant to attack them directly ... Yes, they were fooled by their politicians, just as we were fooled by ours.

He talked a lot about Japan and President Woodrow Wilson until the deputy speaker said: "The Honourable Gentleman is rather far from the terms of the motion." As he became more and more miserable, and he was heckled more and more, he hit back: "I rather gathered that at this time in the evening some members of the House were more in the mood to prefer amusement." There were shouts of "Withdraw!", for MPs in those days knew a code for "drunk" when they heard one, and the House of Commons was a far more bibulous place than it is today. He declined to withdraw, and for good measure added: "There is no point in mincing words ... We are not prepared ... to allow Right Honourable Gentlemen with the war and peace records of some of the Right Honourable Gentlemen on the opposite benches, to handle these matters in secrecy..."

The elderly, patrician Tory Sir John Marriott followed. "I would like to say of the speech to which we have just listened that I am sure there was real sincerity, although some of us took exception to the words uttered."

Then, John recorded, "I went to dinner abject and alone. I chose a small secluded table instead of going to the long table which rank and file Labour members used." To his table came Colonel Josiah

Wedgwood, veteran MP, vice chairman of the Parliamentary Labour Party, friend of Clement Attlee, dedicated parliamentarian and relative of the late Tony Benn, bearing a glass of sherry and a message of hope.

A lot of MPs made fools of themselves, he said; the trick was to get back on the bicycle as fast as you could, and not brood on it. It was good advice, and John followed it. The very next day he asked the Home Secretary whether he would consider making third party insurance a condition of motor car ownership – a rather sensible idea which was eventually implemented in the Road Traffic Act of 1930 – and over the next few days he asked a series of sensible low-profile questions.

He was, in other words, turning himself into a good House of Commons man who expected to be in the cabinet one day. But there was turmoil underneath the surface of the increasingly accomplished young parliamentarian. The House, which he had entered with such pride just three months earlier, now suddenly seemed like a prison. He resented being seen as lobby fodder. He despised the House's antiquated formalities. He found the chamber where MPs debated miserable, stuffy and unhealthy, with its artificial light and its lack of ventilation, and the speeches made there unbelievably pointless and tedious. (MPs now work in rather more comfortable surroundings because the chamber of the House of Commons was bombed in the Second World War.)

The only alternatives, the tea room or the library or the bars, made him even more miserable. "I am not a clubbable type of man," he wrote rather stiffly, "and the library conversations were almost worse than the debates. The main subjects were political gossip, wearisome anecdotage, or, endlessly and tediously, the kind of 'funny' story associated with barrack rooms." Which is an odd thing for him to write; for John had a remarkable talent for embroidering anecdotes, he enjoyed political gossip and he had a wonderfully funny store of the most scabrous stories imaginable, which he told with enormous zest and flair. "There was little else to do," he wrote miserably, "except walk like caged lions up and down the length of the terrace."

Here was a man of just 30, the youngest MP of his Party, tipped for a brilliant parliamentary career, walking on the terrace of the

House of Commons with its wonderful views over the river, rubbing shoulders with the most famous men of his day, the envy of everyone he had ever known, and he felt simply caged up and alienated.

He grew quickly to despise most of his fellow Labour MPs. The safest Labour seats, which had survived the 1924 electoral setback, were generally in the pockets of the unions, and given to elderly trade union officials as a kind of retirement present.

The unions have always tended to see the Parliamentary Labour Party as a sort of junior partner. It is an instinct which persisted until well into the 1980s, and traces of it can still be seen to this day. MPs have their uses, but they do not do the real work of the Labour movement: that's done in trade union offices. Being an MP is seen as a consolation prize for a long-standing union official who has never quite climbed to the top of the tree and is no longer up to the arduous work of union organisation.

"These cohorts of aged men," John raged, "putting on physical and mental flesh daily as they sucked their pipes round the map room in the Library, which became, by ancient lore, their refuge from the cares of the world." Many of them, "through a hard youth in the pits and a too easy middle age in a trade union office", were prematurely aged. John had no patience with them.

Not so his friend Hugh Dalton, who, John wrote, "tolerated fools gladly, spending hours in the library and smoking rooms, listening with an air of cordiality and interest to the dreariest anecdotage". John was the first of many to notice the foundations upon which Dalton built a career which peaked in 1945 when he became Chancellor of the Exchequer.

But John, having no talent for flattery himself, never saw what more perceptive observers saw: that Dalton was not very good at it. Dalton became known as "the man who slaps you on the back and calls you by someone else's Christian name". "Morning, Tom", he called to an aged trade union MP in 1945, and then confided to a much younger politician, Roy Jenkins, "You'll never get anywhere in the Labour Party until you learn to call that man Tom." Jenkins pointed out that the man's name was Bill.

Dalton cultivated obscure trade unionists who had block votes at their disposal, offering his impressive contacts, sophisticated knowledge and extensive intelligence in return for their influence inside the Party, laughing a little too loudly at their jokes. Intending to leave them feeling grateful, he often only left them feeling patronised.

He also cultivated John Beckett, and wrote in his diary years later, after John had imploded, that he was "a friend of mine at that time" who had "great energy and some ability" and he was disappointed when he became a fascist. For by then, with that instinct that politicians have, he knew John's friendship was a liability, not an asset.

But in those early days, John and Hugh Dalton talked for hours, in the House and at Dalton's Westminster flat, John raging against the way things were, Dalton listening with flattering attentiveness. He must have seen that John would either rise to the top or burn himself and his boats with the heat of his passion.

Dalton eventually became more skilled at selecting the young men whom he groomed for high office. After 1945 he had sentimental friendships with many of the next generation of Labour leaders, and consciously advanced their careers: Jenkins, Anthony Crosland, Hugh Gaitskell.

"Had I listened to Dalton's good advice," wrote John, "and to Attlee's, my career would probably have been very much more distinguished in the parliamentary sense."

Instead he listened to Ellen Wilkinson, the young recently elected MP for Middlesbrough, who was to become Education Minister in 1945. She was a tiny bundle of energetic idealism, one of a group of intellectuals who had recently left the newly formed Communist Party. Their friendship began over a weekend spent in her constituency a few months after the election. It was supposed to be a weekend of open-air meetings, but it rained continuously, and they hardly left their small commercial hotel, deserted except for themselves.

She considered herself well to the left of John and his friends Dalton and Attlee, and at first told John he was "one of MacDonald's good little careerists". But they were firm friends by the end of the weekend. "Our friendship," noted John caustically,

> endured until I had become the Parliamentary Whip of the
> extreme left and was almost entirely severed from the Labour

Party, while Ellen was a Parliamentary Private Secretary attached to the Labour government and supporting its most reactionary measures in the division lobby.

Friends they certainly were; lovers they may well have been. John was fast acquiring a reputation for sexual profligacy. The discovery that he was attractive to women, like the discovery that he could move great audiences with his oratory, rather went to his head. His relationship with Ellen Wilkinson was certainly different from that with his other Labour Party friends. Ten years later, when he was no longer able even to talk to them, John wrote of other old Labour colleagues, and they wrote of him, with a kind of affectionate sadness. But he and Ellen Wilkinson wrote of each other with a sharp sense of personal betrayal.

She, footloose, fancy-free and sharing to the full the sense of liberation which radical young women had in the 1920s, was in a position to form a personal as well as political partnership with a young, good-looking fellow Labour MP. John seems to have lived and travelled as though he, too, were footloose and fancy-free; but, of course, he was not. In his Cricklewood house, he had a wife and daughter. It seems quite likely that, in her husband's first year as an MP, Helen was starting to feel more than a little neglected.

But that was not why she left him. Nor was it sexual jealousy which caused her, one day in John's first two years in Parliament, to pick up her child and walk out of his house, never to return, leaving not even a note to tell her husband where she had gone.

It was simply, as her daughter Lesley explained to me, that she watched him spending what seemed like huge sums of money in entertaining, at the House of Commons and in expensive restaurants. She knew that the money was coming from shaky theatrical ventures; and she was a working-class girl who had been brought up to be careful about money.

John was still sure, however, that nothing could touch him. He was driving his life like the powerful racing cars and motor bikes which he soon started driving on weekends at Brooklands.

Helen could not see the immovable concrete obstacles into which their life together could so easily crash, but an intelligent instinct told her they were there. Her warnings may have been too vague for him to understand, or perhaps he understood and thought them foolish. So she left him to live with her mother, and took her daughter with her. John woke up one morning to an empty house. It disturbed him, and upset him, but not enough.

Ellen Wilkinson introduced him into a circle which he had not known before, and which was more radical than that of his London ILP friends Attlee and Dalton. Her friends were communists and former communists, and to John's taste far too much like the Clifford Allen circle which he had grown to dislike so fiercely. "One end of Bloomsbury is very like another", he mused. But they, like him, were impatient with the Labour leadership and not afraid to say so.

Every fortnight he left Westminster for a speaking tour in the north-east, often with Ellen Wilkinson. There he recharged his batteries, rekindled his idealism and remembered his despair. He was a favourite speaker not only in Gateshead and Newcastle, but throughout Durham:

> Each time I spoke in Gateshead I saw huge audiences of expectant and suffering faces; my own friends who had walked in broken shoes and thin coats through the cold and rain of the election period were unable to find sufficient food and comfort for their families. During the war they had managed to accumulate the necessities of life and a few small luxuries. For the first time they had known what it was to have just that little margin which they could use for pleasure and comfort. From 1918 to 1923 this was steadily stripped from them until by 1924 they had sold or pawned the purchases of the war years and were in a worse condition than that they had first known. I felt intensely my powerlessness to help.

As for his fellow Labour MPs, "These smug, comfortable men on the benches beside me, had promised to dedicate their lives to the underdog; yet lived handsomely on pennies extracted from hungry men." One day in September 1926, his hosts asked him to sign a visitor's book and, in his huge, flamboyant handwriting he left an impromptu verse:

> Oh better far to live and die
> Under the brave red flag we fly
> Than play a mean and greedy part
> With a Tory head and a pirate heart.

It was, of course, his adaptation of the pirate king's song from *The Pirates of Penzance*, and the song ran through his tuneless head all his life:

> Oh better far to live and die
> Under the brave black flag I fly
> Than play a sanctimonious part
> With a pirate head and a pirate heart.

Notes on sources

Hansard.
Call Back Yesterday by Hugh Dalton (Frederick Muller, 1953).
Haters, Baiters and Would-be Dictators by Nick Toczek (Routledge, 2016).
Hugh Dalton, A Life by Ben Pimlott (Harper Collins, 1995).

6

THE 1926 GENERAL STRIKE

Trade unions in the 1920s had real power, and a record 45 per cent of the workforce belonged to one. This percentage was not reached again until 1974, when the unions were again stronger than ever – and, again, were within a decade of their most decisive defeat. And the biggest and most powerful of them all was the 900,000-strong Miners Federation of Great Britain (MFGB) – the aristocracy of organised labour.

Britain needed coal. Getting it out of the ground was harsh, back-breaking and horrifyingly dangerous work, and the coal owners had a long record of exploiting the men, forcing them to work long hours for little pay, housing them in hovels and skimping on the expenditure necessary to provide safe working conditions.

So the miners had built up a strong trade union tradition to protect themselves. When they went on strike, they all went, though they knew that after the strike, the owners, if they emerged from the battle strong enough to do so, would victimise strike leaders, and evict them from their homes. "Scab" – strike-breaker – was the most offensive name you could call a miner.

Strikes were frequent, and frequently successful, because unions were well supported. Union leaders became national figures – a tradition that lasted right up to the 1984–5 miners' strike, and then ceased abruptly. From 1920 to 1984, the great union leaders were household names ranking alongside top politicians: Ernest Bevin, Walter Citrine, Arthur Cook, Frank Cousins, Hugh Scanlon, Jack Jones, Laurence Daly, Arthur Scargill and many more.

The new political and industrial militancy, and the vast gap between conspicuous wealth and grinding poverty which had been accepted as the natural order of things before the war, made a mix which many people believed meant revolution.

Miners still lived in some of the harshest conditions, with poverty pay and tied housing that was often not fit for human habitation. Their tiny, basic terraced homes were packed into small spaces in areas where there was no alternative employment. They had outdoor lavatories: "You had to go out the back, go up the steps and walk about 15 or 20 yards and carry a bucket of water with you", recalled one veteran, years later. Their union and their socialist faith told them that they did not need to live in squalor: they could fight for something better.

The mines, nationalised during the First World War, were denationalised immediately afterwards, much to the disappointment of the miners, who blamed the mine owners' greed and lack of enterprise for the unnecessary harshness of their lives. Renationalisation was top of the list of demands put to the government by the MFGB, along with reductions in hours and an increase in pay.

But the Conservative-dominated government under David Lloyd George was determined to disentangle itself from its wartime involvement with mining. The coal owners saw their dividends shrinking as they failed to compete with foreign coal, and resorted to the simple formula of cutting the cost of production by cutting the miners' wages and increasing their hours.

Miners went on strike on 21 April 1921. They held out until June, and returned to work with pay not just reduced but, in many districts, halved. In the increased poverty and squalor in which they lived, they nursed a deep sense of grievance against the fellow trade unionists who they believed had betrayed them – for dockers and railwaymen had promised to come out in support, and failed to do so.

They focused their hopes on political action through the Labour Party. When Labour first took office in January 1924, David Kirkwood, a newly elected left-wing Labour MP, told his cheering supporters as his London-bound train pulled out of Glasgow station: "When we come back, all this will belong to the people." But as Kirkwood was speaking, the new Prime Minister, Ramsay MacDonald, was apologising to King George V for the behaviour of Labour supporters at their victory rally: "They had got into the way of singing The Red Flag ... By degrees he hoped to break down this habit." When MacDonald's government fell the next year without having changed anything very much, the baton passed back to the unions, and the moderate MFGB general secretary was voted out of office, to be replaced by a young militant called Arthur Cook. Miners admired Cook, and they followed him.

John spent much of 1925 touring the Durham coalfields with Arthur Cook, whom he considered an extraordinary orator:

> By every accepted rule he was a poor speaker. His appearance was feeble, his voice high, thin and harsh, and he had no ability whatever to build logical arguments or even construct sentences flowing into a coherent whole. Yet for well over an hour, coatless, with his shirt sleeves rolled up, he would passionately declaim slogans expressing in a nutshell the views he desired his audiences to take.

They spoke together at the 1925 Durham Labour Women's Gala. John spoke first. He was a favourite with Durham audiences. The fire and fury, the noise and the passion, and the belief that this clever young man would one day be in a position to do the things he talked about, drew them to him, and they cheered him. But then Cook rose, and his reception took the roof off.

Cook became general secretary under the Labour government, but had to deal with its Conservative successor, whose huge majority – it had 419 seats to Labour's 159 – made it very powerful. In the summer of 1925 the coal owners announced their intention to cut miners' pay. They argued that they were now losing £1 million a month; the miners retorted that in the previous four years the owners had made profits of £58.4 million. If they had shown any inclination to share the proceeds of the fat years with their workers, their workers might have been more sympathetic when the lean years came.

Arthur Cook tramped the country with a slogan that was to become famous: "Not a minute on the day, not a penny off the pay." And the government capitulated, for the moment. It set up an enquiry under Sir Herbert Samuel, and meanwhile mine owners would get a subsidy sufficient to pay the miners.

It was a great victory for the unions. But the subsidy was to run out on 1 May 1926. What would happen then? Scotland Yard's Special Branch predicted bloody revolution orchestrated from Moscow. Excitable voices in the unions and the Labour Party predicting not just victory for the miners, but a better world.

Ernest Bevin, general secretary of the Transport and General Workers Union (TGWU) and Britain's leading trade unionist, tried hard to insist that, if it came to a general strike, it would be solely an industrial matter, not a political one, but few people on either side believed him. John, playing the statesman for the very last time, agreed with Bevin.

The Samuel Report, when it appeared, solved nothing – but it had bought the government a year in which to prepare for the general strike which most people now considered inevitable. Prime Minister Stanley Baldwin made it clear that the subsidy would not be extended, and the mine owners said that without the subsidy there would be pay cuts and longer hours.

The day the subsidy ran out, a meeting of the executives of every trade union affiliated to the Trades Union Congress (TUC) voted almost unanimously to support the miners with a general strike.

The general strike was called on 1 May 1926, and John threw himself wholeheartedly into it. At least, he tried to. The moment the strike was announced, he went home and fetched his small two-seater car, intending to travel to Gateshead at once, carrying messages and addressing meetings along the way. But first he had to get the messages and an itinerary from TUC headquarters in Ecclestone Square.

He found the headquarters in a dreadful state of panic and confusion, and it was impossible to see anyone with authority, or obtain information or permission to do anything. "I found eventually," he wrote, that the Council was split up into a number of committees which were sitting behind closed doors, and that nobody could do anything until they broke up. Although a large staff of very capable men and women existed, none of these had any instructions, or power to act.

He caught two left-wing General Council members, Alonzo Swales and Fred Purcell, as they came out for some air. Over the third pint, they started to confirm his fears. They told him that the Council had no idea what to do, and was terrified that the strike call would be ignored. Ernest Bevin of the TGWU had been given overall control.

Someone mentioned that there was work to be done in the transport department. There, a harassed official had been told to have cars waiting for all Council members. John hung about until 1.30 a.m., and then was told to drive the TGWU's Ben Tillett – a 56-year-old union leader who had been roughly elbowed aside by Bevin and given the post of International and Political Secretary of the TGWU, and probably had few illusions left – to his home. It was a strange journey, and fed all his worst suspicions and forebodings:

> He gave me first an address in Brook Street. I drove him to a large house, and waited outside nearly an hour. Tillett came out in excellent spirits, and on the journey home gave me a somewhat incoherent account of the rich man he had been and was going to be again. He did not like my little car, and compared it most unfavourably with a Rolls Royce which he had or was going to have, I was unable to make out which. I tried to get some information upon the progress of the strike, but all he would tell me was not to worry, because [railwaymen's leader Jimmy] Thomas was going to see Abe Bailey, "and he's a darned good chap, and a pal of Samuel's". I reached home about three o'clock, wondering what use this wealthy oriental influence was to the working class. [Abraham Bailey was a fabulously wealthy South African diamond tycoon, politician, financier and cricketer.]

They still had no work to offer him the next morning, so he went to Hyde Park and used some of his furious pent-up energy giving an anti-strike speaker the hardest time of his life. He wriggled through the crowd, climbed on the platform and drowned out the speaker with his statement that he would spend ten minutes outlining the real truth. Seeing that only physical violence would stop him, the meeting's sponsors let him go on.

At the end of his ten minutes the crowd kept him answering questions for another hour until the sponsors of the meeting managed to get it closed; then a section of the crowd dragged him to a platform hung about with a red flag, and he gave his speech all over again. It was, though he did not mention the point when he told the story, probably his first speech from a communist platform.

That lifted his spirits a little, and next day he managed to see Arthur Greenwood, then head of the Labour Party's research department and later the Party's deputy leader. "Greenwood was a good fellow, and had he ever been able to discover of what part of the work he had been given charge, he would undoubtedly have made a great success of it."

Greenwood handed over what he assured John were vital and confidential messages to strike organisers, mapped out his route and promised to telephone ahead at all the places he was to visit on his journey north, advising them to organise a meeting for him to address.

John's first stop was Biggleswade. There, he handed over his top-secret envelope to the secretary of the strike committee, who opened it with due solemnity. In it he found the strike instructions sent by post several days previously, a few Labour Party propaganda leaflets and a sample copy of a pamphlet on agricultural policy.

Nearly 60 years later I myself sat despairingly in the Labour Party press office as the 1983 general election campaign sunk deeper into the mire, and watched as huge bundles of paper were despatched daily to agents in every constituency in the country. One day I looked into one of the parcels. The first document I found was an impenetrable analysis of the political situation in Pakistan. "They talk of nothing else in Scunthorpe", remarked Gerald Kaufman, who also saw the parcel.

But Yorkshire, Durham and Tyneside lifted John's volatile spirits again. The TUC pennant on the front of his car ensured that he was cheered everywhere he went. In Gateshead the road was blocked solid with people waiting to hear him for several hundred yards before the Labour Party headquarters, and on the common land opposite he reckoned there were another 20,000 people.

He spent a couple of days there and then drove back to London. As he was entering Barnet in Hertfordshire, he saw posters declaring the strike at an end. "With no attempt at bargaining, with a complete disregard for the loyal hundreds of thousands who had answered their call, the TUC leaders had surrendered unconditionally", he wrote.

By the time he went to Gateshead again he was close to despair. His public meetings were now

> crowded but indescribably dejected and I had no message to cheer them. I had lost faith in the triumphant campaign launched by MacDonald and enthusiastically taken up by the bulk of the Party, to point out that, as industrial action had failed, the thing to do was to return a Labour majority at the next election. I no longer believed that poor people could benefit by spending their few spare coppers and tired evenings working for men who had led them so disastrously in the industrial field.

The victorious mine owners were able to pick and choose whom they took back, and the most prominent strikers were left, with their families, to starve. Neither the Labour Party nor the unions seemed able or willing to help them. The mood in Labour's conference in Margate that year was fractious, and furiously John tried to lead a revolt against the leadership.

According to the *Daily Herald*'s lead story on 15 October, "the principal participants were Mr John Beckett, Miss Ellen Wilkinson and Mr George Buchanan [one of the left-wing Clydeside MPs] on one side, and Mr MacDonald and Mr J.H. Thomas on the other". It was started, unexpectedly, by John, who condemned Labour MPs for their feeble opposition to Baldwin's government and failure to defend the miners. The *Herald*'s front page that day also carried news of the miners' decision to carry on their now doomed battle.

"Mr MacDonald described as humbug most of what he had heard that morning", reported the *Herald*. MacDonald said that you couldn't ask for a finer body of men and women than the Parliamentary Labour Party, and that to say otherwise was to provide ammunition for the movement's enemies.

John said the Parliamentary Labour Party had done nothing useful and had failed to support the miners. Jimmy Thomas said Beckett ought to have made these points at the weekly Parliamentary Labour Party meetings, and John said he had.

But John seems to have badly misjudged the mood and lost the conference. Delegates cheered Thomas and called on John to withdraw. All the same, Ellen Wilkinson came back with a further attack on Thomas's "hysterical" demand that nothing be said to embarrass the Parliamentary Labour Party.

The *Herald* editorialised that Labour had managed to avoid the splits and internecine warfare of the other two parties, and so it should continue, which was why "many delegates at Margate yesterday showed strong resentment at certain remarks of Mr John Beckett, MP for Gateshead". He should "state his case in such a way that it cannot be used by the enemy to the detriment of the Movement".

His week in Margate must have deepened John's certainty that there was nothing to be hoped for from the Labour Party. But what else was there? Did democratic politics offer any hope? In his unsystematic way, John was moving towards the idea that it did not. And if democratic politics offers no hope, then what?

One answer was communism. The Communist Party's membership doubled in the 12 months after the strike, partly because communists alone helped those miners whom the strike left jobless. Money from the Soviet Union was brought in by Comintern agents and distributed by the Party. John himself obtained money for his hungry constituents from the Communist Party and from a Soviet front organisation, the International Class War Prisoners Aid Society.

Nationally, at least £270,000 of Soviet money went into the mining communities. Locally,

> in my own Gateshead mining villages at Low Fell and Wrekenton I watched the slow disintegration, through hardship and hunger, of a fine and courageous community, and had the devil offered the help withheld by their fellow countrymen,

I would have been grateful. Had the CP possessed the smallest ability or tactical common sense, it could have reaped a great harvest.

John himself would probably have been part of that harvest. Ellen Wilkinson, a former communist and still close to the Communist Party, invited John to her flat for parties at which he met leading communists like Tommy Jackson, who told a rally around that time that they would take the Labour Party by the hand "as a preliminary to taking them by the throat".

In 1926, I am sure he could easily have joined the Communist Party. He had become much closer to the Communist Party and its leaders than he ever afterwards owned up to. But the Communist Party turned on him and his friends, and even on Arthur Cook, for it was in one of those self-immolating moods that overtakes the British left from time to time. John probably never knew that Moscow had imposed on the Communist Party a fiercely sectarian policy called Class Against Class, according to which the bitterest abuse had to be reserved for non-communist socialists. As for Cook,

> his will and determination matched his personality, and he was to drag an unwilling leadership into the maelstrom of the general strike, see his beloved miners beaten down to an unbelievably low level, and die a painful and premature death without gainsaying one inch of [his] principles.

John did undertake one mission for the Communist Party. Wilkinson asked him to go to Poland on behalf of Red Aid, and he agreed, though only – or so he afterwards claimed – out of gratitude for its aid to the miners.

In 1926 Marshal Pilsudski led a military coup in Poland, and by the end of that year his government was treating left-wingers and racial minorities with great brutality. John agreed to lead a fact-finding delegation of three, with his friend Arthur Shepherd, MP for Darlington, and Winifred Horrabin as secretary. Horrabin, then a member of the Communist Party, had visited the Soviet Union earlier that year and visited Lenin's tomb.

He spent a month in Poland, playing cloak-and-dagger games with government spies and drinking huge quantities of vodka with revolutionaries of all types. He took to the Polish communists: "A persecuted party is always good as far as its personnel is concerned. These men were hunted like rats and only the utmost courage and sturdy fanaticism could keep them in the ranks." But he could not quite shake off a certain admiration for the brutal old marshal who had replaced a chaotic democracy with what seemed to John to be a relatively efficient and pragmatic dictatorship.

The government gave them access to the prisons. There the delegation found evidence that there was a great deal of torture when men first went inside, to get them to betray the names of their comrades.

But what shocked him most was the condition of Polish miners, working ten hours a day for a miserable wage – and the fact that the pits were owned by two combines, both controlled by British companies. "It was unpleasant to realise that our hungry unemployed miners in Durham had lost their employment in order that 'British' financiers could profit by the callous sweating and exploitation of Polish labour."

The inverted commas around the word British tell their own story. Years later a man called William Joyce was to write that when Polish coalmines offered rich pickings, city investors had starved Britain's pits of capital. It was true. But he wrote in the service of a very different political philosophy; he was by then in Germany, and the work was commissioned by the German Nazis. And John was – but let us not jump too far ahead of ourselves.

Poland added to his stock of entertaining anecdotes. After one all day and all night train journey in a desperately cold and very crowded third-class carriage, sitting on bare boards and watching with growing nausea as all the other occupants ate raw herrings with their fingers, they arrived at a small town, where they were to observe a trial the next day. The owner of the town's only inn showed them to a large room with a stove on one wall and a single huge bed.

The two Polish interpreters settled down on the floor beside the stove, and the parliamentary delegation, fully clothed, made itself as comfortable as possible on the huge bed and fell into a deep sleep:

Early in the morning I awoke intensely hot, and found myself almost smothered by the large form of mine host. I wriggled out and surveyed my companions. On the other side of the bed was the Member for Darlington with our large hostess sleeping coyly beside him. In the middle Winifred could hardly be seen beneath the two daughters of the house. We found that this was the family bed which guests were allowed to share.

When they arrived at the trial, John wished they had stayed away. In the courtroom, the dozen or so prisoners greeted the delegation with communist slogans. "These prisoners were not communists," he wrote, "but simply ill-treated and half-starved peasants who blamed their foreign masters for their ills." They had, he discovered, been told that the delegation would be so pleased by the slogans that it would order their release. The trial was a farce and all the prisoners received long sentences.

A visit to Posen on the return journey may have marked another staging post on John's strange political journey. Posen had been a German city until the Versailles treaty. Now it was Polish. What John saw was this:

> A highly civilised and efficient German municipality has been obliged to revert to a primitive and corrupt system of local government. Heartbreaking as it must have been for the citizens of Alsace and Lorraine to leave German municipal methods for those of France, their lot was easier than that of the Germans in Posen. Every evidence existed that the Poles were deliberately trying to suppress German language and culture, and were smashing the German trade union machine and battering down the standards of life.

Wages, he wrote, were pitifully low, and ownership of industry was shared between Paris and London. "The despairing engineers of Tyneside had fought and defeated Germany in order that British and French financiers should be able to force German workers to undercut them in the world's markets."

He was developing an admiration for Germany, and felt increasingly sure that the Germans had been badly treated. I wondered where this admiration came from. Then I looked back at Eva Dorothy Solomon's family tree and realised that John's great grandfather Isaac Jacobson came to Britain from the province of Posen – a part of Prussia, which became Germany in 1870, but was handed to Poland in 1919 under the Treaty of Versailles.

It is one of the oddest ironies of a story full of ironies that my father's anti-Semitism may have been fed in its early stages by a family memory inherited from his Jewish forbears.

Wherever it came from, in a man who knew no moderation, this perfectly sensible idea could form a poisonous cocktail if mixed with a growing distrust of Jews.

If neither democratic politics nor communism offered hope, what did? In 1926 no one, not even John himself, could have any idea of the answer he would eventually come up with. It was not an answer that the passionate young socialist MP would ever have considered. Unfortunately, that was not his only persona. He was juggling three personas, and was bound to drop something one day.

Notes on sources

A Very British Strike by Anne Perkins (Macmillan, 2006).

A.J. Cook by Paul Davies (Manchester University Press, 1987).

Marching to the Fault Line by Francis Beckett and David Hencke (Constable and Robinson, 2009).

Ramsay MacDonald by David Marquand (Cape, 1977).

7
A COMPLICATED LIFE

The general strike was the moment when the generation of 1918 realised that they would have to learn to live without the dreams that had made their wartime nightmares bearable.

For John, managing the despair was made even harder by the complexity of his life. He was really three very different people.

There was the increasingly bitter militant from a mining constituency whom we met in the last chapter, despairing and angry as he saw the suffering of his constituents, moving leftward at breakneck speed and, in 1926, briefly very close to the Communist Party.

There was the accomplished young parliamentarian, close to Labour's rising stars such as Dalton and Attlee, spending weekends at the country houses of wealthy political heavyweights like Charles Trevelyan, who was the scion of a great political family and minister for education in MacDonald's government; and getting to know everyone who mattered, from Neville Chamberlain to David Lloyd George: the young MP with a great future before him.

And there was the London socialite, seen constantly with leading actors, holding glittering theatrical dinners at the House of Commons and in the best restaurants, apparently very well off, unlike most Labour MPs at that time.

The young parliamentarian enjoyed rubbing shoulders with the powerful, while the young militant stared with horror at their feet of clay.

The young parliamentarian seemed able and willing to play the parliamentary game. He persuaded health minister Neville Chamberlain to give a big loan to the Gateshead Board of Guardians, because they had hundreds of starving families to feed and could not begin to do so from the rates of a poverty-stricken borough, writing later that this loan "was a tremendous fillip to the Labour cause in the town, and [Chamberlain] was far too shrewd a man not to have known it, but he was also too just a man to withhold help in order to make Party capital".

He played the same civilised parliamentary game with Home Secretary Sir William Joynson Hicks, presenting a petition for a reprieve for a Gateshead woman sentenced to death for murder. Joynson Hicks sent for him. "I'm reprieving that woman of yours. The news will be out tonight. I thought you would like to be the first to send it." John telegraphed the information to the people responsible for the campaign, and received credit which he happily admitted was quite undeserved.

The 78-year-old father of the House, T.P. O'Connor, who became an Irish MP 14 years before John was born, once an Irish Nationalist MP and now effectively an independent with a Liverpool seat, sought him out in the library.

> So you're the young man with a ten thousand majority. Well, anyone can get a ten thousand majority, but I'll tell you how to keep it. Never do anything. Never, never do anything. Directly you do something you'll upset someone and if you do enough you'll upset everybody. Look at me. I never do anything and I keep my seat, not like Winston and the other busybodies who rush round upsetting people and are in and out like Jacks in boxes.

John laughed his loud, cracked laugh, no doubt, but really he did not know what to think. The accomplished parliamentarian admired the old man's languid cynicism. The militant in a hurry was disgusted by it.

The militant despised the witty cross-talk in the House between Chancellor of the Exchequer Winston Churchill and Labour's Philip Snowden when "the real struggle was taking place outside Parliament" (that phrase has a contemporary ring to it – I used to hear it in the seventies). But the parliamentarian enjoyed the exchanges, and his memoirs offer that rare and precious thing, a new Churchill story.

Churchill, he says, listened for more than an hour to a storm of angry invective from Snowden, an acid, bitter man who always appeared to loathe his fellow human beings. Then Churchill rose and congratulated Snowden. He had, he said, watched Snowden's brilliant political career with great sympathy, and had noticed that his natural kindliness and charm had been a handicap, making his life one long contest between his amiability and the cultivation of sufficient acidity. "It is with great pleasure," he said amid the growing laughter, "that I notice that the Right Honourable Gentleman has at last won this long struggle against his better self."

The parliamentarian still had lines open to Ramsay MacDonald, and even seems to have made a half-hearted attempt to justify the Labour leadership's role during the general strike. But the militant had already identified the Labour leader to whom he would transfer his disappointed loyalty.

John Wheatley had been housing minister during the short-lived Labour government. He was the only left-winger included in that cabinet, and the government's only real success. He had instituted a programme of council house building that foreshadowed, and laid the groundwork for, the much bigger programme Nye Bevan introduced after 1945. and John had watched him perform in Parliament, later writing:

> Intimates of MacDonald had told me much of an unpleasing nature regarding [Wheatley]. The worst allegation was that he considered himself a better man than MacDonald. Later I knew him well, and it was certainly true that he considered himself, and most of his friends, to be far better men than MacDonald. While I listened to his speech, full of that challenge we longed

for and received from no other cabinet minister, I made up my mind that ... here was a leader of whom I should feel proud.

Wheatley and Jimmy Maxton led the small group of Glasgow MPs called the Clydesiders who, in the 1924–9 parliament, established themselves as the shock troops of the left. These were to be John's new friends and comrades, the men to whom he would take his fierce and muddled loyalty next.

Meanwhile the sophisticated metropolitan socialist was leading what must have looked like the good life. His old friend Arthur Bourchier was nearly 60, while Bourchier's second wife, actress Kyrle Bellew, was still a young and stunningly beautiful woman, just seven years older than John. John and Kyrle began an affair that was known to everyone in their joint circles, which meant both the political and theatrical establishment.

Kyrle was stunningly beautiful and a fine actress. At this distance, it's impossible to say just how good; there was some feeling at the time that being married to Bourchier had brought her starring roles in the West End which she might not have got on her own merits, but maybe that was just sour grapes.

Her name could mislead. It was almost the same as that of a famous male actor from a slightly earlier generation, Cosmo Kyrle Bellew, to whom she was distantly related. She seems to have given the impression that the relationship was closer than it was – she was related to him through her mother, whose maiden name was Harcourt. Her real surname was Falck, and her family were provincial lawyers.

She began her stage career in London in 1914, claiming to have previously acted in films in the USA, though there is no evidence that this is true – she, like John, seems regularly to have provided information about herself which is more likely to be convenient than true. Her birth date got steadily later as she got older. She might have been one of those women of whom Lady Bracknell spoke: "35 is a very attractive age. London society is full of women of the very highest birth who have, of their own free choice, remained 35 for years."

But she certainly acted in the West End throughout the war, often with Arthur Bourchier. She married Bourchier while they were starring together in *Scandal* at the Strand Theatre, on 24 December 1918, six weeks after the armistice and eight months after the draper's manager John Beckett married Helen Shaw. For John in 1918, even getting to talk to the famous and glamorous Kyrle Bellew would have seemed like an impossible dream. Sleeping with her must have seemed to him a measure of the distance he had travelled in less than a decade.

She played regularly opposite Bourchier in the West End, and starred as Becky Sharp in a 1922 film of *Vanity Fair*. She seems to have been a clever and very political woman; but also unreliable, a chameleon, who reinvented herself so often that I think she had already lost sight of the truth about herself. She was also, I think, very aware of the need to keep her name constantly in front of the public.

The affair was not reported in newspapers, as it would be today. This was partly because Bourchier himself knew of it, and apparently had no objection. Newspapers which might have been tempted to write about it saw reports of dinners at the House of Commons given by John Beckett MP and attended by Arthur Bourchier, and concluded that Bourchier would not stand up the story that he was a wronged husband if he publicly appeared at dinners given by the man who was supposed to have wronged him. John once told me that Bourchier was quite happy to see a younger man fulfilling sexual demands which he no longer felt equal to meeting.

All three John Becketts were still much in evidence as 1927 opened, but only two of them celebrated Christmas that year. The young parliamentarian had all but disappeared. He seems to have decided quite early that year that the House of Commons was not for him.

In 1925 and 1926 Hansard is full of dull but worthy questions asked by the honourable member for Gateshead, as well as occasional polite but firm interventions on major issues – opposing plans to remit supertax, seeking to get the government to send an ambassador to Moscow – designed to establish him as a good House of Commons man. All these start to disappear in 1927, and he asked almost no questions in 1928. He did, however, make a speech about an ex-soldier who had sent him his medals with a letter saying they were useless – the pawn shops were full of them; and when he finished speaking, he flung the medals on to the government front bench.

At some stage in 1927 he seems to have realised that his temperament was not suited to politics. He was, of course, right. His contempt for democratic politicians has a remarkably modern and contemporary feel now, when there is widespread cynicism about them, and people are forgetting, as he did, that the alternative to grubby elected politicians is always much worse.

To change anything as a democratic politician, you need great skill, patience and a very high boredom threshold, none of which he possessed.

So that year, realising he was not suited to Parliament, he remembered an old ambition. Ever since he was at school, he had wanted to be a lawyer. Probably it was what his Jewish mother wanted most for him, and perhaps by 1927 she could see that no good was going to come from mixing John and politics. But, having left school at 14, he did not have the necessary educational qualifications to read for the bar.

Sir Patrick Hastings, the Labour Attorney General who had been at the centre of the Campbell affair in 1924, agreed to try to obtain for him an exemption from the preliminary examination, on the grounds of his war service and his public service.

But John was not going to leave the House of Commons without showing what he thought of the place. He started the year by making a radical, and unwelcome, proposal to his parliamentary colleagues about how they might stifle Stanley Baldwin's trade union bill.

The bill's purpose was to take advantage of the fact that the trade union enemy was defeated and helpless, and to ensure that it stayed that way by virtually outlawing the strike, the only real weapon the unions possessed.

The bill was also designed to cripple Labour Party funds by making trade union members "opt in" to the political fund instead of "opting out".

All this also has a remarkably modern ring to it. To a radical Conservative government, trade unions are public enemy number one, and exactly the same arguments have been mounted in the years since 1979.

Typically, John told everyone that he was rather in favour of the second part, making union members opt in to the political fund rather than opting out, because working men should not be dragooned into contributing money to keep politicians in unaccustomed luxury. This stance did not endear him to fellow Labour MPs.

Still, the bill had to be stopped if possible. So he proposed that it should be stopped by filibustering.

Start with one MP making a strong protest in unparliamentary language, and refusing to apologise. With ingenuity, determination and an endless supply of points of order, that member's suspension could be made to last for over half an hour. There were 156 Labour MPs, and suspending them all would take ten days. Once they were all excluded, he believed Parliament would be seen to be a Conservative rump outfit, and would lose all authority.

He had, of course, a better chance of flying to the moon than of persuading the Parliamentary Labour Party to adopt the plan. Yet direct action in Parliament increasingly seemed to John all that was left. After one of his unrestrained attacks on Prime Minister Stanley Baldwin (for whom he had conceived a special loathing), one of the stupider Conservatives, Luton MP Terence O'Connor, crossed the floor and asked him to "come outside and take a damned good hiding". A sensible man would have told the MP not to be such a fool. John said he would follow the man after the vote, and this led to a farcical scene.

They somehow missed their assignation, and both, like schoolboys meeting to fight at the school gates, claimed that the other had chickened out. John insisted that he scoured the corridors and was told that Sir Terence had left, while Sir Terence told a Luton audience that weekend that he had taught John a lesson he would not forget – "the proper way to deal with cowardly socialists".

The ILP's Luton branch sent John a newspaper report of the meeting at which this was said, and John sent a letter to the Luton papers announcing that he would speak in the town and repeat what he had said in Parliament, so that Mr O'Connor could attend and attempt to take retribution.

The idea that two MPs would stand in the middle of Luton market square and slug it out, surrounded presumably by their various cheering supporters, seems rather to have appealed to him.

John was very proud of that Luton meeting. The hall, and an overflow hall, were both full to capacity, the streets were packed, a third overflow meeting was held in the market place and there was apparently no sign of Mr O'Connor.

According to the *Daily Herald* account, O'Connor apologised for the threat, and even Conservative MPs were surprised that he had not turned up to debate in Luton. "The reception given to Mr Beckett in Luton ... was the most memorable political event in that town for over a generation", reported the *Herald*.

A few days later, however, the *Herald* noted that "Mr O'Connor is an ex officer, six feet tall, and has some reputation as a boxer. Mr John Beckett is an ex-Serviceman who was invalided out of the army in 1917 with a disabled right arm and heart trouble." O'Connor lost Luton to the Liberals in 1929, but returned to Parliament to become Solicitor General in 1936, a post he held until his death in 1940, aged just 48.

A month later, in May, Stanley Baldwin told the House of Commons that some of the trade unions were controlled by the Communist Party, and John rose on a point of order to ask the Prime Minister to admit that he had lied. The Speaker, as he was bound to do, ordered him to withdraw, and John offered to do so "if the Prime Minister will withdraw the lie he told". The House voted for a week's suspension by 321 votes to 88. It was the first of several suspensions.

Oddly, he hated it. From the moment he called Baldwin a liar, "I was conscious of a concentrated disapproval and dislike almost physical in its strength. The sense of isolation is acutely painful." It was some compensation that the newspapers printed all the unkind things he wished to say about Baldwin, and attendance at his meetings rose steeply.

But his moment in the spotlight killed his dream of becoming a barrister. Sir Patrick Hastings told him that it had prejudiced the benchers against John, and there was now no chance of him getting the exemption he sought to read for the bar. Sometimes we only know what we really want when we know we can't have it, and he regretted this lost career all his life. Paradoxically, that parliamentary outrage, subconsciously designed to close off politics as a career, was the moment that helped nail him to politics.

John was 33, and had already thrown away four promising careers, in advertising, journalism, politics and the law.

In the autumn of 1927 he travelled to South Africa to join Arthur Bourchier on a tour in which John had a financial interest. The trip changed everything, for two reasons. One reason was personal, and we will come to that in a moment. The other was political, and he anticipated it when talking to a South African Labour MP on the three-week boat trip:

> I sensed that the result of this trip would make me extremely unpopular with the anti-imperialist section of the ILP. Trips abroad contributed largely to my downfall in the Labour Party. Had I not seen for myself, I might have been content to echo the shibboleths of the anti-imperialists.

Men like Fenner Brockway on the Labour left were as committed to equality for foreigners as for the British, for black as well as white people. John's passion for justice did not, in the end, extend beyond these shores, or his shade of skin.

He had been a very active anti-imperialist before his visit to South Africa, though it was not a side of his work that he chose to reveal in later years. As late as February 1927 he had been in Brussels for the foundation of the League Against Imperialism, and the following month he was one of the prime movers in the foundation of its British Section. His friend Fenner Brockway became chairman of the section, George Lansbury treasurer and John (and Kyrle) joined the executive.

Bourchier left for South Africa before him, and was pictured at the station saying goodbye to his wife Kyrle Bellew, who told journalists she had "the best husband in the world". She travelled on later, almost certainly with John, though she is not mentioned in his long account of his adventures on the voyage.

He seems to have had a wonderful time in South Africa, dallying for a month in Natal because of the pleasures of surfing and socialising. He talked at length with Manilal Gandhi, a son of the Indian leader and himself the spokesman for Natal's Indian population, and with prominent white politicians. These white politicians complained that Indians were undercutting white labour, and John remarked on the fact that outside Durban and Pietermaritzburg, the retail trading establishments were mainly Indian.

To repay Gandhi's hospitality, John invited him to lunch at his hotel, and was told that his guest would not be allowed to enter. He was horrified. But it was not the straightforward anti-racist horror that Brockway would have felt. John wrote: "If Mr Gandhi, who was an Oxford graduate and a member of the Inns of Temple, desired to travel by tram, he had no recourse but to share a 'Jim Crow' with the most primitive South African native." It does not seem to have occurred to him that the system of dividing the races might itself be the trouble.

He could not accept Gandhi's wish to give the Indians equal status with the whites: "Although there were a number of educated Indians, the great majority were little more advanced than the South African natives, and in most cases by no means such good physical and moral types." The blame for the situation, he thought, lay with the greed of early white settlers: "Had they not supported cheap Asiatic labour, the country would not now be overrun."

He hired a car and drove through Zululand, seeing "a great deal of these magnificent people". Here again, he found it easy to make sweeping racial generalisations on the briefest of acquaintances. He did not agree with those who told him that Zulus were mentally deficient, and thought they could do well if educated; but on the other hand, "The people seem happy as they are, and I was told that urban life seriously affected their physique."

Once again, he thought the greed of the whites was to blame, for this led them to exploit Zulus in the mines of the Rand, and use them as house-boys and rickshaw runners. "For me the rickshaw runners constituted the one really repulsive feature of life in Durban. The average life of a runner is less than seven years, and the spectacle of these fine men running like burdened animals is a blot upon South African civilisation."

A minister drove him to see a scheme designed to give a fresh start in life to "poor whites" and provide them with the technical knowledge necessary to supervise black, Indian and Chinese labour. John approved wholeheartedly,

> but I wondered whether they could build a white man's
> country unless white men performed the necessary manual
> labour. The argument that white men should not have to do
> hard work in a warm country seemed to me not to carry
> weight.

White men managed, he noticed, to play strenuous games of golf and
tennis there.

He took these views to a rather puzzled South African Trades
Union Congress, and to what was probably an even more puzzled
confidential meeting of the Executive of the South African Native
Congress. He admired its members individually but ended up certain
that the problem should be resolved by setting aside specific native
areas, "rather than in unhappy attempts to mingle the two races, with
hardship and grievance to both". This must deeply have shocked
friends such as Brockway and Lansbury when, as I am sure he did, he
lectured them on his return about how to solve the problems of race
in South Africa. Of course, South Africa did eventually try John's
prescription, with disastrous results.

Thus, as he wrote in his baffled way, "as so often happened in my
political life, I found myself out of step with everyone". It was a
talent he had.

South African newspapers quickly discovered what London newspapers already knew, that John Beckett MP was always good for an
outrageous quote. They asked his view on every conceivable issue,
including a rather arcane dispute about whether the British or Dutch
flag should have primacy, at a time when British South Africans flew
Union Jacks from their cars. His reply was to mock "the love shown
for England by flying German-made flags on American made motor
cars", and he suggested that orders for Birmingham and Coventry
would be more appreciated.

Four newspapers carried furious leaders the next morning, all of
them comparing him with Rudyard Kipling's Pagett MP. It was one
of his own favourite poems:

> Pagett MP was a liar, and a fluent liar therewith –
> He spoke of the heat of India as "The Asian solar myth";

> Came on a four months' visit to "study the east" in November,
> And I got him to sign an agreement vowing to stay till
> September...
> March came in with the koil. Pagett was cool and gay,
> Called me a "bloated brahmin", talked of my "princely pay"
> March went out with the roses. "Where is your heat?" said he.
> "Coming" said I to Pagett. "Skittles" said Pagett MP.

The heat of India, of course, eventually gets to Pagett and he begs to
be allowed to go home:

> And I laughed as a drove from the station, but the mirth dried
> out on my lips
> As I thought of the fools like Pagett who write of their
> "Eastern trips",
> And the sneers of the travelled idiots who duly misgovern
> the land,
> And I prayed to the Lord to deliver another one into
> my hand.

Business beckoned. Arthur Bourchier was to meet John at Johannesburg station. He was not there. Instead, the director was there to tell
John that Bourchier was seriously ill. They took him to the theatre
for the evening's performance of *Ambrose Applejohn's Adventure*. From
the front row of the stalls, he could see that his friend was in a high
fever and very ill. In the first act Bourchier introduced business and
dialogue from the other two acts. The last act became almost farcical,
with the bewildered company striving to adapt themselves to the
jumbled playing of the leading actor.

As John arrived in his dressing-room after the performance, Bourchier collapsed. John and Bourchier's brother-in-law and manager,
Kyrle's brother Lionel Falck, took him back to the Rand Club where
he was staying and went out in search of a doctor. Bourchier died
two days later.

He had wanted to be cremated. The only cremation facility in
Johannesburg was the Indian burial ground. John was one of the four
pall bearers:

As I helped to carry the heavy coffin over broken ground to the Indians' sweet-smelling funeral pyre, I wished that I could believe that dead men still lived and could see their own obsequies. The beautiful semi-tropical gardens and reverential white-robed attendants, the primitive yet impressive log structure on which he was to rest, made an unforgettable scene, and one which could have been appreciated by no one more keenly than the unconscious chief actor.

Lionel Falck placed a match to the pyre and the flames shot up as the mourners were ushered away. There ends John's own account of his South African adventure, and there is one name which is entirely missing from it throughout: Bourchier's wife, Lionel Falck's sister, John's mistress – Kyrle Bellew. Reading his account, you would assume she was not there. But she must have been. She must have been at her husband's funeral, and she probably put a match to the pyre alongside her brother.

I know that she travelled back on the liner with John. But I know that only from reading Hugh Dalton's diaries. John wrote her out of the story. She must have travelled out with him, and round the country with him, too.

Back in England, the House of Commons seemed drearier and more pointless than ever. John no longer believed that the Labour Party was going to do any better than the old parties, or that radical change could be effected through Parliament. "There were also," he writes carefully, "personal matters which made me feel that I should be happier out of public life."

This is a reference to Kyrle's view that, now her husband was dead, there was nothing to stop them marrying, except the inconvenience that John was still married to Helen – not a comfortable position for a rising young politician in 1927.

Not, I think, that any of this constrained his natural sexual promiscuity. He hinted to me that there were a great many young women in and out of his life and his bed, though he made it a point of honour never to name names.

But he certainly met a young Oxford undergraduate named Barbara Betts; for decades later, the former Labour cabinet minister

Baroness Barbara Castle, as she became, wrote to me: "I certainly remember meeting your father who was a bit of a hero of mine in my young days ... He certainly had guts." When we met she added, "I had a bit of a crush on him, you know", but then clammed up. I think she was surprised to find that he had never mentioned her to me.

Some months later, my then publisher wanted to tie up a deal for an authorised biography of Castle, and suggested my name to her as author. He came back crestfallen and told me she had rejected the idea out of hand: "I think the trouble is that your father made a pass at her."

Actually, I think Barbara Castle wanted a woman to do the biography anyway. It was eventually written by that excellent journalist and historian Anne Perkins, who made a much better job of it than I would have done.

The rumours reached Gateshead. John was used to the south, where they were more liberal about sexual behaviour and had a less strongly developed sense of the dignity of their representative. His Gateshead activists had taken to Helen, and felt that their MP had treated his wife badly. And they did not much like the publicity which surrounded his parliamentary scenes.

Perhaps he could have hung on to Gateshead – his campaigning skills were still prized there – but there was likely to be opposition. Most politicians would have trimmed a little and fought to keep their constituency. A man as disillusioned with Parliament as John could see little point in the battle.

But what else could he do? The law was closed to him; he does not seem to have tried to return to journalism. It turns out that he did have an idea in the back of his mind, for early the next year we find him telling the Gateshead Labour Party that he would not be contesting the constituency at the next election.

He told his Party activists how he was feeling. Their conditions had deteriorated steadily:

> I cannot see any hope of improving things for them, even if, as I think probable, they continue to return me for another five years. As you know, I am a person who likes action. I do not find, at the moment, sufficient outlet and hope in Parliament.

The work that really needed doing was that of educating Tory areas to vote Labour.

> I have a considerable liking and aptitude for educational and propaganda work, and I believe I can serve the army of labour better in the field than in Parliament. All these things have been long in my mind, and this letter is the result of months of anxious thought and soul-searching.

There are, he told a local newspaper reporter from the *North Mail*,

> at least five to ten years of hard propaganda work to be done in the country before parliamentary socialism becomes a practicability … I shall devote myself in the new campaign mainly to work in the south of England, which is the great bulwark of toryism.

So that was it. Back to the life he had so loved as part of the ILP's extended family, the confident brotherhood of men and women who took him to their hearts and his message to their souls, and fed him tea and optimism, as he travelled round the country with the gospel of socialism. Back to the draughty meeting halls where bumbling but good-hearted local chairman forgot their visitor's name, and bleared round the room, and talked too long, and John had to step in to make sure the meeting finished before the pubs closed. Back to where there were no hard-faced Tories who had done well out of the war, no smooth-faced Labour politicians on the make, where the air was pure and honest,

> Where the wine is on the rafter
> And the beer is in the wood
> And the God that made good laughter
> Has seen that they are good

(as another of his favourite poets, G.K. Chesterton, had put it).

It would never do, of course. The revolutionary optimism of 1920 had gone, never to be seen in the land again until 1945, by which time John had thrown away his right to be a part of it. And

John had changed, too, though he was quite capable of hiding from himself the extent of the change. He had become much richer, much better known and, crucially, his life was much more complicated.

He was no longer the young man who could travel as cheaply as possible and bed down at the end of a long day in the front room of an impoverished local activist. He must have half recognised the change in himself, because he told Gateshead he would concentrate on the south of England – which would, of course, enable him to keep in touch with his theatrical interests.

Gateshead's Labour Party chose a successful London barrister, J.B. Melville KC, to replace John. Melville seems to have been John's friend and protégé, so perhaps John still dreamed of being a barrister – or perhaps he was repaying a debt. In any case, the candidature caused no end of trouble. Labour's national executive refused to endorse Melville. Dalton's diary records on 5 November 1928:

> National Executive from 10.30. The case of Melville at Gateshead comes up. Robinson threatens, through NUDAW, to circularise trade unions on the incursion of middle class candidates. Quite a sense of class war in the air! We are rather intimidated by this but shouldn't have endorsed M anyway. It is alleged that M offered Forster [the ex-Gateshead secretary, Robinson's chief backer] the refusal of the agency at £350 a year with a five year contract. This greatly shocked constituencies. Agreed that we don't endorse, owing to irregularity, but that Uncle and Morrison see M and try to persuade him to withdraw altogether, and also that they go to Gateshead. A fine mess these lawyers make of their affairs!

"Uncle" was Arthur Henderson, Labour Party secretary and the man John had so recklessly embarrassed in Newcastle, and Herbert Morrison was then chairman of the national executive, and John's enemy from Hackney days.

John probably thought Melville was being victimised for being his friend. In any case, he seems to have taken prompt action in Melville's defence. Just five days after that meeting a local newspaper carried an exclusive and sensational local story. "I have reliable authority for stating that two highly important developments have occurred in the mystery surrounding the resignation by Mr John Beckett MP of his seat at Gateshead, and the circumstances of the selection of a successor", the *North Mail*'s labour correspondent reported breathlessly.

It appeared that Beckett might stay on in Gateshead after all. He had been approached by unnamed members of the Gateshead Labour Party. "I am unable to make public at this stage the details of the terms of the approach, but I understand that they are of a most interesting character", reported the *North Mail*.

Mr Beckett, "contrary to rumours circulating in the party, has no intention of severing his connection with politics, and I am able to announce that he has received a warm invitation to contest a Labour stronghold in the South country".

To those used to the ways of politicians and newspapers, it is clear that the *North Mail*'s informant must have been John. It looks like a warning to the national executive to keep ahold of nurse (in the shape of Melville), for fear of finding something worse (Beckett himself).

Ten days later Henderson and Morrison arrived to meet the local Labour Party and explain why they could not endorse Melville. They left without comment, and the only quote the local press could obtain came from an unnamed delegate who said, "We have no candidate at present. Why not let John Beckett stand for us again? He says he wants to go to Parliament again, and we are quite willing to send him."

Melville was re-selected by Gateshead, and this time the national executive made no objection. He became attorney general in Ramsey MacDonald's 1929 government, but died suddenly within a few months. It was his death which led MacDonald to offer the post to a rising young lawyer with, at that time, no seat in Parliament and no political ambitions, named Stafford Cripps, who was to become Chancellor of the Exchequer in 1947.

So it was over. Except that it wasn't. A part of John must have realised that he was kidding himself, for he seems to have been looking everywhere for alternative ways of living. He increased his involvement in the theatre, for the first time, with Kyrle, financing and managing his own West End production.

And behind the scenes he was soon making plans to get another parliamentary seat, if he could not dowse the fires he had ignited on his Gateshead boats.

His parliamentary work rate increased. Briefly in 1929 he looked once again like a young parliamentarian who cared about his future, producing an elegant parliamentary performance on a bill about pensions, and suggesting that the government should recondition Britain's canals. This was a really good, creative idea, which he probably thought of for himself because the Trent and Mersey Canal flows through the village of Thurlwood and past the Broughton Arms pub kept by his uncle John. Decades later, a future government started to do it.

In later years he claimed that the invitation to seek nomination for the Peckham constituency in south London came to him entirely unasked. That's not quite how his friend, the Peckham MP Hugh Dalton, saw it.

Dalton had fallen out badly with his agent and some members of the Peckham Labour Party, and had decided to decamp to a constituency where the local workers were rather less awkward. In May 1928, according to Dalton's diary, both men were guests for the weekend at the country house of Sir Charles Trevelyan. On a long walk that the three took together John listened quietly as Dalton described what was going on and asked Trevelyan to help him find a northern seat. Dalton's diaries cast a curious light on all this. He already seems to have been rethinking his friendship with the young man from Gateshead who did not seem to mind how many enemies he made. His diary entry for 20 July reads:

> To Liphook to spend the night with the Webbs [Sidney and Beatrice] and walk next morning ... He [Sidney] says he hears that Mrs Bourchier came back from South Africa with Bourchier's ashes and Beckett in the same cabin, and fancies that her wealth may not have been wholly absent from Beckett's mind.

Nor was that all. John's growing friendship with John Wheatley had not passed unnoticed in the household of the influential Webbs. The young and ambitious Dalton seems to have been warned off Wheatley in no uncertain terms: "Beatrice thinks John Wheatley is a real Tammany Hall type – his stock has never been lower."

According to John's account, about that time some leading Peckham activists approached John to stand for Peckham, assuring him that if he did not approve of the agent, the agent would have to go.

John promised to talk to Dalton, and did so in November 1928. John's account of this conversation was that Dalton pressed him to accept, saying that if he would "go there and clean it up", he would be doing the Labour Party a service. Dalton's autobiography records that John Beckett wanted Peckham, and was "a friend of mine at this time, and had great energy and some ability".

In November Dalton was adopted in Bishop Auckland. In his diary of 6 November, he wrote:

> Parliament meets. Everyone very congratulatory about Bishop Auckland. MacDonald in good form in his opening speech … Lunch with John Beckett who is after Peckham. (Good luck to him!) … Beckett says that MacDonald is now being motored about by Paddy Naismith, a film actress, said to be engaged to Derwent Hall Caine – a little bit of fluff with an elegant car. I saw her hanging around at Birmingham. They motored to and from Wolverhampton. People are wondering where they really slept!

Derwent Hall Caine was an actor and a Labour MP with a string of mistresses who had at least three illegitimate children, and who established the Hall Caine Airport on the Isle of Man. Paddy Naismith was not just an actress, but also a pilot and aviator. If the two ever were engaged, they must have broken it off.

The only serious alternative candidate for Peckham was solicitor Lewis Silkin, a Labour member of the London County Council, friend and ally of Herbert Morrison, future minister in the 1945 government, and the founder of a legal and political dynasty. According to John, they had known each other well, and Silkin harboured a grudge because John, as secretary of the ILP divisional council, "had been obliged to take certain steps towards him which he had resented". Unfortunately Silkin has left no papers from which we might learn more.

On 19 December, Dalton told his diary about the Labour Party National Executive Committee meeting: "Beckett endorsed for Peckham! We couldn't, it was felt, be a court of morals, and nothing in this case was really public." It isn't clear what this refers to, but I suppose it must be the affair with Kyrle Bellew. John's account was: "In spite of the fact that Silkin was a far wealthier man than I, and was strongly supported by Herbert Morrison and the London Labour Party, he received few votes, and I was selected."

This game of musical chairs ended in good time for the 1929 general election. Peckham found itself with a candidate who was saying at every opportunity that his support of Labour's leaders was entirely contingent on them carrying out approved Labour policy. His campaign was opened by the Clydesiders' leader Jimmy Maxton, a pretty clear statement of where he now stood in the Labour Party.

Peckham also found itself with a candidate whose turbulent lifestyle during his five years in Parliament provided ample material for whispering campaigns. Naturally the relationship with Kyrle surfaced, but John found, to his delight, that while this would have been deeply damaging in Gateshead, in Peckham it seemed if anything to do him good. Early in the campaign he overheard a conversation between two men on a bus which cheered him up no end. "That John Beckett, 'e's carrying on with that actress, Kyrle Bellew." "Is 'e?" Pause. "Lucky sod."

It was rumoured that he had been thrown out of Gateshead by an indignant local Labour Party for his behaviour. But the rumour seems to have done little harm: he turned Dalton's 800 majority into an apparently impregnable 6,000 majority.

Notes on sources

www.imdb.com/name/nm6788038/bio (for Kyrle Bellew).

The Political Diary of Hugh Dalton, 1918–40, 1945–60 edited by Ben Pimlott (Cape, 1987).

Who was Who in the Theatre, 1912–76 edited by Ian Herbert (Cengage Gale, 1978).

8

THE DEATH OF HOPE

Did Ramsay MacDonald offer his one-time friend John Beckett a government job after the 1929 election – a last peace offering? John certainly thought he did, though in a rather roundabout way.

While Dalton, Attlee and Ellen Wilkinson waited for the call to MacDonald's Hampstead home hoping for the preferment they had earned, John was approached – on his own account – by "one of Labour's leading journalists, known to be in the confidence of three of the big five", who "asked whether I would join the government as Parliamentary Secretary to the Air Ministry". No, John said, he would not: "Tell them to find a conjuror to get aeroplanes out of a hat, as Tom Shaw [Minister of Labour in the 1924 government] gets jobs." They did: the job went to Fred Montague, a well-known member of the Magicians' Circle.

MacDonald signalled early what sort of government he was going to run. He dropped the one left-winger, and the one success, of his 1924 government, the housing minister and Clydesiders' leader John Wheatley. In a pre-election list of possible ministerial appointments, Wheatley was pencilled in for the Ministry of Labour. By the time the results were declared, MacDonald had decided that he could afford to keep him out.

Wheatley was 60 in 1929, a Catholic born in Ireland whose parents had migrated to Glasgow when he was seven. The oldest child of a family of ten, he followed his father down the mines and worked there for 15 years. In 1901, aged 32, he became a reporter and then an advertising canvasser for a Catholic newspaper, the *Glasgow Observer*. Five years later he started a printing business, which prospered and made him fairly rich, allowing him in 1923 to found a weekly newspaper, the *Glasgow Evening Standard*, which lasted until 1960.

A grim, poverty-stricken childhood, and friendships with socialists like James Connolly (a frequent visitor to the Wheatley household until his execution in 1916) combined to add the socialist faith to his Catholic one.

The two faiths co-existed uneasily. The Catholic Church in Scotland thought socialism was godless and wicked, while Scottish socialists saw Catholics as reactionaries whose aim was to keep the workers in their place by telling them that all would be put right in the next world. One Catholic priest persuaded his indignant parishioners to go to Wheatley's home and burn him in effigy in front of it; and in 1909 Wheatley had a public debate with Hilaire Belloc on whether Catholicism and socialism were compatible.

Well before the First World War, he and James Maxton had become, as they were to remain until 1930, the joint leaders of the ILP in Scotland. He was the architect of Labour's extraordinary success in western Scotland in the 1922 general election which saw ten new Labour MPs, including Wheatley and Maxton themselves, elected to Parliament. As their train left St Enoch's station for Westminster, they were given an almost religious farewell. "It is important," writes Sheridan Gilley in the *Dictionary of Labour Biography*, "to understand the almost apocalyptic expectations of the Glasgow poor in order to judge Wheatley's acute frustrations with Westminster politics, and the increasing disillusionment and embitterment of his Clydeside radical colleagues."

That year they supported MacDonald for Labour leader because he was seen as the ILP left-winger, although Arthur Henderson warned them prophetically that it would not be long before "you Clydeside men" started to regret the choice.

It was not just Wheatley's Catholicism which marked him out from his Clydeside colleagues. It was also his distaste for the internationalism of the Labour movement. He, like John Beckett and unlike most of their ILP friends, thought that a British socialist had done his duty when he had seen British workers all right.

In the House of Commons, Wheatley's great strength was his close reasoning and mastery of detail. He was not a flamboyant orator like Maxton, but he could hold the House in his spell in a way that Maxton could never do. He was a politician of immense personal power.

If any of the Clydesiders were to have office when Labour first came to power in 1924, it had to be Wheatley, and he had been given the job that the former Glasgow slum-dweller wanted most, that of Minister of Housing and Health. His Housing Act was the government's main, if not its only, achievement. It provided for a steadily expanding investment in public housing at modest rents, and paved the way for Aneurin Bevan's much more ambitious housing programme after 1945.

After the Labour government fell, it was Wheatley who ensured that the ILP would in future be the vehicle for left-wing opposition to MacDonald. But between 1927 and 1929, Maxton was forced to make the running. Wheatley's health had become poor, and his attention distracted by attacks from the Conservative candidate in his Glasgow Shettleston constituency, who targeted his Catholicism as well as his socialism, and whom he unsuccessfully sued for libel.

Wheatley was short, dumpy, unprepossessing and calculating, peering myopically through thick, round spectacles. Maxton was the opposite in every way: painfully thin, handsome and romantic in a raddled sort of way, with long, flowing black hair. An eloquent former schoolteacher whose spellbinding oratory was legendary, he lived on his nerves and a constant supply of tea and cigarettes.

It was Wheatley, not Maxton, whom MacDonald really feared. Wheatley had one of the finest political brains of his generation. Maxton, though nominally the leader of the ILP, understood as well as anyone the reality of their relationship. "I am asking you because you are my leader", Wheatley once said to Maxton. "Aye, John, I am your leader," replied Maxton. "And you will discover that I am the cutest leader you ever led." Maxton was containable – and when Wheatley had gone, Maxton was contained. Wheatley was not containable.

John wrote in 1938 that he had only known three great men in his time in the House: Winston Churchill, David Lloyd George and John Wheatley. Fifty years later, in 1980, I told the then very old Fenner Brockway that Wheatley had been John's political hero. He was visibly surprised. "That shows his judgement was better than I thought. I'd have thought he would be more attracted by the romanticism of Maxton."

Another Labour politician recognised Wheatley's special qualities. Oswald Mosley, just entering MacDonald's government with a brief to conquer unemployment, said Wheatley was the British Lenin. Wheatley never lived to see the direction Beckett and Mosley took. If he had lived, at least one of them would probably not have taken it. It was, I suppose, from Wheatley that John picked up his romantic ideas about the Catholic Church, and Chesterton and Belloc and wine and good fellowship, and all that stuff.

Very quickly – within a few days of Parliament reassembling in June 1929 – the battle lines were drawn up. MacDonald's decision to exclude Wheatley from the government was greeted by the *Daily Express*, correctly, as a declaration of war on the left. When the Parliamentary Labour Party met, Wheatley said prophetically that the country was entering one of its periodic slumps, and cuts in the standard of living were inevitable. The Labour Party, without an overall parliamentary majority, could only apply capitalist measures and administer those cuts. So it should wait to form a government until it had an overall majority.

Fenner Brockway wrote after that meeting:

> There are few men who can speak so impersonally as Wheatley. His thick-set body did not move. One could not see his eyes behind the thick pebble glasses. Nevertheless he gripped; there was a quality of strength and certainty in his voice and his reasoning was remorseless.

John agreed: "Wheatley was the most effective debater I heard in the House during eight years' membership. Maxton's courage, loyalty and personal charm made an excellent foil to Wheatley's somewhat hard and unemotional exterior."

When the ILP group met, a few days later, Maxton, as chairman, ruled that the group should consist only of MPs who accepted ILP policy. He was saying, in effect, that they must put ILP policy before the policy of the government, and vote against the government if the two conflicted, as they inevitably would. This ruling reduced the ILP from 100 or so MPs to a hard core of just 19. Fenner Brockway wrote in his autobiography:

> We acted closely together, appointing John Beckett as secretary. He … was an aggressive young rebel, but without basic socialist philosophy. I had spoken at one of his election meetings in a crowded music hall. My speech was heard with indifference; then Beckett spoke with unrelieved denunciation of the rich and much abuse of his Tory opponent. The audience loved it.

Years later Brockway wrote to historian Colin Holmes:

> Beckett was young, enthusiastic, dynamic, a tremendous worker. By his energy, spectacular methods and ability to win people by his "rabble-rousing" oratory at street corners, he built up a huge following at Peckham … There was no policy in his speeches, just punch and hit. A boxer.

Fred Brooks, one of Labour's activists in Peckham, wrote to me:

> I heard him speak many times. He had a great personality and could hold a big crowd under almost any circumstances. I once saw him speaking on the corner of Finsbury Circus and it was during the lunch hour. I reckon a good many went without their lunch that day!

Wheatley worked out policies, Maxton articulated them, Beckett worked out the parliamentary tactics. In the debate on the King's Speech, Maxton put the demands of the left.

> I am going to promise the cabinet active hearty support and work on one condition and one condition only, that they will

arrange the affairs of this country that no unemployed man, his wife or child, shall have any dread of starvation or insult.

It soon became clear that this modest demand would not be met, and by midsummer Maxton was asking the House of Commons: "Has any human being benefited by the fact that there has been a Labour Government in office?" In October he said: "It would be foolish to expect the government to deliver socialism but ... the government had it in their power to stop starvation."

John made a close study of parliamentary rules and procedure. With the Liberals and the Conservatives supporting most of the government's measures, he saw himself, and was seen by the ILP group, as the chief whip of the only real opposition party. It was he who knitted the 19 MPs together into an effective force, known before long as the "parliamentary suicide club".

Immersed in the technicalities of organising opposition, John for a time forgot his despair. For the first year or so of the new Parliament he enjoyed himself enormously, showing off his organisation, his flair for publicity, his grasp of procedure and his recklessness; and trusting Wheatley for the grand strategy.

It seems genuinely to have come as a surprise to him that the government, with all its powers of patronage, was able to keep most of its MPs trundling obediently into the government lobby. For one in particular, there were no words too bitter:

My revolutionary mentor Ellen Wilkinson sat demurely on the bench of repentance in the second row, reserved for parliamentary private secretaries who may be seen but not heard. Just after the election Ellen had telephoned me urging me to meet her as soon as possible. She sounded tearful and deeply distressed, and I found her in a state of the most abject depression. At tea she wept, and told me that enquiries had elicited the fact that she was not to be given a post in the new government.

I ... said that surely after her strong opposition to MacDonald and his friends, she could not have thought that she had any chance whatever of being selected, adding that I could not understand her desire to be a member of the kind of ministry we knew would be formed. Sobbing afresh, she said that she had not dreamed her sincere opposition to certain proposals would be punished so severely; that it was an insult that men of the poor calibre of Mr Y and Mr N should be included and she left out. Her last words to me as I drove her home were: "You'll see, if this is what being a rebel does, I'll show them something different in future."

This account is, of course, not corroborated by any other source, and particularly not in the only biography of Ellen Wilkinson. I think it is substantially true, though, like many of John's stories, perhaps a little embroidered. But there is a certain vindictiveness about the way John recounts this private conversation for publication, when he discreetly hid the names of other parliamentary colleagues.

He did not, for example, reveal the name of the Durham miners' MP who had for years been an outspoken supporter of the Minority Movement, the communist front organisation in the trade unions:

> I approached this man to ask him to vote for 5/- a week for the unemployed man's child instead of 2/-. He refused. I reminded him of his past activities and said: "What about the revolution now?" "Och," he replied. "Brother ... can look after that in Durham. I've got economic security for the first time in my life and I'm not going to lose it."

Of course, unlike his Durham friend and many other Labour MPs, John had a source of income outside Parliament. He had his theatrical interests, and was, by comparison with many Labour MPs, quite well off. When MPs were told that the unions would not give rebels financial help in their parliamentary campaigns, and that the Party would withdraw recognition from them and extinguish their parliamentary careers, it was a serious matter – as John recognised – for men "who had been absent from their trades for many years, had no other means of existence, and had wives and families to support".

He was not in that position. He was sending his estranged wife enough money to enable her to send their daughter Lesley to a private school. He assumed he would be able to do so forever. He was wrong.

The first battle was over the government's refusal to raise unemployment benefit to the amounts promised in the manifesto. The ILP managed to get nearly 40 Labour MPs into the division lobbies, and another 50 abstentions, so that in order to get its Unemployment Insurance Financial Resolution through the House, the government relied heavily on the Conservative and Liberal parties.

The ILP decided to smoke out their colleagues. Many MPs liked to appear as good party men at Westminster, and rebels in their constituency. One way – still used today, though made harder by the speed of modern communications – was to move an amendment to a government proposal, and then, when you got a kindly but unhelpful reply, rise and say that in view of the minister's sympathy, the motion would be withdrawn.

John pointed out to his ILP colleagues that, to withdraw a motion in this way, you had to have the permission of the House. Of course normally it was a formality and no one ever opposed a member who wished to withdraw. But they did now. The ILP refused to allow such motions to be withdrawn without a division, placing their Labour colleagues in the position where they either had to face the serious consequences of defying the whips, or vote against their own motion.

John was very pleased with this tactic.

> We forced them to vote against the rates of benefit which they had loudly abused a Conservative government for refusing; against compensation for miners whose pits were closed; and against a dozen other things, in the purely vocal clamour for which they had spent their political lives.

It did not, however, improve the temper of his fellow Labour MPs, among whom he was rapidly becoming hate figure number one.

"He loved it", Fenner Brockway wrote to Colin Holmes. "We continually had to restrain him from going to extremes in action and language ... He was contemptuous of the Labour majority. Couldn't find a word sufficiently bad to say of them."

The Prime Minister himself decided to try to reason with him. John had placed a question on the order paper asking how many commissions and committees had been set up by the government, and how many of the chairmen and members were opposed to Labour policy.

First the whip asked him to withdraw the question. Then Mac-Donald's Permanent Private Secretary asked. Finally, John was asked to see MacDonald. In the Prime Minister's room in the House of Commons, MacDonald talked of their "long friendship" and asked him to abandon "embarrassing and disruptive activities". John said he would withdraw the question if he could have an assurance that no other committees would be set up without a Labour Party or neutral chairman. Unsurprisingly, MacDonald was furious. It was almost the last of John's boats, and he had casually thrown a match on to it.

Old friends were avoiding him now, and he was unsparing with them. "Attlee, Greenwood, Morrison, Dalton and the rest failed," he wrote, "not because a brutal opposition majority was too much for them, but because of their own inability and time-serving subservience to leaders who, when they were no longer in office, they could not sufficiently abuse."

Dalton's references to John in his diary now became positively acid. One of them, in August 1930, reads: "Frank Owen [Liberal MP and future editor of the *Evening Standard*] to dinner. Ruth [Dalton's wife] dislikes him as vulgar, untrustworthy and careerist. She thinks he is the same type as John Beckett."

But John was right to point out that the government's failure was not due to Labour's lack of an outright majority. Theoretically, the Conservatives and Liberals could combine and muster 320 votes, enough to vote out the Labour government with 287. The reality, though, was that nothing of the kind was going to happen. The Liberals had been wounded by their poor showing in the election and their relegation to the status of third party, and did not want to precipitate an early election. In any case they had produced a programme to deal with unemployment which involved public works on a huge scale, so they could hardly have opposed radical measures on unemployment if MacDonald had been inclined to introduce them.

Conservative leader Stanley Baldwin studiously avoided criticising the government too much, to the evident irritation of many Conservatives, and he was severely weakened by internal divisions. At by-elections the government had the benefit of a divided and ineffective opposition, because the press lords put up Empire Free Trade candidates against official Conservatives. The government had the general support of two Irish members, two independents and some of the Liberals, and might even have survived a combined attack by the Conservatives and Liberals, in the unlikely event that such an attack was launched. As Roy Jenkins writes in his biography of Baldwin, "The MacDonald government, despite its many faults and vicissitudes, was left almost miraculously free from strong and sustained attack by its principal opponent."

John bought (or, probably, rented) one of a group of splendid old houses in Lincoln's Inn which were pulled down in the 1930s. He possessed a rare panelled room which had survived the great fire of London, and had it carefully restored and redecorated. Within walking distance of Fleet Street, the House of Commons and the West End, it became a meeting place for journalists and left-wing politicians. Guests regularly included John Wheatley and James Maxton, the miners' leader Arthur Cook, William Mellor, editor of the *Daily Herald*, and Stanley Baldwin's son, the left-wing Labour MP Oliver Baldwin.

He saw a good deal of the left's new rising star, Aneurin Bevan. But John failed to persuade him to throw in his lot with the ILP, although Bevan often voted with them. He put this down to Bevan's weakness: "He is too honest to see eye to eye with the powers which could give him the political recognition his abilities deserve, and too lazy and comfortable to break away."

Among Labour MPs, only his own group of rebels, and those close to the rebels, dared to be seen with him. Old friends such as Attlee and Dalton were lost irretrievably. But like many MPs who are political lepers in their own parties, he started to make friends among the rebels of other parties. They felt something of his impatience with the old leaders such as MacDonald and Baldwin, who belonged to the world before the Great War. New friends included W.E.D. (Bill) Allen, Ulster Unionist MP, who was to play a crucial part in his future.

The Conservative Leslie Hore-Belisha became a regular visitor to his flat, and John wrote in 1938: "It seemed obvious that the heights he could ascend would be restricted only by the extent to which he could mask his enormous personality and intelligence and uproot the social sense he showed in his early political days."

John wrote that years later, in 1938, shortly before his new fascist friends targeted Hore-Belisha, then Secretary of State for War, because he was a Jew. But for the moment, only one of all these men mattered. John Wheatley was John's new leader. Wheatley, with John Beckett at his side, was going to lead the nation to socialism.

Wheatley was respected in Parliament, but not liked. People thought him cold and calculating. He entirely lacked Hugh Dalton's easy familiarity, and could not pretend to a friendship he did not feel. His eyesight was so bad that he was unable to recognise people unless they hailed him. The way to popularity and success in the Parliamentary Labour Party, then as now, was, as John put it, "by an almost repulsive indulgence in affectionate and usually meaningless camaraderie". Wheatley "had everything necessary to a great statesman except the ability to seek friendship or tolerate fools gladly".

In the 12 months after the 1929 election, Wheatley became a close friend. The left-wing Scottish elder statesman of 60 and the London firebrand of 35 dined together, and planned ILP tactics, every week during the winter of 1929–30, either in John's flat or in a favourite Soho restaurant of Wheatley's. John never, for the rest of his life, talked of this friend with anything other than respect.

"Wheatley's only fanatical belief was that hardship and suffering in Britain should be regarded as criminally wasteful and unnecessary" he wrote. "His mind was full of plans for the creation of an effective opposition to the existing palsied leadership."

To John – and to no one else – Wheatley confided his real view of his friend Maxton, as a good and brave man who could not lead an effective political movement. John wrote years later that he persuaded Wheatley that what was needed was a new political party – an organised party, not a loose association. More likely, Wheatley, a better and more experienced operator, allowed John to think it was his idea. Either way, Wheatley took that message back to the sceptical Maxton, and with some difficulty persuaded him.

This strange triangle – Wheatley and John Beckett in London, Wheatley and Jimmy Maxton in Glasgow – decided that the ILP was to be transformed into a new political party, to do all the things they had dreamed of, and to replace the Labour Party. In 1929 John believed firmly that Wheatley, with himself at his side, was going to lead Britain to the new Jerusalem. The exciting times of 1920 had come again.

They planned the new party in detail. They also planned ways in which to asset-strip the Communist Party, bringing its best people over to the ILP – an ambition which has a sad irony to it, because what actually happened in the 1930s was that the Communist Party asset-stripped and destroyed the ILP.

Wheatley was taken ill at the ILP 1930 Easter conference, but recovered and returned to London the next week, dining with John on Tuesday evening.

"He was full of plans for re-organisation," John recalled,

> and we spent several hours checking over the details of a number of schemes he intended taking to the ILP's National Administrative Council to put into immediate operation. On Wednesday he returned home, and on Friday we heard of his death.

That night John travelled to Glasgow for the funeral with fellow London MP W.J. Brown. They were met at the station in the early morning by Jimmy Maxton and David Kirkwood. John joined the funeral procession and later spoke with Maxton at "Wheatley" meetings in Manchester and Liverpool.

But the bottom had fallen out of his life. He had no sense of direction any more:

> We talked of the necessity for carrying on the work that Wheatley had left to our hand, and for a short time that thought did have an inspiring effect upon many, but in our hearts we knew that it could not be done. We were the men with whom Wheatley might have built civilisation in Britain, but without him we could only hope to fight on, whatever the consequences might be.
>
> On Maxton's frail shoulders had fallen the sole burden of leadership, and I saw much of him at that time. I have never

associated with a kinder, more impeccably honest, loyal and courageous man. But he is without ambition, has no patience for detail, and a queer philosophy adapted to his inherent laziness which makes him an impossible leader for any movement. He himself denounces leadership, claiming that he has no right to make up people's minds for them. His politics are socialist, but his habits of thought and temperament are completely anarchist.

Wheatley, says Maxton's latest biographer, Gordon Brown, "was the thinker and strategist, Maxton, sixteen years younger, the popular leader and orator". As Hugh Dalton smugly confided to his diary: "The death of Wheatley will make some difference to the left I think. They will be like sheep without a shepherd."

John was now the most disliked man in Westminster. Maxton and some of the other Clydesiders were popular, but it was John's strategies that were causing Labour MPs embarrassment in their constituencies, and John's attacks on them which were meant to hurt most. It was not in his character to hide his cleverness, even if it would only make him enemies.

It had been his task, as ILP whip, to confront fellow Labour MPs with their own cowardice, and he had done it not always wisely, but always thoroughly. He did not spare the feelings of those he felt had behaved badly. He was "the least likeable of the ILP Members", according to future Labour minister George Strauss, and Fenner Brockway told me: "The Labour leadership wanted John out more than they wanted any of the rest of us out, because he denounced them in more violent terms than the rest of us."

He had gambled everything on Wheatley, and Wheatley was gone. There was no hope, or any way back that he could see. It was, literally, a matter of fighting on, and damning the consequences. He no longer thought he had anything to lose.

The Labour Party machine was fighting back. It was starting to undermine the ILP members in their constituencies, getting loyal MPs to hector them in the corridors of the House of Commons and even denying them a hearing inside the chamber. ILP members found it increasingly hard to get replies to supplementary questions and opportunities in debate. Ministers were able deliberately to ignore their questions, backbenchers produced inspired interruptions to get ministers off the hook when ILP members tried to press their point and the Speaker generally made sure that John did not catch his eye, so much so that at one point an orthodox Labour MP, John's former friend Seymour Cocks, rose to ask whether "it is in order for anyone else to be heard except the Member for Peckham".

While Wheatley lived, it was all bearable. John believed that one day, under Wheatley's leadership, they would triumph. Suddenly, there was nothing left in the world except gestures. Wheatley died on 12 May 1930. By the end of July, John had poured petrol over his political career and put a match to it.

Notes on sources

A Lost Left: Three Studies in Socialism and Nationalism by David Howell (Manchester University Press, 1986).

Baldwin by Roy Jenkins (Harper Collins, 1987).

Call Back Yesterday by Hugh Dalton (Frederick Muller, 1953).

Dictionary of Labour Biography edited by K. Gildart and D. Howell (Palgrave Macmillan, 2010).

Ellen Wilkinson: A Biography by Betty Vernon (Croom Helm, 1982).

Maxton by Gordon Brown (Mainstream, 1986).

Stanley Baldwin: Man or Miracle by Bechhofer Roberts (Robert Hale, 1936).

Towards Tomorrow by Fenner Brockway (Hart-Davis MacGibbon, 1977).

9

LIFTING THE MACE AND
PLAYING TO THE GALLERY

On 25 June 1929 John and Helen were divorced.

In the manner of the time, the divorce had hung about for a while before they got the decree absolute, and someone had to be to blame. Fortunately, someone was. Helen petitioned on the grounds that "the respondent has frequently committed adultery with Violet Marion Bourchier" (Kyrle Bellew) and was living with Kyrle in Bourne End. Helen asked for, and got, custody of their daughter Lesley and John was to pay her, for life, maintenance of £133.6.8 a year, and was to pay the legal costs.

Just four days later, on 29 June, John and Kyrle married in a blaze of publicity. It looked unseemly. He could have waited, and done it more discreetly, and it would have been politically prudent to do so.

Three decades later he gave me his account of how it happened. The two of them, he said, were driving to Glasgow with two other Labour MPs, who turn out to have been Elijah Sandham from Liverpool Kirkdale and John Kinley from Bootle, to help Labour's candidate for John Wheatley's Glasgow Shettleston seat, John McGovern.

At Gretna Green, they stopped for coffee, or so John thought. But as he got out of the car he found Kyrle at his side and the pavement full of photographers.

Kyrle and the two MPs had planned the wedding, as a surprise for John, he told me.

Now, this is very odd. There was no need at all to go to Gretna Green. They were not runaways. But it made a wonderful story for the newspapers the next day. For Kyrle, it was probably welcome publicity. Sandham and Kinley no doubt thought it would please John. It probably did. It also helped to finish him, and surely they must have predicted that too. They may have thought he was beyond caring.

And here is the oddest thing of all. The marriage at Gretna Green was reported in all the newspapers, which treated it as a major news story, and it was told to me 30 years later; but whatever happened at Gretna Green, it was not a marriage.

Doubts surfaced the very next day, and brought another stack of headlines, which may or may not have been welcome to either of the newlyweds. John had told the village blacksmith at Gretna Green, who conducted the wedding, that he had been resident in Scotland for the required 21 days before he was married. But had he?

Kyrle told the *Daily Herald*:

> Mr Beckett had a room in Glasgow for 23 days before our marriage, during which time he was working in connection with the by-election in the Shettleston Division of Glasgow.
>
> It is true that he did not sleep there every night and that he was not in Glasgow every one of the 21 days before the marriage.
>
> During that period he paid one or two visits to London to attend to his parliamentary business. Altogether, I believe he spent about 14 days of the 21 in Glasgow.
>
> But he thought the fact that he had taken a room in Scotland for the qualifying period was sufficient to satisfy legal requirements in regard to a Gretna Green marriage, and I am surprised that anyone should have raised any question in the matter.

He had, apparently, asked the blacksmith, who did not know.

John, described by the *Herald* as "36, with black, curly hair and a fresh, boyish complexion", told the paper: "Everything that is legally necessary has been done and will be done." The real wedding happened quietly, four days later, on 5 July, at a London register office, after which they demanded, and rather surprisingly got, an apology from the *Herald* for casting doubt on the legality of their marriage.

John's second marriage certificate, like his first, is a prosaic, unforgiving and desperately unromantic document. Though even this document misleads: his age is given accurately as 35, but hers inaccurately as 37 – she was actually 43. Kyrle, like John's mother Eva, was keen to appear younger than she was.

The headlines did him nothing but harm in politics, and he must have known they would. He was ensuring that he could never be taken seriously again. Yet he went along with the unnecessary Gretna Green wedding, and even perpetuated it as a myth.

I was probably about 12 when I heard the story, but even a 12 year old can think that through and ask: why on earth did you do that? Well, he said, they were going to get married anyway, so "I might as well be hanged for a sheep as a lamb."

And that bit of unreliable homespun wisdom will recur rather often in this strange story, for it was the axiom by which John drove his life.

A week after they were married, Kyrle announced that she was resuming management of the Strand Theatre, and her brother Lionel Falck was to be general manager. And just 12 days after the real marriage, on 17 July, John found the biggest sheep yet to be hanged for, with the escapade that earned him a permanent footnote in history.

The mace is an important parliamentary symbol. The Sergeant at Arms solemnly bears it into the Commons before each sitting, and carries it out afterwards. The actions of the House have no legal validity when it is not there, and to handle it is sacrilege.

John was sitting in the chamber getting – I suspect – not just angry, but ferociously bored. He listened as one of his ILP colleagues, W.J. Brown, failed to get any information out of the Home Secretary on the matter of a child of eight who was apparently ordered to be birched by a court. Then another ILP man, Fenner Brockway, pressed the Prime Minister for an answer on the matter of the imprisonment in India of Gandhi, Nehru and 6,000 Indian Congressmen. Getting no answer, Brockway refused to sit down. He was "named" by the Speaker, and the Prime Minister moved his suspension from the House.

In the division on Brockway's suspension, only the ILP group supported him. The ILP therefore had to nominate two tellers for the vote, and they put up John and W.J. Brown. As the tellers walked up to the Speaker's table, John told Brown he intended to take the Mace away in protest. Brown wished him luck, and said that he could not himself risk suspension because he had an important meeting with the Chancellor of the Exchequer that afternoon on a matter concerning civil servants, whose trade union he represented.

Brown and Beckett reached the table and Beckett shouted: "Mr Speaker, these proceedings are a disgrace." Then he picked up the Mace, and almost fell over. The Sergeant at Arms always carried it as though it were very heavy, so John was braced for a considerable burden. The Mace turned out to be no heavier than an umbrella. "It was as hollow as the proceedings over which it presided", he wrote afterwards. Recovering his balance, he put it on his shoulder, turned on his heel and walked out of the chamber.

He had rather expected to be relieved of his burden very quickly. In fact, the 30 or so Members at the Bar of the House parted to let him through, and roared their disapproval as he did so. He found himself in the Inner Lobby, wondering what to do with his trophy. He decided to take it to the gents, "and place its head in one of the magnificent porcelain receptacles" to be found there. But at last, two large attendants arrived, and he was relieved of his burden.

"What in the world was the idea, John?" asked Brockway as the two men were escorted through New Palace Yard by the police. John replied, "It came to me suddenly – the House is in session only when the Mace is on the table. If I could get away with it, they couldn't suspend you."

Years later, Brockway told historian Colin Holmes: "I was a bit annoyed about the Mace, felt he had destroyed the dignity of the protest and its purpose. He revelled in the incident. Chuckled hard as the police sergeant escorted us out." In his autobiography Brockway says:

> I first met Beckett in the years immediately after the war; he was organising the National Union of Ex-Servicemen on a socialist and anti-war basis in opposition to the British Legion, and I was able to help him by introducing a number of

subscribers who contributed generously. Despite his subsequent political development, I have a friendly memory of earlier association with Beckett and particularly of the motive which led him to run away with the Mace.

This is a remarkably generous assessment given the rubbish John was talking – just how long could he expect to delay Brockway's suspension? Of course, John's motives were not that simple, and it is doubtful whether he himself ever quite understood them.

He told Brockway part of the truth, but there was a lot more. There was despair in the gesture. Then, too, there was probably some truth in the accusation, most pointedly levelled by Ellen Wilkinson, that it was publicity-seeking. She wrote in the *Daily Mail* four years later (on 22 November 1935):

> The time for the P.G. Wodehouse "silly ass" member is surely gone. The man who wants to carry off the Mace or do a tribal dance before the Speaker to call attention to himself will meet with cold contempt from those of us who have been very close to grim reality in the Distressed Areas during the election.

This, as it happens, was the only mention of the Distressed Areas in the article, the rest of it being on such vital matters as the advantages of knowing when to bow to the Speaker. All the same, and despite the grim loathing which the passage suggests, Wilkinson was probably not wrong in calling him a publicity seeker.

He told me the story when I was a child, and I asked, more for something to say than anything else, "So why did you do it?" He laughed his loud, sudden, cracked laugh and said, "Sheer bloody bravado." And that was part of it too. And he was bored. Bored, bored bored. Parliament is tedious, and he had a very low boredom threshold.

But I fear the biggest part of the explanation lies in that philosophy of life which caused him to have a fake Gretna Green wedding. He had already done enough to earn the undying hatred of his Party's leaders. And I am pretty sure he thought: I may as well be hanged for a sheep as a lamb.

And that's why he refused to apologise, instead making speeches and giving interviews in which he attacked the Parliamentary Labour Party in the most insulting terms he could think of – which were very insulting. He became quite quickly one of the best-known politicians in the country, with headlines every day for his increasingly sensational condemnations of his colleagues.

"For 14 months we have sat in the House of Commons all hours of the night wasting time listening to senile statesmen scoring futile debating points off each other..."

"Why listen for hours to the same century-old abominable drivel?..."

And so on.

When I met Brockway in 1981, he took me to the bar near the terrace of the House of Lords and told the barman: "Give this man a very large whisky. His father and I were thrown out of this place together." (A lifelong teetotaller, Brockway had discovered the joys of whisky in his eighties.)

He told me that John Beckett had been his closest friend throughout the 1929–31 Parliament. "He left his mark on this place, even if it was more of a streak. He wasn't really a socialist – he was a rebel. I was attracted by the rebel in him." To Colin Holmes, Brockway added: "He was sincerely outraged by poverty and injustice and human suffering."

When I told him my father had left an unpublished autobiography, he was very concerned to know what John had written about him, and offered to write an introduction to it for publication once he had read it. Despite everything that had happened, John's good opinion still mattered to him.

(He never did read it. I checked the references to him and decided against showing it to him – a very stupid decision; Brockway would not have minded the occasional slighting reference.) Brockway seems always to have been inclined to generosity where John was concerned. He also told Holmes: "He was loveable in his utter devotion. He might have become a great personal force and it was sad to see him wasted."

But wasted he certainly was. Only six MPs voted against his suspension, though many more voted against Brockway's. The very next day, Labour Party secretary Arthur Henderson told the Party's national executive that John's action "had brought discredit on the Parliamentary Labour Party and had constituted a gross affront to parliament".

Henderson also drew the National Executive Committee's attention to "the unsatisfactory voting record of Mr Beckett". There were reports, probably accurate, that he was raising money to run socialist candidates against official Labour candidates at the next election. The committee decided to discuss with the ILP the problem of this increasingly impossible MP.

John defended himself in the ILP publication, *The New Leader*. The protest was, he wrote, more successful than he could have dreamed:

> The Press, usually blissfully oblivious of the sayings of dissatisfied Labour men, have been good enough to draw the attention of some millions of people to Parliament's disgraceful time-wasting.
>
> For 14 months Parliament has been a grotesque and self-righteous orgy of useless point-scoring. Unemployment steadily grows, wages steadily fall. Armaments are increased and the intensification of British imperial tyranny goes on ... We cling without dignity or decency to office barren of power or prestige. The present government, with the support of the Liberal and Tory leaders, deliberately prevents the socialist viewpoint being put forward in the House. There is time for hours of backchat between Snowden and Churchill.
>
> Time for voting huge sums of money for war. Time for ... endless ceremonials and bowing and scraping. Time for a summer holiday nearly three months long. No time for socialist motions or supplementaries on working class questions.

Parliament may have been affronted, but Peckham seems to have been delighted. Two hastily summoned, but packed, public meetings cheered him to the rooftops, and a specially called meeting of the Peckham Labour Party passed a unanimous vote of congratulation.

Fred Brooks wrote to me: "It was a dramatic gesture of protest against the almost total lack of commitment by the government to the plight of the unemployed … It won support and admiration from the people he had been sent to represent."

It changed nothing though. Two months before, in the month that Wheatley died, May 1930, the government threw out Sir Oswald Mosley's memorandum on unemployment, and Mosley resigned and published it. It called for a programme of public invest-ment, protection of British industry with tariffs, an end to the export of capital for investment overseas and a major programme of public works (which Lloyd George and the Liberals had advocated during the 1929 election).

Mosley spent the summer canvassing support for his proposals among MPs. John on his own account stayed aloof, sharing Maxton's distrust both of Mosley himself and of the proposals. John was cer-tainly not among Mosley's supporters, although on 1 August 1930 Dalton wrote in his diary, rather bewilderingly: "Beckett – Sandham – Mosley. The Posing Peacocks and the Booby. But against the Tired Timidity of Leaders, not a quite unnatural foreground."

Nonetheless, John followed carefully the events which led to Mosley forming the New Party. Strangely, given what was to happen later, John was not an admirer of Mosley. He thought him a spoiled young careerist, with more money and ego than sense, the sort of rich young aristocrat who impressed snobs like MacDonald but whom real socialists, like himself and Maxton, regarded with amused disdain.

He would at that time have agreed with his old friend Clem Attlee's much later judgement: "A wealthy young baronet was just the person to appeal to Mr Macdonald, while his vigorous invec-tive made him popular with the rank and file of the Labour Party." John reports the formation of the New Party with a sort of dis-dainful irony which reads strangely in the light of what he himself did three years later. The New Party on John's account, started "in the fertile brain of W.J. Brown". Brown was the ILP man who had been the other teller when John stole the Mace. He was secre-tary of the Civil Servants Association and an ILP loyalist. A small, delicate, fair man with a quick mind, John thought him the most stimulating conversationalist he had known, but did not take him seriously.

> The intense conviction with which he feels any idea which occurs to him during conversation makes him almost irresistible, but one yields to his arguments on Monday only to give him the trouble, on Wednesday, sincerely and convincingly of showing how wrong a view one holds.

So "the shrewd laziness of Maxton and our natural iconoclasm usually prevented us from acting on his freely dispensed advice".

One of the ideas was of a New Party, backed by Mosley, who would provide both the money and the charisma while Brown provided the ideas. It was of course what John had wanted - but led by Wheatley, not Mosley. Mosley and Brown were encouraged by two ILP men, Oliver Baldwin (son of Stanley Baldwin) and Robert Forgan, as well as John Strachey, the old Etonian left-wing Labour MP, Aneurin Bevan, and John's Ulster Unionist friend W.E.D. Allen.

John wrote this account of how it happened, and it is probably the best inside account that exists, even allowing for John's instinct for not allowing prosaic actual events to get in the way of a good story.

> There are several versions of the manner in which the debacle happened. The truth is that Mosley, after sitting on the fence for some weeks, declared at a small private gathering his willingness to proceed. Strachey and [Mosley's secretary] at once rushed into print with the news ... W.E.D. Allen resigned at once from the Conservative Party; Oliver Baldwin and Robert Forgan, followed two days later by John Strachey, resigned from the Labour Party; and a large number of Conservative and Labour members who had been hanging around the Mosleys for months rushed into print to say that they had nothing at all to do with it.
>
> Brown said that he could not take part because of the attitude of his union and his inability to forfeit their financial support. Mosley guaranteed him against financial loss, and went with Strachey to interview the union executive, who gave permission for Brown to participate. Brown then went to bed, ill. Mosley and Strachey rushed to Highgate to see him, but he was not well enough to be interviewed at any length. Mosley then broke down, and the new movement was ushered in with

little welcome from its leaders and inspirers. Mosley retired to bed in Smith Square the day after Brown retired to his bed in Highgate.

...It is a queer system which drives men of honesty and independence of character to a hopeless and slightly ridiculous mutiny as the only alternatives to the perorations of a Mac-Donald and the narrow cunning of a Baldwin.

When Lord Rothermere's newspapers printed endless horror stories of people getting a few shillings from the dole to which they were not entitled, MacDonald began talking of married women turning up to collect dole in fur coats; and in 1931 the government produced an Anomalies Bill in order, they said, to prevent abuses.

The ILP harried the bill unmercifully in an all-night session, nine ILP MPs including John keeping the House in session until 10 a.m. the following morning. John spoke with bitterness of his oldest friend in politics, Clem Attlee. In those early days in Lime-house, he wrote,

it would have seemed impossible to me that a kind, gentle, love-able man might be so corrupted by the Parliamentary system that he could represent the people of the abyss and yet vote for two shillings a week for their children; and support the Anomalies Act, which swept them away from their meagre dole like flies.

Attlee says in his autobiography that he reluctantly severed his long connection with the ILP because it "became more and more irre-sponsible under the leadership of Jimmy Maxton".

Unemployment rose from 1,630,000 in June 1929 to 1,912,000 in June 1930. Well before the end of the year it had topped the two million mark and rising (it reached three million by the time the gov-ernment fell). By now pretty well everyone shared John's low opinion of Jimmy Thomas, who had been given the task of solving the problem. He was disintegrating before his colleagues' eyes. A man who owed his political career to his superficial joviality, he was petrified by the enormity of the task, and was drinking too much and offering nothing but trite pieces of homespun wisdom.

In the first few months of 1931 the financial situation grew worse almost by the minute. British banks had taken short-term loans from the USA and France, and lent to Germany at higher rates of interest. When the German banks failed, they were left deeply in debt to the French and the Americans. By February Philip Snowden was telling the House of Commons: "The national position is so grave that drastic and disagreeable measures will have to be taken." Labour MPs knew he meant a reduction in unemployment pay.

The next month MacDonald set up a committee chaired by Sir George May, secretary of the Prudential Insurance Company, to recommend "all possible reductions in national expenditure".

In July there was a flight from the pound. That month also saw John's worst and most violent parliamentary scene.

John McGovern, who had succeeded Wheatley as MP for Glasgow Shettleston, was, like John, fundamentally a rebel rather than a socialist. He came to the House one day burning with indignation about the harsh treatment apparently handed out to some lay preachers arrested for preaching on Glasgow Green without a licence.

McGovern, together with Maxton and the other Clydesiders, urged the Scottish Secretary to use his power to release the men. When they failed to get the undertaking they sought, McGovern refused to sit down. Ordered to leave, he again refused, and the Speaker had to despatch four attendants to remove him.

If you read John's account of what happened next, and then read McGovern's, it looks like two quite different incidents. But what seems certain is that McGovern wedged his feet into the paper rack on the seat in front, in order to form a lock, while Maxton, Beckett and some other ILP MPs prevented the attendants from reaching him. Maxton was knocked flying into the seats in front of him, and either John or McGovern knocked at least one of the attendants after him.

In the end, the honourable member for Peckham and the honourable member for Glasgow Shettleston were frog-marched out together, two attendants to each, holding their arms pinioned behind their backs while a Mr Samuel Rosbotham, Labour MP for Ormskirk, seized the chance to punch John in the face. The sitting was suspended owing to "grave disorder".

What on earth prompted John to get involved in this mess? He knew nothing at all about preachers on Glasgow Green. It was the sort of Scottish issue which a wise London MP would have stayed well clear of, and McGovern had given his colleagues no indication of what he intended to do. John knew little about McGovern, though he must by then have realised that this was not a man of the intellectual quality of Wheatley and Maxton.

For John, however, the Clydesiders now represented the only decent force in Parliament. He always had to have people in whom he believed absolutely, who were right even when they were wrong. He needed someone to receive his absolute loyalty.

The Anomalies Bill was to be introduced the next week – the one bill they were most determined to fight – and their escapade seemed destined to ensure that they would be suspended and unable to take part in the debate. So Maxton immediately went into a series of meetings with Party leaders and the Speaker. John had a caravan beside the Thames at Hurley, and it was there that he, Maxton, McGovern and the rest met to decide what to do.

MacDonald had told Maxton that, if he would agree to exemplary punishment for Beckett and McGovern, no action would be taken against anyone else. John wrote: "As Maxton is the only political leader I ever met who was not anxious to pass responsibility to his followers in any moment of pressure, it never occurred to any of us that this offer should be taken seriously."

Their apologies, every word of which had to be agreed by the Speaker, were grovelling. It was the bitterest medicine John had yet swallowed. But it was the price of being there for the Anomalies Bill, and listening, as John put it, to

> speech after speech telling of some Labour MP's relative or friend who knew someone else who had heard of a man who drew ten shillings a week in unemployment benefit when he actually did weekend work and earned a few shillings as well.

Maxton called the bill "a surrender in the face of one of the meanest, ill-natured agitations that have ever taken place by the rich against the worst defences of the poor".

John planned a strategy for the committee stage which he reck-oned would enable the ILP group, now reinforced by Sir Charles Trevelyan who had resigned as Education Minister, to keep the House up all night. Trevelyan and others were sceptical. The Irish republicans, with all their experience of holding up the work of Par-liament, advised that it needed more MPs than the ILP could muster. John wrote triumphantly afterwards:

> The committee stage began at 3.45 p.m. and we kept the House going until just after 10 a.m. on the following morning. Nine of us made over 100 speeches, and there were over 40 divisions. No disorder of any kind took place. But every member of our small group worked in an orderly, disciplined manner, taking advantage of every legitimate parliamentary trick to embarrass the government.

The bill went through, and Parliament broke up for the summer. MPs went on their holidays, not knowing that this summer vacation was to be like no other, and that before they returned after their break the government would have fallen. John and Jimmy Maxton had planned a family holiday in John's caravan at Hurley, with John's daughter Lesley, Maxton's two sisters and Maxton's young son Jimmy who, since the death of Maxton's wife, had lived with his sisters. It was a calm and comfortable few days beside the Thames, and neither man could have known that it was the last they were to have together with the same easy comradeship.

Notes on sources

The Decline and Fall of the Labour Party by John Scanlon (Peter Davies, 1932).
The Fascists in Britain by Colin Cross, reviewed by Earl Attlee (*Political Science Quarterly*, 79(1), March 1964).
Towards Tomorrow by Fenner Brockway (Hart-Davis MacGibbon, 1977).

10
1931

On 1 August the May Committee report was published. Sir George May said that the only possible solution to the economic crisis was to save £97 million of national expenditure by cutting unemployment benefit and teachers' and police salaries by 20 per cent.

MacDonald and Snowden published the report without comment or policy statement, then went on holiday. Throughout August the drift from sterling accelerated, and the bandwagon for cutting unemployment pay, propelled by the newspapers, the banks and the Conservatives, rapidly became unstoppable.

There were, as the ILP pointed out publicly and some cabinet ministers pointed out privately, other ways in which the required savings could be made, without causing the hardship and bitterness among the poorest and lowest paid that May's proposals would entail. John's preference, typically, was to take it from the repayments of war loans – the money that those with capital had lent the nation in order to fight the First World War, and which was being repaid at a generous rate of interest. "A cut of one per cent in war loan interest would solve the whole problem", he said. The TUC wanted at least some of it to come from those who lived on investments or on property. They thought the rich ought to pay as well as the poor –

including the city financiers, whose greedy strategy had collapsed, and who had then run to the government to demand that the unemployed and public servants should pay the price.

"The General Council are pigs", said Sidney Webb to his wife Beatrice. "They won't agree to any cuts of unemployment insurance benefits or salaries or wages." But how could he have expected them to do so? The government was proposing the very measures that the TUC had founded the Labour Party to oppose.

By the end of August MacDonald and Snowden were sure that Britain's salvation depended entirely on obtaining a loan from a New York bank. The bank demanded a 10 per cent cut in unemployment pay as the price of a loan. The cabinet turned this down by 12 votes to nine. MacDonald, "looking scared and unbalanced", according to Harold Nicholson, went to the palace to advise the king to summon the other Party leaders.

But Baldwin and acting Liberal leader Sir Herbert Samuel (Lloyd George was ill) believed the best solution was a National Government consisting of all three parties and led by MacDonald. If unpopular measures hurting Labour's natural constituency were to be introduced, it would be convenient to have Labour implicated. MacDonald put up a token resistance to the flattering idea that he was the indispensable man, and on 24 August told the cabinet that he "could not refuse the king's request" to lead the new National Government.

For a few days John thought this just might be the moment they had waited for. Surely their old colleagues would now see that the ILP had been right all along? If that happened, then there would be no need of the new party he and Wheatley had planned just a year ago. The Labour Party could itself be made into the instrument which changed the world.

He kept in close touch with Maxton and the Clydesiders in Glasgow, and Brockway in London, and established that the ILP would work with the Labour Party, without recriminations, if Labour would work with them.

But as soon as the Parliamentary Labour Party met with trade union leaders also present, it was clear that there was no chance of this. According to Gordon Brown,

At the very moment when Maxton and the ILP could have seized leadership positions in the Labour hierarchy he chose to stand aloof ... Maxton misread the signs and was unable to grasp the opportunities presented to the ILP to recover its leadership of the Labour Movement.

Brown seems to believe that a place on Labour's front bench was Maxton's for the asking, that all the bitterness of the past two years might be set aside. He may be right but it was certainly not John Beckett's view at the time. When Labour MPs met on 28 August, according to John's account:

Maxton's conciliatory speech was violently interrupted from its beginning, and a bitter attack upon us as the root of the trouble, made by an ex-cabinet minister, was roundly cheered. This minister was known to have hung about Downing Street for several hours in a fruitless attempt to see MacDonald after the dismissal of the Labour government, and the burden of his argument was that had we not criticised the Prime Minister so rudely he would not have left the Labour Party.

Sadly he does not name the minister, and there is no reference to this speech or to Maxton's in the fullest account we have on this meeting (in Hugh Dalton's diary). The reference may be to Herbert Morrison, who is known to have tried to get a job in MacDonald's new Conservative-dominated National Government. But if so, why not name him?

Still, Maxton could at least have stood for the now vacant leadership. In the event, 68-year-old Arthur Henderson was elected unopposed as Labour leader. At the meeting of the Parliamentary Labour Party, according to Dalton's diary, just five votes were cast against Henderson: Maxton, Beckett and three ILP Scots – George Buchanan, Campbell Stephen and Jennie Lee. These were pointless votes, because they had no alternative candidate. No one, on either side, was going to forget and forgive. As John wrote bitterly:

Now the whole pack was in full cry. Here was an enemy upon which they could concentrate their chagrin at the early prospect of losing a general election. Arthur Cook tried to speak, and was threatened with physical violence. I succeeded in making a short speech pointing out that more important things remained to be done than to split the Party still further. A gentleman chiefly prominent for his ability to guess by which door any cabinet minister might be leaving, in order that he might open it, was so enraged that he rushed towards me, and when he was safely restrained by two colleagues, threatened violence.

The last six weeks I spent in the House were among the most miserable I had experienced. Until the last few days, the Labour Members believed that if only they did not oppose the National Government too strongly, there would be no general election, and daily they crawled past their lost leader in mute homage, uttering pleas for forgiveness because he had deserted them.

Mr Snowden, addressing the House one afternoon, paused for a few moments to survey the Labour benches thoroughly, and then remarked: "I sat with my back to you for many years. Had I seen you as thoroughly as I do now I face you, it would not have been so long." We sat on the benches below the gangway, and were able to watch the sickly and servile titters with which Labour Members greeted this.

Stripped of its bitterness, expressed here in John's usual pungent and unrestrained language, how reliable is his record? John's account of that meeting of MPs has hardly anything in common with the only other version we have, which is Dalton's. Yet the events reported by both of them probably occurred. It is their selection, and the flavour they attach to it, that makes the difference.

Most of John's charges, and also Maxton's, were accurate. Labour MPs knew that MacDonald had it in his power to destroy their careers by calling an early election, in which many of them would lose their seats. They also knew that there was very little difference between the policies MacDonald was now pursuing, and the policies he had previously pursued with their support. If MacDonald's policies were a betrayal, then they were all guilty.

Perhaps Gordon Brown is right – perhaps there was a moment for Maxton to have seized, a moment that John Wheatley would have seized.

Or perhaps the ILP had made that rapprochement possible – and if that is the case, then the man most responsible for doing so was its whip, John Beckett.

It is an odd irony that John's biggest contribution to history may have been to consign the ILP to the wilderness which it entered in 1931, and from which it never returned.

There are very few Labour people who come out of the 1931 crisis with any credit at all. Jimmy Maxton, John Beckett and their friends may not have handled themselves with much political skill, but they were consistent and they were honest.

Lingering hopes that MacDonald might not call a snap election were swiftly dashed. The government secured the American loan, went off the gold standard which it had been formed to safeguard and, of course, made the reductions in unemployment benefit and public service pay which MacDonald's Labour colleagues had refused to make. Then, six weeks after he had formed his National Government, MacDonald dissolved Parliament for an election.

The Labour Party's first concern seemed to be to get its ILP rebels in line. Maxton and others were sent a form to sign, promising not to vote against the whips under any circumstances. Most of them refused to sign it. They were therefore denied endorsement as Labour candidates.

One of them was not sent a form. John Beckett was not even to be given this last chance to redeem himself. The Labour leadership was determined that, whatever the fate of Maxton and the rest, Beckett at least was to be got rid of.

Peckham Labour Party nominated John enthusiastically. But on nomination day they discovered that Labour Party headquarters had declared a Captain Hubert Beaumont, someone of whom they had never heard, to be the Labour candidate for Peckham.

It turned out that the London Labour Party – then as now the most conspiratorial of bodies – had organised a secret meeting of five local members, together with Lewis Silkin, who had lost the nomination to John for the 1929 election. They nominated Captain Beaumont, a little known Co-Operative movement official, and Transport House declared them to be Peckham's official Labour Party.

A MacDonald National Labour candidate was also nominated.

Although other ILP MPs were refused endorsement, only John Beckett and John McGovern were actually opposed by official Labour candidates. This was partly because they were the two who were most hated. But there seems to have been a more cynical calculation. It was no good opposing Maxton and George Buchanan – they would hold their Glasgow seats against anyone. And there was no need to oppose the ILP MPs in English seats – they were likely to lose anyway, given that the tide was running against Labour. But Beckett and McGovern seemed likely to win if they were left alone. Should the Labour vote be split, there was a reasonable chance that the Conservative could win.

John had no money to fight the election. Since Beaumont was the official Labour candidate, it was against their own rules for trade union branches to finance John's campaign, though they refused to finance Beaumont's campaign.

John, who knew a thing or two about the law of libel, wrote afterwards:

> The origin of the £600 with which Captain Beaumont's expenses were paid is still a close secret. He told me that he was not a man of means, and his expenses were being paid for him. His only constant supporter was Mr Silkin, who succeeded him in the candidature when the unpleasantness of the campaign was over.

It need only be added that Lewis Silkin, a wealthy lawyer and a friend and colleague of John's old enemy Herbert Morrison, became at the next general election the Labour MP for Peckham.

Half a century later I became a friend of his son John Silkin, a senior Labour politician in the 1980s, and helped and advised him in his campaign for Labour's deputy leadership. One day I decided to tell him whose son I was next time we lunched together. But before I could start, he wanted to tell me why he always stayed in an elderly, inconvenient hotel in the centre of Brussels when he was Agriculture

Minister, when all the other ministers stayed in the modern hotels conveniently situated just by the Berleymont building. During the war the Nazi Gauleiter in Brussels used that town centre hotel. Silkin always demanded the same suite that the Gauleiter had. He liked the idea of a Jewish cabinet minister lording it in the room, dancing on the murderer's grave.

I left the restaurant without telling him about my father. I resolved to do so next time. But a few weeks later John Silkin died suddenly, so I never did.

To add to John's troubles, the communists decided to devote all their considerable energies in London to ensuring that he was not returned. His views were closer to theirs than those of any other London Labour candidate, and that was why they opposed him so fiercely. The Communist Party in 1931 believed that its first duty was to destroy other people and parties of the left, because they competed with it for the allegiance of the working class. It is an absurd and self-defeating way to behave, but it is the way in which several left-wing groups over the years have buried the ideals for which they fought.

Their main tactic was to destroy John's meetings. They would turn up en masse where he was due to speak, and sing and chant to prevent him from doing so. His response was to organise a defence force and to put in charge of it a well-known local boxer.

These were the type of bodyguards for which, within three years, Sir Oswald Mosley was to become notorious.

For the last time, John threw his hurricane-like energy and imagination into a furious parliamentary campaign, hampered as never before by lack of funds. His supporters seemed sure of winning right up to the declaration, but John sensed victory slipping from his grasp in the final three days.

The Conservative, Viscount Borodaile, received 19,458 votes to John's 11,217. The MacDonald Labour candidate received 1,442, beating Labour's official nominee, Captain Beaumont, into fourth place with 1,350. The turnout was low, and John was sure that, without the issue being confused by the intervention of two other Labour candidates, he would have won. Nationally, 1931 saw the twentieth century's biggest landslide. The National Government returned to Parliament with 556 seats and a majority of 500 over all opposition parties. Labour won just 46 seats. It was the most crushing defeat imaginable for a Party which, just two years earlier, had become the largest in the House of Commons. Of the ILP rebels, only Maxton, McGovern and George Buchanan remained in Parliament. Of John's list of 53 Labour MPs who had voted against the 1929 government, only nine were left.

Labour's leadership was decimated. Its leader Arthur Henderson lost his seat, along with a huge swathe of his colleagues, including Herbert Morrison and Hugh Dalton. Veteran left-winger George Lansbury, who had made his peace with Labour's leadership a few years previously and was now 72, became leader, and the only other survivor with any ministerial experience, Clement Attlee, who had become Postmaster General just five months before the Labour government collapsed, became deputy leader.

It was another 13 years before Labour was to hold power again. In 1945, led by Attlee, it was elected with an overall majority and for the first time started to implement its own agenda.

The game of historical "what if" is a fascinating one. The 1931 result has provided the material for endless rounds. What if Herbert Morrison, or Hugh Dalton, had held their seats in 1931? Dalton and Morrison tormented themselves with this scenario, probably for the rest of their lives, and their biographers followed them. Either of them, they believed, would have become deputy leader instead of Attlee, and Prime Minister in 1945. I think they were wrong. Attlee would still have won.

Another commonly played version is: what if Oswald Mosley had stayed in the Labour Party? Would he not have retained his Birmingham seat and become leader, and Prime Minister in 1945? Again, my own view is: no, Attlee would still have led Labour.

But what if John Wheatley had lived?

After Wheatley's death, the small ILP parliamentary group began to fall apart, and its parliamentary influence to diminish. By the time the government fell, many natural ILP supporters – idealists, but practical politicians and democrats too – were beginning to distance themselves from an ILP group which was starting to look increasingly desperate, afloat on stormy seas without a rudder. The group was now the Clydesiders, plus John Beckett.

When the 1931 crisis came, Maxton seems to have been frozen by indecision. Should he try to lead the Labour Party, or forge a new political force out of the ILP? Effectively, he did neither. Fenner Brockway believed, as Gordon Brown argues in his biography of Maxton, that had Wheatley lived he would have kept the ILP inside Labour. But Wheatley was dead, and after the 1931 election, the ILP broke away from the Labour Party and was, within a few years, an irrelevance.

Its supporters scattered: John Beckett and Robert Forgan, eventually, to fascism; John Strachey in the direction of the Communist Party. Others, like McGovern and Jennie Lee, stayed in the ILP as it dwindled into an ineffectual fringe, and they eventually rejoined the Labour Party.

If Wheatley had lived, the ILP's 19 parliamentary rebels would have behaved very differently in the last year of the Labour government. Wheatley demanded, and received, discipline from his followers. He would never have allowed them to dissipate their energies and credibility in pointless scenes over preachers on Glasgow Green, nor would John Beckett have run away with the Mace.

In Parliament the ILP would have worked in the disciplined manner in which it opposed the Anomalies Bill, and would have avoided the shambolic scenes created by McGovern and Beckett. McGovern, of course, would not have been an MP (he inherited Wheatley's seat) and Beckett would have been Wheatley's loyal and able organiser.

When the crisis came, the ILP would have made itself strong enough outside Parliament to be a real and credible threat to the official Labour Party. It could not have been excluded without real danger. Wheatley would have been a key power-broker after the 1931 election, and quite possibly Labour's leader in preference to George Lansbury.

The hideous irony for the ILP is that after 1931, Labour was led by its natural friends and allies, George Lansbury, Clement Attlee and Stafford Cripps. These were men with whom Wheatley could have done business.

For John Beckett the difference might have been stark. He would probably have kept his seat in 1931. If not, he would have stayed loyal to Wheatley, and would probably have returned to Parliament at the 1935 election. After 1935, Labour under Attlee extended the hand of friendship towards those rebels who remained, so much so that the ILP's George Buchanan became a minister in 1945. John, if he could have learned a little discipline and self-control, might have returned to the mainstream of events.

Then again, he might not. Perhaps even Wheatley could not have reined in John's self-destructive urge, especially after the personal blows which John was about to suffer. But if he could, then after the 1945 general election, instead of being an outcast recently released from prison, he might have been awaiting a call from his old friend Clem Attlee to tell him which government post he was getting.

Notes on sources

King George V by Harold Nicholson (Macmillan, 1967).

Maxton by Gordon Brown (Mainstream, 1986).

Politicians and the Slump by Robert Skidelsky (Papermac, 1994).

The Diaries of Beatrice Webb by Beatrice Webb, edited by Jeanne Mackenzie (Virago, 2002).

The Political Diary of Hugh Dalton, 1918–40, 1945–60 edited by Ben Pimlott (Cape, 1987).

11

DYING ON STAGE

The election nomination papers in Peckham in 1929 record that John Beckett, Labour candidate, was by profession a theatrical agent.

Back in 1925, a young, handsome and glamorous newly elected Labour MP had begun a love affair with a theatrical profession, which was itself entranced by the radical politics of the time. The 1917 Club saw young socialists such as John Beckett and Fenner Brockway forming close friendships with left-wing actors and actresses.

In 1929 Beckett and Brockway founded the Masses Stage and Film Guild with the help and support of leading politicians like Clynes, Lansbury, Maxton and Trevelyan, and leading theatrical folk including Sybil Thorndyke (later Dame Sybil), John's old friend Denis Neilson-Terry, Miles Malleson, Lewis Casson and of course Kyrle Bellew. It aimed to present plays of social significance and charge affordable prices for seats.

After Arthur Bourchier died in 1927, Kyrle Bellew inherited his lease of the Strand Theatre and John began to take an active part in its management. He also started investing the money he had made with Bourchier, but now without Bourchier's hand to guide him. The next year, still an MP, invested in *The House of the Arrow* by A.E.W. Mason at the Vaudeville Theatre, and seems to have been involved in every aspect of the production. This is less surprising than might appear: the producer was Kyrle, and it was her first venture outside acting.

For the next four or five years John and Kyrle must have lived in each other's pockets. He came into her world, increasingly managing as well as publicising her work. She came into his: a long-standing Labour supporter, she was elected as a councillor in Peckham after John became Peckham's MP, and became a loved and admired local figure of whom Peckham Labour Party was exceptionally proud.

John's managerial duties seem to have ranged from helping select Denis Eadie to play the main part, and taking the certified box office returns to Eadie after each performance (stars in those days were paid a guaranteed salary plus a proportion of the gross takings), to comforting his highly strung leading lady, Valerie Taylor. But after three weeks' run, Eadie died suddenly, and the show was doomed. The next year John was equally involved in *Appearances*, by Garland Anderson, the first play by a black writer to be presented in London. Anderson had got his play, about a black man falsely accused of raping a white woman, produced on Broadway in 1925 with the help of the actor Al Jolson and the US President, Calvin Coolidge. In the light of what John later became, there's a sad irony in the fact that he brought it to London.

In the summer of 1930, just after their marriage, John and Kyrle rented a houseboat near Henley. Paul Robeson stayed one weekend, together with the actor Edmond Gwenn, and they introduced John to a vigorous and exhausting American game called Bumble-puppy.

Robeson was playing Othello in the West End that summer (not a patch on Arthur Bouchier's Othello, John thought), and the *Daily Mail* – later to endorse Sir Oswald Mosley's fascists – asked his Desdemona, Peggy Ashcroft, what she felt about having to kiss a black man on the stage. Miss Ashcroft treated the question with the contempt it deserved, but her quote was enough for a prurient little news story:

> I consider it a great honour to be acting with Mr Paul Robeson, and any discussion about my kissing and being kissed by him seems merely silly to me. I have thought no more about it than I would have would have done if I had to kiss an Englishman on stage.

It was the nearest the newspapers came to hinting at the affair between Robeson and Ashcroft which most of theatrical London knew about. Newspapers in those days were just as prurient as they are now, but more timid, and in 1930 John and Kyrle were still benefitting from that.

John became a sort of parliamentary spokesman for live theatre, introducing a bill to give local authorities the power to fund the establishment of a local repertory theatre and getting all-party support for it. The government, as is the way with governments, did not allow even so minor a backbench initiative any parliamentary time. When the government introduced legislation to allow Sunday opening of cinemas, he put down an amendment extending this to theatres. But the churches lobbied heavily against this, and it lost in committee by a narrow margin.

Speaking to the committee, John noted sardonically that the religious bodies opposing him "have never spent an effort or bought a stamp to urge parliament to feed their lambs, or to protest against the systematic malnutrition of women and children in a Christian state". He was right, of course, but the atheist Clem Attlee and the Catholic John Wheatley would have avoided making unnecessary enemies of such powerful organisations.

The campaign brought him into contact with the great comedian Leslie Henson, who lobbied tirelessly for the reform, and Henson became another close theatrical friend. "Off stage, like most comedians, Leslie is not a very cheerful person", wrote John. "A visit to his dressing room after the show is often enough to convince one that life is not worth living."

Henson became the source of many of those anecdotes which John loved so much and told all his life. Henson, he said, was generous in big things and remarkably mean about small things. He remembered sitting in conferences all morning where everyone, in turn, passed their cigarette cases around the room. Henson's case would not be seen except when, occasionally, he would finish the cigarette he was smoking, glance round the room to see that no case was doing the rounds, then carefully extract one cigarette from a well-filled case and replace the case in his pocket.

It reminded John, a very heavy smoker and instinctively open-handed, of an old Labour Party friend, the miners' leader Bob

Smillie, a pipe smoker who claimed that he never had a decent smoke. When he used his own tobacco he filled his pipe too loose, and when he used someone else's he filled it too tight.

After losing his seat in 1931, John had more time to devote to the theatre. On the face of it, it was a most enviable existence, far better than the average MP who loses his seat and scratches for a way to make a living. He was an established theatre manager, his wife was a famous actress, they lived in considerable style and he liked and admired theatre people – so much better and more straightforward than the greasy politicians he had associated with at Westminster. For a while at least a part of him thought that this was how he would spend the rest of his life.

He helped revive Bourchier's Christmas tradition of a production of *Treasure Island*, with Tod Slaughter playing Bourchier's role of Long John Silver and Kyrle as Mrs Hawkins. The show flopped, a backer let them down and disappeared leaving huge bills, and John, Kyrle and Tod Slaughter were pursued by creditors for months afterwards – an unhappy omen for what was to come.

They salvaged something from the wreckage by taking *Treasure Island* on tour with another actor, Vernon Fortescue, as Silver. John managed the tour. He loved moving about the country, and he loved the freedom and lack of convention of theatre people, so different from the stilted, suspicious company of politicians. He worked hard in the evenings and spent the days on a local golf course.

He even made his first appearance on the professional stage. When some of the cast left and funds were running low, he cast himself as Honest Tom Watkins, who appears in a short scene alone on the island with Silver, refusing to take part in Silver's nefarious plans, announcing his incorruptible honesty and getting killed after a dramatic struggle. It was a three-minute scene and he loved it, but it taught him that he could never be an actor. This, typically, he put down to the fact that he was a great orator, and the two talents, he decided, were incompatible.

John and Kyrle had a wonderful time on tour, and were able to salvage something of their finances, so a few months later they went on another tour, again with John as manager. They thought that if they did what Bourchier had done, and presented a play as nearly as possible in the way that it had appeared in London's West End, there would be an audience for it.

They learned the hard way that the touring theatre in England was almost dead. For the first five weeks, *Firebird* lost a fortune every week, and they had to decide whether to cut their losses and pay a heavy forfeit to the theatres with which they had contracts. They decided to carry on, but to reduce expenses.

One of the ways of doing this was for John to take on a small part himself, that of a famous actor who, after a passionate love scene with the heroine, is shot dead. For the second and last time he died on stage. This time his character, conveniently, wore a dinner jacket, so it was a simple matter to play his part, exit, clean the make-up from his face and go out front to continue the managerial job of counting the house.

Playing the part was less simple, and this time he seems to have made a mess of it. The heroine had to rescue his performance most nights. The heroine, though when John told the story he did not mention this point, was Kyrle, and she seems to have become irritable as, night after night, he ruined the scene with his stage fright and his inability to remember his lines. On his first night, his nerve and memory failed him so badly that he clung to a balustrade repeating any nonsense that came into his head.

In the summer of 1932 Kyrle, as the proprietor of the Strand Theatre in London's West End, appointed John as its manager. It wasn't an easy assignment. The mortgage on the theatre cost £250 a week to service, an enormous sum in those days which had to be found even if the theatre was shut. The job would have taxed someone who knew the theatre inside out and had an excellent head for business. For John, it was a disaster, not helped by the fact that he had the sort of manner which convinced everyone, including himself, that he knew exactly what he was doing.

Their first play, *Sally Who* by Dion Titheradge, starring Jessie Mathews and Sonny Hale, flopped, despite good notices. It was a poor start, and they had to take the show off at the end of June. He had great hopes of a new farce, starring Sydney Howard, but it was not due to open until November, and how were they to fill the theatre during the summer?

John (probably Kyrle was there too) found, at a small theatre in a Paris suburb, a Mexican company performing a kind of musical revue. He took to them at once, and, with his usual method of reaching decisions, agreed terms that evening.

It was a terrible mistake, as he must have begun dimly to perceive the very next week when he travelled from London to Newhaven to meet his new company.

The American manager with whom he had negotiated turned out to be a casual acquaintance whom the Mexicans had picked up in Paris. None of the rest of the company spoke any English. He had not bargained for them bringing an army of wives, children, relatives, friends, two mothers and one grandmother. Most of the company expected to sleep in the theatre with the baggage, except for the principals who went to the Waldorf Hotel next door, and he had to collect them from their various dugouts and find them digs in and around Covent Garden. He lost three, who emerged the next day from the cellar under the stage.

All the financial references they had given him in Paris turned out to be fake; the company possessed no funds whatsoever. John had to advance large sums of money for the production if it was to appear at all.

When they started rehearsing, he realised with horror that, instead of performing the routines which he had so enjoyed in Paris, they were rehearsing entirely new routines they had thought up on the boat across – and the show was due to open the next week.

They must have noticed his growing agitation, because at last their stage manager, with an understanding gleam in his eye, drew John to one side. "We all most grateful to you, Mr Beckett", he said. "All the company wish to show their gratitude. Any lady, any gentleman, show their gratitude, Mr Beckett."

John had invested too much in his Mexicans to let them fail. He set up a press reception at the Waldorf next door, and was delighted to see some key journalists there. But no Mexicans appeared. At last his assistant came in to say that they were rehearsing a new number they had just thought of, and could not be persuaded to break off. He rushed next door to the theatre and hustled and bullied them into the press conference, but it was too late. The key journalists had left, in a bad temper.

The show was appalling, and the press notices said so. He had the reviews translated to his company the next morning. On the second night, he says,

> They gave one of the most beautiful performances imaginable in a theatre containing 40 people who had paid for their seats and 100 deadheads whom the box office manager had whipped up to "dress" the house and prevent general recognition that the show was a flop.

After three weeks they took it off. There were still two months of summer to get through.

Now the theatre, and its manager, were in serious trouble. Each morning he crept into the premises by a different route, avoiding creditors and writ servers. Kyrle went to the countryside in what seems to have been some dudgeon and it may be guessed that she was getting a little impatient with her new manager. John eventually locked up his theatre, wrote a few newspaper articles to provide some sort of income, rented a small country bungalow and retreated there to await November and Sydney Howard's farce.

Then he heard that Howard had been taken seriously ill, and there would be no farce.

It looked like the end. But John was saved, for the moment anyway, by what he called "one of the few acts of really disinterested generosity which I have met". Leslie Henson was rehearsing for a new musical which he intended to take to the Palace Theatre. He brought it to the Strand instead, even though the building was far too small for this lavish spectacle and he would make much less money out of it. In October he opened with what became one of his most famous shows, *Nice Goings On*. It starred Robertson Hare and Richard Hearne, who after the war became famous as television's Mr Pastry, and it kept the theatre full until Easter 1933.

All was right with the world again. That Christmas John again involved himself in *Treasure Island*, with Kyrle again playing Mrs Hawkins and John reprising his cameo role, credited in the programme as John Warburton. As it opened, in November, Kyrle got a little publicity for it by pointing out that, as lessee of the Strand, she was in the van of the movement to get more women at the top in British theatre.

"Not so long ago you would seek in vain for a woman scenic designer, presenter, stage manager or producer", she told the *Daily Sketch* on 21 November. "Now there is practically no aspect of the theatre in which women do not play a part." For modern feminists, the sentiment would be rather spoiled by her explanation: "The feminine eye for detail."

This time Malcolm Keen played Silver, and John and Keen got to know each other well, playing golf together and going to theatrical first nights and boxing matches. Winter 1933 was calm and untroubled. But in March 1934 Kyrle opened in the lead in a play called *The Bride* which had done well in New York. It was another disaster. The *Stage* wrote: "Surely the theatre is the place for plays, not religious songs." On the second night, fewer than ten people paid for seats, and it closed in a fortnight.

John's own account of his stewardship of the Strand ends in Christmas 1933, and *The Bride* is not mentioned at all. I think he and Kyrle blamed each other. Certainly they were by now constantly bickering.

He told me that her spendthrift instincts caused their disaster. She had never had to worry about money, he said, and she had always led him to believe there was, more or less, a bottomless pit. It was, he maintained, a terrible shock to discover suddenly that there was nothing at all to fall back on.

She, on the other hand, seems to have believed that the failure was caused by his bad management. My suspicion is that they were both right. The truth, probably, was that they took on Arthur Bourchier's legacy, but lacked his professional instincts.

Whatever the reason, it was the final disaster for both of them, and for their marriage. John was declared bankrupt early in 1934, with debts of £3,577, most of it to the tax man, and assets of £20. They were living apart and he told the court that the problem was due to debts contracted by his wife. "I managed to persuade her to take up a more modest scale of life, but after about six months she went back to the same scale", he said. He was also, he said, assessed for tax on his wife's private income.

These hearings, and his many other court appearances, received massive publicity which made the damage worse – and the subsequent divorce hearing, as we shall see, was the worst of the lot.

All their money was gone. Her reputation was damaged irreparably, and she lost the Strand Theatre in 1935. She never again appeared in the West End, though two years later we find her at the Alhambra, Glasgow, and she worked successfully with several touring companies.

She still had a profession, however, and the remains of what had been a great reputation in it. He had nothing. He was bankrupt, homeless, jobless and suddenly almost friendless. He had been quite rich for nearly ten years, and had forgotten how a poor man lives.

The person who suffered most was his daughter Lesley, now 11. Until then John had sent her mother Helen regular money, and paid for Lesley to go to an expensive private school.

Lesley's visits to her father and her glamorous stepmother seemed to her like visits to fairyland, in a succession of pleasant riverside homes. She always remembered the day that Kyrle, about to travel to Paris in style, asked Lesley what she should bring back for her. Lesley timidly asked if she might have a pair of silk stockings of the type she had seen Kyrle wear, and was amazed when Kyrle returned with six pairs.

At the beginning of 1934 the money, and the visits to fairyland, stopped abruptly. Helen was forced to take Lesley away from the school, and could not even send her to the local grammar school (whose entrance exam Lesley had passed) because she could not afford to buy the uniform. Lesley left school two years afterwards, and, in later years, although she had a good career, she often wondered what she might have become if she had been able to finish her education.

I suspect her father remembered his own childhood and education, blighted by his own father's bankruptcy. His guilt had a devastating effect on my own life, nearly 30 years later.

What was John to do? He might have revived his dream of being a lawyer, or looked for work in journalism – there were still people who remembered that he had a talent for turning a sentence, even if it was most often used for invective. The trouble with those options was that they might take a little while. More or less destitute, beset by creditors, he did not feel he had time.

The choice he made when cornered destroyed the rest of his life, the lives of those closest to him and those who were to be close to him; and the whole of his reputation.

Notes on sources

The Theatre of the Organised Working Class, by Rose Merkin (PhD Thesis, University of Warwick, 1993).

12

A LIFE IN RUINS

In the three years from 1931, when John lost his seat in Parliament, to 1934, when he lost all his money, a great deal happened, both in the world outside and in John's own life.

Soon after the 1931 election, Jimmy Maxton took the ILP out of the Labour Party and on to the long road which led to its oblivion, and Oswald Mosley turned his New Party into the British Union of Fascists (BUF).

Maxton's lieutenant was now John's old ILP friend Fenner Brockway, who had also lost his seat in the 1931 election. Mosley's deputy was another of John's ILP "parliamentary suicide club", Dr Robert Forgan, and he, too, lost his seat in 1931. Another defeated rebel, John Strachey, was moving towards the Communist Party. The left was splintering in all directions.

For John, the theatre absorbed a great deal of his energy. But politics was in his blood now. When he thought of Ramsay MacDonald and the Labour establishment, or of the communists, or of the poor who had expected so much of organised labour, he could still feel so angry that I guess he found it hard to breathe.

He still wanted to change the world; and he still had friends and admirers in politics. In the first few months after the election, the

Peckham Labour Party was fiercely loyal to John. One activist, Fred Brooks, wrote to me that taking the Mace "won respect and admiration from the people he had been sent to represent". Mr Brooks thought him "a very sincere man whose one ambition was to do all he could to help the working class. I recall that he had an expression which he used often to describe the Conservatives: 'Moral perverts'." Kyrle too was admired: "She was one of the finest people ever to take her seat on the council", wrote Mr Brooks. "Her care and compassion for the poorer folk within her ward would be hard to surpass and she was literally loved by all."

So it is unsurprising that for a time, Peckham Labour Party defied Labour's ruling national executive and continued to support John, insisting that he would be their standard-bearer at the next election. When, in 1932, Labour's executive announced that Lewis Silkin would be Labour's official candidate for Peckham, all except two of the members of Peckham's Labour Party decamped into two ILP branches formed by John and Kyrle. John was starting to create at a local level the great new party of the left which he and John Wheatley had planned in 1930 as a national party. Locally, it was not called the ILP but "the Beckettite party".

Local historian Dave Russell writes: "Regular meetings were held at the Old Kent Road Baths and at the Central Hall, Peckham, where Beckett could be heard 'preaching firebrand politics to rapt audiences'."

But it was no good. The left did what it always seems to do in times of crisis: it degenerated into sectarian squabbling. Preparing for the demonstration against unemployment in February 1933, the chief preoccupation in Peckham seems to have been, not "How many people can we get along?" but "How do we make sure more people march under our banner than under the banners of our rivals on the left?" There were three competing banners: the official Labour Party, the National Unemployed Workers Movement (a communist front organisation) and the ILP.

John wrote later:

> I had hoped that the ILP, freed of its Labour Party commitments, could act as an independent revolutionary socialist party,

using parliamentary action for the purpose of creating a socialist commonwealth upon British lines and by British methods. The stress of the fight with the Labour Party, however, had worn down a great many members who would have been invaluable, and the Communists had skilfully penetrated the movement with men and women who, while they obeyed every instruction of the Communist International, denied any connection with the Communist Party.

The most dangerous communists, he wrote, were those who were not open about their membership.

I know one of our most prominent journalists, holding a key position on a national daily paper, who is often bitterly attacked in the *Daily Worker* [the communist newspaper], and who has been an outside member of the Communist Party for many years.

This is the only reference in John's memoirs to a man of whom he saw much in those years, another strange and foolhardy mixture of idealist and reprobate, Tom Driberg, who in the 1930s was working for Lord Beaverbrook's *Daily Express*, and, his personal finances being chaotic, was occasionally bailed out by his amused proprietor. Beaverbrook was also helping Driberg to evade the consequences of his homosexual activities, which were of course illegal, and John, surprisingly liberal on this, wholeheartedly approved of helping Tom. In 1945 Driberg became a left-wing Labour MP.

It was the communists, John believed, who in the end wrecked his party, and he was at least partly right. The Communist Party of Great Britain was still in the grip of the Moscow-driven policy called "class against class" which required communists to attack other left-wing parties far more ferociously than they ever attacked the supposed class enemies. We now know that Moscow, and Britain's top communists, many of whom had been John's friends and comrades in the heady days of the early 1920s, were now, in the early 1930s, filled with fierce sectarian bitterness and paranoia, and that they deliberately targeted the ILP because its policies were closest to theirs.

Of all the ILP people, John was singled out for special attention by the communists, paradoxically because they saw him as the most left-wing, and therefore the one most likely to lead the working classes away from the true faith.

Douglas Hyde, who was to become one of Britain's top communists before he defected to the Catholic Church, has recounted how, under instructions from communist headquarters, he joined the ILP "as a means of taking my communism into the enemy camp". He became ILP secretary in North Wales. When the ILP left the Labour Party, he demanded that all his members (many of them elderly folk who thought of Ramsay MacDonald with affection) should tear up their Labour Party cards. They refused, as he knew they would, and he expelled them from the ILP. When it had no more members, he closed the branch. He arrived soon afterwards in Surrey to perform the same service for the ILP branch there.

Caught between the Labour Party hammer and the Communist Party anvil, it would have taken exceptional leadership for the ILP to survive. Perhaps John was right, and his hero Wheatley could have provided that leadership. At any rate, Jimmy Maxton could not, and for the first and only time John speaks harshly of his friend and comrade:

> Maxton failed as he was bound to fail in a crisis because he does not want to lead; he has no political ambitions, and justifies his lethargy behind a curious philosophical theory that the rank and file should always lead.

Of his other old friend Brockway, now ILP secretary, he wrote:

> He is the hardest working man I know; but he works in a circle, without vision, and instead of devoting his organising ability and influence to the creation of a militant political party, trails pathetically after the Communists, appealing to them not to abuse him.
>
> Had Wheatley lived, we should not have lost this great opportunity to create a workers' party. In his absence was illustrated how erroneous is the belief that the time produces the man.

In May 1933 Peckham trades council narrowly carried a motion of support for Silkin. Gradually, but inexorably, the political machine was winning back Peckham, and John announced that he was leaving the ILP for "business reasons". He had decided to give up politics and, in May 1933, with Leslie Henson in *Nice Goings On* at the Strand, the theatre must have looked like an attractive way in which to use his talents and energies.

There was, he was now sure, no hope at all in democratic politics, "the sacred principle of nose-counting". There was, however, another sort of politics, the sort where you find a great leader to take decisions, and leave matters in his hands.

Three years earlier, in the summer of 1930, just after Wheatley's death and his marriage to Kyrle, John had visited Mussolini's Italy. He had with him Kyrle's teenage son. In his memoirs, there is no mention of Kyrle being there, but she was. There is no mention of Kyrle in the whole of John's memoir, nor of Helen. It is as though he decided to purge both of his first two wives from history.

As a holiday, it was a disaster. On the train to Naples, where he planned to stay, he felt an appalling pain in his stomach. John's pain got steadily worse throughout the train journey of several hours, and the long taxi run to his hotel some way outside Naples. His stepson had a severe asthma attack. Newspaper accounts tell us that Kyrle was ill too.

They lay in their hotel room for days on end, thinking they were going to die. A local doctor visited them and, apparently, injected morphia, using an infected needle, into the scar of the old war wound in John's right arm. Months later, this caused a swelling so serious that it looked briefly as though the arm might have to be amputated. The doctor put a bottle of laudanum beside the bed and told John to drink some if he could not sleep, but "happily I retained enough sanity to realise the danger of this advice". On the fifth morning they both felt a little better, but they were very frightened, and John was terrified to find that when he lifted his fingers to his face, they were like matchsticks.

His stepson was at last well enough to go and find the British Consul. "Late that evening he returned with the Consul and an English doctor, well groomed and in clean white suit. Never in my life have I so wanted to sing Rule Britannia."

But as research, John's holiday proved much more rewarding. He found that "the working people looked on Mussolini as their man, and seemed quite certain that, in any reasonable dispute with the employers, the fascist decision would always go in their favour". English conservatives living in Italy told him they thought Mussolini's working-class sympathies were too great. "The fact that both conservatives and workers regarded him as the champion of the underdog made me revise my opinions fairly drastically."

The intense nationalism of fascism, which turns so quickly into racism, was no trouble to him at all. He always felt sure that some races were better than others, and that the English were a good deal better than most. He had never in his heart much liked his Labour colleagues' desire to dismantle the Empire. A bit of him was still his jingoistic father's son.

The next year, 1931, he had had some private talks with Mahatma Ghandi, then in London to lobby for independence. John wrote afterwards:

> Remember that he is an Indian, with the poor physique of the natives of the lower part of the country, that he was trained in England as a lawyer (which seems poor equipment for saint-hood), and that he has the greatest personality and one of the most obtrusive egos imaginable. Remember that after living to the age of 48 and having had several wives and a large family, he formed an Order of Celibacy for young men ... A curious exhibitionism led him to walk about London streets and appear at English functions in a quite unsuitable piece of white linen ... I thought him a slightly better type of charlatan than the average British statesman because his will and fanaticism gave him strength to undergo hardships which the average Tory and trade union politician could not endure.

So by October 1932, when Oswald Mosley formed the BUF, John had already acquired some admiration for Mussolini's Italy, and added to his instinctive racism.

Several Labour left-wingers were attracted by Oswald Mosley's New Party, which soon morphed into the BUF, including Robert

Forgan and, briefly, Aneurin Bevan. But John was not. Neither was he there when, as Forgan puts it in an unpublished autobiographical fragment, Mosley "grafted the corporate state onto the social and economic proposals of the New Party, and – against my advice – called the organisation the British Union of Fascists".

On John's own much later account in his memoirs, this was because, if you are joining a fascist party, you need to be pretty confident of the leader, and John considered Mosley to be insincere and foolish.

As usual with John, it's a part of the story, and not the most important part. By the time he wrote his memoirs, six eventful years later in 1938, he had decided to keep one secret locked away where no one would ever see it.

John's mother was a Jew. John was devoted to her. It is true, of course, that she had rejected her Jewish religion and been declared dead by her family, but she must nonetheless have known who she was – and known that fascists were enemies of her people. John was – and I don't know how much of this he knew – the grandson of Mark Solomon and Jessy Isaacs.

Eva was estranged from her family, but she can never have forgotten that she was a Jew. She would surely have been horrified if she had known where it would lead her son. He did not join Mosley when Mosley was riding high and his mother still lived; he joined Mosley after she died, when Mosley's movement was already starting to decline.

There was another factor which, by the end of the 1930s, had become almost as unmentionable as his mother's Jewishness. It is clear from research by local Peckham historians that for a year or so after his 1931 defeat, John saw himself as a potential political leader.

I am sure that for a while, John saw himself as the leader the country needed, the heir to Wheatley, the alternative to Mosley. Perhaps he saw himself as Britain's fascist leader, and he was not short of folk in Peckham to encourage this idea.

Another part of him wanted to leave politics altogether. In 1932 I think he saw the theatre as a more likely future.

But three things happened between 1932 and 1934, with what I think he found terrifying speed. And the most important of them was that Eva Dorothy died, aged only 64 (and admitting only to 60 on her death certificate – since her marriage she had shaved another three years off her age), in March 1932 after a long, painful illness, of breast cancer.

Within two years he had lost his mother and the man who I think was a surrogate father, John Wheatley. It left him forlorn and lost – orphaned, even though his father was still alive.

She died in Wembley, at 5 Chalfont Avenue, and I suppose that must have been where she and her husband William were living. But where was William? After the 1911 census, which finds him running a draper's shop in Pinner, which is near Wembley, William disappears from the radar. My father told me nothing of him. I do not even know when he died. There is no death certificate anywhere, and my father hardly spoke of him. It is as though he simply disappeared off the face of the earth.

I do know that William's money troubles never left him. He is thought to have appealed to the Cheshire Becketts for money, and been turned down with unnecessary unkindness by his well-off younger brother, landlord of the Broughton Arms in Rode Heath. Lesley thought that one day my father had found him in distressingly poor circumstances, but did not know when or where.

I think William was not with his wife when she died, because Eva Dorothy's death certificate records that it was Lillian, the wife of John's brother Cecil, who was present at the death. But before she died, while she was ill, John and Cecil had had a terrible quarrel in front of her, ending with some sort of physical confrontation, and they did not speak to each other again for 30 years.

The Cheshire Becketts were a quarrelsome lot, by all accounts, and it's a trait which has gone down the generations. I have it too.

While the turmoil of these events made it hard for him to think clearly, his marriage was disintegrating alongside his business. The end of John's second marriage was not something he dwelt on in those talks with me. It was certainly tied up with the failure of their theatrical enterprises, for which he blamed Kyrle, and she blamed him. He was also unfaithful, I think – sexual philandering was something of a habit, as it was for Mosley.

He had very little time to keep in touch with old parliamentary colleagues, and the ones he did see were those who sought him out.

He made one visit to the House of Commons to have tea with Maxton, but only regularly saw two of his old colleagues.

The first was W.E.D. (Bill) Allen, an Ulster Unionist MP from 1929 to 1931, from a wealthy Northern Ireland family and, between 1925 and 1970, chairman of the advertising firm David Allen and Sons Limited. "Allen, more than any other man I have met, seemed to represent the spirit of modern chivalry", he wrote, which shows that he had returned to the values of the imperialist children's novelist G.A. Henty, from whom he had first learned his history; and shows also his capacity for completely misjudging his man.

The sentence was written in John's memoirs in 1938 and crossed out after the war, so perhaps before he died he grew to suspect that Allen was not what he seemed.

Allen, he said, was not only sensitive and physically good-looking, but in Parliament had been

> the recognised spokesman for a group of young Conservatives who took "noblesse oblige" in a practical form, and to whom patriotism and imperialism meant care for the British and Imperial peoples, rather than a careful network of financial intrigue cloaked by wild waving of the Union Jack.

Allen was also one of the few MPs who not only joined Mosley's New Party, but stayed with it when it became the BUF. He was personally close to Mosley, and was still supporting him when war broke out in 1939. He paid the salaries of some of Mosley's staff; MI5 thought him the main funder of the infant BUF.

There was a lot about Bill Allen that John didn't know. He was not only putting his own money into Mosley's movement, but also, according to intelligence reports, acting as a conduit for German money. Hitler came to power in Germany in January 1933, and it was as natural for Mosley to look to Hitler and Mussolini for money as it was for communist leader Harry Pollitt to look to Stalin.

Mosley apparently thought Allen had Security Service connections, though at that time he did not, MI5 having decided that he was "completely amoral and politically unstable". In 1933 he had fascist sympathies, Nazi contacts, money and understood the complex international movement of funds. He was very valuable to Mosley, not least in helping him recruit the disillusioned and troubled former MP for Gateshead.

The other former parliamentary colleague was Dr Robert Forgan, a Scottish GP and one of the small band of ILP rebels whose activities John had organised in the 1929–31 Parliament. Forgan had gone with Mosley into the New Party and was now deputy leader of the BUF.

Everyone who knew Forgan seems to agree that he was charming and terribly handsome. John thought him intelligent, too, but Brockway described him as "a charming if rather naive Scot", although he also considered him sincere in his socialism: "He had been a doctor in the Scottish slums and had seen the effects of malnutrition." He had also been an army medical officer in the war, and was an international authority on the treatment of venereal diseases.

In 1933 and 1934 he took the lead in persuading John to join the BUF. John could not have known – no one knew until, 60 years later, Professor Geoffrey Alderman examined some Jewish records in New York – that by the early summer of 1934 Forgan was more or less offering his services to the Board of Deputies of British Jews as a spy in the Mosley camp.

He was supposed to be acting as Mosley's emissary, negotiating a modus vivendi between fascists and Jews. In fact, he told Board Chairman Dr Neville Laski that he found it impossible to work with Mosley, that despite protestations to the contrary Mosley was deeply anti-Semitic and that he intended to leave.

But Mosley was paying him £700 a year, he had a wife and children, and he had to earn a living.

Also, though he did not mention it to Laski at the time, he had serious personal problems. His wife had attempted suicide, and he had sent his daughter to stay for several weeks with another fascist leader, William Joyce, and his wife.

Forgan joined Mosley largely from personal admiration and friendship – he was godfather to one of Mosley's children. While he was having those lunches with John, he was already privately arguing against Mosley's move towards anti-Semitism. He wrote in a private fragment of autobiography shown to me by his grandson:

I remember in late 1933 spending half a night trying to persuade Mosley to alter the tone and terms of an article that he published in spite of me, entitled "Shall the Jews drive Britain to war?" Early in 1934 I was the only Gentile present at a luncheon in the Savoy attended by the leaders of British Jewry, where we discussed the possibility of calling off the "war" between Mosley and the Jews.

But he insisted that the BUF's anti-Semitism was partly the result of Jewish "provocation".

Laski told him rather sharply that the Board of Deputies did not buy opponents. Laski's note of the meeting records drily: "I did mention that a normal method of changing parties was to write a letter to the leader of the party which was being left giving reasons for its abandonment."

Three months later Forgan left the BUF. He and Mosley agreed that it should be done discreetly, and told everyone that Forgan was ill and had to take some time off. Nonetheless, his departure nearly caused an internal revolt, in which members of Mosley's staff "plotted to take over the movement and oust those officers who had crawled in during the booming period of the Mail" (when it had had the enthusiastic support of the *Daily Mail* and its proprietor, Lord Rothermere). Mosley "flew into a rage and threatened to shoot them in the guts", as Stephen Dorril puts it. "The megalomania of 'The Leader' was beginning to show itself", wrote Forgan in the same autobiographical fragment:

> Mosley began to ape Mussolini and to model himself and his party on Italian lines...
>
> Sickened of politics and with no wish to join a political party, I ... nearly starved for a year while trying to build up a medical practice in Golders Green!

He could hardly have chosen a more Jewish area.

None of these doubts surfaced during the series of lunches Robert Forgan held with John Beckett and his wife Kyrle in 1933 and early 1934. John's main concern seems to have been Mosley. Forgan told him that Mosley had changed: "He takes his mission extremely seriously, and is now grown up." Forgan, as Colin Holmes put it to me, "was a lousy judge of character – Mosley remained throughout his life a man-child".

Keen as he was to get John into the BUF, he nonetheless confided in an interview for the BUF official history 40 years later: "I did not believe in Beckett as a political leader. Did not think he had it in him. He was prepared to take all sorts of risks. In fact he might have been a dangerous leader."

Forgan and Allen talked John out of his distrust of Mosley. After that there were several meetings with Mosley himself, and later in 1933 another visit to Italy confirmed John's view that "here was a great new conception of civilisation ... Italy was achieving all those things which I had hoped for from the Labour Party in this country". Italian fascists were, he thought, eliminating class differences, national credit and the power of money. So with twentieth-century power of production, it would be able to organise a life of reasonable comfort for all its citizens.

He did not mind the nationalism – in fact he rather liked it. "Progress in Britain need not wait for the Zulus to join their union and the Japanese to become members of the third international." Nor did he value democracy: "My experience in the Labour and trade union world confirmed my distrust of any organisation pretending to be democratic." Democracy meant giving votes to the ludicrous Colonel Blimps who were the mainstay of the Conservative Party, and even to the appalling communists who disrupted his meetings, "slouching in untidy files through the streets of our cities ... they bear banners urging war in Asia or Spain or some other place where they suspect the prevalence of a spirit of patriotism, discipline or decency".

Was he joking when he added that they should be put in "well run labour camps where, properly fed and efficiently educated ... they could be restored to mental and spiritual health"? I like to think so. But I am not quite sure. Perhaps he was not quite sure, either.

On his return from this second Italian trip, Forgan provided the last push. He told the Italian press that John Beckett was about to become a fascist. According to a report from the British ambassador in Spain to the Foreign Secretary, "the 'conversion' of Mr John Beckett, late MP for

Peckham, was given large headlines by many papers, which represented the incident as an important political event". British newspapers picked it up from them, and when he landed in England he found a battery of reporters asking him about his conversion.

Years later John told me: "I thought, I'm getting all the odium of people thinking I'm a fascist. I might as well be hanged for a sheep as a lamb."

He was still an inactive member. His boats were not completely burned. But in early 1934, after the failure of *The Bride*, the sad and stupid fact is that he was suddenly bankrupt and entirely without resources, and Mosley offered him a salary.

He admitted this to Colin Cross, author of *The Fascists in Britain*, but not, as far as I know, to anyone else. His usual account of the moment at which he became an active fascist is, naturally, rather more elevated.

It happened, he said, when he went to a meeting at Paddington Baths. Mosley was ill, and the meeting was taken by a young man called William Joyce, of whom John had never before heard. He wrote:

> Within ten minutes of this 28 year old youngster taking the platform I knew that here was one of the dozen finest orators in the country. Snowden's close reasoning and unerring instinct for words were allied with Maxton's humour and Churchill's daring.

After that meeting he ordered a black shirt, from Forgan's tailor, naturally.

What could make a man like my father put on a black shirt and call himself a fascist? The question is worth asking because he is as good a case history as you can find, just because he was the most unlikely fascist you could imagine. He was irreverent, spontaneous, funny. He loathed accepting orders. He spoke and wrote with fluency and humour – the weapons of a democratic politician, not a demagogue. He had no time for the "heel-clicking and petty militarism" of fascism.

He had two key qualities for a fascist though. First, intellectual laziness, which led him to grab at something that seems to offer an effortless total answer. And, second, a mystical nature. The sort of person who can believe in ghosts and table-rapping is much more open to be convinced of the mystical qualities of a fascist leader.

Yet he did not have the fascist reverence for the Leader. He was shocked by the people who were attracted to fascism because it enabled them to strut about self-importantly in a uniform. He does not seem to have realised that all this was an intrinsic part of the creed he had embraced. This fascist – for that is what we must call him – was intelligent, sincere, noisy and very human.

His faithful and much-abused friend Brockway found an excuse for him. He told me 40 years later: "I'm sure John thought, I've tried Maxton's romanticism, Frank Wise's intellectualism, let's see what Mosley can do." Brockway did not add that fascism also provided a way out of John's personal problems, which, as we shall see in the next chapter, were multiplying.

He wore his new black shirt first to address a meeting in Uxbridge in March 1934, just 14 months after Adolf Hitler came to power in Germany. He was, he says, feeling "extremely self-conscious and uncomfortable" in the shirt, but not, unfortunately, uncomfortable enough.

And that meeting marks the moment which ensures that John Beckett today is remembered, when he is remembered at all, not as a charismatic and fluent, if muddled, idealist, burning with righteous rage on behalf of the underdog, which he undoubtedly was; but as a racist bigot, which he also was.

Notes on sources

Fragment of autobiography in the keeping of the Forgan family.

Friends of Oswald Mosley archives.

Blackshirt: Sir Oswald Mosley and British Fascism by Stephen Dorril (Viking, 2006).

Dr Robert Forgan's Resignation from the British Union of Fascists by Geoffrey Alderman (Labour History Review, 1992).

Enemy Within by Francis Beckett (John Murray/Merlin Press 1998).

I Believed by Douglas Hyde (Heinemann, 1951).

National Socialism Now by William Joyce (National Socialist League, 1938).

Searching for Lord Haw-Haw by Colin Holmes (Routledge, 2016).

The Fascists in Britain by Colin Cross (Barrie & Rockliffe, 1961).

Tom Driberg: His Life and Indiscretions by Francis Wheen (Pan, 1992).

13
ANNE

Anne Cutmore was an aspiring actress of 24. In 1933 she was training at evening classes at RADA, and at night, when not training, she queued outside West End theatres for seats in "the gods" – the galleries, where a place on a hard wooden bench could be purchased for a few pennies.

During the day she did secretarial work – she had learned shorthand and typing so that she could live while nurturing an acting career. Decades later she gave her daughter a solemn warning: a woman should never learn shorthand

She lived with her mother and her two sisters near the Portobello Road in London. Her mother Florence's brother Ernest Holford ran a pub in the East End and died young, in 1931, at least partly from failing to keep away from his stock. His son was too young at 17 to take over the running of his pub, so Florence looked after it until it was sold, and then took her nephew to live with her and her three daughters: Hilda, the oldest, just five feet tall, musical, with quick movements, and Jo, the youngest, languid and athletic.

Anne was registered with Pitmans, which farmed out secretarial staff. One day in about 1932 they sent her to an address in Chelsea and told her to ask for a Dr Forgan.

Dr Forgan, she discovered, was the deputy leader of something called the British Union of Fascists. His correspondence was considerably more interesting than that of the dull commercial organisations she had been sent to before, and he and his colleagues were more exciting. He was, she found, a former MP, and very handsome.

Forgan, for his part, was delighted with his magically pretty, dark-haired new secretary with her mobile oval face, musical voice, flair for mimicry, her entertaining and literate conversation and her smile that lit up a room.

Forgan had an eye for a pretty girl. His marriage was crumbling and he told Anne years later that he would have married her if he she would have had him. How close they became, it's impossible to say, but in later years each spoke of the other with great affection to their children.

He invited her to make up a four at lunch with an important politician whom he hoped to recruit to the BUF, together with the politician's actress wife.

John Beckett was, he said, a clever and charismatic former MP whom they were very anxious to win to the party, and she must be charming to him. He told her "He was one of the most brilliant young men in the ILP. We must get him in."

At lunch, Anne could see John's and Kyrle's marriage literally disintegrating in front of her eyes, and she could sense John's immediate and keen interest, both in her physical charms and her lively conversation.

In the office, Anne had become part of a circle of intellectual young men and women in the BUF. They went to theatres, to the country, to clubs, they talked and danced, and they took their politics just seriously enough to be a common intellectual base, but not so seriously that they had to examine them too closely.

She was especially close to a young composer named Selwyn Watson, who wrote the music for the song which was intended to become the British version of the Nazis' "Horst Wessel Lied". She thought him kind, talented and sensitive. One day Selwyn lent her his car, and she crashed it. She rang him to confess. "Are you all right?" he asked. She gave him full marks for not asking first if the car was all right, but from the moment she met John, the dalliance with Selwyn was effectively over.

Selwyn, disappointed, told John: "You're old enough to be her father." "I'd have had to be pretty precocious", replied John. Anne's mother and sisters felt as Selwyn did – they did not like the idea of Anne, at 24, attaching herself to a man a few months short of 40. They would have liked to see more of Selwyn, who eventually made a solid career for himself as an advertising copywriter – though Anne thought he ought to have stuck to his guns and carried on composing music.

One day John came to the office for an appointment with Forgan, who was on the telephone. While he was waiting, John said to Anne: "You know, you and I between us could turn Bob Forgan into something." That, she said, impressed her: that John could see the emptiness beyond Forgan's charming facade, yet want to build him up, not tear him down. John, by this time, had fallen hopelessly in love again, and I doubt if he gave a damn whether he built Forgan up or tore him down.

Anne's first name, which she hated and never used, was Doris, which sounded a little like Dorothy, the name of John's mother, so he always called her Dorothy Anne. He thought she would be pleased. Maybe she was.

They made an odd couple. She was light on her feet, she could dance and she could sing. She loved 1930s musicals, and if I close my eyes I can still hear her going around the house singing them:

Let him go, let him tarry, let him sink or let him swim
For he doesn't care for me, nor I don't care for him.
Let him go and find another who I hope he will enjoy
For I'm going to marry a far nicer boy.

He was heavy and clumsy and tone deaf, he couldn't dance – much to her regret – and his musical tastes ran to Gilbert and Sullivan. If he could have sung, he would have sung their political satire:

I polished up those candles so carefullee
That now I am the ruler of the Queen's navee.

Like John, she had a tongue which could make enemies, but she was kind and generous, and loyal to a fault.

Her father James Cutmore had worked his way up to be a law writer for the Solicitors Law Stationery Society, drafting legal documents in a beautiful round hand. He was a gentle man who had nicknames for each of his three daughters. Hilda was Froggy. Anne was Topsy.

Anne remembered all her life the hurt face he turned towards her when she had done something naughty; she remembered the night she spilled ink over a law document he had been working on, so that he had to sit up all night and redo it, but he never complained. She remembered that when the war came, he tried to join up, out of a sense of duty, but was turned down because he was short-sighted.

Most of all, she remembered with dreadful clarity, though she was only seven, the evening in 1916 that her father arrived home in Clapham and said that while he was walking from the city, a woman came up to him and gave him a white feather. Guilt overwhelmed him, and he spent the next day persuading the army to let him in.

Florence kept all his letters to her and her daughters. They were long, long letters, in his fine law writer's script, and he only commented on what the children were doing, almost nothing about himself because he didn't want his wife and daughters to be sad or frightened, except once when he sent a registered letter to Anne, and all it said was:

> Celer et Audax
> Domine Dirige Nos

The little girl cannot have had any idea what it meant, but she must have known it mattered, because she kept it through a difficult and muddled life in its original envelope, in which I found it after her death.

There are dozens of letters, all running to several pages, all in his small, neat writing, all now where I have placed them, in the Imperial War Museum. He must have spent every moment he could writing to his wife and children.

> My dear little Doris, I was very pleased to receive your very nice letter and to hear that you are not frightened when there

is an air raid on, of course you know that all the banging you hear is not made by the air ships but by our own guns firing at them, so you need not be frightened because our own guns would not hurt you, would they?

I am glad to hear that Mother still has a few cups left with handles on them, but we don't trouble much about cups out here as we generally use an old corn beef tin or anything else that we can find, but never mind it will soon be over and we will all have a nice holiday by the seaside.

My dear little Doris, I am quite well and glad to hear that you are well also and that you would like me home again ... I should like you to study your spelling as much as you can because when you grow up I shall want you to go to business with me in our office.

He was delighted with Hilda's school report but didn't want her to be satisfied with third place. He was writing to her while "sitting on a heap of bricks and using an old shrub as a desk" but he still managed three very full pages.

"Believe me my darling I think only of you and our babies", he wrote to Florence. "When I was home I feel I was more a nuisance to you than I was worth but I will make sure that it does not happen again."

She must have written saying she had not been as kind to him as she ought to have been, because he rushed to tell her it was not so. "I want to return to you, life would not be worth living without you, and when I return I want you to be my only companion."

So why did he leave her to join the army? "I am fit, a good shot, and it is not in my nature to hide behind the men who have the courage to join and leave them to protect you and my babies." There are eight more pages of that letter.

Getting into the army had been easy. By 1916 they cared nothing for short-sight. They just wanted a body which could stop a shell, which he duly did two years later, in March 1918 at the age of 40, after serving in France and Flanders.

There is a letter from his commanding officer to Anne's mother. You can see that the poor man had had to write dozens of such letters, that day and every day, and he does his best, but the words are joined to each other, showing that he did not have time to take his pen off the paper, and that he knew the formula far, far too well. "Death was instantaneous" the kind but harassed man wrote. It wasn't; it occurred three weeks after the injuries. It was probably a dreadful, lingering death, full of unimaginable pain. I suspect Anne and her mother knew that.

All her life, Anne loathed the white feather women. "Women of Britain say GO" said the poster, and decades later she saw it reproduced in a poster advertising the film *Oh! What A Lovely War*, and she said to me: "Not very loudly they didn't." She loved telling the story of the woman who asked G.K. Chesterton: "Why aren't you out at the front?" Chesterton looked down at his enormous stomach and said: "If you look closely, madam, you will see that I am."

She always remembered her father's last leave, early in 1918, when he was so shell-shocked that he could hardly speak to her, and her mother spent every day ironing his uniform in the vain hope of killing all the bugs.

James had always wanted a boy, but his only son died before the war of one of those childhood diseases that cut a swathe through the childhood population at the start of the twentieth century. The boy was called William after James's father, and "little Billy" was never quite forgotten in the family.

So when he went to war, he had no son to whom to say, "If anything happens to me, look after your mother." Instead, he said it to Hilda. Hilda knew a sacred duty had been laid upon her; she never married and lived with her mother until Florence died in 1965, when Hilda was near retirement as a personal assistant at the Central Electricity Generating Board.

The general manager of the Solicitors Law Stationery Society wrote to Florence: "Your Husband was a man for whom I had the greatest respect and I have been keeping the position of Manager of our Chancery Lane Writing Department open for him when he should return from the War."

Anne was nine when her father died. Florence, in deep shock, sold their south London home and took her three daughters to New

Zealand, where she had relatives. They went out by ship through the Suez Canal, and lived in Gisborne, a small coastal town in the north island.

But Florence found that her relatives were not able to find her work and an income as easily as she had been led to expect. She had been in service, and uncomplainingly returned to cleaning people's homes to make a living. Anne remembered the wonderful Waikenae Beach in Gisborne all her life. Never again could she come home after school and go straight to the beach to swim.

They returned in 1924. Anne's version was that Hilda had started to go out with a Maori, and her mother was so horrified that she immediately packed up her daughters and returned to England; but by the time she told me that story, Anne had acquired John's habit of embroidering her anecdotes, and I think it was at least exaggerated. It is true, though, that in New Zealand Anne had a hope of going to Wellington University; in London a university education could not be afforded.

They returned via the Panama Canal. The excitement of the sights and sounds of Panama and Suez were with her always, and friends made on the ship remained with her all her life.

Back in London, Florence lived mainly on a war widow's pension. Anne always remembered an inspector coming to check on her circumstances and remarking that she had had a good deal of money from the government over the years. "I'd rather have had my husband", she told him quietly.

When she met John in 1933, Anne was still mourning her father. She mourned him all her life. In her last years, with her brain crippled by dementia, when she had forgotten everything else about her life, Anne still remembered her father and his useless death. She carried to her grave the unconditional love that the luckiest fathers inspire in their nine-year-old daughters.

I think she was, unconsciously, looking for an older man, a man who knew the world and its ways and could instruct her in them, as her father would have done had he lived, and she felt (probably wrongly) that her mother could not do.

She wanted guidance. John needed guidance. They both chose a partner who was unable to supply it. Anne was too young and innocent, and John was too foolish.

His personal life was more complicated than ever. Years after my father died, I discovered that Kyrle refused him a divorce; and that my parents, whom I had always assumed to be married, were not, because my father was not free to marry.

So I went in search of a divorce petition. It turned out to contain a rather extraordinary piece of information.

John's petition for divorce is dated 9 October 1934 – a few months after his bankruptcy hearing, at which he blamed Kyrle's lavish lifestyle and the fact that he had to pay tax on her private income for his financial troubles. John was by now living in Maida Vale, and "the respondent's address is unknown to your petitioner but she carries on business at the Strand Theatre".

The petition alleged "That the respondent [Kyrle] has frequently committed adultery with James Carlyle Elliott who resides at 8 Saltwell Place, Gateshead." Elliott was alleged to have stayed with her overnight on 27 August 1934 at 10 Pond Place, and that was the beginning of an affair.

The judge didn't like it, or else Kyrle denied it and the judge believed her, because the petition was refused.

Who was James Carlyle Elliott? He does not figure in any of my father's reminiscences, but it's intriguing that he came from Gateshead, the constituency John left in 1929, partly because his relationship with Kyrle caused a scandal there.

In 1939 the National Register was compiled to ensure everybody got a ration card, and Elliott is listed as a cinema house manager and treasurer. In his house lives a lady whom the compilers first entered as Anne Elliott; but they crossed out the name Elliott and substituted Bourchier.

This must be Violet Marion Annie Falck, a.k.a. Kyrle Bellew. Her occupation is given as "unpaid domestic", not a difficult euphemism to translate. The date of her birth is given as 1894, so it has moved forward a few more years a little smoke and mirrors, and she has become John's age.

And that is all I know. Like Eva Dorothy Solomon, like John himself, Kyrle guarded her secrets.

Whatever is going on here, it's clear the breakup with Kyrle was messy. On top of his beloved mother's death and his bankruptcy, John's life in 1934 was a war zone.

His solution was typical. He told Anne, "We'll tell everyone we're married, and no one will ever question it." They even had a wedding picture taken.

It was his second fake wedding. Four years earlier the witnesses in the picture had been two Labour MPs. This time they were his fascist friends William Joyce and John McNab.

Anne suggested changing her name by deed poll, but John said it would only draw attention to the situation. She should just call herself Anne Beckett. No one would question it, any more, perhaps, than anyone had ever questioned that his name was John Warburton Beckett, or that his mother's name was Dorothy Salmon, or that he had married Kyrle at Gretna Green.

It worked, more or less. For the rest of their lives, most people did not know that they were not, legally, man and wife. Their children certainly didn't. The security services knew, of course – but we'll come to that.

She must have ignored the advice of Mosley's mother, who had an office in BUF headquarters and, according to an internal report quoted by Nicholas Mosley,

> kept a motherly eye on some of the less staid and prettier ones and warned them of the hungry looks being cast in their direction by appreciative Blackshirts, and by one high-ranking officer in particular who was both an experienced politician and an experienced womaniser.

This, almost certainly, was John.

He made her the drama critic for all the fascist newspapers, and when Forgan left, she went to work for the chief of staff, Ian Dundas. She thus became one of the few people who knew for certain that Mosley was being funded by Mussolini, because Forgan and Dundas both boasted about it to her, and showed her the cases full of banknotes. She was the sort of woman who has that effect, quite unintentionally, on rather vain men.

She loyally identified with John's politics, but she was not a fascist at all. Set her apart from John, and you would not find any of the racism or fanaticism that a fascist requires. Even after she had lived with him, listened to him and been loyal to him for 30 years, and suffered for his politics, she seldom talked about his political views, and never with much conviction. She was an early and thoughtful feminist, but apart from that, what she understood and cared about was literature and the theatre, not politics. But personal loyalty meant everything to her, and the more of an outcast her husband became, the more strongly she felt the need to be loyal to him.

In later years, she sometimes thought that with different breaks (and perhaps a different husband) she might have been a considerable actress. Her drama training never left her. "I'm a teapot", she would say, and bend over and make one arm into a handle, and she was amazingly like a teapot. She was offered a season at the Shakespeare Memorial Theatre in Stratford-upon-Avon but got laryngitis that winter and could not take it up.

I don't know how good she really was. She was certainly a talented mimic, and her writing was stylish and fluent. She was capable of great love and great loyalty.

She wrote, and typed up on BUF headed paper, a poem about unrequited love, which she dated 12 September 1934.

> ....Must I lust and yearn
> For ever vainly, nor expect return?

It ended:

> Yet blind and silent are the barren skies
> And unresponsive as my lover's eyes.

Was this John? Or Forgan? Or someone else? John, I suspect. She had something special. I know that much.

But in 1934 she took a decision, and she stuck to it. No married woman could have been more loyal, through thick and, far more often, thin.

Notes on sources

Peter Holford (*Cockney Ancestor*, 142, Spring 2014).
Beyond the Pale by Nicholas Mosley (Secker & Warburg, 1983).

FIGURE 1 J.B., Wanstead, 1918.

FIGURE 2 The Becketts of Cheshire at a family wedding in 1908. On the far left is John Beckett, aged 14, and his father William is (probably) third from the left in the back row. The patriach, farmer John Beckett Senior, is seated, fourth from right, with his wife Hannah seated beside him. Centre, the bride and bridegroom, John's youngest aunt, Clarissa, and George Knowles.

JOHN BECKETT,
PROSPECTIVE LABOUR CANDIDATE.

(COPYRIGHT)

WALTER SCOTT,
BRADFORD

FIGURE 3 Prospective Labour candidate for Gateshead, 1924 (Beckett family).

FIGURE 4 The fascist orator in the East End of London in the 1930s.

FIGURE 5 Clem Attlee as J.B. knew him, wearing his chain of office as Mayor of Stepney (Anne, Countess Attlee, reproduced with permission).

FIGURE 6 James Cutmore at the front, not long before he was killed. He is standing on the left, looking at the camera (family picture).

FIGURE 7 Anne (on the throne) when she still had theatrical ambitions. I wish I knew what the play was, or where it was staged, but it might have been a RADA production (family picture).

FIGURE 8 Anne as a young woman in the late 1920s/early 1930s (family picture).

FIGURE 9 Anti-Semitic cartoon from Mosley's *East London Pioneer*, 1936.

FIGURE 10 Speaking for Mosley's candidates in the east London council elections of 1936 (Beckett family).

FIGURE 11 The Duke of Bedford (Beckett family).

FIGURE 12 Major General "Boney" Fuller (left) and Major Harry Edmonds (right) with Mrs Sonia Fuller seated. Fuller "foresaw disaster after disaster for the world until it acknowledged that there were superior men and inferior men, and saw to it that the superior men were permitted to take their natural place in the leadership of the world." (Edmonds family, reproduced with permission).

FIGURE 13 The middle-aged savant: posed photograph used as a byline picture in the *People's Post*, late 1940s (Beckett family).

FIGURE 14 The family man: early 1950s (Beckett family).

FIGURE 15 Somehow this picture sums up my parents' life towards the end of the 1950s: outside this lordly mansion perches their tiny, elderly, unreliable Fiat 500, which every morning the children pushed down the gentle slope ahead of it so that my father could bump start it. Bump starting motor cars was a skill I picked up early (Beckett family).

FIGURE 16 In the grounds of St Joan of Arc Convent in Rickmansworth, early 1950s, with a visiting Bishop (Beckett family).

FIGURE 17 A Catholic parish garden party in Rickmansworth in the late 1950s. Father Brendan sits at the head of the tale, rubbing his hands in the way he always did (Beckett family).

FIGURE 18 My parents loved this picture. "Just like his father", they'd say, and laugh indulgently (Beckett family).

FIGURE 19 Resplendent in Beaumont suit, with my sister Clare (Beckett family).

FIGURE 20 This picture seems to me to be almost unbearably sad, though I am not sure why. I think I took it myself in about 1957, when I was 12, while we were on holiday, perhaps in North Wales; and it shows my parents with my younger brother and sister. It seems to me now that I can sense in it the burden of the past and the terror of the future that they were carrying.

14
THE STREETFIGHTER

In 1934 the BUF had the support of Lord Rothermere's newspapers, the *Daily Mail*, *Evening News* and *Sunday Dispatch*. The *Mail* acclaimed it in January 1934 with a famous front page lead headline:

HURRAH FOR *THE BLACKSHIRTS*

It had perhaps 40,000 members.

But it had failed to make much impact on the working class and the unemployed (which no doubt was why Mosley was so anxious to get the left-wing hero John Beckett) and its headquarters was sinking under the weight of its own bureaucracy.

It was much more than a political party: a home, a comfort blanket, an entire way of living. Its headquarters, Black House in Chelsea, was a social centre for fascists as well as a political headquarters, and housed several younger male members, many of whom Mosley employed for a pittance. It had lecture rooms, dormitories, a gymnasium and a parade ground, and many central London-based Blackshirts regarded it as their home.

It was pretty ridiculous. An announcement in the *Blackshirt* for February 1934 told readers:

The infant son of District Officer and Mrs Point was christened in Holy Trinity Church on Sunday February 18. The Leader, represented by the chief of staff, and Captain Lewis, represented by Mr Risdon, were godfathers. The child was given the names of Robert Oswald Frederick – Oswald after the Leader and Robert after Dr Forgan.

Poor young Robert Point! It was far worse than naming your son after the entire Manchester United football team – at least footballers don't become non-persons, as Bob Forgan did.

The paper also carried a note from Ian Dundas, chief of staff, reminding members that when they wore the black shirt or a fascist badge they should "conduct themselves in a manner worthy of the Cause they serve". Cause, like Leader, always had an upper case initial letter.

Fascism demanded total obedience. The *Blackshirt* sternly reminded its readers:

> Members whose points of view do not coincide with their local leaders are required to surrender them for the good of the Cause. A member who does not pull his weight in the branch fails in his duty to the Leader. The fascist method is not the democratic method. Fascism does not submit matters to a show of hands.

What on earth could have made John – who, whatever else he lacked, did not lack a sense of humour – attach himself to this sinister yet ludicrous outfit, which might have come straight out of one of his beloved Gilbert and Sullivan operas? He must have needed the salary really badly.

He tried to explain explaining his conversion to the cause (sorry, Cause) on the front page of *Fascist Week* in March 1934.

> During my life I have roamed a good deal. I have lived in Limehouse and Mayfair, have known intimately dockers and big business men, Boers, Indians, Australian and English Tommies, all sorts and conditions. In the Parliamentary Labour

Party I discovered a new low level ... Those who mattered would have disgusted Tammany and nauseated a cosmopolitan crook. Some sold themselves openly for a job. The majority succumbed to a double whisky and a condescending nod from a real "gentleman".

He elaborated on the theme in the more intellectual *Fascist Quarterly*. A Labour government, he wrote, "means spineless government by nonentities without any guiding principles". He was quoted, in a fawning biography of Mosley written at the time by A.K. Chesterton as saying:

Mosley had the worst possible temperament for success of Westminster. He suffered fools badly. He wanted to work – not to listen for hours to the wearisome babblings of decrepit trade union leaders sent to the House of Commons as a place of pension.

From all of which we might gather that John's main justification for joining the fascists was his loathing for the Labour Party establishment: a loathing so intense that he could not see clearly for the fog it created in his mind. But there was a philosophy of sorts, though it, too, rested on the failings of his former political home.

In the *Fascist Quarterly*, John said that there were three basic ideas: fascism, communism and social democracy. Social democracy had failed in every country where it was tried: "It not only failed to effect the peaceful transformation from predatory capitalism to socialism, but it failed to provide the slightest check on the robber." It attempts to have things all ways: "Promise the rich and poor alike that you will be their friend. Abolish the slums and dine with the slumowner."

The problem was democracy. The working class did not want to govern. They wanted comfort and security, and could get it by discipline. "If the nation is to be reorganised and regenerated," he wrote later, "either Parliament must be reconstructed first, or we must face the inevitability of extra-constitutional methods."

So he put on his black shirt, submitting, so he said, to the discipline that it demanded. The reality, of course, was that he had no talent at all for submitting to discipline of any kind, and fascist discipline required an uncritical acceptance of authority compared with which the Parliamentary Labour Party was positively liberal.

"Beckett, a tall red-faced handsome man with a tendency to lose his temper, was among the most interesting figures who attached themselves to Mosley", wrote Colin Cross.

> His career inside and outside politics has been marked by a combination of recklessness and an intelligent instinct for self-preservation. Over a somewhat arrogant belief in his own abilities lies a jovial charm and a boyish delight in elaborating an anecdote. His native ability might have carried him to a leading place in the labour movement, but, like Mosley, he was a casualty of the 1929–31 parliament.

I think it's a pretty good assessment, with serious reservations about the "intelligent instinct for self-preservation".

Nicholas Mosley describes him as "histrionic and pugnacious" and adds: "A good public speaker, in the hierarchy of BUF speakers he soon gained a position second only to Mosley and William Joyce."

The libel courts were soon seeing a lot of John. He won £700 in libel damages from one Maurice Isaacs who had falsely accused him in print of diverting some of the funds of the National Union of Ex Servicemen for his own use. But he lost an action for libel he took against a Mr Emanuel, and was ordered to pay 30 shillings a month towards Mr Emanuel's £135 costs.

In fact, he seems to have spent a good deal of the early 1930s in courts of one sort or another. If it was not libel, or bankruptcy, or an unsuccessful petition for divorce, it was some sort of altercation with a policeman over his car, in which he accused the policeman of assaulting him.

His court appearances were well covered by the newspapers. John Beckett was always good copy.

I don't know whether he was there when, as reported in the *Blackshirt*, the London BUF rugby team went to Old Windsor to play the old boys of Beaumont College, a very posh and expensive Catholic public school run by Jesuit priests. The fascists won, and

Beaumont became one of only four public schools with a fascist cell. A quarter of a century later, my father fulfilled a dream by sending me to Beaumont.

The month after he joined, in April 1934, the *Blackshirt*'s lead headline read:

LIVELY SCENES AT BRISTOL
The Leader's inspiring speech at Colston Hall
Many Reds ejected

On 7 June, Mosley addressed a big rally at Olympia in London. Police records now available show that the Communist Party and its allies carefully planned to disrupt and destroy the meeting, but the fascist reaction to the threat was sinister and equally deliberate.

As he heard interruptions, Mosley would stop speaking while the searchlight sought out the perpetrators. Stewards then advanced on them and removed them with ostentatious violence, and some of them were then beaten up in the foyer.

As near as you can date it, this marks the moment when the BUF turned into a gang of racist thugs, fighting Jews and communists for control of the streets. The whole of the next issue of the *Blackshirt* was devoted to it, and its headline writers did their best with the impossible task of taking the moral high ground while stoking up street hatred:

THE TRUTH ABOUT THE OLYMPIA DISORDER
Communist Determination to "kill Mosley"

HOSTILE DEMONSTRATION CAREFULLY PLANNED
Blackshirt Assaulted Hours Before the Meeting

The following month Rothermere withdrew the support of his newspapers, citing the BUF's growing reputation for violence as well as its burgeoning anti-Semitism.

This was not, however, the moment the BUF became anti-Semitic. It was when the BUF formally adopted anti-Semitism. Mosley, Beckett and even Forgan claimed ever afterwards that anti-Semitism was the result of Jewish hostility to the BUF. As late as 1975 Robert Skidelsky placed much of the blame on Jewish anti-fascists.

But Daniel Tilles points out that as early as April 1932, before the BUF was even founded, Mosley invited two of Britain's most notorious anti-Semites, Arnold Leese, leader of the Imperial Fascist League, and Henry Hamilton Beamish, founder of the Britons (and a man, as we have seen, whom John already knew), to address the New Party's youth wing on the subject of "The Blindness of British Politics under the Jew [*sic*] Money-Power". A close New Party associate of Mosley, Harold Nicolson, has attested to anti-Semitism in Mosley's thinking at that time.

Tilles writes: "The foundations for the BUF's antisemitism were in place from the outset ... Anti-Semitism had always been intended to play a role in BUF policy."

And Jews in east London, and the enemies of Jews in east London, knew it. Peckham, which is a working-class area of south-east London, knew it, and Peckham's high-profile ex-MP knew it. I think his Jewish mother Eva Dorothy Solomon knew it. And I think that is one of the reasons why he did not join Mosley until after her death. There was a persistent rumour among Jewish East Enders that one of the top fascists had a Jewish wife or parent; I heard it years later from the historian David Englander, who was brought up in the East End.

It was after Olympia, however, that the BUF lost its apparent respectability, its influential newspaper support and any chance of bringing in the left. It became increasingly reliant on anti-Semites and Blimpish ex-army officers. The hostility of organised labour became implacable, but ex-officers and former public schoolboys queued up for two days outside the Black House headquarters to join.

The best known of these was General J.F.C. "Boney" Fuller, who applied to join the BUF the day after Olympia. "You should always join a man in his worst moment", he told Mosley. Fuller is said to have been a great military strategist, and I expect he was, but in politics he was a caricature of the upper-class solder: ignorant, arrogant and super-stitious. He thought the League of Nations was "a pink Jew-Bolshevik baby" and the Jewish conspiracy was "the cancer of Europe".

Fuller was a short, abrupt man with the sort of army officer's political opinions that can easily spill over into fascism, coupled with a nutty theology which led him to the view that "mentally and morally, the Jew does not fit into the Christian World Order".

He had been associated with Aleister Crowley, the self-styled apocalyptic "beast", and it was probably through Fuller that my father was introduced into such circles, which included Tom Driberg and the fascist turned agent runner Maxwell Knight. He talked of it very little, and wrote not at all, but I know he saw things which frightened him, and left him convinced that, in some ill-defined way, he had seen an evil spiritual force at work.

Fascism and superstition often go hand in hand. William Joyce, A.K. Chesterton and John were all, as we will see, deeply superstitious.

By October 1935 the best estimates we have suggest the BUF was down to 5,000. The movement John had chosen now relied on the people who in 1926 had broken the general strike and the spirits of his Gateshead constituents; and on people who would shun him if they knew who his mother was. His friend Bob Forgan, the last former MP in its leadership apart from Mosley and John Beckett and the man who had recruited him, left six months after John arrived.

Hitler and Mussolini were also losing faith in Britain's fascist leader. Mosley always claimed his movement got neither money nor guidance from German Nazis and Italian fascists, but he lied. Colin Holmes has studied documents in the Russian State Military Archive, which the Nazis seized from French intelligence when they occupied Paris, and the Red Army seized in Berlin in 1945 and took to Moscow.

In 1934 Holmes finds Mosley telling German emissaries that his movement would sweep to power at the next general election, and several BUF members being warmly received in Cologne. The Leader sent Hitler a signed copy of the German edition of *BUF: Oswald Mosley. Portrait of a Leader* and attached a letter emphasising the need for their continued close co-operation.

The same year secret meetings, organised by Rudolf Hess, took place in Germany, and that autumn in Munich Mosley met with leading members of the Nazi hierarchy – Hess, Himmler, von Ribbentrop – along with French and Spanish fascists. In October 1936 we know that he married his second wife, Diana Mitford, in Joseph Goebbels's house on Hermann-Göring-Strasse. Berlin had become his spiritual home.

In March 1935 Mosley abruptly suspended the head of the BUF's external relations department, who had given offence to Berlin. When leading Nazi Julius Streicher, pathological anti-Semite and editor of *Der Stürmer*, complained of BUF policy towards the Jews, the Leader replied:

> Please accept my very best wishes for your kind telegram ... I value your advice greatly in the midst of our hard struggle. The power of Jewish corruption must be destroyed in all countries before peace and justice can be successfully achieved in Europe. Our struggle in this direction is hard but our victory is certain.

In 1936 he changed his movement's name to the British Union of Fascists and National Socialists.

Mosley was meeting Nazis, trying to bond with and impress them. In return Berlin offered advice, support and funding.

Most of Mosley's top people were secretly entertained in Berlin, and John was one of them. There is no record anywhere of this, as far as I can establish, and I only know it because he once told me about a Berlin night club which he had been taken him to. It sounded very like the Kit Kat Klub in the film of *Cabaret*, only much sleazier. The girls who brought him his drinks were naked, and, unasked, performed some fairly explicit sexual acts in front of him. William Joyce went to Germany some time in that period, too. Perhaps they first bonded in Hitler's Berlin.

But by 1936 Hitler was losing patience with Mosley. It no longer looked as though the Leader could deliver.

For John, despite Forgan's departure, there were still a few familiar faces in BUF ranks. The most prominent was John Scanlon, a left-wing journalist and an old Glasgow chum of Maxton's. Scanlon's book, *The Decline and Fall of the Labour Party*, was the political history of the 1920s and early 1930s according to Maxton and the ILP. He continued well into the 1930s writing for fascist newspapers under pseudonyms, and was still working with John when the war came.

John and Scanlon shared a bitter sense of betrayal about the Labour Party. One of John's more thoughtful articles for *Fascist Quarterly* was "Fascism and Trade Unionism", in which he accused union leaders of using their members' money to feather their own nests, and of stifling internal union democracy.

> For years, for example, the active members of the National Union of Railwaymen were extremely anxious to be rid of Mr [Jimmy] Thomas's highly expensive services. Mr Thomas stayed on in compete autocracy until a better offer arrived and the unfortunate nation took him off the railwaymen's hands.

This is a roundabout way of saying that he joined the cabinet. He achieved this, John wrote, because he had the power to sign or refuse to sign the expenses chits of his executive members.

But what John offered in place of our fallible trade unions was a tame corporate union.

> Strikes and lockouts will be relegated to the barbarous past, but ... we are fully alive to the fact that adequate machinery must be devised that will safeguard both employer and worker ... In each industry these governing bodies will be set up, armed with whatever authority is necessary, and responsible to the government through the Minister of Corporations.

This socialist, who had condemned Labour leaders for failing to help the working man, had nothing to offer the worker but a state run workers' council, against whose decisions there was no appeal, and the outlawing of the workers' only weapon, strike action.

He behaved as though he really believed all this, and I suppose he must have done. He certainly did not behave as though he had joined a lost cause. "Beckett threw himself into his new career with gigantic enthusiasm, addressing 100 meetings in the first six months, leading his stewards in two-fisted battles against violent opposition", writes Colin Cross. He spoke all over the country, at small street corner meetings, in large halls, on village greens and at open air rallies. He claimed that his speeches "were practically the same as those I had made in the ILP, because my change of organisation had no effect on my socialist convictions". Fenner Brockway would have recognised them: no policy, just punch and hit, very effective.

John always maintained that the violence at his meetings came from fascism's opponents:

> Blackshirt speakers were always assured of a good audience, but almost as soon as they began to speak, a small section of it would begin to shout or sing, and if it was thought that the speaker was alone or only had a few companions, the platform would be rushed and often considerable physical damage done. Some half a million hooligans in this country have taken it upon themselves to decide what speakers may be heard, and what meetings shall be closed down.

At Marylebone, a lump of lead narrowly missed his head. A meeting at Plymouth degenerated into a free fight before he had even begun to speak, and John went down from the platform to rally his stewards and lead them to the rescue of four of them who were on the floor. He was brought down by a flying rugby tackle and his head was being beaten on the floor when the police arrived. Both sides accused the other of starting the trouble. When order had been restored, he gave his speech.

He might just as well have remained an MP: he could have had all that in the chamber of the House of Commons, shoulder to shoulder with John McGovern.

As often as not, Anne Cutmore went with him. At one open-air meeting in the East End, he needed to climb down from the roof of his loudspeaker van and make his way through hundreds of opponents who looked and sounded as though they were ready to tear him to pieces. Anne, a diminutive but elegant figure, wormed her way to the front of the crowd so that she could walk beside him, and though there was much shouting, the crowd parted to let them through and no one touched them.

"I think," he would say jovially in his comparatively mellow old age, "that they thought: he may be a bastard, but he's got a nice wife."

Anne's younger sister Jo watched it all apprehensively. "John had the courage to tackle anything and Anne always backed him, whatever she thought", she told me.

He toured the north-east, where he was greeted with cries of "Traitor Beckett" in his former Gateshead constituency and ran the gauntlet of 2,000 protesters, many of them throwing missiles, to get to his orderly ticket-only meeting; he addressed friendly meetings in Durham mining villages; and, in Newcastle, he was the key figure in what was probably the biggest pitched battle the fascists ever fought.

Accounts from both sides of the barricades, and the police and local Press, agree on the essential details of what happened. Local fascists were holding Sunday meetings at Cowan's Monument, a well-known Newcastle landmark. The local Anti-Fascist League was determined that these meetings should stop, the more so after fascists had disrupted an ILP gathering, and the last four meetings before John arrived had ended in fighting.

John went to see the deputy chief constable, who told him that the trouble was caused by the presence of uniformed fascist stewards. John asked: if he were to go to Cowan's Monument alone that Sunday, would the police protect him? He was told that they would. So that Sunday, typically, he mounted the monument alone.

A vast army of people on one side of the platform – all estimates put it at about 1,000 – moved ominously towards him, shouting abuse, and for a few seconds he felt something like panic. He looked for the police: he could see two constables and an inspector on the outside of the crowd, far too far away to help even if two men were of any use.

But in the front of the crowd, although he always insisted that he did not know it, were six fascists in plain clothes, sent up from London to see how it all went. "I truly believe that to these men I owe my life", he wrote afterwards. John was pushed off his platform, which was smashed to pieces, and the policemen advanced through the crowd and ordered him to close the meeting.

Then, on John's account, the fascists literally fought their way, inch by inch, through the streets of the city to their own headquarters, carrying two of their comrades who were unconscious, and reinforced by 20 or so more. Sometimes they had to rescue a colleague; sometimes they would themselves dart into the crowd and set about an opponent.

The official report claims that the police escorted them, but both John and his enemies seem agreed that it was the other way round: the fascists escorted the police. "The crowd was particularly incensed against Beckett and were determined not to allow him to speak", states the police report.

Just a decade earlier, cheering crowds had carried him shoulder high through the streets of the same city to share a platform with the city's other Labour candidates. Almost certainly some of those who cheered him then were in the angry crowds now, ready to tear him to pieces. Did that not make him sad and thoughtful? Perhaps he was too busy.

A *Newcastle Journal* reporter inside the headquarters that day described it as "exactly like a first treatment centre behind the line". About 15 injured fascists were helped or carried inside, and the floor of the big meeting room was covered with blood and groaning men.

John told me about Cowan's Monument in the 1950s. He said that the story had appeared in A.K. Chesterton's hagiography of Mosley, and that he felt aggrieved because, when the book was reprinted, after John had left the BUF, it no longer contained the episode. Even I could see that a fascist organisation was bound to erase this episode from its history when its leading actor defected. At 10 or 11, I already knew something about totalitarianism which my father went to his grave without understanding properly.

He never, as far as I know, mentioned one detail which I think is almost unbearably sad. Most of the anti-fascists, when they dispersed, went to the Palace Theatre, to listen to John's old friend Jimmy Maxton. John could, and should, have been at Maxton's side.

Back in London, John went to address an open air meeting at Parliament Hill Fields. As he was standing beside the platform a 22-year-old labourer called Anthony Yates shouted, "Beckett only left the Labour Party because they would not give him enough money", and John hit him. The police broke up the fight and both men were fined 40 shillings. Yates went to prison rather than pay, but he had the last laugh: there was no other way he could have got that allegation into the national press, where I found the story.

Within weeks John and Mosley were speaking in Hyde Park, and a meeting in opposition was being addressed by other old friends

Fenner Brockway and John McGovern, together with communist leader Harry Pollitt. Police estimated that 60,000 people were there – pro-fascists, anti-fascists and curious onlookers. His own speech, or those parts of it the police reporter could hear, still contained passages that could have been delivered had he been sharing the platform with Brockway, but others that could not:

> Thousands of men and women here today defying the mob ... Declaration of war against poverty ... Some of them are misguided enough to let the poison from Moscow get into their veins; many of them are decent English working men and women, but lots of them, thrown out of the sewers of Moscow ...

Despite the battles – perhaps partly because of them – he was happy on the road for those six months. He had probably never enjoyed politics so much since he stomped the country as one of the roving band of ILP speakers, before he went into Parliament.

Notes on sources

Fragment of autobiography in the keeping of the Forgan family.

Beyond the Pale by Nicholas Mosley (Secker & Warburg, 1983).

Blackshirt: Sir Oswald Mosley and British Fascism by Stephen Dorril (Viking, 2006).

Blackshirts in Devon by Todd Gray (Mint Press, 2006).

British Fascist Anti-Semitism and Jewish Responses 1932–40 by Daniel Tilles (Bloomsbury, 2015).

Fascism in Britain 1918–1985 by Richard Thurlow (Basil Blackwell, 1998).

Ideology of Obsession: A.K. Chesterton and British Fascism by David Baker (I.B. Tauris, 1996).

In Excited Times: The People Against The Blackshirts by Nigel Todd (Bewick Press, 1995).

Oswald Mosley by Robert Skidelsky (Macmillan, 1975).

Oswald Mosley: Portrait of a Leader by A.K. Chesterton (Action Press, 1937).

The Fascists in Britain by Colin Cross (Barrie & Rockliffe, 1961).

The Fascists in Britain by Colin Cross, reviewed by Earl Attlee (*Political Science Quarterly*, 79(1), March 1964).

15
FOLLOWING THE BLEEDER

John returned to London and occupied an office in Black House. There he put the energy which had served him so well on the road into his schemes for reforming the BUF's organisation, where it was to serve him rather less well.

In headquarters he found a mess, that particular sort of mess which goes with a totalitarian organisation revolving around a leader whose pronouncements are considered infallible:

> A huge staff of badly paid and useless people had been gathered together, and there were probably at least 200 full time organisers and speakers, paid anything from ten shillings and their keep to two pounds a week. They made trouble wherever they went, and their only qualification seemed to be their cheapness and extreme servility. Some of the senior officers seemed quite happy if they could sit at their ease while a few underpaid hacks clicked their heels and saluted ... A part of national headquarters staff were unbelievably like the caricatures of fascists in the *Daily Worker* and the *New Statesman*.

A successful businessman came to Black House offering voluntary service. He was kept waiting for a long time, then shown into the office of a young blackshirt officer who, a few months previously, had been a door-to-door salesman. The businessman took a seat and the young fascist shouted: "Stand to attention when you are talking to me."

John himself tried to recruit a prominent Catholic, arguing that if you accept the authority of the Pope, why not that of the fascist leader. "I don't mind the Pope laying down a dogma every thousand years," said the Catholic, "but I'm not having Tom Mosley lay one down every five minutes."

John did not see that all this came with the creed he had embraced. He thought it could be solved by better administration if only Mosley were made to understand; and once back in London, he told Mosley what he thought, several times, in person and by memorandum, in his trenchant and rather tactless way. Mosley quickly came to resent his counsel, according to Colin Cross, but "it would not have occurred to Beckett to stop giving advice".

At first he thought he had been successful. The Black House was sold in 1935 and, in the new and more modest Great Smith Street headquarters, Mosley set up a Central Council, including John and the two men who, after Forgan's departure, John liked best: William Joyce and A.K. Chesterton. Major General Fuller was put to work to report on the organisation, and John felt optimistic.

Fuller produced an 11-page report which said that the objective should be to obtain power through parliamentary means, not by violent revolution. This meant reducing the influence of the paramilitary elements, and restricting the wearing of the black shirt to a few chosen people. Britain, he said, is an old country, solid, instinctively feudal. "The masses of the people will always listen to men and women of experience and importance but not to youngsters."

He wanted Mosley to become one member of a "triumvirate", "the hidden dictatorship". "This trinity will represent the soul of the Movement", Fuller wrote. "Its existence should be kept secret."

He seems to have been pretty clear about the identity of at least one of the two men who should assist Mosley with the burden of leadership. "I am ready to assist anyhow for a period. I reckon it will take about 3 months to get the organization pulled together and three more before full results are seen." I suspect Fuller lived all his life in expectation of the military coup which would bring him to power as part of a British junta.

But if Fuller, or John, thought Mosley was going to share control, then neither of them had the first understanding of the man they were dealing with, or of the creed they had embraced.

"We understood," wrote John,

> that this council would discuss the whole work of the move-
> ment, and although there were also a number of bureaucrats on
> the council, they were not gifted men, and we felt confident,
> once we were sure of being consulted, of our ability to sway
> Mosley by the force and sincerity of our arguments.

I am quite sure that John wrote this rubbish entirely seriously.

The Central Council was naturally a waste of time. Apart from General Fuller, himself, Joyce and Chesterton, "the other members sat silent and stupid, occasionally starting up with fury when it occurred to them that someone was arguing with the Leader. After three months General Fuller declared he had no more time to waste, and attended no more."

Mosley spent much of 1935 in Italy. He was there when Italy invaded Abyssinia, and John effectively took control of strategy and propaganda, launching a campaign against intervention under the slogan "Mind Britain's Business".

One secret purpose of Mosley's long Italian sojourn was to ensure that Mussolini continued to fund his movement. The BUF, we now know, received £40,000 in 1933 and 1934 from Italy, probably £3,000 a month throughout 1935, and £1,000 a month in 1936, until Mussolini grew disillusioned with Mosley and stopped the money in 1936 or 1937. These were huge sums in those days. As Richard Thurlow puts it, "The Mind Britain's Business campaign ... was a true quid pro quo, the price of foreign funding."

The implementation was John's. He invented the slogan, and he took the opportunity to drop the fasces symbol, a picture of several sticks bound together, which Mosley had inherited from the Italian fascists. Instead he adopted a flash and a circle, designed by a member, which became the movement's symbol from then on, and soon became known as "the flash in the pan".

The new symbol moved the BUF in the direction Mosley wished to go, more towards German Nazis than Italian fascists. Leaflets were issued, meetings were organised, members were encouraged to chalk "Mind Britain's Business" on walls throughout the country and a cable was sent to Mosley in Italy asking him to return, which he did within a week.

John became director of publicity, editing the BUF's two weekly newspapers, *Action* and the *Blackshirt*, and controlling the rather heavier quarterly, as well as handling all publicity material. He assembled a small staff of younger people, and acquired a reputation as a maverick.

Mosley asked him to form what he called "an anti-libel front". In Germany, he said, Nazi propaganda chief Dr Josef Goebbels had fought dozens of libel actions and been bankrupted several times before his party achieved power. All it needed was to ensure that publications were run by an official who did not mind being made bankrupt, and to arrange that publishing and printing were done by companies with no assets. Then, when he received a writ for libel, all the editor had to do was to go into court and make a propaganda speech repeating all the libels. The BUF would incur no costs, and the paper would appear the next week with another printer and publisher.

John considered it a splendid idea. He, of course, had no money or assets at all, and had already been bankrupt once. He thought it would enable him to expose scandals which could not be proved in court. On his own account, he set up the trust so effectively that, when he was fired two years later, he realised it would be a waste of time to sue his employer for the money he was owed.

He lost a libel action to eight members of the Amalgamated Engineering Union, whom he accused of corruption, but the damages were not great and I think they were never paid.

He was, as Clement Attlee and the Gateshead Labour Party had discovered, a talented propagandist. He understood how to make a newspaper at once a propaganda vehicle and a paper that people really want to read. It is a hard trick to pull off, and few can do it, even today. Most people either fall into the marketing trap, and produce wall-to-wall breathless good news which no one wants to read, or they produce journalism which forgets that it is also supposed to be propaganda.

John was proud of pushing the circulation of the *Blackshirt* from 13,000 to 23,000 and that of *Action* from 5,000 to 26,000, and bleakly satisfied that, a year after he left the papers, the latter was down to 14,000.

He discovered, nevertheless, that the reality of power inside the BUF was very different from the appearance. The real power lay, not with the flamboyant figures like himself and William Joyce, but with the BUF Trust Ltd, which controlled the money.

The BUF headquarters was now split into two factions. Thurlow writes:

> The dispute was between those who saw the BUF's future in terms of a military organisation appealing to law and order, and emphasised a style of disciplined marches and demonstrations, and those who saw a need to expound propaganda and convert the masses to fascist ideology. The first faction was led ... by ... Neil Francis-Hawkins [the chief administrator] and Ian Dundas, the latter group by William Joyce, John Beckett and A.K. Chesterton.

Francis-Hawkins was the key figure among the bureaucrats. A short, stout former maker of ophthalmic instruments, in the 1920s he had been in a small fascist group, the British Fascists, a bitter group of extreme right-wing anti-Semites who had argued that the way to deal with unemployment was to lower income tax so that wealthy people could hire more servants. (We should not laugh too loudly. Some perfectly respectable mainstream politicians make essentially the same argument today.) Like most of the British Fascists, Francis-Hawkins transferred his loyalty to Mosley in 1931.

He was a bachelor, a homosexual and a workaholic, and said he preferred working with unmarried men because they could give more time to the cause. He was, unsurprisingly, popular with the regiment of Colonel Blimps who attached themselves to fascism.

Joyce, too, came from the British Fascists, and perhaps the two were working out antagonisms first developed in this tiny, obscure and rather ridiculous organisation, for Joyce and Francis-Hawkins were as different as two human beings could be. Joyce was a remarkably effective platform orator, and between 1933 and 1937 he addressed hundreds of meetings all over the country, to great effect. He could have been a fine writer, too, if some stylist had found him early enough and trained out of him a certain wordy sententiousness.

He was an Irishman from Galway, though he had been born in Brooklyn in 1906, and had a first class honours degree in English literature from Birkbeck College, London, where he had been president of the university Conservative Society. He was physically small, but pugnacious and brave and a good boxer.

At home he regularly consumed huge quantities of a cheap Spanish drink called Segavin, but he was not an alcoholic: he could go for weeks without alcohol. When people came round and talked politics, his wife Margaret said he became "segovinned". His daughter Heather remembers a loving and affectionate father who would deal with his explosive temper by taking long walks, from which he returned quite calm.

Born in 1928, for the first seven years of her life she told me she saw him every day:

> He'd be coming back from work, carrying his briefcase, he'd be coming up the road and my mother would say, go to the pillar box to meet Daddy, and as soon as he saw me coming he'd smile, I always remember that. I'd wait for him to come in if the weather was too bad to go and meet him.

Some researchers doubt Heather's account, suspecting a need to imagine an early childhood she did not have. I think they are mistaken: I found her entirely credible. She went on: "He was a great raconteur. And he would sing all sorts of songs: Hearts of Oak, Bonnets of Bonnie Dundee. Also some Irish rebel songs but he rather parodied them."

He would. Joyce was a passionate opponent of Irish Home Rule, and like Victor Grayson, he was scorched by contact with spying in

Ireland. As a teenager he informed on the IRA for the British security services, and once narrowly escaped an IRA assassin's bullet.

With the British Fascists, he was fighting street battles with communists as early as the early 1920s, and he had a long scar down one cheek which, he said, was inflicted when two communists (sometimes he said they were also Jews) held him down and a third slashed his face with a razor while he stewarded a Conservative Party meeting.

That account has always been accepted, but it isn't true. Recent research by Colin Holmes tells a different story. The wound was inflicted by an Irishwoman. "Joyce's Galway activities had followed him to London. The IRA had missed killing him in Ireland. But he was not forgotten. Irish nationalists had found him in London."

While in the British Fascists, he was in regular contact with its intelligence chief, Maxwell Knight. Afterwards, in 1929, Knight joined the security services, but he may already have been secretly on MI5's payroll when organising the British Fascists' intelligence activities. The security services at that time, paranoid about communists, found in the British Fascists a group which felt the same way, and some MI5 officers felt at ease with its ideology. So it was blessed with several spies.

At any rate, we know that once in the service, Knight never forgot his old friend "Joycey". John, I am sure, never knew of this friendship, or of the part Knight later played in Joyce's life. If he had known that, he would not have become so close to Joyce. And if Joyce had known a little more about John's Jewish mother, he would have shunned him.

Joyce often talked of his political beliefs in near-religious terms, and Colin Holmes thinks they provided a substitute for his lost Catholicism. He would not be the only person of whom that's true.

Joyce was a generation younger than John, too young to have fought in, and been shaped by, the Great War. But A.K. Chesterton, born in 1899, arrived as an officer in France in the spring of 1917, and the things he saw and did stayed with him in nightmares all his life. Eleven years later, reviewing R.C. Sherriff's First World War play *Journey's End*, he became carried away with his memories:

> Think of the effect on a man of seeing friends, fellows who he has learned to love during the sharing of unspeakable experiences,

following each other post haste into screaming death, while he himself must go marching on, watching the world become a vast Necropolis, keeping his head the while, leading his men, enheartening them, planning his defences and waiting, waiting, waiting for the day when he too will be a stinking corpse, grinning at the moon.

Chesterton was awarded the MC at the age of 19, after leading his men in seven hours of hand-to-hand fighting in the German trenches in September 1918. After taking the trench he returned to inform his commanding officer, and reached his objective almost without touching the ground, which was covered by a vast carpet of German and British bodies. For years he had a recurring nightmare of walking over a mass of dead bodies stretching to infinity.

Like many First World War officers, he made the trenches bearable by drinking whisky. He became an alcoholic, and alcoholism alternated with periods of total abstinence for the rest of his life.

Chesterton, a distant cousin of G.K. Chesterton, spent the 1920s as a journalist with literary tastes, a drama critic and something of a Shakespeare scholar. The theatre in Stratford was burned down in 1926 and Chesterton played a prominent part in the campaign to have a modern theatre erected in its place. Then he went to work on a local newspaper in Torquay. In 1933 he met Mosley and was mesmerised by him, seeing him, apparently, as the last representative of the spirit of the Tudor aristocracy.

He was a tall, slender, very vain man with piercing eyes, a faintly aristocratic manner and an even more overblown literary style than Joyce's. His fawning 1937 biography of Mosley ended by telling his breathless and probably exhausted readers:

> If the hearts of his followers prove one tenth as great as Mosley's heart, their courage one tenth as high as his courage, they will not relinquish the struggle until the heights of fascist power be won; until Britain's great revolutionary leader, sprung from one thousand years contact with British soil, achieves power to act for and with the British people, in the name of their ancient sanity and splendour, that there may be built up in their peerless

land a corporate life which shall ensure that her million hero-
sons did not die to make a mock for history. Their battle-shouts
sound above the discords and semi-tones of a fading age: hail
Mosley, patriot, revolutionary, and leader of men.

In his first three years at BUF headquarters he was frequently too
drunk to work, and John remembered several times, when Chesterton had been missing for a few days, touring his known haunts,
finding him, drunk and filthy in some dive, and returning him to his
wife to be cleaned up. Eventually Mosley paid for him to go to a
special clinic in Germany where they specialised in alcoholism,
throughout the winter of 1936–7.

After that he was dry until half-way through the Second
World War.

Chesterton was brought up largely in South Africa, and believed
all his life in the superiority of the white Anglo-Saxon.

His wife Doris believed none of these things. She had fallen in
love with a rising young journalist whose principal interest, like hers,
was in theatre; they had met when she was a member of an amateur
drama society in Torquay and he was reviewing their work for the
local paper. She seems to have been utterly horrified when he threw
it all up to go and work for Mosley, instead of taking up an appointment he was offered as director of publicity for the Shakespeare
Memorial Theatre. She told Chesterton's biographer David Baker: "I
was shocked to find him in sympathy with the fascists. We were in
love, with shared interests, but we never talked deeply about
politics."

Doris had a diploma in history from University College London,
and she was also a medium. She could foretell the future, or so her
husband and his colleagues William Joyce and John Beckett believed.
Belief in spiritualism was common in fascist circles, as was Catholicism, and no one should be surprised at that. If you are willing to
believe that Oswald Mosley is bound to lead you in the right direction, you'll believe anything.

John told me a story of how he had once visited the Chestertons,
and found them surprised to see him because Doris had predicted
that he would by now have murdered someone and been on trial for

his life. And the extraordinary thing (you're way ahead of me) is that just the previous week, he had come within an inch of murdering someone.

Years later I discovered from Mary Kenny's biography of Joyce that he told the same story about himself. Then, rooting around among Chesterton's papers for this book, I found he too told the same story about himself, only this time the medium was not his wife, but a professional medium later exposed by the *Daily Mail* (wrongly, in Chesterton's opinion) as a fraud.

Maybe it happened to all three of them. Maybe it happened to one of them, and the others appropriated the story. Maybe it never happened at all. How should I know? The spirits don't confide in me.

Sitting on top of the heap, because it was his money which had founded the movement and which, together with Mussolini's and Hitler's and Bill Allen's, maintained it, was the extraordinary figure of Sir Oswald Mosley.

Mosley's image had a remarkable makeover in the 1970s and 1980s, from which he emerged as he might have hoped history would see him: a politician of genius, a man of passion, the best platform figure of his generation: with flaws of course, but a great wasted talent.

Six feet four inches tall and apparently irresistible to many women, he has been presented as somehow different from the brutal dictators and would-be dictators of Europe in the 1930s, more civilised, less likely to send his foes to concentration camps. He was, after all, a peer, an army officer, an Olympic fencer, a sophisticated, cultivated and educated Englishman. Even after the Second World War he could still count millionaires, dukes and top politicians among his friends and admirers. So, the theory runs, he must surely be superior to a brutal Bavarian corporal who slaughtered millions of Jews.

Yet those who worked with Mosley, and knew him closely, describe something much more sinister, and that should not surprise us. Fascism requires its followers to subordinate their own views utterly to those of the Leader. If that requires a remarkable faith in its followers, it requires a far more remarkable trick from the Leader. He has got to believe, really believe, that he is infallible, and that is as good a definition of madness as I know.

"I have finished with those who think. Henceforth I shall go with those who feel", said Mosley when he founded the movement. But, of course, that meant his followers had to feel, and to leave the thinking to him.

Clement Attlee thought Ramsay MacDonald guilty of something like fascism in 1931, with his call for a "doctor's mandate", a call which the nation was sufficiently panicked to heed; and it was that panic on which Mosley, at first, hoped to capitalise.

Soon after that the communist *Daily Worker* identified Mosley as a fascist, long before he came out as one, though we should not be too impressed by that. If you call almost every political opponent a fascist, you're bound to hit a winner sometimes.

John seems to have thought in the end that the creed might have worked if the Leader had not, unfortunately, been mad. The trouble is that the creed is the Leader. When he described Mosley, John, without knowing it, described exactly how an authentic fascist leader must be:

> Mosley ... has enormous personality which dominates any conference or committee. He is capable of inspiring great love and great enmity. Yet ... during the whole of his career not one person of intellect and integrity has remained his associate, although his brilliance and magnetism have drawn to him the best of his generation. This is the fault of his enormous ego, combined with a peculiar shallowness of judgement and ability to deceive himself. The man who brings him good news is his friend, the carrier of unwelcome tidings slowly becomes his enemy.

How did it take him so long to see that? As John's old friend Clem Attlee – whose friendship was now irrevocably lost to him – wrote: "Able and sincere young men like Bevan and Strachey soon found their leader intolerable. Throughout his career Mosley failed to keep the allegiance of men of character and standing."

Richard Thurlow confirms their judgement: "Those who had access to Mosley's ear realised that ... the best way to advancement was to tell him what he wanted to hear, whether it was true or not."

A fascist leader has to be like that. Think of Hitler in that bunker in Berlin in 1945, taking furious revenge on any subordinate who suggested that victory was less than certain. A fascist leader has to believe that he is always right – must, in some mystical way, always be right. If he did not, the strain would blow him apart.

John goes on to describe the public image:

> Several times a month, [Mosley] addressed large audiences, and saw hundreds of members and great enthusiasm. He did not realise, and I suppose does not realise now [1938], that a great part of this is a stage army which attends him everywhere. In the north the same 100 or so have been his "brothers in arms" in every place at which he speaks; in the south, Bethnal Green and Shoreditch fascists have represented the growing strength of fascism in every town south of the Trent. In every county are several dozen Mosley fans and whenever he speaks within 50 miles of them, they are harried by paid organisers sent on ahead, and pressed to collect parties and "get there somehow". They are given reserved seats in the front rows, and they behave as hysterically as film star fans.
>
> The Communists … stage flattering scenes outside his meetings. He drives through streets alive with opponents shouting his name and calling attention to him, to a hall where admirers greet him with enthusiasm all the more boisterous because of the "dangers" which their hero has just escaped. A far stronger brain than poor Tom's might well fail after five years' food for the ego of this description.

The only people he valued were those who gave him absolute and uncritical admiration. The late John Warburton (by coincidence he shared John's first two names), who as late as the 1990s was still running an organisation called The Friends of Oswald Mosley, told me: "When I was young I thought OM [Mosley] was a god. Now I realise that he wasn't a god, but he was the nearest thing to a god that I'll meet in this world."

Colin Holmes writes that Mosley (and William Joyce) had a condition which psychoanalysts call narcissistic personality disorder, whose symptoms are self-importance, preoccupation with fantasies of unlimited success, a belief he or she is special, arrogance, haughtiness, need for excessive admiration, sense of entitlement, envy of the strong and powerful who can be seen as gods, exploitative approach towards others and absence of empathy in personal relationships.

Only such a man could, without a trace of humour, call his associates by their unadorned surnames and expect them only to call him the Leader. To friends and associates of his own class, he was Tom. To fascists, he was the Leader, always written with an upper case L. John, who in the House of Commons had, like his other parliamentary colleagues, called him Tom, started the habit of referring to him behind his back as The Bleeder, a term of abuse in those days. It was one of many ways in which John swiftly ensured that, should the fascists ever come to power, his reward was more likely to be a firing squad than a job as Gauleiter.

Notes on sources

Beyond the Pale by Nicholas Mosley (Secker & Warburg, 1983).

Blackshirt: Sir Oswald Mosley and British Fascism by Stephen Dorril (Viking, 2006).

Fascism in Britain 1918–1985 by Richard Thurlow (Basil Blackwell, 1998).

Germany Calling by Mary Kenny (New Island, 2003).

Ideology of Obsession: A.K. Chesterton and British Fascism by David Baker (I.B. Tauris, 1996).

Oswald Mosley: Portrait of a Leader by A.K. Chesterton (Action Press, 1937).

Searching for Lord Haw-Haw by Colin Holmes (Routledge, 2016).

The Fascists in Britain by Colin Cross (Barrie & Rockliffe, 1961).

16

JEW-BAITING AND STANDING BY THE KING

The year 1935 saw unrelenting trench warfare in BUF headquarters, chronicled in detail by MI5. In January "John Beckett is spreading rumours that the Blackshirts are finished and it is all the fault of F.M. Box" (an ally of Francis-Hawkins). By July Mosley is censoring Beckett and two others for "having aired their grievances among themselves instead of 'coming forward in a fascist and comradely spirit'".

There was hardly a meeting or discussion of the smallest importance which MI5 did not record. I suspect that without MI5 agents to do the work, fascism in Britain could have caused even the small ripples it did make.

They included the BUF chief of intelligence, P.G. Taylor, who was in reality an agent named James McGuirk Hughes. Mosley is thought to have known this, but considered Hughes to be "on our side", presumably because Hughes had a history of helping with strike-breaking operations and stealing documents from communist offices. His enthusiasm for fascism seems to have been quite genuine.

The strange and sinister spymaster Maxwell Knight, responsible for monitoring fascists, communists and their sympathisers at MI5, had in 1924 been a member, with Joyce and Francis-Hawkins, of the British Fascists, and had become their director of intelligence.

But, before they parted company, John and the Leader were to have one big adventure together. In 1936 it became clear that the government was going to force the new king, Edward VIII, to choose between the throne and his lover, Wallis Simpson.

Both John and Mosley had met the king, as Prince of Wales, and taken to him. John, as a Labour MP, had been impressed that the prince was visibly shocked at the poverty and malnourishment that was allowed to co-exist with great wealth in his future kingdom. On a visit to south Wales, shocked at the condition of miners' families, he had caused anger in establishment political circles by saying, "Something must be done." To John, the young, handsome king represented their generation, and his enemies, principally Prime Minister Stanley Baldwin, represented the old men who had profited from the war.

So John and Mosley threw themselves into a campaign to rally public opinion on the king's behalf. John again designed the campaign, under the slogan "Stand By The King". He wrote the leaflets and pamphlets, organised chalking on walls and produced a special newspaper called *Crisis* which sold 37,000 copies.

When the crisis became front page news, Mosley was in Liverpool. John wrote:

> He telephoned to London and asked Joyce and I to drive there and discuss the position with him. A Bentley was placed at our disposal, and we reached his private suite at the Adelphi Hotel at about seven. Mosley was in a state of great excitement. He claimed to be in direct communication with the court. The king, he said, was strengthened by the knowledge of the support of him and his movement, and for this reason would accept Baldwin's resignation and call upon Mosley to form a government.
>
> Standing in the middle of the room, he detailed his plans for governing without parliament until the budget, pointing out that the financial estimates until then had already been passed, and he strode about the room in excitement as he explained that millions of pounds would be available to fight an election in such a cause, and that as Prime Minister he could broadcast as often as he wished. This, he was certain, could not fail to turn the electorate in his favour.

At this point a telephone call came through from London. Explaining that this was an important call for which he had waited all day, he seized the instrument and began rapidly speaking in back-slang. When he replaced the receiver he turned to us and explained that he had received most important news from court. He apologised for speaking in cipher, but said that he always used it because his calls were intercepted by the CID.

I had learned this simple method of talking at school, and Joyce said that he thought every London schoolboy understood it ... I am sure that Mosley really believed he was on the threshold of great power. The conversation confirmed my suspicion that he was deluded, and was dangerously near the borderline between genius and insanity. I knew the man to whom he had spoken. He was a dilettante society friend of Mosley's, who lived in as fictitious a world of grandeur as Mosley himself...

We left Tom that night convinced that he already believed himself in charge of the nation's affairs, and agreed that his powers of self-delusion had finally conquered his sanity. He could not realise that nobody except himself and the comical little group of ex-peddlers and humourless ex-officers with whom he was surrounded took him at all seriously.

Edward VIII abdicated and married Wallis Simpson. For John, Baldwin and his friends were:

the preachers of Christianity without Christ, of churches without charity, of humanity without dignity ... Paying lip service to the Cenotaph and the Unknown Dead, these crabbed, aged and wartime stay-at-home heroes hunted, in a self-righteous pack, the finest symbol of the living whom they had betrayed ... Always in my heart, as in the hearts of millions of my generation, we shall think regretfully of the dethroned king who represented the new ideas of the wartime generation and was crucified by malice and hatred disguised as righteousness, and hypocrisy enthroned as principle.

John could get carried away by his own rhetoric, so much so that at a demonstration outside Buckingham Palace just after the abdication, he was arrested and fined for obstructing the police.

Mosley, in the light of what we now know about Edward VIII, may not have been quite as deluded as his publicity director thought. Edward VIII had some sympathies with Hitler and the German Nazis, and during the Second World War the Duke of Windsor (as he became after his abdication) made efforts to secure peace which seem to have bordered on the treasonable. After the war the duke and duchess's closest friends in their Paris home were their near neighbours Sir Oswald and Lady Diana Mosley.

In 1937 the BUF mounted its first electoral challenge, putting up candidates in three east London council elections. Right up to the count, Mosley, against all the evidence, was certain of victory, telling John the canvass results proved it. John said his reading of the results was that they could not possibly win. Mosley was furious, and later severely reprimanded the man who had showed John the canvass returns. William Joyce picked up, and passed to John, a rumour that Mosley wanted to be rid of both of them.

The results were an utter humiliation. John and Mosley were together as they came in. Mosley sat at his desk working out figures for some time, then looked up with an air of triumph. "I've got the stuff for the papers, Beckett", he said. "The percentage of our vote is slightly higher than the percentage Hitler polled at his first big election." John pointed out that the BUF figure was in three carefully selected constituencies, whereas Hitler's was over the whole. But he left his leader drafting a preposterous announcement of victory on percentages.

Mosley was quoted in a German newspaper:

> Our position is now nearly equal to that which was formerly in existence with you in Germany ... In the east end of London we have now gained the absolute majority ... Our struggle against the Jews ... helped us to win ... Britain and Germany must be in the closest possible alliance.

The security services noted:

Beckett is very bitter about the conduct of the campaign. He stated quite bluntly that he considered Francis-Hawkins and Donovan [Captain Brian Donovon, a Catholic former headmaster, generally regarded as an incompetent martinet] to be utter fools and that if Sir Oswald Mosley was not as great a fool as they are, he is certainly far too complacent; that perhaps the shock will induce Mosley to place less credence on the counsels of Francis-Hawkins and his friends ... The headquarters staff who went to east London ... were worse than useless ... Raven Thompson [the BUF ideologue and philosopher] is a dangerous idiot who frothed about the Jews and boasted that he would soon be elected and giving orders ... Beckett ... confided that he felt so exasperated at the incompetence and lack of realism ... on the night of the election that he had very nearly resigned ... Headquarters officials who were sent down to work did nothing but sit around the fire in the election agent's room ... and order or bully the voluntary workers.

Five days later, in a cull of full-time staff, Mosley fired John, William Joyce and, according to John, "every other man or woman on his staff who had ever reasoned with or contradicted him or his henchmen". An MI5 report said, correctly: "The significant feature of this upheaval is the complete victory of the Francis-Hawkins 'blackshirt' clique, which has practically eliminated those who were opposed to its conception of the BUF as a semi-military organisation rather than an orthodox political machine."

It also noted that cuts were needed because Mussolini had stopped funding the BUF after its failure in the East End. Mussolini's subsidy plummeted from £86,000 in 1935 to only £7,630 by 1937.

After Beckett and Joyce had gone, A.K. Chesterton's loyalty could not last long. His wife Doris told Chesterton's biographer David Baker that John was Chesterton's closest friend in the movement, sharing a sense of humour with him: "John was roguish in the endearing sense."

Chesterton was still being treated for alcoholism, and Mosley saw a means of splitting his opponents. He wrote a flattering letter to Chesterton:

> Do not feel that our present necessities compel you to cut things short as you seem able to write about half the paper in the present circumstances and you are certainly writing at the top of your form. It will be a great thing to have you back on the spot again but don't take risks with your health ... There will be a great burden of work waiting for you in the future and you want to be thoroughly fit for it ... I need not assure you that the great amount of writing you have been able to do at this juncture has been of inestimable service to the Movement.

It was no good. Quite soon Chesterton was throwing in his lot with John and William Joyce.

I used to think the far left was fissiparous, prone to splitting into ever tinier fragments, but that was before I studied the far right in full cry. Mosley on one side, and John and Joyce on the other, began a brutal, undignified and entirely unscrupulous war for the loyalty of the tiny and diminishing band of people who still wanted to call themselves fascists.

A circular went out from Mosley's headquarters:

> District Leaders should be ready to inform any members of the facts of the recent reorganisation which despite economy will now enable the life and work of the Movement to continue as before. This has been made possible by the splendid spirit of National Socialism shown by those who are no longer members of HQ staff but have offered voluntary service ...
>
> ... 104 members of NHQ salaried staff had to be dispensed with for reasons of economy alone. Nearly all ... have offered voluntary service in their spare time. The exceptions among so many are Messrs Joyce and Beckett who have not emerged in the same manner from this stern test of character ...
>
> It is probable that these two men will try to make any little trouble that they can and to that end will circulate all kinds of stories ... District Leaders should at once notify NHQ of any such activity.

Joyce and John sent their own letter to local BUF leaders: "If we march without Mosley, it is because he gladly permits his pace to become a dawdle lest perchance the unwieldy functionaries who cling to him should be left behind."

Years later, after the holocaust had so discredited anti-Semitism that no politician could profit by it, Mosley found it convenient to say that Joyce and Beckett were fired for their extreme anti-Semitism. This was never suggested at the time. It does not figure in the lengthy, self-serving explanation Mosley sent to his district leaders at the time.

The truth is that that Mosley himself was the leader and inspirer of the BUF's Jew-baiting campaign. In late 1933 Jews were excluded from BUF membership, and November saw the Mosley article Forgan had tried to stop – "Shall Jews drag Britain into war?" On 28 October 1934 Mosley declared an anti-Semitic policy, and thereafter he frequently mimicked Jewish accents in his speeches. By 1938 he was arguing that Jews who "engaged in practises alien to the British character" must leave the country. His Final Solution was a national home in some waste but fertile area.

The likelihood is that John and Chesterton became much more anti-Semitic than they had been before, as a result of absorbing the atmosphere of the BUF.

Chesterton was brought up in South Africa, a good place to learn theories about the superiority of white Anglo-Saxons. His embryonic anti-Semitism was fed before the First World War by the Marconi scandal, which his famous cousin G.K. Chesterton had helped expose, and he had absorbed the languid anti-Semitism of the Chesterton–Belloc circle.

But his most strongly anti-Semitic writings were directly inspired by Mosley, who commissioned a special task from him: to research "the Jewish question". David Baker's remark is even more applicable to John:

> What is often ignored ... is the degree to which he gained his more extreme ideas from within the movement – as a result of concentrated exposure to these beliefs. This process of socialisation must have been important as there is little evidence of such extreme or systematic anti-Semitism in his pre-fascist writings.

John, no doubt, had imbibed the ideas of the turn of the century imperialist from his own father, as well as the mild anti-Semitism of Labour leaders such as Dalton in the 1920s. He had, in a vague and unfocused way, felt that war profiteers like Sir Alfred Mond were most often Jews, he had almost certainly met and been influenced by the extreme anti-Semite Henry Hamilton Beamish, and he had felt that there were powerful Jewish interests in the London theatre in his time which were hostile to him. But up to the time of his beloved mother's death in 1932, he was not, and could not have been, the rabid anti-Semite that he later became, under Mosley's tutelage.

From the time he lost Rothermere's support, Mosley seems to have decided that he had everything to gain and nothing to lose from constant and brutal assaults on the Jews. At one fairly typical meeting in Manchester in late 1934 quoted by Colin Holmes, he talks of "sweepings of the continental ghettos hired by Jewish financiers", "these Jewish rascals", "this little crowd brought here by Jewish money", the "yelping of a Yiddish mob", "alien Jewish finance" and the "alien faces" in his audience. From then on, few Mosley speeches were complete without many if not all of these references.

International Jewish finance was "that nameless, homeless and all-powerful force which stretches its greedy fingers from the shelter of England to throttle the trade and menace the peace of the world".

Fighting the 1937 east London council elections, Mosley, according to police reports, was telling East End audiences:

> The Jews already in this country must be sent to where they belong ... You have seen the foreign Jews brought in here and making the goods under your noses ... No more of admitting foreigners into this country to take British jobs and those who are already here can go back to where they belong ... There are many people in the East End of London who have received notice to quit from the Jews, but this time you are going to give the Jews notice to quit.

In east London, the BUF emphasised anti-Semitism. So, while Jews made only sporadic appearances in the *Blackshirt*, the *East London Pioneer* (the name seems to have been taken from the paper John once started for Clem Attlee in Limehouse) was relentlessly, obsessively, boringly anti-Semitic. Mosley took the conscious decision to concentrate his resources in the area where Russian-Polish Jews had settled in the late nineteenth and early twentieth century. So on 4 October 1936, Mosley, finding his path blocked by political opponents, retreated from what had been intended as a major demonstration of the BUF's strength in east London. It became known as the Battle of Cable Street.

The next month the *East London Pioneer* went after Jewish chemists. It's not at all clear why they chose chemists, but it was another moment which should have given John pause, for when he was working for Attlee in Limehouse he must have worked closely with the key Labour activist in the constituency, a Jewish chemist called Oscar Tobin.

Two months later an article headed "Jew-Controlled Tailoring Shops" began: "It would be interesting to know how many Jewish tailors from Germany are among those who deprive British tailors of work."

There was a rumour that Mosley's wife's mother was Jewish, and it always provoked violence at fascist meetings when it was repeated. In Hornsey town hall one evening, drunk BUF stewards singing the Horst Wessel song attacked a man and a woman who shouted out the rumour. Mosley stopped speaking each time he was interrupted, telling his stewards to eject the hecklers "with old-fashioned fascist courtesy".

Internal BUF documents which fell into the hands of the security services show that the policy decision had been made to put "the Jewish question" at the heart of the campaign.

Mosley, the man who said of the Abyssinian crisis "Stronger even than the stink of oil is the stink of the Jew", did not dissociate himself from anyone because he was embarrassed by their anti-Semitism.

None of this, of course, excuses any of his lieutenants. Whatever John or A.K. Chesterton were when they joined Mosley, they were both racist bigots by 1937.

Joyce is a different case, because he seems to have been pathologically anti-Semitic all his adult life. His anti-Semitism corroded his whole personality, and touched everything he said and did. Nonetheless, Mosley's post-war repudiation of Joyce – "that horrid little man" – stinks of hypocrisy. Joyce's anti-Semitism was not expressed in language any more extreme than Mosley's, and Mosley never once attempted to curb it. Nicholas Mosley, in a mostly honourable attempt to come to terms with his father's life, suggests that Mosley simply failed to restrain Joyce's anti-Semitism, but there is no evidence that he ever tried, and every reason to suppose that the violence of Joyce's tongue suited Mosley's purposes at the time.

John's anti-Semitism was different from the pure hatred preached by Joyce or even Mosley. John, who in everything else used the bludgeon, in this used the rapier. His method was the indirect one, the sneer rather than the assault. Attacking trade union leaders in the *Fascist Quarterly*, he analysed the expenditure of the miners' unions, ending with an item called "Fees and grants", and translated this for his readers as "Hungry Jews etc.". At one meeting, according to an observer for the Board of Deputies of British Jews, he talked of the national press and "delighted his audience with stressing the Jewish names of the persons either owning or being part owner". A fascist who came to our home when I was a small child told me how a Jewish heckler once interrupted John with Shylock's words: "If you prick me, do I not bleed?" John replied: "If I prick a pig it'll bleed."

I like to imagine that he went in for this uncharacteristic way of doing things because his heart wasn't in it. I have no idea whether I am right.

The split had nothing to do with any other policy, either. As Colin Cross put it, William Joyce and John Beckett were bad at taking orders, and therefore bad fascists. Colin Holmes puts it this way: "The victory of the Francis-Hawkins faction was a triumph for those members wedded to a bureaucratic and quasi-military form of organisation over the likes of Joyce and Beckett, whose chief interest lay in propaganda activities."

Under totalitarian regimes, apostates are written out of history. Even half a century later, when John's existence could, with difficulty, be acknowledged, the BUF's official historian, Richard Reynell Bellamy, wrote of John rather as Stalin's official biographer might have written of Trotsky: "A clever and able man, who held the mentality of the masses in contempt, and who was well versed in serving up what his readers wanted, had been editing *Action* with success, and adding to his own reputation."

Others in the BUF remembered mainly his jokes and his stories. Many remembered him telling the story of the Mace, and how it was so light that he almost fell over backwards – "He made it sound hilarious", writes one. They remembered his breezy manner and scabrous jokes. William Joyce's six-year-old daughter Heather remembered hearing one of the adults tell her mother, "That John Beckett, he's got a filthy tongue", and the next time Heather met John, she watched him, hoping he would stick his tongue out so that she could see what a filthy tongue looked like.

Few people can make as many mistakes as John had made, and still get yet another chance. John was getting one, if only he could see it. He was more or less destitute, his salary was gone and for most of his old friends he was now beyond the pale. But he had his native talent. It was a chance to rethink and remake his life. What would he do with it?

Notes on sources

Blackshirt by Stephen Dorrill (Penguin, 2006.)

BUF official history by Richard Reynell Bellamy, in Sheffield University Library.

Anti-Semitism in British Society by Colin Holmes (Edward Arnold, 1979).

Beyond the Pale by Nicholas Mosley (Secker & Warburg, 1983).

Ideology of Obsession: A.K. Chesterton and British Fascism by David Baker (I.B. Tauris, 1996).

In the Highest Degree Odious by Brian Simpson (Oxford University Press, 1995).

Searching for Lord Haw-Haw by Colin Holmes (Routledge, 2016).

The Fascists in Britain by Colin Cross (Barrie & Rockliffe, 1961).

17

THE NATIONAL SOCIALIST LEAGUE

The break with Mosley was bitter. Neither man ever forgot or forgave. Neither was ever again able to speak of the other without contempt and loathing. It is lucky for them that the fascist state they dreamed of never came into being. One of them might not have lived long.

Mosley regularly accused John, as well as William Joyce, of misappropriating BUF funds, quite wrongly as far as anyone has ever been able to discover, while they regularly pronounced him delusional.

According to a police report, Joyce's friend John McNab, still on the BUF staff, went to see Mosley to complain about the treatment of Joyce:

> He thought Mosley was going to strike him or have a seizure. Mosley went livid and thumped the desk and shouted that Joyce was nothing but a traitor; that he would never rest until he had broken him; that he would roll him in blood and smash him. He also threatened he would smash [McNab] and everyone else who acted as a traitor.

McNab, apparently, returned to his own room, and a uniformed guard appeared. He was given ten minutes to clear his personal belongings and then escorted to the main entrance.

Mosley had another visitor, 23-year-old Sylvia Morris, a clever, attractive, thoughtful young woman, one of the BUF's few rising stars, a friend of John and Anne and one of Anne's few really close women friends, who probably had an affair with William Joyce around that time. Mosley seems to have decided to try to bully her. Sylvia wrote to her sister:

> The first thing he said to me when I got into the room was "I suppose you realise that by rights you can no longer be a member of this movement" ... There followed an argument on which I admit I was beaten (I am told that one invariably is with Mosley). He then made the statement that neither Beckett nor Joyce had ever disagreed with nor criticised his actions in conference or in private until they were removed from the salaried staff. I knew this was not true so I said "for that I have the word of two men against yours." ... He said: "Then if you cannot believe the words of your leader there is no sense in your remaining a member of this movement – you are expelled."

Very soon after the split, Lord Camrose, the owner of the *Daily Telegraph*, sued the fascist weekly, *Action*, which John had edited, for suggesting that he was, in the words of Camrose's barrister, "a Jewish international financier with no loyalty to the crown and no sense of patriotism, and that in his conduct of the Daily Telegraph he allowed his duty to the public to be subordinated to his own financial interests".

The first six paragraphs of the article John had written were what many people today would want to say about media ownership: that the places people get their news are controlled by "the great financial houses of the city of London" and wealthy newspaper magnates. But the seventh paragraph says: "The Berry family is of Jewish extraction and has intimate contacts with international Jewish interests."

As it happens, Camrose was not Jewish. Roland Oliver KC for Camrose said there was nothing derogatory in calling a man a Jew or a Jewish financier, but if one proclaimed that all Jews and in particular Jewish financiers were unscrupulous and dishonest and then called a man a Jewish financier, it was defamatory.

John was not called by either side. He was not worth suing, since he could not pay any damages, and Camrose's principal target was Mosley. But John turned up in court anyway and asked to make a statement.

He said he had been given the information about Camrose by "a titled friend" (obviously Mosley):

> Unfortunately I have discovered that the facts were not true ... the two cardinal facts that matter above all are entirely wrong and to my mind they were two of the deadliest insults.... To tell a man that he is a Jew, to tell him that his financial interests were far greater outside this country than inside, are two of the greatest insults that can possibly be offered to any man.

Mosley's lawyer had attacked him.

> Mr Gardiner said that so far as he knew, my only qualification for journalism was a scurrilous pen.... I have been using my pen and earning the bulk of my living in journalism since I joined the staff of the Harrow Observer at the age of 16 ... I have had nearly 2,000 articles in the published press ... it is as unfair and unreasonable as for me to say, without any other knowledge of Mr Gardiner, that the only qualification for his silk gown is the gift of petty impertinence.

Then he hit back. Gardiner had claimed that Mosley had nothing to do with the article – he had flu when the paper went to press. But that was a lie: Mosley had seen and approved it.

Camrose was awarded £20,000 damages and costs. *Action*, still owned by a £100 company, went bankrupt, and Beckett told the press of his disgust at a man who could hide behind a £100 company – the very scheme he and Mosley had contrived together as a "libel-proof front".

Neither John nor Mosley came out of this affair with any credit.

Mosley, who had used anti-Semitism cynically to buy members and loyalty, now wanted the odium for this decision to fall upon his followers. It was all the fault of his scurrilous editor, and he did not know about the article, he claimed, but everyone who ever edited one of his publications has said he was the most hands-on proprietor, interfering at every stage and signing off every page personally. Whether or not he instigated the article, he certainly approved it.

John wanted to damage Mosley, and he succeeded. But his second objective was to establish that it was libellous to call someone a Jew. It was the idea of a brilliant propagandist whose brain had been scorched and distorted by disappointment and hate, and it was utterly, irredeemably wicked.

Both men thirsted for revenge.

Fascism had become a far, far bigger part of Anne Cutmore's life than she had expected when she went there as a temporary secretary to Robert Forgan, when I think she knew next to nothing about it.

She could hardly go on working at the BUF, so she and John were both out of a job, and neither of them had any money. She used (presumably) her experience of newspaper production at the BUF to get a job with Corvinus Press, which published rare books. She saw all the books through the press.

I don't think she ever had a job she liked so much, and the published history of Corvinus Press makes clear that she was its key figure. Corvinus was a private press established by Viscount Carlow in Red Lion Court, off Fleet Street, in 1936. She joined him then, and stayed until the outbreak of war in 1939.

Carlow was a keen book-collector, amateur linguist and typographer, and he grew to rely on Anne. He was friendly with many leading literary figures, some of whom allowed him to print their works at his press, so he published new work by T.E. Lawrence, James Joyce, Wyndham Lewis, Edmund Blunden, Stefan Zweig, Walter de la Mare and H.E. Bates. His taste in binding was individual, and he generally produced a few special copies of each book which he had bound by a leading craft bookbinder. I still have a few of them.

John, I think, waited for something to turn up. Anne, seeing him flailing around, told him that he should write his memoirs. He wrote them, very quickly, with all his usual verve and lack of restraint.

They are very strange. At one level, they are the work of a natural journalist – racy, readable and anecdotal, with the sort of gossip from his days in Parliament that newspaper diarists love.

The information they give is generally reliable, and they contain authoritative accounts of major political events which are better and more detailed than you will find elsewhere. He knew every politician who mattered in the 1920s, and many of the most important actors and theatre directors, and has something interesting to say about most of them. The memoirs are a political historian's treasure trove, and a good resource for theatre historians too.

They are very selective in what they cover – though that's hardly surprising: show me a politician's memoir that is not.

But the really odd thing about them is the personal information. There isn't any. There are a couple of sentences in the introduction about his parents, both of which are, to put it mildly, misleading. Also in the introduction is thanks to "my wife Anne Beckett" who, he says, has given the memoirs what literary style they possess; and that is the only mention of any of his three wives.

It is as though Helen and Kyrle never existed. Detailed accounts are given of many events in which either Helen or Kyrle were active participants, but they are never mentioned. They have been written out of his history, just as he was written out of the BUF's history, just as William Joyce wrote his first wife out of his history.

Anti-Semitism is written out too. There is hardly any anti-Semitism in his memoirs, if you discount the odd code, like "his original name was not Day", which hardly counted in those days. One of the politicians he most admired, he writes, was the Jewish Leslie Hore-Belisha, who by then was a hate figure among anti-Semites.

The memoirs begin after he leaves the army, and even then tell us only that by the time the war ended he had "a fairly good job" in Sheffield – I have had to find out myself that it was in his father's trade, as a draper. They tell us nothing about how he earned his living before he went to work for Attlee.

It's what he wanted the world to know about him in a brief few weeks of 1938, when I think he was ready to put fascism behind him. He wanted to be remembered as a parliamentarian, not a fascist.

The admiring passage about Hore-Belisha contrasts strangely with the view of Collin Brooks, the editor of *Truth* – the pro-appeasement magazine controlled secretly by Conservative Central Office. Brooks wrote in his diary in 1939, when Hore-Belisha was Secretary of State for War:

> On his visit to the front ... he arrived arrayed like a Bond Street bum-boy, even wearing spats. They took him through all the mud they could find and tired him out. At the chateau there were two privies, one upstairs which was civilised with running water and one outside which was primitive. They concealed from His Majesty's Secretary of State the existence of the civilised one, so he excreted in extreme discomfort. He repeated some remark that Winston, he said, had made in a cabinet ... which annoyed somebody, coming from this pushing Jew-boy.

Hore-Belisha seems really to have got up the noses of the anti-Semites. One of Lord Haw-Haw's wartime broadcasts promised bombs on Warren Farm, Hore-Belisha's home and farm near Wimbledon, and a note in the leading pro-Nazi Admiral Barry Domvile's diary on 10 July 1938 says: "I object to paying for police protection for this Jewish Don Juan." He seems to have found it terribly upsetting that Hore-Belisha owned this farm – he keeps mentioning it in his diary, and at one point he writes of how he got some young friend to take scarlet paint and deface the farm sign.

So it is especially strange that John should write about him with admiration and affection in these very strange memoirs, now housed in the library of the University of Sheffield, the city where his strange political journey began.

Writing them whiled away the time while waiting for something to turn up. What turned up was William Joyce, with a pot of gold.

Joyce had planned for this situation. In January 1937, well before the great split that spring, his friend John McNab was writing to the American poet Ezra Pound on National Socialist League (NSL) notepaper – even though the NSL did not yet exist – to express his exasperation about the "total torpor of English people", who would never be stirred politically until "a big bolshie comes & whacks them on [the] head".

The pot of gold came from Alexander Scrimgeour, a rich admirer of Joyce's who was said by MI5 to have contributed at least £11,000 to BUF funds. Scrimgeour was willing to fund a new fascist party fronted by Joyce and Beckett. Thus was born the National Socialist League.

Within a few months A.K. Chesterton, too, had left the BUF. The NSL published his pamphlet attacking Mosley, and he spoke at several of their meetings.

Gossip in MI5 had it that Bill Allen helped fund the NSL. He split with Mosley after a quarrel over money, and his Security Service connections begin about this time.

Those interested in Bill Allen catch up with him again in 1956, when MI5 was at last closing in on the Soviet agent Kim Philby, and Philby had been fired from the Foreign Office. Allen, back on the family estates in Northern Ireland, offered Philby a bolthole, and Philby stayed with Allen for several months, out of the eye of the storm. He was also for a time MI6 Head of Station in Ankara.

Perhaps the NSL also had Nazi funds from Germany, as Mosley had done. If so, they were not very substantial and they quickly dried up. Certainly Christian Bauer, a German journalist who had covered London for several papers including Goebbels's *Der Angriff*, attended its launch; and John had written to him giving an account of the split with Mosley, saying he was anxious that "our German friends should know the truth". Later that year, Bauer returned to Germany for a holiday and the British authorities refused to allow him to come back. Joyce stayed in touch with Bauer, signing off his letters "Heil Hitler".

Anne loyally tried to like John's new hero William Joyce, but she only saw a small, square, pugnacious man drinking constantly to keep away the pain behind the eyes. Her younger sister Jo saw a man who tried too hard to please: "I was introduced to him once and he said, oh, I've heard of you, of course, and of course he hadn't at all."

One old BUF hand recalls going to see them in their Vauxhall Bridge Road office:

> Up several flights of uncarpeted stairs. The HQ was on the top floor in a single room, also uncarpeted, the only furniture a desk and two or three chairs. In a corner of the room were a couple of piles of leaflets. When I went in, having knocked on

the door, both Beckett and Joyce were there. I told them I wanted to hear their side of the argument. They sat me down and for the next half hour they explained the policies in great detail.

A few weeks later the same man saw, at a street corner, a portable platform with one of them (he could not remember which) standing on it and speaking, and the other heckling – a way of trying to attract an audience to an open air meeting. "What a terrible comedown from the great meetings I had heard them speaking at!"

But Joyce's anti-Semitism was by now so violent, bitter and obsessive that it frightened away both John and Chesterton, neither of whom were particularly squeamish about such things. Joyce's attitude to the danger of war worried them too. At one meeting, Chesterton reported:

> He brought the meeting to an end by calling for the National Anthem to be sung. That done, he shouted the Nazi cry of triumph Sieg Heil. I did not attach much importance to the episode, if only because the unpredictable little man was quite as capable of closing the meeting in Icelandic or Old Norse, both languages, incidentally, which he had mastered ... [At another meeting] I expressed my concern at the growing danger of war. Joyce arose vehemently to dispute my contention. "There will be no war," he thundered. "I trust Adolf Hitler to see to that." Something had happened to Joyce's clarity of vision.

Perhaps Joyce had changed: he had parted from his wife in 1936 and shared a flat with his friend John McNab, who had left the BUF with him, and he was drinking heavily. His wife Hazel said he was "terrible to live with", had a "vile temper" and was often "very sarcastic".

Rather like John, he married his second wife, 24-year-old Margaret White, five days after Joyce's decree absolute, on 13 February 1937, and she moved into the home he shared with John McNab. Joyce appears on the marriage certificate as "University

Tutor (retired)" and "of independent means". Like my father's marriage certificates, and John's mother's, it was largely a work of fiction.

McNab, Joyce's closest friend, was about Joyce's age, a tall, thin product of public school and Oxford, whose "Jolly Judah" column in the *Blackshirt* had concentrated on attacking Jews. "Master" as Joyce called him was the son of a distinguished Harley Street ophthalmologist who had been bayoneted to death in November 1914 while attending the wounded at Messines.

After failure in business he became a schoolmaster, and joined the BUF in April 1934 aged 27, working alongside Joyce in its propaganda wing. They shared passions for alcohol, chess, classical music (particularly Wagner) and literature. They also had sporting interests, Joyce in boxing, McNab in mountaineering. McNab hero-worshipped Joyce.

But John had looked over the abyss, and, quietly, he parted from Joyce. Joyce wrote to his members to tell them of "the resignation of Mr Beckett, who felt that greater moderation was necessary, especially in relation to the Jewish problem".

The NSL was declining irrevocably. Joyce was having constant rows on the telephone with his first wife Hazel, who, with her new husband, had remained loyal to Mosley. She was now refusing to allow him to see his children. The oldest, Heather, told me of happy weekends they had spent in his flat, and how, curiously, he used to tell her tales of German mythology.

Heather's parents parted in 1935, when she was seven. At first she told me that she saw him most weekends but one day her mother said: "I don't think you should telephone Daddy any more. He was so rude to me last time we talked." "He wasn't rude to me", said Heather, but not aloud.

Scratching around for a way to earn a living, Joyce found his way to Gabbitas Thring in Sackville Street, off Piccadilly, a firm which for generations has provided teachers for private fee-charging schools and tutors. He didn't, he said, want to teach any Jews.

Notes on sources

Diaries of Admiral Barry Domvile, housed in the National Maritime Museum.

Fleet Street, Press Barons and Politics: The Journals of Collin Brooks 1932–40 edited by N.J. Crowson (Cambridge University Press, 1998).

Lord Haw-Haw: The Full Story of William Joyce by J.A. Cole (Faber & Faber, 1987).

Searching for Lord Haw-Haw by Colin Holmes (Routledge, 2016).

The Corvinus Press: A History and Bibliography by Paul W. Nash and A.J. Flavell (Scolar, 1994).

18

THE ANTI-WAR FACTION

We tend to think that from the moment Hitler took power in Germany in 1933, the Second World War was inevitable. It did not seem so at the time. The generation of 1918 splintered in extraordinary and unpredictable ways, and a substantial section of it was against fighting Hitler.

In 1914 many of them had rushed loyally to the trenches to defend civilisation against what they were told was a German antichrist led by a mad and evil Kaiser, only to discover afterwards that they had been told lies. So why, they reasoned, should they now rush out to fight because the same elderly and comfortable statesmen told them about a German antichrist led by a mad and evil Führer?

Fascists, socialists, right-wing conservative peers and pacifists united against the threat of another war, and were joined (and sometimes, it seemed, almost outnumbered) by a set of grubby spies and *agents provocateurs* from MI5.

John's next creation was the British Council against European Commitments (BCAEC), founded at the time of Munich in 1938 and bankrolled by Lord Lymington, a Conservative MP between 1929 and 1934 and later to become the Earl of Portsmouth.

Lymington had been a leading figure in English Mistery, a right-wing group of wealthy farmers and landowners which praised "tradition" and "race" and condemned "moneyed interests" and "aliens" (no prizes for guessing who those were). In 1936 English Mistery had split, and Lymington now led its more pro-Nazi faction, The English Array. Lymington believed that a war against Germany "would benefit no one but the Jews and the international communists".

John often took something of value from the people with whom he associated, and from Lymington he took an abiding belief in organic farming and a hatred of farm chemicals. I expect he also told his new landed friends, in his loud, cracked, street-corner orator's voice, all about the Cheshire Becketts and his "yeoman ancestry", and, like the English gentlemen they were, they hid their contempt beneath polite expressions of interest.

John was secretary of the BCAEC. The socialist who had fought for starving miners and East End slum dwellers had come a very long way in a few years. He also, presumably, produced the one-off newspaper on 1 October 1938 welcoming Chamberlain's trip to Munich to confer with Hitler, though it was not done with his usual flair. It was headed, in huge capital letters, "WAR CRISIS", and its lead headline was:

BRITAIN ON THE BRINK OF DISASTER!!
PATRIOTS! SMASH THE WAR CONSPIRACY!

It also contained an article called "What War Means to Women", signed simply A.C.:

In the spring of 1918, my father came home after ... service in France. A quiet man, and a scholar, he returned a shell-shocked and physically ruined man, who could neither recognise a neighbour nor write his own name. At the end of fourteen days leave he went back to the battlefields of the Somme, to be blown to pieces by a shell.

Her heartbroken mother, wrote A.C., had then been forced to work in a kitchen to feed her three children while the War Office quibbled about her pension, and then struggled to bring up the children on the meagre pension ultimately provided.

A.C., of course, was Anne Cutmore, and the story was true, but someone got hold of her article and put a lie in. According to the article as printed, the kitchen Anne's mother worked in belonged to "one of the Rothschilds". Many of the anti-war faction were unable to see any bad thing that did not have Jews at the bottom of it.

The newspaper's appeal was to avoid a repeat of 1914–18, and a powerful appeal it was too. An article bylined "A.K. Chesterton M.C." began: "After 20 years of the fullness of peace you will now be suitably fattened for the slaughter which last time you were fortunate to escape."

John Beckett's article recalled Ramsay MacDonald saying at a meeting in 1918 that the dismemberment of Germany and Austria was laying the seeds for future wars. "At the same meeting Jerome K. Jerome talked, amidst great applause, of 'the devil's kitchen at Versailles brewing the bones of the future's youth'." Yet now, "with the exception of Jimmy Maxton and his ILP group, they are all clamouring for another 'war to end war'."

In poured the leading lights of the far right. Major General Fuller and A.K. Chesterton joined. So did Admiral Sir Barry Domvile, a former Director of Naval Intelligence and the founder of the biggest and most successful pro-Nazi group called The Link.

Domvile's racism was of the upper crust military sort. "Spoke on Anglo German affairs and a dirty little Jew called Leon got up afterwards and made a speech about his beastly race instead of asking questions", he wrote in his diary on 5 April 1938. He wasn't even sure about the dark-complexioned Mosley, who did not "look English ... but a touch of something east of Suez. Perhaps his ma stayed out late."

Domvile had visited Germany with his Anglo-German Fellowship in 1936: "Standing in the crowds I saw HITLER arrive – drive past standing up and looking A1 – terrific reception of Heils – absolutely genuine – I looked at all types of faces to see – they worship him ... Hitler spoke very well." He was briefly introduced to the Führer: "We shook hands and I looked into alert, magnetic, honest eyes." It was only spoiled for him by the presence of John's old nemesis,

Labour's Clifford Allen: "Dirty little abortion Allen has arrived – I wonder he has the cheek to accept German hospitality."

A year later a man called Paul von Shwaback came to see him: "He is a half Jew and has just been refused permission to marry an Aryan – he thought my great influence with the German Govt. could help!!... I did feel sorry for him – the way of the Jew is hard." The next year the young man died – Domvile did not record how, but wrote in his diary: "My poor young Jew. Very cold." The last two words referred to the weather that day.

He was in close touch with the British Ambassador in Berlin, Sir Nevile Henderson, who was doing his best to avert war, as well as Joachin von Ribbentrop while he was German ambassador in London, and he exchanged regular letters and telegrams with Himmler.

From the NSL came William Joyce. From the Imperial Fascist League, the most extreme of them all, came Arnold Leese, who had always refused to have anything to do with Mosley, whom he denounced as a "kosher fascist". Leese, a former vet, had been inspired to an anti-Semitism even more violent and obsessive than William Joyce's, partly by disgust, apparently, at the kosher method of slaughtering animals.

In too came the members of all the strange pro-Nazi and anti-Semitic bodies which sprang up in the 1920s and 1930s, some of whose names bear witness to the presence of swivel-eyed loons: the Nordic League, the White Knights of Britain, the Militant Christian Patriots, British Vigil, The Britons, The English Array. The most mainstream was the Anglo-German Fellowship, which attracted some respectable names.

From the left came Jimmy Maxton's old ILP chum John Scanlon, as well as Ben Greene. A cousin of the novelist Graham Greene, Ben Greene had known John back in the early 1920s and, like John, had been close to Clem Attlee, who was godfather to his son. In the 1930s Greene ran a successful campaign to change the Labour Party's voting system so as to give less weight to the views of the trade unions and more to the views of the ordinary Party member. It was an important battle, making Greene for a time a key player in Labour Party politics and enabling Attlee, now Labour leader, to bring in much-needed reform.

Greene's importance in the history of the Labour Party has been overshadowed by his subsequent association with other former Labour Party left-wingers like John Beckett and John Scanlon. He resigned from the Labour Party in 1938, encouraged by John Scanlon who wrote to him: "I do not regret having made my break."

Greene was an enormous man, six feet eight inches tall and broad and fat to match. He had been at Berkhamsted public school at the same time as A.K. Chesterton. Ben and A.K. hated the place, and Greene had a sort of constant melancholy lying underneath his surface panache.

His size made him feel something of an outsider. He was a Quaker and a pacifist, and had done famine relief work with the Quakers in the Soviet Union and Germany. His family despaired of his melancholia.

Anne thought he was always running away from himself. She said: "If Ben was in London he would say he could not stand it, and rush off to Scotland. But then he couldn't stand that either, because he took himself with him."

With Ben Greene came much of his family: his sister Kate Greene, and his brothers Felix and Edward Greene, the latter known in the family as Tooter, as well as their German-born mother Eva Greene. Edward complained that John "had Ben very much under his influence". These were "the Hall Greenes" from one end of Berkhamsted, the ones whose ancestors had made money in commerce. The other end of Berkhamsted boasted their cousins "the School House Greenes", who included the novelist Graham Greene and the future BBC director general Hugh Carleton Greene, the sons of the headmaster of Berkhamsted School, Charles Greene.

The BCAEC, in fact, was a front organisation for every fascist, neo-fascist and anti-Semite in London, and a way in which they could link up with socialists, pacifists and anyone else who might be recruited to the anti-war cause in the wake of the 1938 Munich agreement, when Prime Minister Neville Chamberlain returned from meeting Hitler and announced "peace for our time". The BCAEC lasted only about six weeks, but the coalition it represented stayed more or less together until most of the leading figures were imprisoned.

After Munich, Lymington bankrolled a new monthly magazine, the *New Pioneer*, which John edited. It tried to be the thinking right-winger's paper – a kind of *New Statesman* of the anti-war faction. "Let us not blind ourselves", it editorialised with studied moderation just after Munich, "to the fact that something of the old Prussian spirit of Weltmacht is still extant, and we must be prepared for any eventuality if the present regime of Herr Hitler should be overthrown."

It contained literary and theatre criticism by Anne Stone (a pseudonym for Anne Cutmore) although the review of a film of Gilbert and Sullivan's *The Mikado* was naturally signed J.B.: "It cannot possibly injure the susceptibilities of even the most traditional Gilbert and Sullivan follower." It offered several pages of reviews of political books, many of them signed A.K.C. But John chose to review a biography of Ramsay MacDonald by MacDonald's former Permanent Private Secretary, L. MacNeill Weir.

Weir was unsparing about his old master, writing that everyone of any decency and humanity pleaded with MacDonald to raise the allowance for the child of an unemployed man. John wrote:

> On December 3rd 1929 Miss Jennie Lee and I moved an amendment ... to increase this figure. Not only Mr MacDonald, but Mr Attlee, Mr Greenwood, Sir Oswald Mosley and some 200 other Labour members voted against any increase, and in the 37 who voted for "decency and humanity" the name of MacNeill Weir was conspicuous for its absence.

Ben Greene and John Scanlon also offered disillusioning reminiscences of Labour Party politics, and Major General Fuller offered gloomy assessments of Britain's military strength.

It cannot have been easy, even with memories of the First World War in your mind, to enter 1939 still believing in the goodwill of Adolf Hitler, after the destruction of the synagogues and Jewish shops and businesses on Kristallnacht and the invasions of Austria, Czechoslovakia and Poland, but John Beckett and his friends and associates managed it. Ben Greene actually went to Germany to see persecution of Jews for himself, and came up with the extraordinary idea that the way to help them was to send money into Germany for them. That this would have been confiscated at once, as the Jews' own property had been confiscated, does not seem to have occurred to him.

They kept it up even after Hitler's march into Prague in March 1939. In fact, the very next month John founded his last political party, the British People's Party (BPP), bankrolled this time by the Marquis of Tavistock, the future Duke of Bedford.

This was quite unlike all the other fringe anti-war groups at the time, with their predictable right-wing enthusiasms for the English countryside, class system and racial purity. Tavistock was an enthusiast for social credit and for monetary reform, and the BPP put social reform at the top of its agenda. It rejected fascist totalitarianism, insisting that change must only come about in the democratic parliamentary way, and John was now saying that he was no longer a fascist.

He had, I think, at last realised, as Churchill once put it, that "democracy is the worst form of government, except all those others that have been tried from time to time". Mosley, he said later in his appeal against imprisonment, had cured him of dictatorships:

> One feels one must put up with this one-man dominance for the sake of the objective, then when you get inside it cures you of all that. You realise you must have democracy, otherwise you get palace politics ... A leader sitting in a room in the palace by himself, as happened in the bad old days with kings, with the courtiers intriguing in the outer rooms.

Many of the BPP's ideas would not have been out of place in a left-wing party, and its leaders had started their lives on the left: John Beckett, John Scanlon, Ben Greene. They married this, however, with a delicate dose of anti-Semitism.

This was not to be the raucous hate of a Joyce or a Mosley. At its inaugural meeting, John, defending the BPP from barracking by Mosley supporters who condemned his weakness on the Jewish question, was quoted by the police observer as saying that more could be achieved by refraining from direct attacks on Jewry: a campaign against "usury" would bring about the same results.

"From now on," writes Richard Griffiths, "we shall find the terms 'usury' and 'money power' used continually by people such as Beckett and Greene, as a coded reference to Jews, to be understood by their members." It joined the other code-words for Jews which had been common among British anti-Semites for decades: aliens, cosmopolitans.

It enabled John to claim, unconvincingly, that anti-Semitism was no part of his politics. Asked "do you consider antisemitism to be a form of anti-capitalist protest?" he had replied:

> I am not in favour of antisemitism and never have been. I cannot say whether antisemitism is a form of anti-capitalist protest. If it is, it is extremely ill-informed, as if every Jew disappeared tomorrow, the finance-capitalist problem would still be with us.

The month after the foundation of the BPP, May 1939, saw the first appearance of the Right Club, started by the Conservative MP for Peebles, Captain Archibald Maule Ramsay, another aristocratic back-to-the-soil pro-Nazi and anti-Semite. If the BPP was designed to take the anti-war message to the left, the Right Club was to take it to the right. Its first object, wrote Captain Ramsay, was "to enlighten the Tory Party and clear it from any Jewish control".

Its second meeting, on 10 July 1939, ran into trouble. "Ramsay's meeting at Wigmore Hall cancelled by management at the last moment", Admiral Domvile confided to his diary on 10 July 1939. "The power of these bloody Jews is alarming."

That month, the BPP put up a candidate at the Hythe by-election, to fight on an anti-war ticket: Harry St John Philby, who had a long association with the Middle East, starting in Iraq during the First World War. Arabists do not, of course, have to be anti-Semites, but many of them are, and Philby was.

Today St John Philby is much less well known than his son Kim, who, it later transpired, was at this time embarking on his career as a Soviet spy at the heart of the British establishment. Kim Philby had also worked for the Anglo-German Fellowship in order to spy on it, publicly breaking with left-wing friends so that he could do so, and associating closely with people like Domvile and Fuller. The anti-war camp was stuffed full of spies, English, German and Soviet. Without them there might not have been enough people to get any work done.

John was the election agent, responsible for trying to mould the strange coalition of racists and pacifists that turned up in Hythe to support Philby into some kind of campaigning machine.

Domvile turned up to speak for Philby, and noted in his diary:

> Not a very big afternoon meeting – Hythe is sticky – about 50 or so. [Ben] Greene in chair – he, I, Philby spoke ... Tea with the Becketts at their hotel... A lot of BU [Mosley's BUF had been renamed] are helping Philby ... A big meeting at 8 pm – several hundreds – very appreciative. Beckett, in the chair, spoke awfully well – the Philbys – self – Greene – questions – over at 10 – an excellent meeting.

John had not forgotten the lesson he learned from those early ILP meetings: get it over before the pubs close. "Mrs B is a nice little thing", added Domvile.

"Pudd" (Domvile's name for his wife Alexandrina) is "much struck with BPP – prefers it to BU". She had been a fervent Mosley fan. She was 46; her husband was 60. Ten days later they had dinner with Mosley; she sat beside the Leader and he flattered her with his attentions: "Pudd resumed her allegiance to BU and deserted BPP!"

What on earth was John thinking? He had never taken any particular interest in the Middle East, or in land reform. Even with his catholic tastes in human beings, he cannot have been excited about the snobbish, dim right-wing grandees he had to work with, even less that of the pacifists whose support he had to try to obtain.

He had not, this time, found a leader. Lord Tavistock was no powerful and brilliant politician like John Wheatley, no glittering charismatic figure like Oswald Mosley, not even, as William Joyce had been, a man with sufficient force of personality to enable John to imagine himself, if he tried very hard, in the presence of greatness.

Was he thinking single-mindedly about the cause, putting in the same work rate and the same passion that he had once put in for Clement Attlee among the slums of Limehouse? Apparently not. In Hythe, he was the most neglectful election agent, unable to bring himself to make any real effort for the doomed cause of getting St John Philby elected to Parliament. Meeting Anne for canvassing, she thought she was in for a hard and dreary afternoon. But he took all her canvass cards from her, filled them in on the spot, writing "Conservative" against some names and "Labour" against others, and said, "That's done. Let's go to the pub." Even his old energy could not, I suspect, have improved much on Philby's 578 votes.

He was probably able to convince himself that he believed in what he was doing. He did have a well-grounded horror of war. More than that, he was in love, as fiercely as when he first fell in love as a soldier in 1915. He knew his past would damage Anne's future, and he could not offer her financial security.

"I know I ought to leave you alone to make the best way you can in this vale of tears", he wrote to her. "But I DON'T WANT TO. Here's the five pounds. I'll send the rest when I can." And, in another a letter dated simply Monday, 11.30 a.m.:

> Here's the dough, precious, and after great difficulty, Ann Black had no money, I succeeded in getting Lewis to cash the fiver so can now get away to Middlesbrough.
>
> Have I mentioned that I am wildly, devastatingly, most passionately and really generally very much in love with you...
>
> Bless and keep you, sweetheart, I'll only really be human again when I get back to you.
>
> Yours only and ever, John.

One day, about to rush off to another pointless meeting, he paused and looked at her. "I wish I could just go and do an ordinary job", he said, and was gone. But the Marquis of Tavistock was very rich, he needed John, and John was still broke. He took his first wife Helen out to lunch and told her of his despair.

His heart had gone out of his work. But, in the frantic and self-deluding circles in which he was now moving, no one knew it, least of all the spies.

He was, however, not quite so lost to sense as to listen to the next idea that came his way. Sometime between the Hythe by-election and August, William Joyce told him secretly that, if war broke out, he intended to go to Germany and offer his services to Hitler, using an old German embassy contact, with whom they had both associated, as an introduction.

I imagine John knew that Joyce had prepared the ground by sending the faithful McNab to Germany the previous year. On the way there, McNab stopped off in Brussels, where he got drunk and told a chance companion that he was journeying to Cologne to meet Christian Bauer, an influential Nazi. Next day McNab begged his drinking companion to forget it. Too late – the man was an MI6 informant. In Germany, McNab sounded Bauer out on what might be awaiting Joyce.

William Joyce, we now know, had advance warning on 24 August from his MI5 contacts – possibly direct from Maxwell Knight – that the Emergency Defence Regulations were to come into effect on 26 August, giving the government power to intern anyone who might harm the war effort; and that his own detention order had already been signed. Joyce and his second wife Margaret left for Berlin on the morning of 26 August.

Nine days later, on 4 September, Special Branch heard there were some people in Joyce's flat. They rushed round there to find Joyce's mother Gertrude and two younger women, one of them Sylvia Morris. What they were doing there, Special Branch seems to have been unable to establish.

Joyce, according to Colin Holmes,

> was not essentially *pushed* to Berlin. The Nazi state *pulled* him into itself. A 1938 Intelligence report presents him as hysterical, tears streaming down his face, proclaiming: "I am convinced that one day we shall see Germany the master of Europe." Britain had to be destroyed, put under Nazi tutelage before it could be revived. Joyce hoped his full commitment to Nazism would guarantee him a major role in this process.

War was declared a week after Joyce left for Germany, on 3 September 1939. At first the anti-war campaigners seemed inclined to give up, but soon they were making plans to stop the war even at this stage. On 19 September, John and Ben Greene had lunch with Admiral Domvile and then drove straight to a flat owned by Captain

Robert Gordon-Canning, another old BUF hand, now a key supporter of the BPP and an admirer of Hitler. There they met five of
Domvile's supporters in The Link.

Thus was founded the British Council for a Christian Settlement
in Europe (BCCSE) to work for a negotiated peace. Lord Tavistock
was chairman and John Beckett secretary. The headquarters were in
Ben Greene's Berkhamsted home. The intention was to create a
broad front of everyone who, for whatever reasons, wanted to see a
quick end to the war.

All the usual suspects attached themselves to it, including Harry St
John Philby and the writers Henry Williamson and Hugh Ross Williamson. But so, too, did Christians and pacifists with no connections
at all with the pro-Nazi right. The Peace Pledge Union supported it,
as did the left-wing Methodist minister Donald Soper, the sculptor
and designer Eric Gill and the writer Laurence Housman.

So did Labour MP Richard Stokes, who the next month brought
together a group of Labour MPs to oppose the war, providing a link
with some more of John's old friends, the ILP MPs Jimmy Maxton,
George Buchanan and John McGovern. McGovern especially was a
strong supporter, and it is likely that he and John met several times in
this period and co-ordinated their efforts. Landed gentry were well
represented, the outright pro-Nazis now being reinforced by some of
the foremost peers in the land.

It even brought in the anti-war faction of the Conservative Party,
and its views were faithfully represented in a monthly magazine called
Truth, which was secretly controlled by Sir Joseph Ball of the Conservative Research Department, the principal adviser to Prime Minister Neville Chamberlain, and edited by a friend of John's and A.K.
Chesterton's called Henry Newnham.

John was full of ideas for getting the anti-war message across, but
the dim aristocrats and former military grandees he was associating
with were not ideas men. "I don't like Beckett", Domvile wrote on
20 November. "He had a particularly futile proposal about acquiring
a ladies' paper. He talked such rot."

In December 1939 the BPP produced a pamphlet, "The Truth
about This War". No author was given, and historians have variously
ascribed it to Beckett, Tavistock and Greene. They are all wrong. It

has a literary style which none of these three could have managed, and it was in fact written (to a brief, no doubt) by Anne Cutmore.

John's old friend Clem Attlee saw it and was shocked by its contents. He was godfather to Ben Greene's son, and sent the boy a panda that Christmas, with which he enclosed a letter to Greene's wife:

> Frankly it strikes me as one of the nastiest pieces of pro-Hitler propaganda that I have met for a long time ... When you told me of the formation of your Party I said I thought its whole tendency was fascist. This book confirms my view. I think it would be better, if these are the views that you and Ben now hold, that we should not meet.

The next month the German government published an exact translation into German. It was a prelude to a series of "peace initiatives", one of which was a deal discussed between Lord Tavistock and the secretary to the German embassy in Dublin.

Tavistock told Foreign Secretary Lord Halifax that his soundings indicated German willingness for Czechoslovakia and Poland to have independence so long as they remained neutral, and for Germany to disarm if everyone else would and to join a reformed League of Nations. Germany, he said, is thought to want to help find a national home for the Jews.

Tavistock remained one of the few people in Britain who thought the top Nazis were people you could do business with. He had, he said, been a prison visitor, and this had brought him into contact with several "rough diamonds" like Hitler and Goering.

Halifax replied: "You suggest that Herr Hitler's breaches of faith may be explained by unsympathetic treatment. I do not think this can be so, since Hitler's breaches of faith to his own people have been flagrant and frequent."

In October Domvile started to try to bring the anti-war group together, hampered by the fact that Beckett and Mosley were not on speaking terms. They were never to speak to each other again. It seems likely that they refused to be in the same room, because all meetings recorded by MI5 contained one or the other, but never both.

When Special Branch went to see Mosley, he told them what he thought of the leaders of John's British People's Party: Lord Tavistock "a good fellow" but "woolley-headed"; Ben Greene "a good fellow but not very intelligent"; John "a crook".

The officers thought Mosley was

> immensely vain, a bad judge of men, extremely urbane and cunning. He is absolutely insincere. His chief handicap is probably his excessive vanity, which must make it difficult for him to take an objective view of any situation. It also makes it impossible for him to tolerate any other outstanding personality in his entourage.

Perhaps for this reason, negotiations floundered, and the anti-war movement fractured and splintered, as tiny extreme groups are liable to do. Ramsay, feeling dominated by Mosley, stopped meeting him. Domvile worked mostly with Mosley, reporting to him privately on his meetings with Beckett and Tavistock.

But the anti-war campaign was reinforced from two unexpectedly mainstream sources. In March 1940 three ILP MPs, Jimmy Maxton, Campbell Stephen and John McGovern, were invited to newspaper proprietor Lord Beaverbrook's home, where he put to them an extraordinary proposition. If they would introduce a "peace candidate" into every parliamentary constituency in the country, Beaverbrook would pay all the election expenses.

I think that McGovern kept in close touch with John throughout this period, but if they met, it was with great care and in secret, because the meetings do not figure on MI5's comprehensive records. John certainly introduced McGovern to Tavistock, and McGovern's support for Tavistock's peace efforts was well known.

Beaverbrook told McGovern that "the nearest approach to peace we were and will ever be able to have was when the Marquis of Tavistock tried to arrange an honourable peace".

But two months later Churchill appointed Beaverbrook as Minister of Aircraft Production, and suddenly Beaverbrook was anxious to pretend that the meeting with the ILP had never happened, which he did successfully until 1941 when McGovern revealed it.

This might explain why John always regarded Beaverbrook as one of the few truly evil men he had ever known – an opinion shared by an old friend from whom he was now estranged, Clem Attlee. I'm guessing that he first heard the opinion from Attlee, and the events of 1940 simply confirmed it for him. I do not think he ever understood how much Attlee had been a mentor, almost a father figure, to him.

McGovern was certainly willing to be publicly identified with the BCCSE, and spoke at several of their meetings, strongly supporting the "Tavistock peace proposals". At the Kingsway Hall on 3 April 1940, John chaired a public meeting at which the speakers were Tavistock, McGovern and Hugh Ross Williamson, a well-known Catholic writer and historian.

It was McGovern whom the security services were most worried about that day:

> It was one of the most seditious meetings they had ever attended in their lives, and the speech made by John McGovern was particularly treasonable. One phrase which may be quoted was: "The people must refuse to fight. When the people refuse to fight we shall get peace on the peoples' terms."

The meeting seems to have been peaceful. Both Beckett and McGovern were older and stouter, if not wiser, than when they had forced attendants to frogmarch them off the floor of the House of Commons. And the breadth of the anti-war coalition was evident that night. You approached the packed hall past communists selling the *Daily Worker*, Peace Pledge Union members selling their publications, as well as pro-Nazis selling theirs.

I suspect that for a moment, John might have believed he was on the road back to the mainstream. He even compiled, for the Marquis of Tavistock, a list of names for an alternative government. Tavistock would become Prime Minister, James Maxton Foreign Secretary, Mosley Lord President of the Council and J.F.C. Fuller would run defence. McGovern would be Minister of Labour, and Bill Allen would run Scotland.

MI5 reported that details of Beckett's alternative government might have been sent to Berlin. It's possible. It would have been difficult and dangerous, and distinctly unpatriotic when John prided himself on his patriotism, but John and Tavistock might have wanted Berlin to know that Mosley was not the only deserving cause in London; there was going to be competition for the role of Britain's Quisling.

Note on sources

Diaries of Admiral Barry Domvile, housed in the National Maritime Museum.

Greene family papers.

TNA: HO 283/26.

TNA: KV2 1510.

In the Highest Degree Odious by Brian Simpson (Oxford University Press, 1995).

Neither Fear nor Favour by John McGovern (Blandford, 1960).

Patriotism Perverted by Richard Griffiths (Constable, 1998).

Searching for Lord Haw-Haw by Colin Holmes (Routledge, 2016).

Shades of Greene by Jeremy Lewis (Cape, 2010).

19
PRISON

Anne Wolkoff was born in St Petersburg in 1902, and in 1917 at the time of the Russian revolution, her father, Admiral Wolkoff, was the Tsar's Naval Attaché in London. So he and his family wisely decided to settle in London, and in 1935 Anna began a haute couture business which attracted royalty and Mrs Wallis Simpson. Briefly successful, by 1939 her firm had gone into liquidation.

A rather more successful enterprise was Admiral Wolkoff's Russian Tea Rooms at 50 Harrington Road, South Kensington, a meeting place for Russian exiles, opened in 1923. In the late 1930s, fascists, fellow travellers and German embassy staff crowded into the small 12-seater café and exchanged gossip, and perhaps more than gossip.

The Wolkoffs were for Hitler and against Jews, and joined Captain Ramsay's Right Club with enthusiasm. Through the Right Club they met Tyler Kent, a cipher clerk at the US embassy in London and a frequent visitor to Wolkoff's Russian Tea Room.

Kent shared Wolkoff's fiercely anti-communist views, and he started to take home the most interesting of the documents that passed through his hands – and a great many did, for part of his job was to encode and decode sensitive telegrams. The most sensitive of them all were those between the new First Lord of the Admiralty,

Winston Churchill, and US President Roosevelt, which, if made public, would seriously have damaged Roosevelt's chances of re-election in 1940.

He kept the documents in his flat, and Ramsay also gave him the Right Club's membership list for safekeeping, hoping to benefit from Kent's diplomatic immunity.

Anna Wolkoff made copies of some of the cables, and passed them to Berlin through an intermediary. She then asked fellow Right Club member Joan Miller if she could pass a coded letter to William Joyce in Germany. Miller was an undercover MI5 agent; she agreed to take the letter but instead of taking it to the Italian embassy, showed it to Maxwell Knight. The letter contained advice on radio propaganda. MI5 arranged to have it delivered – there was nothing terribly secret in it.

Wolkoff always maintained she did not write the coded message to Joyce; she had been given it, she said, by James McGuirk Hughes, who had been Mosley's head of security as well as an MI5 mole in Mosley's organisation. The message offered advice on the best radio frequencies to use, plus some very crude political analysis:

> antisemitism spreading like flame everywhere all classes. Note refujews [anti-Semitic name for refugee Jews] in so-called Pioneer Corps guaranteed in writing to be sent into firing line. Churchill not popular, keep on at him as [American financier Bernard] Baruch tool ... Nearly all your friends still sound ... Family not persecuted by public but only by [Home Secretary John] Anderson who keeps Q [Joyce's brother Quentin] imprisoned without trial and got [Joyce's other two brothers] sacked ... master [McNab] teaching school again.

It asked that its arrival be confirmed by a broadcast reference to Carlyle. On Saturday 27 April 1940 German radio broadcasting to Britain commented: "We thank the French for nothing; where is their Shakespeare? Who is their Carlyle?" (Colin Holmes, *Searching for Lord Haw-Haw*).

Who wrote it? Was it the British security services? Was it Admiral Domvile? Colin Holmes makes out a strong case for fingering Joyce's admirer and friend, John McNab.

On 10 May 1940 Churchill became Prime Minister. Exactly ten days later, on 20 May, Wolkoff and Kent were arrested. It helped convince ministers that there was a fifth column in Britain, and top fascists could not safely be left at liberty. By the very next day, the British Expeditionary Force had been trapped in northern France, along with the remains of the French and Belgian armies. On 22 May, as the government prepared to snatch its army from the Dunkirk beaches, the security regulations were tightened.

And that was the day John chose to speak to a public meeting in Holborn on "Can Democracy Govern?" He attacked the parliamentary system of government and contrasted it with the efficiency of the totalitarian machine.

About 11 a.m. the next day, 23 May 1940, Kate Greene, Ben Greene's sister, bounded up the stairs of 13 John Street, near Victoria Station, which was the BPP office and which had a flat on the top floor where John and Anne lived during the week. (At weekends they lived in a small cottage in Berkhamsted rented from Ben Greene.) She was shouting, "John, the police are here!" In a well-rehearsed manoeuvre, John's secretary took the files with many of the BPP's names and addresses along the parapet and into the empty adjoining building.

That night, Anne picked them up and dumped them in the pond at Hampstead Heath. In the rush, most of John's correspondence over the years went with them.

While the documents were disappearing, John was meeting Superintendent Joss, whom he seems already to have known, and two other plainclothesmen on the landing. "John, we have come for you", said Joss.

"Have you got a warrant, and what for?" John took Joss through the formalities, to make sure his secretary had plenty of time.

"It's under Regulation 18B and here is the Home Secretary's certificate."

"What can I take?"

"You are not an ordinary prisoner. You can wear your own clothes and smoke and so on. It won't be for long."

Anne helped John to pack in their flat above the office. The police opened the empty filing cabinets, and, unsurprised, shut them again, taking what little there was to take. John came down with his suitcase and Joss asked, "Would you like to go by taxi?"

"If you pay for it", replied John, and Joss said, "That will be all right."

John and Joss went to the street to look for a taxi, while Joss's two colleagues stayed to ransack the office. John stopped the taxi in Kingsway to buy a large supply of cigarettes, and they drove on to Brixton prison.

John was sure Joss was right – it wouldn't be for long – and he had never been inside an English prison, only a Polish one. He liked new experiences. He had no idea, as the great iron doors slammed behind him, that he had seen the last of freedom and of Anne for almost four years, and that he would come out ten years older and with a prison pallor on his skin that was never to leave him, and a dark, impotent rage inside him.

He should have realised. A glance through the cuttings shows that he was one of the most hated men in the country. The day he was arrested, a Liberal MP asked the Home Secretary in Parliament not to forget that Beckett had been associated with William Joyce. The *Daily Express* report of the exchange says: "[Home Secretary] Sir John Anderson, smiling grimly, said: 'I will bear that in mind.' He did not add that almost at that moment Mr John Beckett was being arrested."

They drove into the yard and Joss took him to a little bare room with a counter at the end of it. Behind this, a small man in uniform signed for John as though he were a parcel and said, "This way, Beckett."

Now, the familiar figure of the policeman gone, doors clanging shut behind him, John began to feel very alone. He went with the little uniformed man through a long, grimy passage, on each side of which were doors which started at about two feet off the ground and were about five feet high. These were the reception cells, and John was locked in one of them. And suddenly, he was terrified. There was barely room to stand up, no room to walk, and only a small wooden ledge, about four feet long and fixed to the back of the cell, to sit on. He thought this cell was where he was to be kept.

After an hour, someone handed him over the top of the door a greasy tin with something inside which made his stomach seize up, and said, "Here's your dinner." By this time he knew he was not alone:

> Voices all round me proclaimed the presence of what my friend A.K. Chesterton has so aptly described as the "Mosley Circus". I had not heard them for three years – had I never heard them again it would have been too soon. And yet, in all their pompous raucousness, I heard them shouting comments from their various dens.

After the meal had been consumed, the door opened and another man in uniform said, "Come on, Beckett." They went along a corridor and into a small, bare room with a weighing machine and several warders. John stripped and was weighed.

"I suppose you had a bath this morning", said the chief warder, and allowed him to dress. In the next room, they shut him in another small pen for a couple of hours, then a warder took him outside and told him to strip again for the medical examination. He lined up with a few others and "an extremely shabby and weary little man shuffled in front of us with a stethoscope hanging from his shoulders and said to each of us in turn 'You all right?'"

They let him get dressed, and someone said, "Come on Beckett", and took him to his cell. His watch had been taken from him, but he heard 6 p.m. chime on a church clock. "The weary prelude to incarceration had taken all day."

An hour later,

> I had a pressing call of nature, and seeing a bell by the door of my cell, I began to ring it. It rang loudly through the hollow prison, and after intermittent ringing for nearly an hour, I heard a voice outside: "What's the matter with you?" and saw a baleful eye looking at me through a tiny peephole in the centre of the door.
>
> "I want to go to the lavatory."
>
> "Well, you don't bleeding well ring, you use the tin thing under the washstand", and with various imprecations the voice died away in the distance. Making it as best I could in the small

> filthy utensil with no lid, I settled back to look at the bible
> which was the only printed thing in the room, and examine
> the wooden board with two or three unhygienic-looking blan-
> kets on it, on which I was supposed to sleep.

He was woken the next morning by his cell door being flung
open with the cry of "slop aat".

> On looking out I saw my fellow prisoners, in various stages of
> undress, coming out of their cells and along the corridor, car-
> rying before them with careful dignity small tins just like the
> one to which my attention had been drawn the previous night.
> As I joined them, Captain Ramsay MP, whose cell was one
> away from mine, passed with his burden. The other side, Sir
> Oswald, surrounded by several miniature followers, was
> engaged in the same useful task.

John Beckett was moving into Brixton prison just as his old
friend Clem Attlee moved into No. 11 Downing Street as the key
figure in the coalition wartime government. How far they had both
travelled since those comfortable evenings over their pipes in
Limehouse!

Another former friend was becoming Minister of Economic
Warfare, and gloating over John's predicament: "Ramsay's arrest
announced by the Speaker", wrote Hugh Dalton in his diary.
"Mosley, Beckett and others also in jug. This is some compensation
for the loss of Boulogne! Ruth [Dalton's wife] says 'We had to lose
Norway to get rid of Chamberlain, and to lose Boulogne to get rid
of Mosley.'"

Other one-time friends must have noticed, then quickly got on
with something else. In the 1930s Ellen Wilkinson had embarked on
the great love affair of her life, with Herbert Morrison. John never
spoke of it, but I think that the blackest moments in his wartime
prison cell after 1940 were when he contemplated the nocturnal
activities of the man whose orders kept him locked up.

Two years earlier, reflecting on his visit to Poland a decade before,
John wrote:

> In considerable wanderings around the world I have come to consider the right of immediate trial one of the greatest assets of Englishmen. Any government having the right to keep people in prison indefinitely without trial, will abuse that right.

That is true, and no less true because John admired regimes which had that right, and did abuse it. The British government, in suspending habeus corpus and imprisoning John and hundreds of others in May 1940, had removed a key civil liberty from its people.

But the Tyler Kent affair rather forced its hand. They must all have seemed very dangerous people to have running around free at a time when the Germans had swept through Norway, Holland and Belgium, and France was on the point of surrender.

More than 700 were imprisoned, including Mosley, Ramsay, Greene, Harry St John Philby, John McNab and William Joyce's brothers Quentin and Frank Joyce.

Tavistock and Lymington remained free, presumably because they were peers, for they had done as much as anyone who was in prison, and more than most, to earn incarceration. As late as 1941 Tavistock was still telling audiences: "Very few of us have heard, or have had the chance of hearing, Hitler's case stated fairly and fully, as he himself or a close friend might state it." In March 1942 he predicted that "we shall have to overcome our objection to trusting Hitler and accept him as a feature of the post-war world."

More surprisingly, A.K. Chesterton remained free; apparently MI5 thought him "a patriot" and let him join the army. John laughed hollowly, saying that no one had been more emphatic than Chesterton about the immorality of fighting Germany. General Fuller had written to John saying that he had taken a war office appointment and could not therefore proceed with the new campaign they had planned together – an ex-servicemen's movement to ensure "that the young men who are fighting should not have the empire pawned behind their backs, as was the case last time".

John had joined the home guard a few days earlier, and no doubt rather hoped that would protect him from prison, but it didn't.

John's situation was pretty unpleasant. Not only was he locked in a tiny cell for 20 hours a day: in his brief time in the exercise yard, he was surrounded by bitter enemies, the Mosley loyalists. They looked at him, he felt, as though they longed to back him up against a wall and break his bones. He did not think the prison guards would rush to protect one fascist from attack by other fascists.

In those first few months in Brixton, he and the obsessive anti-Semite Arnold Leese became close to each other, mostly because they both, for different reasons, loathed Mosley. He recalled standing with Leese in the exercise yard and watching Mosley and his supporters walking up and down. "There goes Tom Mosley and his bunch of kosher fascists", said Leese loudly. My father told me this story admiringly, and I remarked it was a rather stupid thing for Leese to have said. "Yes, but it was very brave", he replied. "There were twenty of them and only two of us."

One day, a member of Mosley's entourage called Hector McKechnie broke away from the group, presented himself in front of John, and gave the fascist salute.

"Hail Mosley. The Leader says that at this time of danger for our nation, past disagreements should be put to one side. He offers you a place in his government in exile." John, whose many faults never included lack of a sense of humour, simply laughed. The man turned away, but returned a few minutes later.

"Hail Mosley. The Leader says, if that's your attitude, you shan't be in the government at all."

John could see the absurdity far more clearly than when he himself had compiled a list of ministers earlier in the year.

John's contempt for Mosley's dreams may have been misplaced just as they were at the time of the abdication crisis. Hitler's plans for Britain are thought to have involved Lloyd George as figurehead Prime Minister and the Duke of Windsor, the former Edward VIII, as king, with Mosley as deputy Prime Minister and the real power in the land. Mosley must have known something of this, for he always cast Lloyd George as Britain's Quisling.

If that had happened, John Beckett would have seen a firing squad before he saw the cabinet table. He knew it, telling the appeal against his internment:

> Probably more than anyone I have reason to fear a German invasion here … I can produce three reliable witnesses to tell

you that I was put on the "to be shot" list two years ago. Mosley has told these personal friends of mine, one of them known to you … My name has been at the top of that list for two years, ever since the Camrose case.

This is almost certainly right. Mosley's revenge would have been far more lethal than Morrison's.

When the blitz began that summer, and each night the air was dark with German bombers dropping their deadly cargo over London, the inmates of Brixton prison were perhaps the most frightened people in the city, for they were locked in their cells. They did not think that, in the event of a bomb falling on them, the guards were likely to risk their lives to free their prisoners.

Some of the men went to pieces very quickly in prison. Joe Beckett, former British heavyweight boxing champion and former Mosley bodyguard, had a cell close to John, and night after night John and the others could hear him crying and weeping to be let out.

John was always rather proud of the fact that he coped better than most. He did it by feeding his mind, by discovering reserves in himself which he could enter, and ignore his surroundings. He found he could read anything at all and absorb himself in it, however trite it was or however often he had read it before. When the governor stopped prisoners lending each other books, the bible and old newspapers did fine for a while.

He played chess constantly with the German in the next cell. They drew chess boards on the floors of their cells with pieces of chalk, and worked out an elaborate code so that they could convey their moves to each other by knocking on the wall. By the time they were both transferred out of Brixton they had played over 100 matches, and the German was two or three games up because his play was more careful. John approached chess rather in the way that he lived his life, with a certain flair but a fatal disregard for the messier consequences of his moves.

A radio would have helped, but his request to have one was turned down. Mosley's request, on the other hand, was agreed, and night after night he could hear Mosley's radio from a few cells away. It was too distant to make out the words. He found that maddening:

too loud to ignore, too soft to hear properly. He was not on the sort of terms with Mosley where he could ask him to make his radio louder.

Jimmy Maxton came to visit the two detainees he knew, John and Mosley, and spent an hour or two with John. The visit caused a serious row on the ILP National Council. "God's truth, Jimmy, how could you lower yourself – especially to visit that bastard Mosley?" said one of its members. John McGovern, who had known about the visit, writes in his autobiography: "I do not think any other person in the party would have got away with it so easily as Jimmy, but his personal popularity allowed him to ride the storm."

On 10 July John's appeal against internment was heard by a committee set up to hear such appeals under Norman Birkett KC. Birkett asked him about William Joyce, now broadcasting for Germany:

> Q: Joyce is Lord Haw-Haw, I am told. Have you listened to Lord Haw-Haw?
>
> A: Very often.
>
> Q: Do you confirm it?
>
> A: I cannot confirm it, but I think it is very likely.
>
> Q: Not that it matters, but we are told that it is so. We know Joyce has gone to Germany.
>
> A: He is in Germany. Of course, he was never a British subject.
>
> Q: Was he not?
>
> A: No. He was an American subject, he was born in America, but I did not find that out until after we had parted.

This exchange was the first time that anyone mentioned the defence Joyce was to use at his trial. It is almost as though John was preparing the ground for his friend.

They asked him about his letter to Christian Bauer after he and Joyce left Mosley saying they were "most anxious that our German friends should know the truth". He told them:

> Mosley had spent a great deal of time in Germany and the Germans looked upon him as being the great head in this

country for the kind of doctrine they believed in ... Mosley is
a very vindictive man if you disagree with him, he told the
press a lot of stories about us here and I expected worse in
Germany, and I was keen to see Bauer so that he might know
why we had left Mosley.

His experience with Mosley, he said, had convinced him that, after
all, governments should be democratic; and he was able to show that
the BPP constitution, which he had drafted, made it an ordinary
democratic political party.

Over a full day of questioning, John was taken through pretty well
every word he had spoken and written in the previous three years. His
account of himself, though sometimes self-serving and occasionally economical with the truth, is for the most part honest and fluent. He could
not change his private views, he said. He was not a pacifist, as Tavistock
was; he just did not believe in the rightness of this war. But he had
stopped all anti-war propaganda, and issued instructions that the BPP
was to stop it, on 12 May. The so-called phoney war was over and the
real war had begun and, "I could not go in front of an audience whose
young men folk were fighting, and take all the heart out of them by
telling them exactly what a swindle I thought they were fighting for."

So, if they were to order his release, this is what he would do:

I have enough land at Berkhamsted which I have already dug
up and cultivated ... to keep me fairly active, and I have a very
cheap cottage there which I very much like and where we live
whenever we can.

He would live there, dig his ground, join the home guard – "I was a
sergeant instructor of signals when I was discharged, I know all about
signalling, and so I can instruct in signalling."

But of course none of that mattered, and both John and Birkett knew
it. The justification for locking him up was contained in one paragraph
of an MI5 report which Birkett had in front of him, and which read:

In conversation, Beckett has been more frank. In January 1940
he stated that he was making efforts on behalf of his organisation

to get in touch with the men in the forces, so that, when the time was ripe, they would "turn their rifles in the right direction". Quite recently he has stated that he would like to join the local Defence Volunteers so as to obtain a rifle and ammunition, and he reproved his associate, Greene, for refusing to do so when given the opportunity on account of pacifist principles. Finally, he has stated that the names and addresses of members of the fifth column, among whom he ranks himself, are recorded in Germany for use when the Germans arrive.

Of course, this was terribly serious. If even half of it were true, the government would have been grossly negligent had it allowed him to walk the streets, and ought to be putting him on trial.

But not a word of it was true. He knew exactly where the first part of the story came from, and told Birkett's committee. In January,

A man I had known for some time, I had met him first in the Mosley movement, came to see me, and he told me a long story about his own illegal activities, of which I did not believe a word, and he then told me a long story about Mosley's illegal activities, of which I did not believe a word either, and then he leaned forward to me and said: "I hope you are doing something of the sort, what are you doing." He is a man I have suspected for a long time of being some kind of agent.

John had not used the words quoted, "but I am quite confident he would have gone off and said I did".

Birkett asked the name and he told them. It was James McGuirk Hughes, alias Major P.G. Taylor, Mosley's head of security and the man whom Mosley knew was an MI5 agent in his organisation.

Hughes, as researcher John Hope put it in *Lobster* magazine in 1998,

was of central importance to the organisation and development of the BUF … During the crisis which engulfed the BUF following its dismal performance in the local elections of 1937, it was to Hughes that Mosley first turned to salvage the disaster.

Hughes was Mosley's emissary to Ramsay and the Right Club, and "threw himself wholeheartedly into the intrigues in which Ramsay engaged in 1940".

Hughes was Maxwell Knight's man and Mosley's man, and on behalf of MI5, he provided lying evidence to fit up Mosley's enemies for internment.

John did not know where the second part of the story, about the fifth column, came from. We know now. It was invented by a young German who spied for MI5 called Harald Kurtz, who also provided false evidence on which Ben Greene was imprisoned.

Greene was able to prove that it was untrue, and was eventually released. But for John, the entirely false allegations reappear over and over again in MI5 documents explaining why his continued detention was necessary, with embellishments. By 1941 it was being confidently asserted that he believed Kurtz to be a Nazi agent and that he "openly refers to himself and his colleagues ... as members of Hitler's fifth column".

Another agent claimed to have had a story from *New Statesman* editor Kingsley Martin, that John had "stored somewhere in this country a supply of arms which he was not able to get rid of to Spain".

The business of spying, then as now, is full of men like Taylor and Kurtz, to whom the secret power it gives them over people's lives are all the reward they want. They do no end of harm.

John was desperate to get out. He told the committee that his whole view had changed when France fell. He added that he dreaded a German invasion, and this was certainly the truth, if only because, as he put it, "The associations I have been forced into during my imprisonment have strongly sharpened my fears of the consequences of defeat, and I am genuinely anxious to do my part in avoiding this disaster."

It didn't work. In theory, the allegations of Taylor and Kurtz were discounted, but they must have influenced the decision. "The committee considered the whole of the evidence in this case with the most anxious care", they reported to the Home Secretary. They were

> not unimpressed by the personality of Beckett, who gave his evidence in a very frank and attractive way. They entertained no doubt that Beckett was a politically minded man who held

his views with great tenacity, and was not lacking in courage in
expounding them.

But they concluded:

> The history of Beckett's political activities indicated a great
> element of instability in his character ... It was impossible to
> be quite sure that a man so unstable in his mental and politi-
> cal outlook would not be led into activities which would
> cause great trouble. The committee also considered the fact
> that Beckett had been associated with Joyce in the public
> mind ... Whilst they did not regard Beckett as a highly dan-
> gerous man, or one who would willingly do injury to the
> country's efforts, they yet felt that if they were to recommend
> his release, it would be done with very considerable
> misgivings.

In 1940, with invasion expected daily, it's hard to fault the decision
to keep John locked up where he could do no harm. All the same, as
Professor Brian Simpson has pointed out, there was no great difference between Greene's case and Beckett's, particularly because the
graver accusations against Beckett depended principally on the evidence of Kurtz.

> In fact, as one senior civil servant pointed out, the cases of the
> Duke of Bedford, Beckett and Greene were much the same,
> but in the event Greene went free, the Duke remained free,
> and the unfortunate Beckett, detained solely for his propaganda
> against the war, spent two more years in detention.

In September 1940 John heard the committee decision, and was
moved to Stafford jail. The next month he had even worse news.
With London being bombed heavily, Prime Minister Winston
Churchill brought a famous Londoner to the Home Office to oversee
the improvement of air raid shelters: Herbert Morrison. And the only
person who could order someone to be arrested or released under
regulation 18B was the Home Secretary. There were no checks, no

other legal process. The Home Secretary did not have to listen to his advisory committees and did not have to give a reason for his decision.

John and Morrison still loathed each other. Twice during the hearing before the committee, John's emotions ran away with him, and both times it was because he had somehow managed to remind himself, in passing of Herbert Morrison:

> I have known Morrison a long time, I knew him in the last war when I was a soldier and he was not, and I do find something extraordinarily wrong in a man who was a conscientious objector when he was of military age ...

It was one of the few occasions when the tribunal interrupted to bring him back to the point.

The point John had wanted to make to the committee was made in Parliament by Labour MP F.J. Bellenger, who quoted from a First World War pacifist leaflet Morrison had written:

> Go forth, little soldier. Though you know not what you fight for, go forth. Though you have no grievance against your German brother – go forth and kill him. Though you may know he has a wife and family dependent on him – go forth and slay him; he is only a German dog.

"A man who could write that stuff in the last war," thundered Bellenger, "when many of us were defending our country and he was not, is not the man to be the judge of subversion on this occasion."

Lady Davidson, who tried to do something for the 18B detainees, made some discreet enquiries in government circles and wrote to Robert Forgan:

> Mr Beckett's chances, however, are not improved by the fact that he and the Home Secretary have never been on friendly terms since – some twenty years ago – Beckett carried a vote of censure against Morrison for his conduct of the affairs of the electricity department.

John had two mortal enemies in politics. Mosley was the first, and John believed that he was still in prison because of the lies of Mosley's friend and confidante James McGuirk Hughes. Morrison was the second, and I believe he pictured Morrison laughing at him as he jangled the keys. For the first time he realised that he was likely to spend a long time behind bars. Despair mixed with a sort of black anger.

And things were not going well outside prison either. A lifetime of making enemies was coming back to bite him. His old ILP friend John Scanlon, who had been with him throughout his strange political journey, was seeing the Duke of Bedford. "Scanlon does not think the Duke will be of much use unless he can be detached from Beckett and Mrs Beckett, whom he does not trust", minuted an MI5 spy.

The governor of Stafford Prison minuted in November:

> Beckett was on report on three occasions:
>
> (a) On 14/10/40 he was reported for (1) Causing a disturbance during an Air Raid Warning and (2) Insolence to a Principal Officer on 13/10/40. For these offences he was deprived of privileges for 3 days.
> (b) On 16/10/40 he was reported for (1) Disturbing the quiet of the Prison and (2) Threatening an officer with the Governor. He was deprived of privileges for 7 days.
> (c) On 12/11/40 he was reported for attempting to pass a letter to his wife during a visit on 11/11/40. He was deprived of privileges for 14 days.
>
> His general conduct during the time that he was in my custody was such that I have every reason to suppose that he would be a nuisance in a camp and his detention at Brixton Prison as a disciplinary case would seem to be merited.

"I have twice travelled to Stafford from London," wrote Anne to the new Home Secretary,

> to find on my arrival that I could not see him because – for some action the wrongness of which he was not even aware –

he had been deprived of "privileges" which included my fifteen minute weekly interview. He is quite willing to give his guarantee not to take further part in political work for the duration of the war – and to this I would add my own guarantee and most earnest request for a reconsideration of my husband's case.

Ben Greene's relatives knew something Anne didn't – or maybe they could afford it and she couldn't. They bribed the warders. "They kept us hanging around waiting for their 'Christmas present'", says Greene's daughter Lesley von Goetz.

Notes on sources

Confidential 1946 report for Institute for Jewish Affairs on Organised Antisemitism in Britain.

John Hope (*Lobster*, 1998).

Robert Forgan's letter to Colin Holmes about JB.

TNA: HO 283/26.

TNA: KV2 1511.

In the Highest Degree Odious by Brian Simpson (Oxford University Press, 1995).

Neither Fear nor Favour by John McGovern (Blandford, 1960).

Searching for Lord Haw-Haw by Colin Holmes (Routledge, 2016).

State Secrets: The Kent Wolkoff Affair by Bryan Clough (Hideaway Publications, 2005).

The Political Diary of Hugh Dalton, 1918–40, 1945–60 edited by Ben Pimlott (Cape, 1987).

Very Deeply Dyed in Black by Graham Macklin (I.B. Tauris, 2007).

20
MR MORRISON'S PRISONER

When John was arrested in May 1940, a German invasion, for which Britain was not at all prepared, was expected at any moment. But by 1941, the justification for keeping men and women locked up without trial became thinner, especially those like John who were clearly not spies or fifth columnists.

The authorities recognised this by releasing some of the internees. But many remained inside, including most of the best-known names: Mosley, Domvile, Ramsay, Leese – and Beckett. In March 1942 a Home Office memorandum suggested that some of them should be taken off the review list and interned for the duration of the war. This should apply to Mosley, Ramsay, Domvile, Leese – but not Beckett.

John's lawyers repeated his assurances about his behaviour, and another old political friend was found to back them up, because they wrote to Morrison: "Mr Beckett is prepared to take no part in politics and he understands that Mr Frank Owen, editor of the *Evening Standard*, will guarantee this if it is necessary." Frank Owen had been briefly a Liberal MP from 1929 to 1931, and a friend of John's, before returning to journalism. He and Michael Foot wrote the anti-appeasement book *Guilty Men*.

John wrote to Morrison that he had never knowingly been associated with anyone connected with a foreign government, or done anything to help a foreign government. Yet,

> I am in a prison, and, with some slight amenities, treated like a convict. My letters and visits are severely restricted, my wrist watch and razor have been taken away and I am not even allowed to have the writing pad and pencil I brought with me. I am locked up in a cell for eighteen hours a day, cannot tell the time, and am not even allowed to leave my cell to satisfy the demands of nature. I am told to use a very small tin receptacle which makes the cell thoroughly beastly ... Does the government really desire to inflict vindictive punishment on those who disagree with it?

It did not help to discover that Mosley was no longer sharing these hardships. He spent most of his internment in Holloway, where he lived in a small but comfortable flat with his wife in an otherwise empty prison. Their son arrived with fine food and brandy which he was allowed to enjoy with them. The governor looked in, sat down and accepted a glass, remarking: "You don't often find brandy like this these days."

It had something to do with the deference due to a wealthy baronet.

The advisory committee heard John again in 1942, by which time he had been moved, after what he told Anne was "a four month nightmare in Stafford", to the Isle of Man. They spent a long time questioning him about a report that, in the prison camp where he was one of the elected "house leaders" responsible for organising one of the houses, he had said to another house leader: "Why do you keep your house so clean? It is toadying to the authorities." This, apparently, was supposed to show that he still had a bad attitude and should remain in prison. He denied it, and so did the man to whom he was supposed to have said it.

A secret Home Office minute complained that John should not have been told who accused him: "This disclosing of an informant's identity seems quite wrong, and it is only natural, now they are together in Brixton, that Hudson should deny having given the information against Beckett." MI5 had placed spies among the prisoners, so that they should never know whom to trust.

"Beckett's influence in the Isle of Man camp was found to be bad", noted Birkett's committee. "As a house leader, he condoned dirt and untidiness and he was thought to be at the root of every movement intended to embarrass the authorities. Consequently he was transferred to Brixton Prison."

Early in 1943 he had to have an operation and was allowed to spend a month convalescing in Robert Forgan's home. When he was due to return to Brixton, Forgan, who had returned to medicine after his ill-fated time in politics and worked for pharmaceuticals company May and Baker, wrote personally to Morrison to ask for an extension. John Beckett's health was still very poor, he said. He offered a financial guarantee for John's behaviour.

The prison doctor responded that the main trouble now was not the aftermath of the operation, but the heart disease, and that the prison hospital was just as healthy a place as Forgan's home. Morrison minuted: "I can only be influenced by medical evidence, and it must be medical evidence in which I have confidence" – his way of saying what he thought of his old parliamentary colleague Forgan.

About the same time, the advisory committee heard John again and were told that he had developed a heart condition in prison. It was the condition he had brought back from India with him in 1916, and the committee saw for themselves that he fainted and collapsed as he left the hearing. Forgan treated him, and again wrote asking for his release on medical grounds, offering to put him up in his own house and guarantee his good behaviour.

The committee reported to Morrison:

> Health considerations are not to be ignored, but apart altogether from these ... Beckett does now consider that there is no alternative to the course upon which the nation is set. The committee think that Beckett could now be released and they recommend that he should be released.

Home Secretary Herbert Morrison overruled them, and decided that John should stay in prison.

The committee's recommendation to Morrison was secret. All the same, some of John's friends suspected the truth. John McGovern, still an MP, wrote to Morrison that September:

> In enclosing a letter from Mr John Beckett, Brixton Prison, I ask you to seriously consider – free from personal bias – the releasing of this man … Do not allow personal spleen to operate in this case … Please do the generous thing in this case, as he will give any reasonable undertaking concerning the future.

But MI5 was determined that John should stay behind bars. An eight-page paper for Morrison, signed G.R. Mitchell (Graham Mitchell, a key MI5 figure), asking him to reject the committee's recommendation for release, began with a highly selective collection of quotes from John's pre-war articles, showing what everyone knew: that up to May 1940, he advocated a negotiated peace.

Mitchell stated that, appearing before the advisory committee, "Beckett made no secret of the fact that all he did in May 1940 was to abandon the public advocacy of negotiations, and not his view that peace ought to be negotiated." On this question he was "quite frank". And so he was. He said that he could not change his private views, but would not speak of them publicly. Mitchell was arguing that private views, even if never publicly expressed, are a sufficient reason to lock a man up.

Every letter John had written to Anne and everyone else had been opened. Mitchell boasted: "We have copies of dozens if not scores of these letters in our files." And none of them contained a seditious word, Mitchell admitted. But "it should be remembered that Beckett is not a fool, that he very much wants … to be released from detention, and that he has always known that his letters were subject to scrutiny".

So they set him up. "He thought he had succeeded in smuggling out a letter to his wife." Yet even then they got nothing on him.

> He says in the letter: "It is nice to write and to know nobody but you will see the letter" and the rest of the letter is purely personal, its tone is even more affectionate than usual, and there is no political or military comment at all.

In the absence of anything incriminating from him, Mitchell turned to Anne's letters. There was not much more there either. The best Mitchell was able to find was a plea to John not to criticise the government in case it affected his chances of release.

The only serious evidence Mitchell could find was a pro-German entry in an autograph album. The fellow detainee who offered it turned out to be another of MI5's prison spies. John told the advisory committee that this was written in a fit of temper after hearing that his previous application for release had been turned down. The committee believed him. Mitchell said that MI5 did not. He said it proved that he wanted a German victory.

Mitchell, knowing his audience, took care to point out "the virulent invective which Beckett has expressed over the past three years against the Prime Minister and the Home Secretary in particular". It dwelt lovingly on quotes from purloined letters intended for Anne in which John said unkind things about Morrison. Mitchell knew his Home Secretary.

I find it impossible to read Mitchell's paper without feeling that I have touched something unclean. It reminded me of a Comintern (Communist International) paper I read when I was researching Britain's communists, written about the same time, which began: "The leadership of the Communist Party of Great Britain contains a number of people who were formerly connected with enemies of the people."

There is the evident pleasure in the secret power Mitchell has over the life of another man. There is the assumption that it is right to lock a man up because you think that secretly, though he says nothing, he harbours unreliable opinions. Quotes are manipulated in the safe knowledge that they will not be examined publicly, and that no right of reply is available to the victim. Possessing the man's love letters to his wife is an occasion for prurient gloating.

Perhaps the creepiest thing in the document is the sly way in which it makes sure Morrison understands that John Beckett has, and expresses, a low opinion of Morrison. This does not, of course, prove that Morrison would keep a man behind bars for saying rude things about him; only that Mitchell thought he would.

Graham Mitchell, educated at Winchester and Oxford, had started his spying career in the research department of Conservative Central Office, led by Sir Joseph Ball. This, at that time, was a spy operation which had infiltrated Labour Party Headquarters; and it also secretly controlled the magazine *Truth*, which was run by neo-fascists and campaigned vigorously against fighting Germany. Sir Joseph got Mitchell into MI5, where Ball had himself worked.

Secret at the time, the document is now available in the Public Record Office in Kew, and it is worth reading in full if you are ever in danger of forgetting how fragile our liberties are. Locking people up without trial places them at the mercy of men like Graham Mitchell.

Morrison's civil servants pointed out that the government had been obliged to release Ben Greene because the evidence of the MI5 informer Harald Kurtz was found to be unreliable, so they could no longer use Kurtz against John. Nor could they use the evidence of McGuirk Hughes, alias P.G. Taylor, because the Advisory Committee had recommended that it was not safe.

This left a legal problem which John himself summed up for them:

> Everything I am accused of here, if it were all true and all proved to the hilt, would be roughly that I was concerned with two organisations and one publication which it was not in the national interest to allow to continue ... The 18B Regulation was not intended to deal ... with such cases.

A civil service brief to Morrison stated that, nonetheless, there was a case for keeping John Beckett in prison. It was true that his detention rested upon the evidence of Harald Kurtz, now known to be unreliable, but it was likely that he still privately would like to see a negotiated peace. There were, still at liberty, an ill-assorted collection of eccentrics who wanted the same: the Duke of Bedford, Lymington, the Peace Pledge Union and others:

> These people have hitherto been harmless, partly for lack of organising ability and political experience, partly because they have often been too obviously fascist, and partly because the idea of a negotiated peace has been so unpopular. It is not beyond the bounds of possibility, however, that some of them might be organised by a man such as Beckett to form a

far more effective crypto-fascist party than we have yet seen ... Beckett is opposed to Mosley and the dictatorship principle and is not, therefore, tarred with the BUF brush. He has the skill and plausibility to take advantage of such a feeling.

There was "no evidence that Beckett or the Duke contemplates such a thing". But "to release a man of Beckett's views and abilities would be to risk more than a mere increase in anti-war propaganda".

Morrison seems to have had two civil service briefs, one recommending release, the other agreeing with MI5 and recommending continued detention. Morrison wrote on one of them in his own hand: "I think the reasons are so substantial that detention is necessary."

John was a resentful and difficult prisoner in Brixton and Stafford jails and in prison camps on the Isle of Man and at Huyton near Liverpool. "His conduct in all places of detention except Brixton have been the subject of adverse reports", Morrison's permanent secretary wrote, but his fellow prisoners remember him fondly.

"He taught me to play chess in Stafford prison", recalled one old Mosleyite. "He organised a chess competition there. I was with Mosley and he was not, so we did not talk politics."

On the Isle of Man they were accommodated in old-fashioned boarding houses on the seafront at Peel, behind barbed wire. Each house elected its own "house leader" and was issued with rations.

The inmates were responsible for cleaning and cooking. John was house leader for the house containing the non-BUF people. From there he wrote to Anne:

I got your letter written in town. I am now beginning to hope for another, to wonder which day I shall see you. The illusion of partial freedom here seems to make things more acute and I have never pined for anything as I have longed to be with you again since I saw you last. It is as if the whole monstrous absurdity of that nine months in a prison cell has now accumulated and I understand why prison turns men into wild beasts.

Like every letter he wrote to her, many of them containing nothing but love and affection, this one was painstakingly copied out, word for word, for the delectation of senior MI5 officers.

"Some of the soldiers are very vicious and I fear 'accidents'", he told her.

> Two evenings ago a sentry came up to me while I was standing quietly inside the compound. As I did not move, he took the bayonet off his rifle, clicked the bolt to load it, aimed it at me and after some seconds pulled the trigger – fortunately it was not loaded. I always understood that the sentries had loaded rifles ... I reported the matter to the sergeant but no disciplinary action seems to have been taken.

He tried to write to MPs who had questioned his incarceration, thanking them, but the letters were "lost" by the censors. An internal memorandum points out that the Home Secretary had assured Parliament that 18B prisoners should be given every facility to write to MPs. So some explanation would have to be given.

In a letter to Rhys Davies MP he told the story about the soldier and the rifle. The letter never reached the MP. After it had been passed from hand to hand several times, the censors realised some account of it would have to be given. "Lost in the Blitz?" suggested one memorandum helpfully, but another writer thought that wouldn't do. "If Beckett could be sent for and told some story about holding the letter up while we investigated the story of the soldier..."

John was briefly part of an ambitious escape plan jointly organised by BUF and IRA internees. A tunnel was built under a road at the back of the camp, with the intention of finding a fishing boat to take them to neutral Ireland. John seems to have opted out at the last minute because each escapee had to get money brought in. He could only ask Anne to do this, and that would put her in danger. The organiser of the escape attempt, Arthur Mason, wrote to me: "John stood up to internment very well, except he was worried about Anne."

The escape attempt went badly wrong. The fishing boats in Peel had had their spark plugs removed to immobilise them, and the men were arrested after they had rowed several miles out to sea. Three days later, a rumour spread that they were being ill-treated by the guards, and a riot began, with John as one of the leaders. The guards started shooting, and he claimed that one of them shot directly at him, missing him by a whisker. A few days later he and several others were returned to Brixton as punishment, then to the dreadful Huyton prisoner of war camp near Liverpool.

Conditions there were primitive, but John's "spirits and gift for repartee had not been diminished despite months of incarceration", says Mosleyite Bob Row.

All the same, something very odd happened to him at Huyton:

> Rations were short and we were all more or less permanently hungry. Long before meals were due there was a steady procession three times a day to join the cookhouse queue. Having nothing to do when we reached it, we talked, and often there were arguments because there were various factions in the camp apart from mainstream BUF ...
>
> A rumour was put around in the queue ... firstly that your father's mother was Jewish and her name was Salmon or Salaman, and later in the day that his grandmother was Jewish and her name was Silver. Naturally he blew his top about all this.

Arthur Mason confirms the story. "His mother I believe was Salmon or Salaman and someone started a rumour that John was therefore Jewish, which he resented."

The rumour, says Mr Row, was started maliciously by a small group of anti-Semite extremists from the East End of London. It was also, of course, true, and it seems likely that a group of obsessive East End Jew-haters knew perfectly well that it was true. But I suppose John could not own to it now, when he relied for friendship and protection on people like Arnold Leese, who would recoil from him if they thought his mother was a Jew.

Anne conducted a relentless letter campaign for her husband's release. She was helped and supported by the socialist pacifist Lady Clare Annesley, whom she got to know well; and her principal lieutenant was the young Sylvia Morris, who had bearded Mosley in his den on John Beckett's behalf.

Sylvia, I think, was already at least half-way out of the extreme right anti-Semitic laager into which she had stumbled, but she thought it wrong to imprison people without trial, she liked John and Anne was her friend. Like Anne, she was instinctively loyal.

She and Anne became very close in the war years, writing to everyone they could think of and lobbying Parliament. Sylvia was a source of strength and humour. Anne, typically, wrapped it up in an affectionate anecdote. The two women were in the House of Lords, looking for a toilet, and they saw a door marked "Peeresses". As they were going through it, an attendant shouted "Are you peeresses?" Sylvia replied: "No, but we function" and in they went. The male attendant could hardly follow them.

William Joyce's mother Gertrude also took comfort from Sylvia's company, judging by a letter she wrote to Anne in March 1941. With one son in Germany, and two more in prison, she thanked Anne for help and support: "I cannot describe how glad we were to see you again, and to see Sylvia ... it was very comforting."

Sylvia's own letter to Morrison on John's behalf appeals to the Home Secretary "as a socialist". It took MI5 a while to work out who she was. An internal memo headed "Sylvia", Church House, nr Spalding, Lincs, reads:

> The above named lady has been writing to Anne Cutmore, unmarried wife of John Beckett, and appears to be sympathetic with these people. We would be grateful if you could let us have her surname ... and any other information you may have about her.

Anne also worked with Tavistock, who was now the Duke of Bedford, his father having died in 1940. MI5 thought she was delivering leaflets for him. The duke helped her a little financially, I think, but not much, because she was also forced to find secretarial work in London. She seems to have applied for a job at the BBC but MI5 heard about it. "We have considerable records of this woman whose husband is at present interned and we would advise that she is quite unsuitable for any form of employment at the BBC", they wrote to the BBC.

Bedford's ancestral seat, Woburn Abbey, had been taken over by the Special Operations Executive, and several times a month Anne travelled to his almost equally opulent Scottish home.

It looks as though she was left at liberty mainly so that MI5 could follow her, note the names of her associates and record her visits to the duke. She found that a member of the BPP and of the NSL, Major Harry Edmonds, seemed remarkably often to be travelling in her direction. John became convinced that Edmonds was spying; and also suspected him of taking a predatory sexual interest in Anne, which, judging by his letters to her in the MI5 collection, he was.

Edmonds was a friend of Major General Fuller. His politics stood somewhere between Colonel Blimp and Adolf Hitler, and he fancied himself as a ladies' man. During the 1930s, he founded the Wagner Society while involved with the German Zeppelin Company and coming into contact with the Wagner family. The Wagner Society continued well into the 1950s, and was always concerned with much more than musical appreciation. Edmonds had written a few novels in the 1930s, too – sub-Bulldog Drummond stuff. One was called *Red Invader,* and its title tells you all you need know about the plot.

In August 1943 John wrote a remarkably intemperate letter to Herbert Morrison. Headed "John Beckett, Political Prisoner", it ended:

> In several cases lately you have caused this type of enquiry to be made by a "Major Edmonds" and last week my wife received a most unpleasant letter from this man asking her to see him. Ever since my arrest he has pestered her in every possible way and plagued her with improper and indecent proposals. This letter is written mainly in the hope that it will supply you with sufficient information to avoid the necessity of exposing my wife to further worry and insult from this nasty piece of work whom you employ to obtain information.

Edmonds was not MI5, though he seems to have had a rich fantasy life in which he was a sort of James Bond figure, and Anne felt less animosity towards him than John did. According to Edmonds's son, she was staying in his home in Hythe, Sussex, on the night of 7 September 1940 when a bomb fell in the garden at 4 a.m.

Years later, after John's death, she was willing to have meals with him, and spend weekends in Hythe.

But I do not think she was attracted to Edmonds, though he might have wished her to be. During the war I know that there was a man she felt a strong affinity with, and I think it was Ben Greene's brother Edward "Tooter" Greene, whose wife had died young in 1936. Lesley von Goetz told me that he was in love with Anne. "I always assumed," she said, "that she was Tooter's mistress and he kept her going." Ben Greene's daughter Margaret said the same to author Jeremy Lewis. But Anne was deeply loyal. She would not leave John while he was a prisoner and he needed her.

And how he needed her. His letters make sad reading. "Could you not get a pass? Some of the others had visitors and I feel sure you would be there." "I live for a visit or a letter from you."

John's imprisonment had made him paranoid. The petty restrictions of prison life, and the complacency and occasional vindictiveness of those who had him in their power, were jangling his nerves. This must have aggravated his heart condition, which had been with him since his wartime service and which was to remain with him for the rest of his life, and was eventually diagnosed as angina.

He spent some time in the prison hospital, where Jimmy Maxton visited him, this time in secret so as to avoid the political storm which his first visit provoked. Anne remembered arriving at the hospital bed to find Maxton already sitting on it, and John turning to her and saying, half humorously, "Jimmy doesn't believe I'm ill."

They eventually let him go to live with Bob Forgan in October 1943, well after Domvile and just a month before Mosley, on conditions that amounted to house arrest, and forbidden to stray more than five miles from Forgan's home near Brentwood in Essex. Anne had asked Forgan to provide asylum for them, and Forgan's loyalty was far more to her than to him. She told Colin Holmes: "To his credit he did so, though I think he was reluctant."

Anne stayed there with him at night, but had to travel to central London to work as a secretary during the day, because they still had no money.

He hated living with Forgan. He had no work and nothing to do. He did not get on with Forgan's second wife Jan, who had met

Forgan in 1938, after he left the BUF. "Forgan's friendship with Mosley was never discussed at home. She found the whole thing very frightening, and was frightened by having John staying", her daughter Valerie Forgan told me. "When my father was at home, he and John talked politics constantly. When my father was at work John typed."

He bitterly resented the five-mile restriction, pointing out that all the other former detainees had a ten-mile radius, except Mosley who had seven miles: only he had five miles.

One day Anne came home from work and found him sitting on the bed looking as miserable as she had ever seen him. "If I had £5 in my pocket I'd get out of here", he said. She produced the £5 and they went illegally to London together and lay low in a tiny flat in Victoria. John grew a moustache to make recognition harder, and seldom or never went out. They were very happy for a few days.

Their idyll was interrupted by a call from Forgan to say that the police were searching Essex for John, and that Mrs Forgan had been unwise enough to tell the police that he was in London.

"She saw John by chance on a street in London when he was supposed to be at home, and the police asked her directly and she told them", says Valerie Forgan. "Your father was not pleased." John returned in haste to the Forgans' home and denied that he had been out of Essex. "During the interview," the Essex detective wrote to MI5, "Beckett appeared very agitated; in my opinion his demeanour showed that he had been caught out, but realising he had his freedom at stake he very cleverly avoided the issue."

Years later, I heard her mention the moustache and he firmly denied ever having grown one. I was not sure of the truth until I read the MI5 reports. Rewriting his own life became a habit.

MI5 opened all his letters, even his Christmas cards, in order to obtain ammunition with which to argue that his five-mile restriction should remain. Graham Mitchell, who had fought so hard to keep him in prison, and whose name John probably never knew, wrote:

The card sent to J.A. McNab, William Joyce's friend, contained the following verse:

> God send us men with hearts ablaze
> All truth to love, all wrong to hate,
> These are the Patriots Britain needs,
> These are the Bulwarks of the State.

Added in ink were the following words: "So Plutocracy put them in Concentration Camps."

At the end of a series of similar quotations Mitchell wrote:

> We quote the above passages from intercepted correspondence, but we most particularly request that no hint of the source of our information be given to Beckett at his hearing ... They are not apparently aware that their correspondence is subject to scrutiny.

Morrison went out of his way, in a speech in Parliament in 1943, to mention John in a debate about the imprisonment of Mosley:

> There was the case of John Beckett in connection with which a number of people approached me, not only on this side but in other parts of the House as well, to let him out ... John Beckett is a man I have known since 1920. He was a troublesome left wing member of the Hackney Borough Council when I was its leader. He is not a wealthy person; he is a proletarian gone wrong. He is what I would call a political organiser and lives as best he can.

I am sure John thought this was a coded way of telling him that Morrison had had the last laugh. But it wasn't a bad summary.

Morrison seems to have interested himself in the most trivial aspects of John's life. A decision as to whether John might be permitted to travel to London for the day to see his optician because he had broken his glasses received the personal attention of the Home Secretary; and by the time it reached Morrison, it had been considered by four civil servants.

The first, G.W. Sturt, wrote a long briefing. He said Beckett had already been allowed to London to visit his mother-in-law in hospital:

> This seems most undesirable, both on account of the very grave view taken of this man by the security services, and from the point of view of possible reactions upon political or public opinion and morale of allowing this traitor free access to London and elsewhere.

There was no justification for the word "traitor", but John could never see the document or know the word had been used.

The minute suggested telling him that if he were ever allowed to travel to London, it would be under escort and he must meet the costs. They knew he had no money, and that this would therefore ensure no further requests. Meanwhile, the request should be refused.

Morrison's minute reads: "I agree. He is being vexatious if not frivolous in his excuses. I rather liked the escort idea of Mr Sturt except his proposal to charge police expenses. Try to tighten up on Mr Beckett within fairness and reason."

After the war, when Forgan applied to rejoin the Labour Party, he was turned down because he had given John asylum in his home. Morrison, as wartime Home Secretary, had only released John on condition that Forgan would put him up. Morrison, as a key member of Labour's National Executive Committee, now punished Forgan for it.

Whether or not Morrison used his power to take revenge on an old rival – only Morrison knew whether that is true, and he is long dead – he certainly enjoyed the power he had to lock people up. But he was also subject to pressure from MI5 and his own civil servants. Their notion of the liberty they were defending seems to have been pretty sketchy, and their spitefulness considerable.

Throughout the war, Morrison was the government's leading enthusiast for locking people up and suppressing newspapers. All his colleagues seem at one time or another to have urged less draconian measures. He kept the communist *Daily Worker* closed long after most people thought it was no longer justified. Even Churchill was rebuffed when he wrote to Morrison asking for the release of the German-born Prince of Pless whose family he knew well, and offered personally to guarantee the man. Morrison wrote back huffily saying no: "I note you say you have only met him twice."

In the summer of 1940, when invasion was thought likely and a well-organised fifth column was thought to be in place, it was probably right that the government should put security before liberty. After that, ministers and civil servants found they enjoyed the power. That's a slippery slope.

It is a tribute to the Attlee government which took office after the war in 1945 that it managed to make a break, more or less, with the wartime attitude towards freedom. It could have poisoned our democracy for decades.

This account has been put together largely from the documents which the government has released. There are gaps where papers are still withheld, allegedly for security reasons. More than seven decades after the event, it is most unlikely that there could be any valid security reasons. It is much more likely that these papers contain material which would damage the reputations of ministers, civil servants and security services.

Sometime in 1944, Anne miscarried their first child. They never spoke of it.

Around him, all the old ranters who had not been to prison were getting ready for a post-war world. There had been secret meetings since 1942 of those of the usual suspects still at liberty – Bedford, Fuller, Harry Edmonds, all the rest, not forgetting the man from MI5.

St Ermins Hotel in Victoria saw a meeting on 5 December 1944 designed to found something called the National Front. Collin Brooks (editor of *Truth*, the magazine run by Joseph Ball of Conservative Central Office to oppose going to war), A.K. Chesterton, who was now Brooks's deputy, and Ben Greene were joined by a man called Waveney Girvan who ran a magazine called the *Patriot*, started by the Duke of Northumberland in the 1920s and still influential in far right circles. They planned "a patriotic and Christian movement" and the MI5 mole who reported on it speculated that they intended to hand it over to Mosley as soon as Mosley was ready to take it on.

Brooks was supposedly at the respectable end, though his views seem to differ from those of the outright fascists only in that his anti-Semitism has a cruel, snobbish edge to it. He was editor of the *Sunday Dispatch* in the late 1930s, then editor of *Truth* after the war broke out and Henry Newnham resigned the job. Brooks lived and died an establishment figure.

His diaries reveal that he was a member of English Mistery, one of the nuttiest of the pro-Nazi groups; and that he and his proprietor Lord Rothermere pro-fascists and anti-Semites long after Rothermere formally broke away from Mosley. In January 1939 Brooks celebrated the elevation of "the first Mistery Man to take cabinet office" (Agriculture Minister Reginald Dorman Smith). As war approached, his diaries are full of meetings with leading fascists, and of Rothermere's freelance attempts to prevent war by placating Hitler.

John was not there. He could not have been, of course, without risking a return to prison; but I don't think he wanted to be. He was looking for a normal job. At last, it seemed, he had had enough. He was 50. He wanted peace and a family.

Anne got some commissions to write theatre criticism for the *Queen* magazine, and had a couple of short stories accepted by the *Evening Standard* under the pseudonym Anne Stone. She found a job as secretary to the Jewish comedian and musician Vic Oliver, who was married to Winston Churchill's daughter Sarah. I suppose she must have kept from Oliver the identity of her husband.

When Anne knew she was pregnant again, she asked the Duke of Bedford for a cottage in a small Buckinghamshire village which he owned. There John fretted under his five-mile restriction, but started slowly to recover his health.

Notes on sources

Fleet Street, Press Barons and Politics: The Journals of Collin Brooks 1932–40 edited by N.J. Crowson (Cambridge University Press, 1998).
TNA: HO 45/25698.
TNA: KV 2/1514.
TNA: KV 2/1521.
Neither Fear nor Favour by John McGovern (Blandford, 1960).
Time at War by Nicholas Mosley (Orion, 2006).

21

A BIRTH AND A HANGING

In 1945 the charming Buckinghamshire village of Chenies, with its fine manor house and church, its two pleasant pubs and the River Chess bubbling over the stones in the valley below, was owned in its entirety by the Duke of Bedford, and its solid and attractive brick cottages were occupied by his tenants.

I was born on 12 May 1945, four days after VE Day, right in the centre of the village, at 29 Chenies, the two up two down cottage on the corner as the road turns right to go down to the Chess Valley. Opposite was the old wishing well which I used to stare into.

The cottage a few yards away was occupied by a very elderly lady called Mrs Puddephat, who must have been an old ducal retainer. My mother used often to visit her, and take me with her. A little farther down, on the other side of the road, lived Dick and Stella Franklin, a kindly childless couple who used often to welcome me into their house. Stella showed me how to stroke her cat properly – like many small children I was trying to stroke the creature against the grain of the fur.

My father went to work in London every day. What he did there, I neither knew nor cared, but it was part of the secure, ordinary life I had, and I was glad to see him when he came back.

As you entered the cottage, you could turn right into the big kitchen where we ate, or left and down a big stone step into the small, cosy, beamed sitting room, and one of my earliest memories is seeing my father there one evening, in his business suit, tired, in an armchair. I was cutting corners from pieces of paper with scissors and showing them to him. He lifted a smile wearily on to his face and told me what a nice shape it was.

At weekends he took me for walks in a nearby small patch of woodland. Today it's been privatised and fenced off and no one is allowed in, but then it was public land and we roamed over it, my father and I, played hide and seek, and got to know every inch of it. There was a huge hole in the ground, and he explained that this was a bomb crater, and the bomber pilot was not supposed to drop his bomb there, but he dropped it as fast as he could and turned and flew home to safety. All this was apparently part of something called The War, before which, I was given to understand, you could get real cream.

The wood, he told me, was full of fearsome brutes called turkey tigers. Turkey tigers were an inspired concept: frightful and mysterious enough to be interesting, not so frightful as to give me nightmares. In fact, in Chenies I never remember being frightened, except once and I think it is my earliest memory. I was lying in bed beside my mother, hearing my father's rhythmic breathing from the other side of the bed, when I saw a dreadful striped creature. My mother showed me that I was looking at the corner of the pillow as it peeked out of the pillow case.

No worse thing than that disturbed my peace in my first four years on Earth when we lived in Chenies, or the next two when we lived in Croxley Green, hearing my beautiful and carefree mother cooking and cleaning and singing:

Oh don't deceive me, oh never leave me
How could you use a poor maiden so?

Some children came to play in our small garden, and introduced me to little packets of crisps with a tiny blue paper bag inside. Inside the blue bag was salt, which you shook on your crisps, and no one my age thinks ready salted crisps will ever quite hit the spot.

Sunday lunch we often took at the Bedford Arms, the pub a short walk up the road, the other side of Mrs Puddephat's cottage. It was then a very small village pub with a bar and a dining room.

The three of us would walk to the pub. My parents would go into the bar for a pre-prandial drink, while I sat on the chair at the entrance to the bar with my orange juice.

They didn't leave me long – one drink, probably whisky or beer for him, pink gin for her. Then my father and I would head off to the very primitive outside toilets.

This was a treat, for at one end of the ancient steel tube which served as a urinal was a deep hole with no covering, and a small boy with reasonable aim could create a very satisfying resounding echo as his contribution hit the water far below. My father, who understood these things, always let me have the end with the hole, even if it meant waiting until another customer had vacated it.

But then risqué jokes were part of my father's stock in trade. Walking in the fields around Chenies with both my parents, I stopped to relieve myself. After some time my father said, "Come along, Francis, put it away." "Yes", said I dreamily. "Put it away, Francis, nobody wants it." I saw my mother look accusingly at my father.

It felt as though Chenies was a settled family home. I was sure my security and happiness were forever. I knew that my parents loved me with an overpowering love that had caught them by surprise. For the first 19 years of my life I was constantly warmed, and often scalded, by their love. If I had known a little of the past, I might have been more prepared for the future.

When my parents moved to Chenies, a few months before I was born, John was 51, and had no home, no money and, with one of the most hated names and faces in Britain, no prospect of getting any work. They were living on what Anne could earn as Vic Oliver's secretary, and I suppose some handouts from the Duke of Bedford.

John felt keenly his inability to keep her properly. He did not want to go back to politics. But who else was going to employ the notorious fascist John Beckett, 51 years old, whose main skill was propaganda, and who was not permitted to travel more than five miles from a tiny Buckinghamshire village?

He had a son and a grandson on the way – for Lesley's child was due about the same time as Anne's.

Anne suggested that John should revive his childhood ambition and train for the bar, but he said he was too old. She suggested that they should set sail and start a new life in New Zealand. She still had relatives there who would surely help them. But John had turned down the chance to accompany his friend Ernest Mander to New Zealand when he was a young man with the world at his feet. He was not going to set sail now, and struggle in a strange, harsh land through his declining years.

He had various surprising ideas. When another advisory committee met in 1944 to consider his appeal against the five-mile restriction, he told them that the only work you could get in Chenies was farm labouring, and his health meant that he was not up to that. But if he were allowed to travel the six miles to Watford, he could get a job. Maybe in advertising, or newspapers. Maybe in factories, fire-watching. Maybe driving heavy lorries. He got quite enthusiastic about the idea of driving heavy lorries, and the committee cross-questioned him as to why he could drive a heavy lorry, but was not up to being an agricultural labourer.

MI5 was opposed, naturally. "We regard Beckett as a potentially dangerous fascist and enemy sympathiser and are anxious that he should not have any chance of resuming political activity", wrote Mitchell. So the committee turned him down, and it was not until 1945 that he got his radius extended to ten miles.

Then he surprised everyone by getting a job, as an administrator at Shrodells Hospital in nearby Watford, now Watford General Hospital. Some of his old fellow 18B internees were very envious that crafty old John Beckett had fallen on his feet again, when no one would employ them.

When Anne became pregnant she felt her baby was taking everything away from her, even draining her brain. She could no longer find the eloquent flow of words for theatre criticism, the imagination which enabled her to write stories. She had to give up working – Vic Oliver was a demanding boss who rang the office at odd times, in order – so she believed – to check that she had not gone home.

Anne's dreams – she would be a famous actress, she would write – now came down to this: that she might have a peaceful life with her husband and child, and he might do a normal job and bring home a modest but regular wage; and she would take no more shorthand dictation. They would live humbly, below the radar, not attracting attention. They would "live small" as she put it. And they would be happy.

But one dreadful day soon after I was born, a doctor at Shrodells told John that a child in the hospital would die unless it was given bananas. Bananas were not obtainable in those rationed times, so he bought some on the black market, and they fired him.

That's what I heard, but I doubt if it's the whole story. Graham Mitchell minuted in January 1945 that Beckett had "a good job – £600 a year as assistant administrator of a hospital at Watford. This is almost certainly yet another case of Beckett's evasion of his 10 mile restriction." The spooks were rather pleased that they could get him fired, and it looks as though they did. If Anne had had her way, he would have lived out his life as a blameless hospital administrator.

Perhaps he couldn't "live small", not if there was an alternative. And there was. The Duke of Bedford wanted to revive the BPP, and wanted John back in charge.

He started going for very long walks several times a week, something he did for the rest of his life. Partly, I am sure, this was a reaction to being locked up for nearly four years. Partly, too, it must have been where he did his dreaming, where he imagined that one day the 18B prisoners would be viewed in the same light as those who had suffered imprisonment for their pacifism during the First World War.

It is not hard to imagine what he might have been thinking as he walked the Buckinghamshire countryside in the summer of 1945. VE Day was four days before I was born; and when I was just over two months old, on 26 July, John's old friend Clem Attlee was forming a government, making John's one-time friend Hugh Dalton Chancellor of the Exchequer and putting his old enemy Herbert Morrison in charge of the government's nationalisation programme.

They were preparing to do all the things that John, as a young socialist in the 1920s, had fought and worked for. Clem Attlee was to create the welfare state, so that the unemployed in Limehouse, Gateshead and Peckham would no longer starve. Nye Bevan, the "armchair revolutionary" as John had called him, was to build the National Health Service so that they need not die of treatable diseases, and build the council homes John Wheatley had dreamed of so that they need not live in slums.

Ellen Wilkinson, whose betrayal in 1929 he had found so shocking, was to implement the 1944 Education Act so as to give the poor an education and a chance to compete with the rich. Hugh Dalton, with his ingratiating ways, was to find the money for all this "with a song in my heart" as he told the House of Commons.

The army was bringing another friend, William Joyce, back from Germany and putting him on trial, and around the time I was born, John was drafting letters asking for clemency, to go over the names of everyone he knew with a title.

Joyce's defence, that he was an American citizen, failed because he had obtained a British passport, though he had lied to get it. When his friend John McNab asked if Joyce would return to the Catholic Church and see a priest, Joyce replied in words which John always quoted: "I've got into enough trouble with false passports without trying to get one into heaven."

He shouldn't have been hanged, but in the immediate post-war atmosphere there was no doubt that he was going to be. John visited Joyce in prison in June, and just before Christmas 1945, while I suppose I was sleeping upstairs, he sat down at his typewriter and wrote the hardest letter of his life.

> I feel an urgent need to write to you, yet find it very difficult to say anything very adequate to the occasion. Certainly I know you too well to imagine there is any need to offer you consolation or exhort you to courage.
>
> Our children will grow up to think of you as an honest and courageous martyr in the fight against alien control of our country.

Years later, John would run down his other old friends to me, but of Joyce he spoke only with respect and affection. That was one promise he meant to keep.

He did not want to buoy his friend up with false hope. "Some of our friends are working very hard to get a petition signed and I shall do my best to help them, but you will not be optimistic as to its results."

He added, obliquely because both men knew their letters were being intercepted:

> No one knows better than myself the sincerity of the beliefs which led to the course of action you chose. You remember we discussed the position in 1938, and the disagreement and respect I showed for your opinion then, remains.

He promised to look after William's wife Margaret. And he ended: "Goodbye, William, it's been good to know you and there are few things in my life I am prouder of than our association. Yours always, John."

Joyce wrote back, a long letter – four cramped pages, his tiny handwriting covering every part of the little sheets of Wandsworth prison paper.

> Of course I remember, quite vividly, how we discussed the situation in 1938. I do not, in the most infinitesimal degree, regret what I have done. For me, there was nothing else to do. I am proud to die for what I have done: but, on the other hand, I feel that I could well have shown you a little more courtesy and understanding than I did. I was bull-headed as usual! But I can make amends now by saying that I recognise your way to be harder than mine.

This suggests to me that Joyce had tried to persuade John to go with him to Germany.

He was reconciled to his fate:

> As you rightly say, I need no exhortation or consolation: but to know that my motives have not been misunderstood by those whose regard I do value is to know that I shall not die in vain, and to suspect that my service in dying may be greater than my service in living. May it be so!

John's letter "could have come only from a real friend". But the petition was unlikely "to stand between me and Jewish revenge" and he would not seek mercy "from those who have denied me justice".

He was worried about his wife, who had gone with him to Germany and was still in prison. "Yes, John," he wrote, "I do believe that my friends and kinsmen will regard my dear wife as a trust from me: and I have been doing my best, and I think with some success, to enable her to bear the blow." But "another long period of solitary confinement now might do her irreparable damage".

He ended by recalling their long talks and their "pauses for refreshment".

> Our friendship, as you say, has been long and chequered: I should like you to know that I look back with great affection on the many happy hours we spent together, and can now see the funny side of our differences ... In gratitude and comradeship, yours aye, William.

A few days after he wrote that letter, William Joyce was hanged on 3 January 1946. John and Anne wrote to his wife Margaret, his brother Quentin and his faithful friend and disciple John McNab. But Margaret declined into alcoholism, and Quentin decided to stay away from all his old fascist friends for the rest of his life.

With McNab, John quarrelled within weeks of Joyce's execution. I don't know why, but John sent him a handwritten letter on 29 January: "I am hurt, but not surprised, that you have not responded to my letter." McNab emigrated with his wife, a former secretary from the NSL whom he married in January 1945, to Franco's Spain, where he stayed for the rest of his life, and wrote a book about bullfighting.

John could not do much, either, for William's 17-year-old daughter Heather. Her mother Hazel decided that she should not see her father in the condemned cell. It might upset her.

So on 3 January Heather went to her vacation job, teaching English to three French girls at a convent school in St Leonards on Sea, and was told not to tell anyone her dreadful secret about what was to happen that day.

But before she went, "I went to Mass, felt peace in the offering of the Mass." She confided her secret to the priest and he agreed to say a Mass for William Joyce.

After the morning's lesson, she and the French girls went to the cinema to see an American war film. She remembers that they all laughed at a scene where the US air force men sang "My Name is Macnamara, I'm the Leader of the Band" and danced round the room. The French girls said it was just the crazy way American soldiers they had seen in France behaved.

The secret Heather carried that day was buried so deep inside her that when, years later, she started to talk about it, it dominated the rest of her life.

Later that year Jimmy Maxton died. Perhaps John felt that his place was following the coffin through the streets of Glasgow, as he had followed Wheatley's. But, of course, it was out of the question.

And so John went back to earning his living by running a tiny, doomed splinter on the far right of British politics. The BPP was nothing without John. It wasn't very much with him, either, but that little was enough for the Duke of Bedford.

But he was rubbing shoulders with the aristocracy and great wealth, and he seems to have decided to try to go native. He asked the duke to be my godfather, but the duke turned him down, apparently because John had declared his intention of becoming a Catholic, and the Catholics had executed one of the duke's ancestors. Thinking a titled godparent would be in some way advantageous, my parents turned next to Lady Alexandrina Domvile – Pudd, the wife of Admiral Sir Barry Domvile.

She agreed but does not seem to have taken her duties very seriously. I never met her or heard from her in all my life, as far as I know, though I have now looked at her husband's diary in the National Maritime Museum, and seen the entry on 12 June 1945. Domvile was having lunch with Arnold Leese, but his wife could not go: "Pudd off to christening of Beckett infant at Watford." And it seems that when I was 15 months old "Beckett + wife + infant" went to tea with the Domviles. "Made themselves pleasant" Domvile records laconically. The Domviles were supposed to go to Chenies for lunch the next month, but on the day "neither of us wanted to go" so they sent a telegram.

Our summer holidays were spent at Cartha Martha, a fine house in Cornwall owned by the duke, and when I was a baby we drove there in a stately old Rolls, also loaned us by the duke, which had some sort of governor preventing it from going at more than 30 m.p.h. On the first three mornings at Cartha Martha John woke up and said to Anne: "This is a wonderful view." On the fourth morning he said: "This is a wonderful view, but I've seen it."

Lesley came with us one year, with her son Patrick. One day she took the two of us out, and got talking with a woman who looked at the two small boys and said: "I can tell which one's yours. The little dark one looks just like you." Lesley decided not to try to explain that the little dark one was her brother.

They relaunched the BPP in December 1945 in Holborn Hall. "Opening the meeting in typical style," reported the communist *Daily Worker*, "Beckett addressed the audience as 'friends, Londoners, countrymen' and went on to say, 'we are here not to praise victory but to analyse it.'" The next month the *Daily Worker* was able exclusively to report that the BPP was planning another meeting. The censor had opened a letter addressed to John and another addressed to *Daily Worker* news editor Douglas Hyde, and had put them back in the wrong envelopes by mistake. John sent on Hyde's letter with a courteous note, but, wrote Hyde, "communists do not send courteous notes to fascists" and he used the information to ensure the meeting was broken up.

Its meetings were regularly broken up, and at 51 John found himself again involved in fights to protect his speakers. He was punched in the eye while guarding the door at a meeting at St Ermins Hotel in London's Victoria.

The BPP chairman was Air Commodore Gerard Oddie, and the right-wing economist Professor Frederick Soddy joined. John said that his party had attracted all the oddies and the soddies. They put Oddie up as a candidate in the Combined English Universities by-election of 1946. He got 239 votes.

As early as the end of 1945, the far right was starting to splinter again, amid mutual recrimination. Mosley's former supporters formed three separate groups, which only came together in 1948 under Mosley's leadership.

John tried, without success, for a rapprochement with Ben Greene, with whom he seems to have fallen out terminally. Perhaps it was about money. Perhaps it was a hangover from imprisonment, where, according to his daughter Lesley von Goetz, Greene "loathed everyone in Brixton Prison with him except those who had been at public school – Domvile, Ramsay, Robert Gordon-Canning".

A.K. Chesterton, according to an MI5 intercept, claimed in October 1945 that for every £1,000 the Duke of Bedford gave John, John appropriated £750. But by March 1946 Chesterton was negotiating fees for his articles with John, and writing to him: "No, of course we will never quarrel about anything so vulgar as money."

That summer John and A.K. they were very close, frequently lunching together at Gows, a splendid restaurant in St Martins Lane frequented by theatre folk as well as by wealthy Catholics, where the manager knew John and let him sign the bill.

Chesterton, John told me, used to pester him over lunch for praise for his articles. But there was great affection between them. Doris Chesterton told Chesterton's biographer David Baker:

> John was a great friend of Kenneth. John was the master of telling a story. He was also a gossip. If the truth suffered on the way to giving the story a good zip, so much the worse for the truth. He was impish in the endearing sense.

It's not a bad summary.

Chesterton had managed to return to his old trade after he left the army, becoming a sub-editor on the *Sheffield Telegraph* in 1943 before becoming deputy editor of *Truth*. He was almost a mainstream figure, with a regular salary and a nine-to-five life, and John must have envied that, and envied the respectability that went with never having been interned.

When not lunching at Gows with Chesterton, he often lunched at the Savoy with Henry Newnham, the former editor of *Truth*, who had a regular table there and fed John fine meals and good political gossip. Once he bought Newnham lunch there, and took me. I was probably about six. He took me to dinner at Gows, too. He thought he was going to die young, as his mother (and perhaps his father) had done, and I suppose he thought he would not have the chance to take me to fine restaurants when I was old enough to appreciate them.

Domvile records that on 28 June 1946 he was at John's Maiden Lane office – "a good chat with JB" – and that he met A.K. Chesterton there for the first time: "Very different from what I expected – elderly and good-looking – a clever face."

Major Harry Edmonds, who had followed Anne about during the war, founded something called the Constitutional Research Association, of which Major General Fuller was vice president and whose lunches were regularly attended by Admiral Domvile and Lord Sempill. However, the "inner circle" according to Edmonds was to be "our gang" consisting, according to an MI5 report, of "himself, Norman Hay, Ben Greene, Barney Seale, Russell Grenfell, Harold Strong, Rex Tremlett and the source of this report".

At their inaugural meeting at Browns Hotel, Fuller

> said that he looked upon man as a beast of prey, the lord of the jungle. But man ceased to be that and became something better when he acknowledged an authority based on something higher than himself; based, in fact, on a myth. Where there had been belief in the myth things had, in general, gone fairly well. But when the myth was no longer accepted, men decayed...
>
> There are too many cads in the world at present and not enough gentlemen – and in using that word he said he meant men of honour.
>
> He foresaw disaster after disaster for the world until it acknowledged that there were superior men and inferior men, and saw to it that the superior men were permitted to take their natural place in the leadership of the world.

That's probably a pretty fair summary of the sort of constitutional research that this collection of arrogant and dim-witted army officers and Right Honourables had in mind.

Lord Sempill seems to have been a Wodehousian silly ass, with added anti-Semitism, who was related to the royal family and had spied for the Japanese before the war.. He spent much of the war years in Canada, apparently on some mission for the Catholic organisation the Knights of St Columba. According to MI5, he

> has caused a great deal of trouble, and dropped a number of bricks, and has run up an overdraft with the Bank of Canada, apparently on the strength of a rather loosely worded letter of introduction from the Knights of St Columba. He applied to the Knights of St Columba recently for money to meet this and ... they have refused.

In a letter from Canada to Lady Sempill they found an account of a court case in which the old American families tried to stop new immigrants taking their names. The old families lost.

So, said Sempill, the old rhyme used to be:

> Here's to good old Boston
> The home of the bean and the cod
> Where the Cabots speak only to Lowells
> And the Lowells speak only to God.

Now it should read:

> Here's to good old Boston
> The home of the bean and the cod
> Where the Lowells have no one to talk to
> For the Cabots speak Yiddish, by God!

Domvile, horrified as he was by the Labour election victory, nonetheless saw a silver lining: "I was delighted [at] so many ministers losing their seats in the general rebuff to Churchill & all the evil he has brought on our land."

In later years Edmonds's associates included Michael de la Bedoyere, editor of the *Catholic Herald*, and, according to Edmonds' son, Denis Thatcher. Increasingly this was the political ground occupied by John Beckett, though of course the poorly educated son of a draper was never really acceptable in these circles.

Graham Mitchell got another sly laugh at the expense of the men he spied on. "Mr Mitchell", reads an internal memorandum of 8 June 1945. "You may be amused to know that John Beckett is certain that Major Edmonds gave information to MI5 ... Beckett believed that Edmonds tried to seduce his wife while Beckett was in prison."

The BPP, of course, did not answer John's need to have something he could believe in with all his heart. But he had that in hand. While in prison he had asked to see the Catholic chaplain, and was now being instructed with a view to being received into the Church.

Catholicism was the faith of John Wheatley and, like fascism, it offered a total answer, which is why there has been a constant coming and going between the Catholic Church and the Communist Party as well as fascist parties. And the Catholic Church was also in those days mildly, carefully, but unmistakably, anti-Semitic. The *Catholic Herald* had been much admired in anti-Semitic circles before the war, and the *Jewish Chronicle* reported in February 1946 that the BPP's "main drive for members is among Catholic elements".

Anne loyally tried to follow. But her instinct to subjugate her own intellect and judgement to her husband's was weakening. She was no longer the impressionable young woman he had met in 1933. She went with him for instruction to the Jesuit priests in Farm Street, in London's Mayfair, but pretty soon she stopped going to Mass. They also never quite resolved the awkward fact that they were not married, and therefore, according to the Church, were living in a state of mortal sin.

The Jesuits sent John on a retreat – the Catholic name for a period of quiet religious contemplation – at a very splendid and expensive Jesuit boarding school called Beaumont College, just outside Windsor, in Old Windsor, where many of the oldest and poshest Catholic families sent their sons. In the 1930s just four public schools had fascist cells, and Beaumont was the only Catholic one. The other three were Stowe, Winchester and Worksop. William Joyce had been educated by Jesuits, at St Ignatius College in Galway, and so had Air Commodore Oddie, at Wimbledon College.

They did a wonderful selling job on him during the retreat. Beaumont had splendid buildings and an air of unobtrusive gentility, and called itself "the Catholic Eton". When it was founded, so the rector told John in his beautifully modulated vowel sounds, the head boy at Eton had written to the head boy at Beaumont: "Harrow we know, Winchester we know, but what is Beaumont?" And the head boy at Beaumont had written back: "Beaumont is what Eton used to be: a school for the sons of Catholic gentleman."

The most splendid Catholic families in Britain sent their sons to Beaumont, and John came back determined that, come what may, he was going to send his son to Beaumont, too.

Ben Greene, according to his daughter Lesley von Goetz, thought John was infiltrating that Catholic Church as he had done with many other organisations. Ben Greene was really, really fed up with him. Even A.K. Chesterton was cynical about it, according to Lesley von Goetz; he thought John must have found a wealthy Catholic patron.

John was still a witty, fluent, compelling speaker, but he had lost the passion that electrified his pre-war speeches. He now often included diversions about people he had known, Attlee and Mosley in particular.

In addition to the old faces, the BPP attracted an undergraduate of 23 just demobilised from the army, who quickly rose to prominence while gaining a double first at Cambridge. His name was Colin Jordan, and he started his political career by writing articles for the *People's Post*, the BPP organ, and organising the Cambridge University Nationalist Club, a front for the BPP. More than half a century later, Jordan wrote to me: "Next to Arnold Leese, my prime political mentor, I rate John Beckett the most impressive political figure I then met."

John went to Cambridge a couple of times to address meetings which Jordan organised. The first time, they tried an open air meeting, but the amplification equipment failed. The second time, there were more protesters outside the school where the meeting was to take place, with placards saying "Schools for education not hate", than there were auditors within. John said it would be ridiculous to address so few from the platform. "At least we had a pleasant hour or so with him in a pub before it was time for him to catch his return train", Colin Jordan told me.

John, he said, was "a witty and fluent speaker, a big, bluff, physically commanding figure on a platform, full of tales of persons and events he had experienced, ranging from Attlee to Mosley".

Jordan soon started to fret at the BPP's moderation and cosiness. Council meetings were held over a weekend at the Duke of Bedford's ancestral seat in Woburn Abbey:

> I can picture the evening meal with the duke at the head of the table, and doing the carving – I have an idea we may have had bison and not just venison – and your father sitting next to him. In the lounge where the discussions took place, steered by John Beckett, I can picture the gentle gentleman, the duke, with his slippered feet resting on a footstool by the log fire. It was all very cosy and amiable, if, in the outcome, hardly productive in the advancement of the party.
>
> On the Sunday mornings the duke led a walk through the grounds, the rest of us following in pairs behind ... I remember your father, probably out of earshot of the duke, telling some of us of the connecting doors between many of the principal bedrooms, affording facility for liaison between guests of different sexes.

It was not what the obsessional young nationalist had gone into politics for, and Jordan was soon out of the BPP and mixing with German and American Nazis, as well as being courted by Mosley's supporters. His real hero was always Arnold Leese, who put up the money that kept him in politics.

Leese had the money because, in 1948, H.H. Beamish, the virulent anti-Semite who had written the "Jews' Who's Who" and fled to South Africa rather than pay libel damages to John's early enemy Sir Aldred Mond, died. He had made money in South Africa, and he left it to help fund the post Second World War British Nazis.

Nick Toczek found a letter from Beamish to Archibald Maule Ramsay the year before Beamish died: "I hear that Dell [secretary of The Britons] has handed over to John Beckett and Carroll [C.E. Carroll, founder of the Anglo-German Fellowship]." Presumably this was one poison chalice which John had the sense to decline.

Of course it could never have come to anything. Before handing The Britons over to him, Beamish and his friends would have done their genealogical research, and would probably have discovered

John's secret. His career on the anti-Semitic right would have been finished.

The BPP rented offices at 33 Maiden Lane, WC2, and held a series of meetings, some of which were broken up by the 43 Group, a militant group of Jewish ex-servicemen. The 43 Group also targeted Mosley's meetings, breaking up a march through Brighton in 1948 and hospitalising Mosley's lieutenant Jeffrey Hamm. In response Mosley's organisation hired several Maltese gangsters, and there was a pitched battle in Romford, Essex, between Mosley's gangsters and other Soho gangsters hired by prominent Jewish entertainers like Bud Flanagan.

John's primary task seems to have been to make the BPP the strongest party on the fascist right, and his main efforts were directed at siphoning off Mosley supporters.

"A great part of my work since 1937 has been acting as a stretcher bearer and medical orderly behind the progress of the Mosley juggernaut", he wrote in June 1948 to one disillusioned Mosley supporter, Michael McLean, suggesting that McLean meet Colin Jordan. Presumably the appeal did not work, because a month later he was writing to McLean: "Surely you can see that you could not help Mosley more than by allowing him to represent your sincere disgust with his movement as being a Jewish-Communist stunt." McLean, however, really was finished with the far right, and passed the correspondence to the Board of Deputies of British Jews.

For at least five years after the war, and I think much longer (the files are not open after 1950 yet), Special Branch was still following John and Anne about, opening their letters, tapping their phones and laboriously writing up the most banal conversations. If John telephoned from the office to say he would be late home that night, the conversation, word for word, can still be read in the National Archive.

It looks as though they may have caught him out in a couple of brief extra-marital affairs, or at least they thought they had, and were rather pleased with themselves about it.

There is naturally a stream of calls to Woburn Abbey. Harry Edmonds called from time to time inviting John to lunch, but John always found that he was too busy.

We find John writing to Bedford about the prisoner of war camp in Chorleywood, near Chenies – a lot of the old fascists were much exercised by the fate of German prisoners of war. He says he and Anne welcomed prisoners into their home and give them some decent food as the camp is "shockingly uncouth".

In February 1947 we find John getting the Duke to fund the defence of Arnold Leese and Tony Gittens, a member of the BPP's national council and a key figure in The Britons, on trial for helping the escape from Kempton Park prisoner of war camp of two Dutch SS officers.

In safe houses in the East End, the two officers received money from Anne's friend and John's supporter Lady Clare Annesley, an old friend of the Duke of Bedford and of Unity Mitford.

The MI5 transcript of John's telephone conversation with A.K. Chesterton reads:

> AK: What's all this about old man Leese and Gittens and co?
>
> JB: Well, you've seen in the papers.
>
> AK: Yes.
>
> JB: They're all charged with conspiring.
>
> AK: With persons unknown?
>
> JB: With persons unknown.
>
> AK: Who are persons unknown?
>
> JB: Well, if they are unknown I wouldn't know. (They laugh.) Well, if I did know, for the sake of the fellow listening I'd give you the names but unfortunately I don't. (AK laughs.).... We have engaged Head [C.B.V. Head, the solicitor who had represented William Joyce] to defend them and seven of them have actually had these men sleeping under their roof, because they weren't Germans, you see, they were Dutchmen.
>
> AK: Really?
>
> JB: Yes, they were Dutch SS and apparently they passed themselves off as Dutch seamen who were stranded for the moment.
>
> AK: Do they look upon it as being serious?
>
> JB: Well, you can get up to 14 years under the regulation they have charged them with, regulation 90, and Arnold's going to defend himself, so I think it's possible he'll get 15. (AK roars with laughter.)

Leese and Gittens went to prison for 12 months.

John's conversations with Chesterton are often about the latter's many articles, often published by the former's papers. A letter to A.K. in April 1947 tells him:

> My dear AK
> Your letter received this morning.
>
> I think we had better have a telephone code for our bomb operation, as it is possible that the gentleman who reads our letters is a Fascist and the one who listens on the telephone is a Communist, and therefore their activities may not be fully synchronised! This probably explains why our good friends of the Irgun Zvei Laumi get away with it so successfully; I do not suppose anyone in the security service dares to give information about Jews.
>
> I enclose, after much consideration, a letter for your private eye which I have received from Oddie with regard to your pamphlet. I do not send this to annoy you, but in order that you should not feel that it is any arbitrary decision on my part which prevents its publication.

But the letter that made me sit up was to the duke. It is about the Protocols of the Learned Elders of Zion, the forged document which extreme anti-Semites believed proved a world Jewish conspiracy. John writes:

> Of course I will stop advertising the Protocols if you are not happy about it. We bought 500 at a bargain price and they are quite our best selling book as ... hardly anyone dares to stock them. Do you not think this is a trifle unfair? If they are a crude forgery as the Jews maintain they still have the right to be circularised and readers can form their own opinion.... In case you have not read the protocols I enclose a copy with your parcel of charters and remind you of Henry Ford's saying: "I do not know if they are a forgery or not, but I see happening around me exactly the things they describe."

Here's the best plea in mitigation I can offer.

I am sure now that my father emerged from prison more than a little mad. He had spent nearly four years locked up, pushed around and punished at whim in order to humiliate him, and the committee set up for the purpose said he ought to be released. He was not a spy, or a traitor.

A friend had been hanged, and most lawyers now agree that he ought not to have been.

In prison he had had to turn for companionship and perhaps protection from Mosley loyalists to obsessive anti-Semites like Arnold Leese. Richard Griffiths has noted that many of the internees came out of prison with their own opinions exacerbated, and John emerged far more anti-Semitic than he went in. He and the Duke of Bedford were among the first holocaust deniers, both describing the war as a "Jews' war".

Even years after his release, he was still watched, and followed, which is not a good feeling. He had tried "living small" as a blameless hospital administrator, and perhaps he knew the security services had even smoked him out of that bolthole. He never, I suppose, heard the name Graham Mitchell in his life, but he knew someone was enjoying having power over him.

The powerlessness a man feels against the faceless people who spy on him and manipulate him does strange things to the mind.

He decided there was a plot. And who had a motive for targeting him? Why, the Jews, for he had attacked them. So what should he do? Why, attack them again. He had served nearly four years in prison for being an anti-Semite. May as well be hanged for a sheep as a lamb.

Imprisonment had a corrosive effect on his personality as well as his opinions. Ben Greene, who was in prison for less than half as long as John, came out "a mental and physical wreck ... his personality and reputation were irreversibly impaired" according to his family. For the rest of his life, Greene was "convinced that virtually any setback in personal life or work showed that 'they' were still out to get him". Graham Macklin quotes one internee, Heather Donovan, as saying internment

> was the sort of experience that could easily and often did breed the hardest sort of bitterness. I thank God in my own case it didn't. In the case of many others, bitterness started and ended up as a lot of other unhealthy things.

Notes on sources

Archives of the Board of Deputies of British Jews.

Greene family papers.

TNA: KV2/1521.

TNA: KV2/874.

Haters, Baiters and Would-be Dictators by Nick Toczek (Routledge, 2016).

I Believed by Douglas Hyde (Heinemann, 1952).

Patriotism Perverted by Richard Griffiths (Constable, 1998).

The 43 Group: Battling with Mosley's Blackshirts by Morris Beckman (Center-prise, 1993).

Very Deeply Dyed in Black by Graham Macklin (I.B. Tauris, 2007).

22
INDIAN SUMMER

As well as running the BPP and editing its regular publication, in 1948 John began to publish a fortnightly called *Fleet Street Preview*. This was not fascist or anti-Semitic at all, claiming to be simply well informed, and aimed at an intellectual closed-circulation readership. "*Preview* does not pretend to give all the news – only that which is unobtainable through ordinary channels", it said.

It had some well-informed comment and a few genuine scoops, especially on Labour Party affairs. It predicted the TUC purge on communist trade union officials, as well as the dismissal of Soviet Foreign Minister Molotov.

A few things it got spectacularly wrong, though probably no more so than regular newspaper pundits. In September 1948 it claimed that Stalin intended to retire. It thought that "Truman, tolerated because he was a nonentity, has no chance of re-election" but that the Republican candidate would not be Dewey: "Governor Dewey has steadily lost ground ... Our information is that Senator Vandenberg ... is the safest long range choice." Dewey became the Republican candidate, and Truman won the election.

A sensational piece headed "Where is Hitler?" claimed to have information from S.S. Colonel von Mackenson, son of the former German ambassador to Rome, that

> Hitler and Eva Braun escaped on or about May 6 1945 from Templehof, Berlin's airport, in a Junkers bomber. There were three Junkers protected by seven Messerschmidt fighters. They flew to Tondern in Denmark. All the planes took off for Spain but were shot down over France. But Hitler and Eva Braun were in Denmark being picked up by a U-boat. Hitler is now almost certainly outside Europe.

But it was genuinely ahead of the pack in reporting of the former Chancellor Hugh Dalton, forced to resign in 1948 after a budget leak, that "Dr Dalton, who a month ago was openly aiming at the succession to the Foreign Office, has been informed that he is persona non grata in that capacity and has transferred his ambitions to home affairs." Dalton always wanted the Foreign Office – John would have known that – and we now know, though only a few political insiders knew then, that the king himself stood out against having Dalton there.

"Should circumstances force a general reorganisation, Mr Morrison would take over the duties of the foreign secretary." He did, three years later. Some of John's old political friends were feeding him good information.

Its interview by "our correspondent in Madrid" (McNab, I imagine) with Myriam Petacci, sister of Mussolini's mistress Clara Petacci who was killed with Mussolini in 1945, was probably a genuine exclusive. But one cannot say the same for the unnamed "socialist veteran" interviewed in August 1949, who remembered Herbert Morrison as a mean and vindictive leader of Hackney Council in 1920.

John Beckett's name was nowhere to be found in any issue of the magazine for the six years in which it appeared. Its regular political commentator was bylined Henry Alexander. A breathless note MI5 received from the Ministry of Defence in 1951 said that the MoD had a very good source who told them that Henry Alexander was a communist.

Security Service director general Sir Percy Sillitoe wrote back to say, correctly: no, he's a fascist called John Beckett. Perhaps, he said, you are thinking of John Alexander who writes for the *New Central European Observer*. No, no, said the MoD, he's a communist, we've got a secret source who tells us so. Sir Percy didn't bother to argue any more. Thank you, he wrote, we'll make a note of it.

In 1949 John and Anne were at last free from financial worry, and they may even have felt that *Preview* was the beginning of their road back to respectability.

That year they persuaded the duke to buy a huge, splendid house in Croxley Green, near Rickmansworth in Hertfordshire, set in 13 acres of fields, lawns and a tennis court.

In theory it seems to have been bought as the headquarters of the BPP. In fact we lived in ostentatious splendour in the front of the house, the ground floor at the back (once the servants' quarters) housed the BPP offices, and the first floor was divided into three: one-third our bedrooms, with two flats in the other two-thirds to provide an income.

The house was called The Firs because of some wonderful fir trees in the grounds, but John at once renamed it Thurlwood House after the farm which had once been leased by what he still called his yeoman ancestors, though the Becketts had lost the farm in the years between the wars.

An ample driveway swept round a small spinney, lush if over-grown, to a pillared front porch in front of a very big flat-fronted Georgian house. John Beckett walked leisurely around his 13 acres, a shotgun in his hand, potting the occasional bird which might other-wise have gorged itself on his strawberries, or on the apples from the small orchard in one corner of his estate. He looked like a real country gentleman. I did not know then that it was the latest of many parts he had played.

One day he saw a small bird perched near the fruit, and shot it dead, and then looked at it. He was so mortified to have destroyed that tiny, noisy piece of vibrant life that he went out and sold the gun that very morning.

With the house came a gardener's cottage, complete with gardener who had worked for the owners of Thurlwood House for years. My parents called him "Fulford" so naturally I did too, and my mother squirmed with embarrassment as she told me that he ought to be "Mr Fulford" to me. My poor mother. She had been poor all her life, and was to be poorer. How would she know how one addressed one's gardener?

John's daughter Lesley came to Thurlwood just once, and I never saw her or her son Patrick again until I sought them out, more than 30 years later, long after John was dead. I think Lesley knew too many secrets. She reported back to her mother Helen that John seemed at last to have fallen on his feet, and could help them financially. Helen knew her man, and advised caution. "Anne will have a difficult time", she predicted, correctly.

He lived, as I suppose he must always have lived in his brief periods of affluence, as though money were never the slightest obstacle. When his Harley Street dentist told him that the biggest Rolls Royce in the world, the Phantom III, was "a poor man's car" because it never needed servicing, he seized on the excuse and bought an enormous second-hand Phantom III that very day. It succeeded a succession of wonderful old Alvises which must have cost a fortune. He loved driving them all, but never bothered to learn how they worked.

They bought a houseboat in Burnham on Crouch, *Paula*, the sad but still elegant remains of what had been a first class ocean racing sailing ship before the First World War. I think that might have been Anne's one extravagance – she had happy memories of sailing in Burnham in the 1930s, before she knew John, and she loved the *Paula*.

But it was John who bought a yacht, the *Golden Fleece*, and, rather typically, never learned to sail her.

He looked like a million dollars, in his splendid cars and boats, with his fine embossed notepaper and his huge house with odd pieces of elegant furniture which had once been at the duke's seat in Woburn and had come to us I know not how: a grand piano of such distinguished make that it was always called by its make, not just as the piano; Waterford glasses, hand-carved; glass fronted bookshelves. Each year he sent out great big pompous Christmas cards. One year I cringed with embarrassment when his huge, expensive card included a Hilaire Belloc verse which had taken his fancy:

> Of Courtesy, it is much less
> Than Courage of Heart or Holiness,

> Yet in my Walks it seems to me
> That the Grace of God is in Courtesy.

I cringed, yes. But I also thought money would never be any object to any child of this obviously rich and solid citizen.

"Live small", Anne had said, despairingly. She had the wrong man for that.

MI5 was not the only organisation which was spying on us. "We are aware of the existence of Thurlwood House and in the past this has been given attention", wrote David Cohen of the Board of Deputies of British Jews in a memorandum in October 1950. The Board of Deputies liked to know where potentially anti-Semitic gatherings were taking place, and its informants had received notice of a BPP social to take place in November, with Air Commodore Oddie and the Duke of Bedford.

John had tried, not very convincingly, to distance himself and the BPP from anti-Semitism. "No Christian can accept a policy of discrimination owing to race or creed", he had said in 1945, adding: "If, for example, a chemical cartel is thought to be a bad thing, we are sure that Lord McGowan and his Gentile associates could carry on quite well if Lord Melchett and his fellow Jews were deported tomorrow."

"Beckett's chief stratagem," said a confidential report prepared for the Institute of Jewish Affairs, "would seem to be to identify Jews with moneylenders or usurers ... He also of course identifies Jews and Communists, referring for example to the Jewish Chronicle and the Daily Worker as 'the two Jewish papers.'"

The security services noted that on 12 September 1950 "a German alien came and was employed at Thurlwood, Marlies Ilse Johanna Haussler, born 8/7/29". I remember Marlies. A big, jolly girl, she helped look after me and my baby brother while my mother was coping with an enormous house which was built for an army of servants to look after it.

I've no idea how Marlies came to be there. But in a speech about that time, transcribed by MI5, John said he had living in his house "a refugee from East Germany, which is starving because the food has been taken to provide Poland's surplus".

A.K. was a regular visitor to Thurlwood House in those days; a tall, dignified, rather distant and patrician figure with what seemed to me, as a child, to be an almost ducal disdain for the lower orders. I would travel with John in the car to Rickmansworth Station to pick up A.K. and Doris for lunch. If it was near to my birthday, he would solemnly take me to a toyshop along with my father and buy me a small toy car, but otherwise he never seemed to notice me.

Once, at the station, a porter accidentally ran his big luggage trolley over A.K.'s foot. A.K. made a huge scene about it, everyone gathered round to see what the fuss was, and even John was a little embarrassed. The station master came out and said: "'E said, mind yer backs, dinne?" A.K. explained at some length that saying "mind yer backs" was not, in his view, good enough.

I could see that my father was different from the fathers of my friends. He was older, for one thing. He was also much, much noisier. In Hertfordshire's middle-class green belt, his loud laugh and emphatic speech were noticeably out of place.

The local Women's Institute asked him to be a panellist on their brains trust, probably because they had heard he was a former MP. He must have sent them a brief CV, because when we arrived – Anne and I went along to hear him – the male chairman apologetically asked what he meant by: "Six years in Parliament and four years in Brixton". "The prison", John cackled at once. The man looked so crestfallen that he took pity on him. "You don't have to mention that if you'd rather not." It wasn't mentioned.

That evening he was a great success, offering vaguely reactionary prejudices I had absorbed from as early as I had been able to understand anything, expressed with an attractive humour.

People these days use each other's Christian names too readily: "When I was young, if someone you hardly knew came up and said, hallo John, you buttoned up your pockets and moved away", he chortled to people who had never seen pockets with buttons. And of course, the best small car in the world is the Volkswagen, a word which means people's car, created by the German government in the 1930s to democratise car ownership.

My younger brother was born in Thurlwood in 1950, the year I started school at St Joan of Arc's Convent in Rickmansworth, a girls' school which took boys up to the age of seven.

Perhaps a year after we moved to Thurlwood, we moved again. Thurlwood was rented out, and we rented a slightly less splendid (but still very large) house called Readings, in nearby Chorleywood. Today it has been pulled down, and in its place is a small street of modern town houses called The Readings. I remember my father saying airily: "I don't want all my capital tied up in bricks and mortar." How was I to know he didn't have any capital?

My sister Clare was born at Readings in 1952. My parents still seem to have thought there was some advantage in having a titled godparent: her godmother was Lady Clare Annesley, and Clare has never heard anything from her in her life, though Lady Clare lived until 1980.

It was while my mother was in bed with the baby, after what I think was a difficult birth, that I first saw panic in her eyes.

I cannot remember what she said to me, but she was ill and frightened, and I had the feeling, just for a moment, that our happiness and security were not as solid as I thought. I also had an urgent desire to go to another room and play.

Children have to learn fear some time. I found it in those few months in Chorleywood. On top of a realisation that all was not as it seemed at home, there was that particular fear that went with being a Catholic child. In bed one night, I started to put together the logic of what I had been told at the convent. I had told my teacher some trivial lie. Lying was a mortal sin; if one died in a state of mortal sin, one went to Hell for all eternity; the only way out was confession; I could die at any minute; and the confessional was not open until Saturday. I cried with fear.

My mother came in and tried to untangle the logic for me, but I already knew she was theologically unsound. She had given up going to Mass on Sunday, and so was in a permanent state of mortal sin. I did not, of course, know that she was in a permanent state of mortal sin anyway, since she was not married to the man she lived with.

I got to confession, and later I tackled my father on the problem of my mother, who never went to Mass and never went to confession, so was destined for Hell. John said that there were just a few very good people to whom the rule didn't apply.

That satisfied me for a while. Much later, he told me what he really thought. We had to believe that God created Hell, because the Pope said so. But we didn't have to believe that He ever sent anyone there.

There never was anyone so good at convincing himself of comforting rubbish. A clever man who could believe that Tom Mosley was an inspired leader, and Doris Chesterton could see the future, and the Protocols of Zion were proof of a Jewish plot to take over the world, was not going to have any trouble with a Hell no one ever went to.

He could also convince himself that the flow of money was going to go on forever. Anne, I think, saw that it might not. The BPP was about as doomed as any organisation with access to the wallet of a very rich man can be. It was fighting Mosley for the tiny and diminishing extreme right. It relied on the talent and charisma of its general secretary, and his heart wasn't in it.

Three of his staff were discharged in 1949, including Kate Greene, Ben Greene's sister, according to the MI5 watchers. They seem to have thought the BPP folded up in 1950, but I think it staggered on for another couple of years; certainly its journal *People's Post* was still going in 1953.

The money which sustained our lavish lifestyle was all the duke's, and the few other members of the BPP were complaining. They could see a Party doing not a lot, with a general secretary living in magnificent homes, driving splendid cars and lunching at Gows and the Savoy.

The duke seems by then to have regarded John not just as a political colleague, but as a friend and financial adviser.

After what cannot have been more than a year at Readings, we moved back to Thurlwood. I have no idea why we moved to Readings, or why we moved back. I was sent to the poshest preparatory school for miles around, St Martins in Northwood, Middlesex. Most of the boys there were destined for one of the local public schools, generally Merchant Taylors, but a much more splendid future awaited me. I knew that I was to go to Beaumont, the Catholic Eton.

That must have been when John started bringing me a stream of public school novels – *The Sixth Form at St. Dominic's*, *Stalky & Co.*,

Billy Bunter. I got an idea of public school life as a long, sophisticated holiday, full of jolly japes with noble upper crust comrades, punctuated by the occasional beating, stoically borne except by cads. I couldn't wait.

Then it all went wrong.

Early on the morning of 9 October 1953 the Duke of Bedford went out shooting on his Endsleigh estate in Devon (he had estates all over the country). When he did not return for breakfast, a search was mounted. He was found a few days later. He had apparently shot himself by accident.

His son, who loathed him and succeeded to the title after him, has suggested he killed himself. My father confided to Colin Jordan that he did not think the duke's death was an accident, but he may have thought he had been murdered, perhaps by the security services.

In the next issue of the BPP paper John wrote an extraordinary obituary which tells us more about the writer than about the subject:

> The British aristocracy very occasionally produces a unique character, who does odd, courageous and independent things ... He was surrounded by every circumstance of training likely to turn out another well-behaved, well dressed nonentity. Instead he became the last representative of the traditions of aristocratic radicalism and nonconformity ...
>
> He never deserted his friends. My wife telephoned to Scotland on May 16 1940 to tell him I had been taken to Brixton prison that morning. He came from Scotland overnight to visit me and see if help could be obtained.
>
> James Maxton was my second outside visitor. These two men had much in common. Of all those I have known in 30 years of public life they were the only two completely honest men that I have met ... I like to believe that today they sit together in some pleasant part of Purgatory happily knowing that the Lord, whom they served by their lives, has not turned his face from them.

It would of course have to be Purgatory. John was now a Catholic, and accepted the orthodoxy that non-Catholics cannot go to heaven.

It was one view of the duke. His son, who succeeded him to the title, has another: "My father [was] the loneliest man I ever knew, incapable of giving or receiving love, utterly self-centred and opinionated. He loved birds, animals, peace, monetary reform, the park, and religion. He also had a wife and three children."

In the 1930s the duke had been the centre of a sensational court case, when his wife sued for "restoration of conjugal rights". She called him "the most cruel, mean and conceited person she had met". He wrote to her:

> My health has been seriously affected by the strain, and as for a long time you have made it very clear that you do not wish to live with me as my wife, there is really nothing you want from me but my money.

Summing up, Justice Bucknall said:

> Lord Tavistock takes a rigid and austere view of life and dislikes many things, some of which he calls "pagan", but which most men do not actively dislike. He dislikes boarding schools for boys, alcohol, tobacco, playing cards for money, and betting. He does not play games, and said he took very little interest in his wife's dress.
>
> I think what concerned him is that his wife has completely turned away from his work and his ideals. Is that treatment a sufficient reason for Lord Tavistock refusing to go back to his wife? In my judgement it is.

John, who loved tobacco and alcohol and dreamed of sending his son to a top boarding school, was an odd companion for this austere figure; he thought the duke considered him a likeable rogue.

The BPP was wound up. *Fleet Street Preview* lasted another year. The hope that the duke might have left John and Anne money was quickly dispelled: he had left John just £600, which was not going to last very long in the hands of a man of 59 with three children under nine, expensive tastes, no income, no home, no work, no prospect of work, no common sense and a name and a face which people stubbornly declined to forget.

Everything we owned, including the roof over our heads, and every penny my parents had, was the duke's. They were now the property of the new duke, who had a thoroughly low opinion of his father's fascist friend, and wanted to sell our home to help pay nearly £3 million death duties.

My mother was beside herself with worry. She said to her daughter Clare that John always believed there was money so long as there was a cheque in the cheque book. My father carried on as though nothing had happened. His own father had become bankrupt when he was 14, forcing John to leave school and abandon all his hopes for the future. John had himself been declared bankrupt at the age of 38, forcing his daughter Lesley to leave school. Christians, he once told me, thought it a disgrace to go bankrupt, but Jews thought it was a normal part of business. Which did he think he was, I wonder?

From the conversations going on around me, I gathered that John had advised the duke to place all his property in a Trust, with John as one of the Trustees, in order to avoid death duty. But for this to work, the duke had to live for another five years, and he died a few months short of that.

Examining the duke's affairs, civil servants noted "certain sums misappropriated by one Beckett under an alleged power of attorney to deal with deceased's investments". Things were looking black.

Notes on sources

TNA: KV2 1521.

The 43 Group: Battling with Mosley's Blackshirts by Morris Beckman (Centerprise, 1993).

23

THE CATHOLIC CHURCH AND THE SOUL OF THE FAR RIGHT

While John's star on the far right was descending, A.K. Chesterton's was rising.

The year the duke died, 1953, Chesterton fell out with the new management at *Truth*. Collin Brooks was forced by the onset of Alzheimer's Disease to resign as *Truth*'s editor and sold his shares in the journal, triggering its sale. In a parting message to Chesterton, Brooks recorded

> my great appreciation of your devotion and industry as my senior colleague over the past ten or twelve years ... your unusual knowledge of foreign and imperial affairs, your wide general culture and your forceful prose style, have been of inestimable value to me, as editor.

Graham Macklin describes what happened next:

> Much to Chesterton's horror Truth was sold to the Staples Press whose owners appointed liberal journalist George Scott editor. Scott immediately began fumigating Truth's reputation for noxious anti-Semitism by appointing Jewish journalists like

Bernard Levin to its staff. Indeed, when Scott's secretary showed him Levin's application he was delighted by the Jewish name and stated: "Show him in, he's got a job". Chesterton was aghast. His response was a visceral diatribe entitled Truth Has Been Murdered, distributed gratis with copies of Free Britain, newsletter of The Britons.

None of that stopped Lord Beaverbrook offering him a job. He became Beaverbrook's "literary adviser", which meant, partly, ghost-writing Beaverbrook's autobiography. Labour MP and journalist Tom Driberg was already working on a biography, and perhaps Beaverbrook wanted to make sure that the authorised version hit the streets first, although Driberg was Beaverbrook's creature. More likely it appealed to Beaverbrook's sense of humour to have the ex-communist Driberg in one pocket and the fascist Chesterton in the other.

The finished book, *Don't Trust to Luck*, was "a terrible book, which nevertheless received sycophantic reviews from the Beaverbrook papers", Chesterton wrote afterwards, truthfully.

The next year, after John lost his wealthy patron, Chesterton found one – a reactionary millionaire living in South America, who funded Chesterton's new League of Empire Loyalists (LEL). Since *Truth* had abandoned the true faith, Chesterton named the LEL journal *Candour*.

Candour was startlingly clear where it stood on the empire and on race. A piece in January 1956 by the South African born Chesterton began:

> There is being reproduced on the Rand, in gangster form, much of the savagery and violence that had been the almost invariable pattern before the Whiteman [*sic*] arrived. As the Whiteman's laws alone had power to stop the internecine tribal warfare, so today only the Whiteman's law, remorselessly enforced, can bring release from their present nightmare to Africans terrorized by the vile creatures of their own race who thus exploit them.

Ben Greene was a keen LEL supporter. So was his daughter Lesley Greene, later Lesley von Goetz, who participated in some of its sillier stunts. So was Herbert Greene, a cousin of Ben's, one of the School House Greenes. Herbert wrote a poem which *Candour* printed on 13 January 1956:

> It's not among the Union Men
> Or Bureaucratic spivs;
> It's not among the Parties
> That the heart of England lives.
> You'll find that heart in wayside pubs
> And in quiet home retreats,
> For there, amidst the smoke and pipes
> The heart of England beats.

Mr Greene was presumably trying to capture the tone of A.K. Chesterton's more famous cousin G.K., hampered by a complete lack of literary talent. Herbert was the problem Greene: his brothers Graham and Hugh Carleton Greene seem to have spent much of their time and money bailing out Herbert's failed business ventures and trying to prevent him from publicly embarrassing them.

With the BPP out of the way, Chesterton's LEL and Mosley's Union Movement fought for the soul of the far right. It was a very bitter battle, all the nastier because the stakes were so small.

You get a flavour of it from a wonderful little spat between Chesterton and Mosley. Back in 1946, when William Joyce was executed, Mosley had lost support to Beckett and Chesterton over his contemptuous disavowal of the dead man, whom he called an "offensive little beast". In 1953 Beaverbrook had asked Chesterton to write about his old friend Joyce for the *Sunday Express*.

Chesterton did his best for his friend, but could hardly avoid making any criticism at all. Mosley's organisation saw a chance to grab back some of the prestige in fascist circles that came from supporting the martyred Joyce, and Alf Flockhart, who ran Mosley's London office, wrote to John McNab in Spain from Mosley's London office.

Chesterton, he said, was

> recently dismissed from the staff of Truth and finding it very hard to obtain a living, perhaps this is a help to him, at the

expense of William. Would you like to give us a comment upon it all, anything you say I will ensure is widely circulated.

Even McNab could see through that. He wrote back that everything Chesterton wrote was true, and copied the correspondence to Chesterton, who wrote to Mosley:

> Dear Mosley, I am enclosing a copy of a letter sent by one of your sweet young things to McNab. It is really rather amusing, considering the blast that has reached the Sunday Express about my endeavouring to make a hero of Joyce...
>
> As I have in my possession a long letter you wrote to me in 1937 bitterly denouncing what you called Joyce's treachery to you, this sudden solicitude is strange.
>
> Before I left Truth I secured an important temporary post with the United Central Africa Association, and before that came to an end ... I jumped into my present position [with Beaverbrook]. The suggestion that I am finding it very hard to obtain a living is therefore a lie and could be considered professionally damaging. Perhaps you could restrain this sweet boy as I do not think he would be a particularly bright ornament in a witness box.

Alf Flockhart was a key figure in Mosley's organisation, which was still giving its most devoted members much more than just membership of a political party. It was a home, a comfort blanket, a way of life, a reason for living. When young Trevor Grundy, the son of two devoted members, passed his eleven-plus, his proud mother told Trevor: "Alf said The Leader is delighted. He telephoned him in Paris."

Most of the old BPP people decamped into the LEL, and John helped the LEL to recruit them by passing Chesterton the *People's Post* mailing list – gold dust if you wanted to found a party of the extreme right.

But John refused to join, to Chesterton's disgust. Maybe, too late, he really had learned better. Maybe he could not play second fiddle to Chesterton. Maybe he couldn't take the LEL seriously – I know I used to laugh out loud when *Candour* arrived and I read it.

Sometime around then, Beckett and Chesterton fell out. John once told me that he wrote A.K. a letter, and the letter came back to him with the word FUCK scrawled over it in huge capitals. I was shocked because it seemed so unlike the dignified figure I knew. John said the kink that made Chesterton an alcoholic was always there, and when he was dry, it came out in other ways.

Whatever the full story, the falling out was terminal and irrevocable. I do not think they ever spoke again. I think too that A.K. was the last of John's old friends to have a relationship with him. I never saw any of them. He'd fallen out with the lot.

John and Anne no longer had much time for old friends. They had to find a way of providing for their family, and it looked as though they were going to lose their home. And about this time, John's past came back in a way that scared all of us.

As you drove out of the main gate of Thurlwood House, facing you, on the other side of the road, was a long, high brick wall. One morning we woke to see it full of huge white-painted slogans, carrying on for 100 yards. The one in big letters right opposite our gate read FASCIST GO HOME, and the others were along similar lines. Even a child could see clearly that they were aimed at us.

The police were called, the wall eventually cleaned. But John and Anne knew they were still watched all the time. Graham Mitchell of MI5 still had reports of their every movement. My brother remembers John "driving for miles through the countryside following a car that he had seen parked at the end of the drive, with strict instructions 'not to tell your mother.'"

But my father was still turning up in flash cars to collect me from the most exclusive prep school for miles around. One day a kindly teacher joined me at the school gate and asked where my father was. He went to the car and said: "Hallo, John, don't say you don't remember me – Bill Wright." John told me later that Mr Wright had been in prison with him during the war. I now know Wright was Mosley's district leader in Hampstead.

Sometime later, my father told me the teacher had worried that the school might find out from us about his imprisonment. John wondered aloud: why would Bill Wright suspect that he might give him away? I said nothing but nursed my guilt. It had been far too good a story to keep to myself, and within a day half of my class had heard it. They probably understood it even less than I did.

I needn't have worried. Bill Wright worked at St Martins until he retired. Years later, long after Wright's death, I corresponded with Mrs Wright, who told me that in those days, St Martins had a quota for Jews to keep the numbers down. That's not in the school's official history.

St Martins was a typical private prep school of that time, a little like Evelyn Waugh's Llanabba House, but not as grim as some. It was a bit of private enterprise by the headmaster, Lionel Woodroffe, to make use of his big house and grounds. Teaching was aimed firmly at Common Entrance, the entrance exam for public schools. They gave me a firm grip of English grammar which I have been grateful for all my life. They weren't as addicted to beating as a lot of private schools in those days, and the preferred instrument of chastisement was a relatively harmless gym shoe.

I did very little work, came regularly top of the class in English and near the bottom in Maths, and was not, I think, unhappy there.

The new duke's trustees demanded vacant possession of Thurlwood House, which was not only the roof over John's family's head but also, with the old duke dead, almost John's only source of income.

He and Anne stalled the trustees. The duke, they said, had given them Thurlwood House to live in for their lifetimes. He had died unexpectedly, otherwise he would have revised his will and left them their home. He would not have had them homeless. They trawled their correspondence with the duke to find letters that suggested this.

But the trustees were trying to raise the money to pay the death duties – at one stage they even offered to hand Woburn Abbey and all its treasures over to the taxman. They had already sold the whole of the village of Chenies, which had belonged to the Dukes of Bedford since 1526.

John had to find a way of earning some money. He knew he was unemployable. So, in 1954, the year after the duke's death, he created a business for himself.

He had been (anonymously) the stock exchange tipster for *Fleet Street Preview*, and still had the *Preview* and the BPP mailing lists. Both of these lists contained several men with a fair amount of money and not much brain. He wrote offering an investment advisory service, calling himself J. Barclay (Financial Consultant) so as to be able to attract subscribers who would not have anything to do with the notorious fascist John Beckett. For a modest subscription you could have a fortnightly stock exchange newsletter and a certain amount of free advice on your investments. He called it *Advice and Information*. A few fivers rolled in – enough to provide hope that all was not lost.

Then he tried to expand it beyond the very small circle of people who had joined the BPP or subscribed to *Preview*. He handed me the Bournemouth telephone directory, and told me to go through it picking out anyone with a senior military rank, or a title, or anyone who lived in a house with a name and no street number. These then received his promotional material.

Former military officers, John explained, were his best market. They had a lump sum from the army and little experience of the world outside it, and they needed someone like him to guide them about what to do with their money.

Politically, the newsletter ran with the sort of respectable right-wing Conservatism which John was adopting for what he still hoped might be a comfortable and respectable old age. The first issue, in November 1954, talked of "Mr Butler's businesslike control of the national finances" (R.A. Butler had become Chancellor of the Exchequer when the Conservative government took over in 1951) and asked: "Will his firm adherence to the welfare state, with its high taxation, prevent a swing of the have-nots to the opposition?... Experts think that Mr [Nye] Bevan will just succeed in keeping his party out at the next election."

Later he expanded on this thought: "Like everyone else who has enjoyed the personal friendship of Mr and Mrs Bevan I am very fond of them ... Together with charm, intelligence and wit, they both have a complete lack of commonsense."

That established the tone. *Advice and Information* was going to sound rather like a *Daily Telegraph* leader, with a few share tips thrown in. A few issues later he was writing: "It is time that the solid middle class people of this country made a little money for themselves as well as for the welfare state and I do sincerely hope to assist you in this endeavour." The man who had disrupted Parliament because of the low rate of unemployment pay had travelled a very long way indeed.

John was able to boast that all the shares he mentioned in his first three months showed a profit, most of them a substantial profit. He made his subscribers money by correctly predicting a Conservative election victory in 1955, and advising them to buy in anticipation, when Fleet Street financial editors were counselling caution.

He made no money for himself because he had none to invest, but one or two of his subscribers were willing to hand their whole share portfolio over to him to manage, in return for a modest percentage, and that produced a little extra income.

Like *Fleet Street Preview*, the newsletter made the most of the qualifications of its author, and then added a few, though always obeying John's golden rule: give your lie some elements of the truth. "For many years," he wrote in January 1955, "I was connected with the investment office of one of our few remaining very wealthy men." This was one way of expressing his role in the Duke of Bedford's life.

In February he claimed that he had "consulted associates in Paris and Washington". His Washington contact was, apparently, "one of the few men who really knows both President Eisenhower and world communist politics". I do not know who this remarkable man was, but I expect it was Colonel Ulius Louis Amoss, known to his friends as Pete, who got in touch with John, so he said, because he had seen and admired *Fleet Street Preview*.

Amoss had founded something called the International Services of Information Foundation, Incorporated (ISI), which called itself a non-profit, privately owned and operated intelligence service collecting and disseminating information from overseas.

It was a CIA front, of course. Whether John knew that or not, I have no idea.

Amoss had CIA connections but was probably not directly employed by them. Google him and you are straight into a peculiarly American form of right-wing craziness: long, long paragraphs written by seriously unhinged folk with no sense of humour but lots of guns.

In order to counter the communist threat, in 1953 Amoss developed an idea which he called "Leaderless Resistance" or "Phantom

Cells" – spontaneous, autonomous, unconnected cells seeking to carry out acts of violence, sabotage or terrorism against a government or occupying military force.

Amoss apparently wanted to use them to prevent the penetration and destruction of CIA-supported resistance cells in Eastern European countries under Soviet control. The idea was revived later by the Ku Klux Klan as a way for white nationalists to fight the US government, and is the theory behind several recent "lone wolf" acts of terrorism within the US. Amoss's long-term legacy may be ISIS's most successful method of terrorising Americans, and Europeans too.

Amoss commissioned John to write a monthly Letter from London, for which he offered very substantial payment. He came to London partly to tie up the deal, and I remember John coming home very impressed after he had been tucked up with a blanket in the back of a Rolls by the chauffeur and taken to lunch at the Savoy.

Amoss, according to Stephen Dorril, who writes about security services, was rather like Britain's Kenneth de Courcy, who was close to MI6, and who during the war had been secretary of the Imperial Policy Group, a bitterly anti-communist and anti-war organisation. De Courcy had been prominent among the anti-war faction in 1940. He had founded a pro-Franco body, the Friends of Nationalist Spain, and ran a conspiratorial publication, *Intelligence Digest*.

Amoss wrote to John and asked what he thought of de Courcy. As it happens, John thought de Courcy was a crook who had cheated some of his clients, and told Amoss so. He had warned his subscribers against de Courcy in Advice and Information. By that time, Amoss was probably already working with de Courcy.

I am not sure whether Amoss ever paid John, but if so the money soon stopped, and John worked on for a long time hoping it would be resumed. When he asked for the money, Amoss explained that his wealthy backers had pulled out and he could not pay. John asked if he could just have some money for expenses. Apparently that wasn't possible either, and Colonel Ulius Louis Amoss disappeared from our lives.

Then John had one of those really clever ideas which are often the foundation of enormous wealth.

He took it to lawyers and accountants, and they all said the same thing. It was so simple and beautiful that there must be something illegal about it, or someone would already be doing it. But they could not find anything wrong. So John wrote to all the subscribers to *Advice and Information* offering £10 units in the Thurlwood Investment Fund. He would invest the lot, and everyone would share in the fruits of his expert husbandry.

The idea of unit trusts is well established now, and fortunes have been built on them. But then they were unheard of. The Thurlwood Investment Fund was probably the first.

The money flowed in. The fund had tens of thousands of pounds within weeks. And then came a letter from the Board of Trade. I do not know exactly what it said, but there was, apparently, no way round it. The Thurlwood Investment Fund had to be wound up, and all the money sent back.

I think John thought that the security services had had a word with the Board of Trade, and from what I have seen of Mr Graham Mitchell's correspondence, he was probably right.

By now even John could see that some economies needed to be made.

A St Martins teacher called Mr Anderson inadvertently helped to find one economy. Mr Anderson was a very tall and unhealthily thin man with an extraordinary cadaverous face and a stoop. He was skin and bones, towering over you – a frightening figure to a small boy, like being menaced by a skeleton. His life, rather than just his job, was teaching in a prep school – he lived in a bedroom in the house of the deputy head next door to the school.

He instilled Latin in the traditional way – you recite declensions, and get hit every time you get one wrong. "A howl for a howler" was how Mr Anderson put it. As a pedagogical method, it has limitations, but it often works.

He ran a "court" for playground malefactors. What my crime was, I have long forgotten, but at the time I was sure I was not to blame. Mr Anderson thought otherwise, and sentenced me to six with his specially adapted gym shoe – he had cut the uppers off his size 12 shoe, to make it more whippy. He told off a senior boy to administer the punishment while he watched.

Anne thought hitting children was dreadful, and when she heard about it, she was determined not to send me back to a place that had

Mr Anderson and his specially adapted gym shoe in it. I didn't like to tell her that the beating was nothing new or particularly dreadful, and my distress was due entirely to my sense of injustice.

St Columbas in St Albans ticked all the boxes. It was much cheaper, Catholic, run by an American order of brothers which had burned all the canes they inherited from the previous owner, and I don't think they had heard of Common Entrance. My parents started to introduce me to the idea of the eleven-plus, which got you into grammar school. I now realise how sad that made John. Of all the dreams he had ever dreamed, the only one he had left was that his son should go to a top public school.

My brother was taken out of St Joan of Arc's Convent and sent to the local primary school, a light, airy, modern school called Little Green Lane, close to the house.

The next economy was more radical. Mr Fulford the gardener having been, with some difficulty, persuaded to retire and vacate the gardener's cottage, we moved into it.

Our quarters in Thurlwood were rented to a very rich American called Colonel Minehan, who I imagine was a CIA chum of Colonel Ulius Louis Amoss. (I know he was very rich – or else had access to unlimited US government funds – because when he moved out, it was to go to a far more splendid house, which I once visited with my father. When we got there, I was sent into the enormous, sculpted garden to play by myself. It was not, I think, a social call.)

I liked the cottage. I could happily have stayed there, and I could have brought my friends home without the embarrassment of having to explain why I lived in a mansion. It was a bit cramped for the five of us, but nothing like as cramped as we were to know quite soon.

The next move was back to Thurlwood House.

As Anne's sister Jo told me: "Thurlwood was far too grand a house to run without servants, which she did, leaving her no time to think of herself, her looks or her health."

She had, a couple of mornings a week, some help with cleaning from Mrs Williams, who lived on the nearby council estate. Phyllis Williams was a large, cheerful Geordie lady from Gateshead who, when she found out that John was the great socialist Gateshead MP, begged him to come home with her and meet her mother, who remembered him. John never would. Perhaps it would have been too sharp a reminder of what he had thrown away.

Nineteen-fifty-six was the year Britain invaded Suez, and the Soviet Union invaded Hungary. It was the year Nikita Khruschev's "secret speech" exposed the crimes of Stalin and the Royal Court Theatre unveiled John Osborne's "Look Back in Anger".

Tommy Steele and Lonnie Donegan leapt to fame. Jim Laker took 19 Australian wickets at Old Trafford, and Britain deported Archbishop Makarios from Cyprus and suppressed the Mau Mau in Kenya.

It was the first full year of independent television, and I remember watching the very first television advertisements. "Murray Mints, Murray Mints, the too-good-to-hurry mints". It was somehow irreverent, like strobe lighting in a cathedral.

All the old assumptions about being British that my father had grown up with before the First World War were shattered just as he needed them most: the assumption that Britain was a great power, that being British was special, that the British Empire was strong and benevolent and forever. After Suez he told his subscribers: "It is ironical that this final degradation of our national prestige will probably be accompanied by substantial profit for those subscribers who took our advice to buy Suez Canal Company shares at around £58."

It was also the year I started at Rickmansworth Grammar School, a ten-minute walk across Croxley Green from Thurlwood House. For the first time, my parents were not paying school fees for me and I could walk to school.

It was a revelation. I thought schools were dim old houses converted into dingy, oppressive classrooms presided over by chalk-stained pedagogues.

Here was a new building, just the fifth new grammar school to be built in Britain since the war; a monument to the Attlee settlement of Britain's affairs, purpose-built, opened just two years earlier to cope with the new customers created by the swift implementation of the 1944 Education Act and the raising of the school leaving age; light, airy and modern, with young and idealistic teachers who enjoyed what they did.

A splendid English teacher called Mr Arch gave me the lead part in a school play and taught me how poetry worked. Even Latin, which I thought consisted of mindless rote-learning led by bloodless elderly men, took on some meaning when Miss Collings taught it, for she started with Caesar's Gallic Wars. There were woods to play in and clubs to go to at breaktime. I never knew school could be like that.

Advice and Information was never going to make a fortune, but John's small band of faithful subscribers thought he was a well-connected genius, some of them demanding that he should send his newsletters to Downing Street so that the nation might be better governed. Few things embarrassed John: in March 1956 he reassured them that he had "the best of grounds for believing that *Advice and Information* is studied in Downing Street". I imagine it only got as far up the government tree as Mr Graham Mitchell of MI5.

Not that Mr Mitchell had a lot of time to study it any more. That year he became deputy director of MI5, under Sir Roger Hollis, and was busy producing a White Paper on the defections of Soviet spies Burgess and Maclean; a task he was performing with all the accuracy and fairness with which he had briefed ministers about John and Ben Greene.

The Mitchell White Paper lied about the time Maclean had been under suspicion, reducing it significantly; suggested Maclean had been tipped off when in fact he had detected the surveillance; understated Burgess and Maclean's access to secrets; and pretended the authorities had no legal power to prevent the men from absconding. It even got the name of Maclean's Cambridge College wrong. It was quickly christened the "Whitewash paper".

MI5 had been spending its time and money on detailed surveillance of easy targets like John Beckett and Britain's communist leader Harry Pollitt, who couldn't possibly be spies because everyone knew who they were. They paid no attention to the likes of Burgess and Maclean, who had been at public schools and were Mitchell's colleagues.

Somehow, John still had good political contacts who fed him accurate gossip. After Anthony Eden's disastrous invasion of Suez and his illness, the newspapers were tipping Rab Butler to become Prime Minister in his place; but my father said: "They won't have Butler, it's going to be Macmillan."

And, in January 1957, it was Macmillan, and my father got out his unpublished memoirs and added a sentence to a passage about newly elected Labour members from the north-east travelling to London by train together in 1925: "We were frequently joined by a pleasant young Conservative who had just won Stockton. His name, he told us, was Captain Harold Macmillan."

He did not add, but he told my mother and me, that Macmillan had a secret, known at that time only to political insiders. His wife had for years been conducting an extra-marital affair with fellow politician Robert Boothby, and the fourth and youngest of the Macmillan children, Sarah, born in 1930, was biologically Boothby's child. When I repeated this at school, they thought I was making it up.

Advice and Information did not expand a lot beyond the tiny base provided by *Preview* and the BPP. To save money, John and Anne took to typing and duplicating it themselves, and even despatching it. They got hold of a remarkable steel machine, and the children operated it twice a month. You passed a metal address label through it, placed an envelope over it, and banged the heavy handle down, and with luck a blurry and just about legible name and address appeared on the envelope.

John's heart murmur grew worse and was diagnosed as angina, and I remember him fainting fairly spectacularly a couple of times, while Anne's nerves were shredded to pieces with worry.

But it was in those years, between 1953 and 1958, that I learned about the extraordinary characters who had populated his life. He took me for long car drives, and talked and talked. I never met any of them, though. It was odd, having in your mind vivid descriptions of famous people, who still lived, but whom I never met and would never meet.

I hoped Leslie Henson was going to be the exception. We had bought a caravan, in which we holidayed one mid 1950s summer in the West Country, and one day my father said he would take me to the theatre in the nearby Somerset seaside town of Minehead, where Henson was playing.

After the show, he said, we would go round to the stage door and I would be introduced to his old friend.

He told me his Henson stories again, and in the theatre that night, Henson lived up to his billing. He had the rich, fruity voice and the comic timing that I had been promised. My one ambition in those days was to be an actor, and perhaps this famous actor friend of my father's could help me. I waited breathless to be taken backstage to meet him.

After the show, without a word, my father led me back to the car, and started on the drive back to our caravan. So, I said, what about going backstage to meet Leslie Henson? He said he thought it might be a nuisance to Henson after a show.

We drove back, my father speaking gently and levelly as he usually did with me, smoking cigarettes one after the other and throwing the butts out of the car window. I suppose he must have put a note into the stage door and got a brushoff. My father really was an outcast.

Then we took the caravan on to Woolacombe in Devon, and John wrote to Kyrle, to whom – I now know – he was still married, and who lived in Devon, in Paignton. I only know he wrote because I saw the reply, though I wasn't supposed to. It came from someone close to her – her sister? – and told John she was not well enough to see him. I am almost sure it ended: "I hope you will understand, John." Even he must have been starting to understand that he had become an untouchable.

Soon afterwards, he read that Henson had died. My mother never knew Henson, and my father had no one to mourn with but me; for I had listened, and knew all about him. He brought me the obituary, told me he'd always liked Henson and sauntered back to the room he kept as an office. Years later I saw, in the *Guardian*'s birthdays column, that Henson's son, the actor Nicky Henson, was born on the same day in 1945 that I was born. I don't suppose my father knew that.

Clem Attlee hung on to the leadership of the Labour Party until Herbert Morrison's chance of succeeding him had gone. To someone who knew the people and the politics, Morrison's frustration was evident, and John laughed loudly and shared the joke with anyone he thought might appreciate it, which, sadly, did not include most of the Catholic community in Rickmansworth who were his principal companions now.

Attlee finally retired in 1955. J. Barclay in *Advice and Information* told his readers: "Many years ago I shared a house in Limehouse with him." Perhaps subscribers were puzzled about how a story of a cowardly attack by Herbert Morrison on the imprisoned George Lansbury might be relevant to their investment portfolios. The point turned out to be that Attlee had "resigned at the precise moment when it would be most difficult for Morrison to assume the leadership. After 34 years the chickens have come home to roost. Although the markets have been quiet they have been firm."

John was returning to the values of his own childhood and his own boyishly jingoistic father, returning with renewed affection to the literature he had once loved before 1914, before the war and the world of labour movement politics scarred his soul. To these he was adding what he saw as the humour and gallantry of the Catholic Church.

He carefully introduced me to the authors he considered vital for the intellectual development of a young boy: Kipling, G.K. Chesterton, Belloc, G.A. Henty, Evelyn Waugh and the like, of course, but also Conan Doyle and Somerset Maugham, as well as his old friend Hugh Ross Williamson, Whittaker Chambers (the man who shopped Alger Hiss to Senator Joe McCarthy) and Douglas Hyde (the *Daily Worker* news editor who joined the Catholic Church) to show me what he considered to be the true nature of communism; more surprisingly, the autobiography of British Communist leader Harry Pollitt; and a book which I disappointed him by finding simply boring and lacking in style or elan. This was *My Struggle* by Adolf Hitler, and to this day I do not know what he expected me to make of it.

My mother introduced me to Shakespeare, and transmitted her own enthusiasm. By 1957, I was easily the best-read 12 year old I knew.

Of them all, G.K. Chesterton was the most important, and I spent happy hours with my father's copy of his collected works, and remembered his imposing, patrician cousin A.K., who no longer came to see us. Forty years later I put the two together, in an article for the *New Statesman*:

G.K. Chesterton wrote cheerful ballads about the pleasures of wine and beer. His cousin A.K. Chesterton was an alcoholic. G.K. was full of noisy, jolly pre-First World War imperial jingoism: "The earth is a place on which England is found/And you find it however you twirl the globe round." A.K. founded the League of Empire Loyalists in 1954.

G.K. was languidly anti-Semitic in the 1920s. A.K. wrote anti-Semitic diatribes in the 1930s as chief propagandist for the British Union of Fascists, and became the first chairman of the National Front in 1967. Yet A.K. was not a monster, any more than his more famous cousin. The line between writing jolly little verses about races you dislike, and writing vitriolic attacks on them, is remarkably indistinct.

Even at 12, I think I saw how G.K.'s dislike of Jews littered and disfigured his poetry. My father recommended, among others, a poem in which Chesterton's dog Quoodle laments the lack of a sense of smell in humans. It's a happy little poem until you get to the jarring, gratuitous second verse:

> They haven't got no noses,
> They cannot even tell
> When door and darkness closes
> The park a Jew encloses,
> Where even the law of Moses
> Will let you steal a smell.

John, who had once seen himself as a sort of Henty swashbuckler, now, I think, started to see himself as a sort of strong, wise Catholic Chestertonian hero, the sort who had a rakish past. He even had a Father Brown to play opposite his Flambeau, in Father Brendan Fox, the Irish parish priest in Rickmansworth.

Father Brendan fitted the bill rather well. A cheerful Galway man, he had been educated by the Irish Jesuits at St Ignatius College with William Joyce. He trained for the priesthood in Normandy, where he had acquired a taste for fine red wine and calvados, tastes which could not be easily satisfied in Rickmansworth in the early 1950s.

Father Brendan dutifully visited all his flock and drank the endless cups of tea they made for him, but he visited us more often than most because my father gave him wine instead. He was a kindly, devout, essentially simple man who was renowned all over Hertfordshire for his skill at tipping the winners in horse races. I think he was John's last real friend, in the end the only friend who remained to him.

My mother complained bitterly that she would like to have notice when the priest was staying for supper. For a pre-prandial snort he usually asked for "gin and cin" (gin and Cinzano), I think only to give my father the chance to say yet again "that's a fine thing for a priest to ask for" and laugh his loud, cracked laugh.

It was my allotted task to see that Father's glass was always full. If I fell down on the job, Father Brendan's kindly voice would pierce my reverie, and I would look round to see him with his glass held out while he looked the other way and said casually: "Oh, well, then, just a small one, Francis."

I saw his flock mostly at Mass on Sunday and confession on Saturday, the men in grey suits with baggy trousers and spotlessly clean white shirts and ties, the women in flowered dresses and hats (a woman was not supposed to enter the church with her hair uncovered). They were decent, pious middle-class 1950s folk, cradle Catholics and easily shocked; not people in front of whom you could express doubts about God or Holy Mother Church. The Pope could do no wrong, and neither could Father Brendan.

Among them were the Creeks, who lived near us. Mr Creek was something in the city, and Mrs Creek taught at St Joan of Arc's Convent. They had two daughters. My parents decided the older daughter was a suitable friend for me, a view not shared by either her or me, and made us spend excruciating afternoons together. Her slightly younger sister, Hilary Creek, in the early 1970s served a long prison sentence as a member of the Angry Brigade, which had carried out a series of amateurish bombings. I think I can understand how Hilary Creek, brought up entirely inside Rickmansworth's Catholic community, might have been filled with inchoate rage about the things the 1950s cheerfully tolerated, and the things they would not tolerate.

John was noisy, and could not help saying things to shock. He had the convert's problem with Catholic jargon. He would "take" communion and I cringed because the nuns had drummed into me that you "receive" communion. He asked Father Brendan to "make" a Mass for the Duke of Bedford, not to "say" a mass.

But he thought he had at last come home. He read, and recommended to everyone who would listen, Francis Thompson's "The Hound of Heaven":

> I fled Him, down the nights and down the days;
> I fled Him, down the arches of the years;
> I fled Him, down the labyrinthine ways
> Of my own mind.

In Hertfordshire's middle-class green belt, his loud laugh and emphatic speech were noticeably out of place.

But not his racism. That was OK. He explained to me, when we saw a mixed race couple in the street, that there were a few inadequates who could not find partners of their own race. And just sometimes – not often – he would say something that was so gross, so crude, that even in the 1950s when racial abuse was an everyday accepted occurrence, even I as a child would look twice and wonder whether I had heard right.

In a roomful of some of the most respectable people in Hertfordshire, he once talked of seeing a "big buck nigger" in the street. No one protested. They would have been horrified if he had said "fuck".

In the four years after the duke's death, John started to think things were going to turn out all right. *Advice and Information* might yet turn into a living. The duke's trustees were negotiating. The house, for as long as we could hang on to it, provided an income of sorts. They had got themselves out of the school fees trap. With luck, care, good judgement and a following wind the family might just make it through.

None of these were available. My family was on a precipice, and in 1958 we fell off it.

Notes on sources

Memoir of a Fascist Childhood by Trevor Grundy (Heinemann, 1998).
MI6: Fifty Years of Special Operations by Stephen Dorril (Fourth Estate, 2000).
Shades of Greene by Jeremy Lewis (Cape, 2010).
Stalin's Englishman by Andrew Lownie (Hodder, 2015).
Very Deeply Dyed in Black by Graham Macklin (I.B. Tauris, 2007).
White Racial Nationalism in Britain by Graham Macklin (Routledge, 2017).
With All Thy Might by Clive Powell-Williams (St Martins Trust, 1995).

24
A FAMILY IN FREEFALL

There were signs that disaster was coming. I just didn't recognise them.

One day the duke's wonderful grand piano turned up in the hall at Rickmansworth Grammar School. I had no idea it was coming. Mr Arch, a keen musician as well as an English teacher, was overwhelmed by this wonderful gift from my parents. I was miserable and embarrassed. The duke's grand piano was to reappear in my life once more.

My five-year-old sister Clare was taken out of school, to be educated at home. My mother had decided to use the vast expanse of Thurlwood to take in and teach local children whose parents were, like her, instinctively protective. She knew nothing about teaching or school curricula.

One day Anne did not get out of bed. She stayed in her room for what I felt was several weeks, but perhaps it was less. Each time I looked in, I saw looking up at me from the pillow the frightened face I had once glimpsed in Chorleywood, and I had the same instinct to run away.

The doctor came often. My father told me that around my mother's age, women went through a change, and in some women it caused illness and distress. But I do not think it was the menopause, or not just that. I think now that she was having a nervous break-down, and that she was never quite the same woman after it.

One day, as I passed her room, I heard her call me. She gave me an envelope, addressed, I think, to a firm of solicitors, and told me to take it quietly and post it, and not to tell my father. She said "they" would not let her send it.

All my life I have run away from decisions. I told my father I was going to the shops, and I let fate decide. He said he would walk with me, and as we walked he told me my mother was not quite rational just now, and much as he hated to ask ... I gave it to him. To this day I don't know if I did right, or what it said.

In 1958 an agreement was finally reached which enabled my parents to buy Thurlwood House from the trustees for considerably less than its market value. With great difficulty a bank loan was secured; my parents joked that a bank would always lend you money, so long as you could prove that you did not need it. The *Paula* and the *Golden Fleece* were sold.

John, typically, was immediately sure that his financial future was assured. There were dinners at Gows again, and he put into effect his cherished, and expensive, plan for my education.

This was to be his gift to his older son. John had been in the army as an ordinary soldier, and knew how much better army life was if you had a commission. Beaumont had a compulsory College Cadet Force, and John was sure that no Beaumont boy went into the army as an ordinary soldier, to be treated like dirt, as he had been. There was still conscription in 1958, and old Beaumont boys became officers.

The bar, that most snobbish of professions which my father had wanted so badly to join and which he now hoped I would join, was stuffed full of old Beaumont boys, and he thought the old school tie would be a great help there – as I'm sure it would have been.

I was beginning to see that my parents had given up on their own lives, and were investing all their hopes in mine. I had to be a top lawyer for my father, and a great actor for my mother.

Beaumont would make me what he now wished he had been: a gentleman, with the right accent and the right contacts.

He had felt patronised in Parliament by men from public schools; he wanted his son to do the patronising. He wanted to ensure that I would not end up with foolish notions of creating a better world, in the pursuit of which I might ruin my life as he had ruined his. He repeated the line credited to Churchill: "If a man is not a socialist by the time he is 20, he has no heart. If he is not a conservative by the time he is 40, he has no brain." I do not know whether he believed this rubbish, but he wanted me to believe it.

He adopted, then preached to me, ideas which he thought would ensure a comfortable life for me.

It was the sort of conservatism that was confined to grumpy colonels in the corner of the Athenaeum until long after John's death when Margaret Thatcher made it respectable. Low unemployment, John wrote in *Advice and Information* in 1956,

> may seem a desirable state of affairs, but it means that, in present circumstances, the "workers" are in a position to dictate what wages they will accept, irrespective of economic facts … Discounting miracles, there must either be a show-down with the unions, something on the 1926 model, or there will be a heavy fall in the value of the pound.

He wanted to convey to me the desirability of behaving conventionally and not rocking any boats; to give me a comfortable and respectable right-wing conservatism to follow. It didn't work, but the love in the effort is enormous.

So I was taken out of the grammar school and sent for two terms to a crammer, because the Jesuits had convinced John that their academic standards were much higher than those of the despised state education system.

It was an entirely unnecessary expense. The Jesuits had lied to him. I had been well taught at Rickmansworth Grammar School, and, in most subjects, was well ahead of what Beaumont had to offer.

Beaumont was the last example of my father's style of decision-making which led him to take his battered idealism to Oswald Mosley in 1933 and William Joyce in 1937. In 1958 he took me away from an excellent local grammar school where my education was free, to a virtual prison where a thoroughly inferior education was provided at enormous cost, thus ensuring a poverty-stricken old age for him and my mother.

At Beaumont we slept in tiny cubicles, each furnished with a steel bed, a bowl and a jug of freezing water. In the first year, my short, stout, emphatic class teacher, Father Bamber, made us learn three questions and answers from the Catechism every day. Failure to reproduce them word for word incurred a visit to Father Brogan, whose melancholy duty it was to spend each morning break hitting boys' hands between three and 18 times with a flat, whippy instrument made of whalebone and rubber, called a ferrula.

After my first visit to Father Brogan I ran about for ten minutes, clutching my hurt hands and vowing I would never do anything again that would bring this misery upon me. But I couldn't keep it up, and I collected ferrulas most weeks for the next four years. After a while they didn't hurt so much.

I was always being beaten, by somebody, for something. Cheek a 17-year-old monitor and you would find yourself bending over a chair to be caned by the head boy – the school captain, as he was called – who held court in the captain's lounge every morning after mass, examining offences and deciding how many strokes to administer.

A frequent offence for younger boys was to fail to march properly down the "higher line gallery", a corridor reserved for older boys who were in the "higher line". When younger boys' business took them down it, for example to go to the library, they had to button up their coats and march down the centre, making a neat right or left about-turn at the door they needed. Older boys lounged along the walls, inspecting marching styles, languidly abusing their marching juniors, making them go back and start again, ordering lines or a visit to the captain's lounge.

But the real terror was called a panning, Beaumont's version of the formal flogging beloved of public schools. Apparently after lights out, two Jesuits, in their long black robes, collected the condemned boy silently and took him downstairs to be ceremonially laid out and beaten on his pyjamaed bottom. I believe someone said a prayer. The mere threat of it caused me nightmares for a week.

Every Thursday afternoon we shined our army boots and paraded to the clipped but perfectly formed vowels of Major Roddy, a sort of military caricature, with the handlebar moustaches which I had seen in war movies. The major also taught history and art. By the end of my first year I had detailed maps of the dispositions at the battles of Hastings, Agincourt, Crecy and Bosworth, but little idea of what happened between these events.

He had a theory that wars were caused by the straight edges of the houses in which we lived, and could be ended if all rooms were round. I told my father this theory, and he said that military men tend to be naïve. I suppose it was nothing to the sort of mystical rubbish he had heard from Major General "Boney" Fuller.

I learned quickly that my grammar school background was not something to boast about. I was the only boy who had seen the inside of a state school, and it led to awkward questions. An older boy asked how much my father earned. I did a quick sum in my head, multiplying the number of his clients by the amount of the subscription, and came up with a figure which I knew would provoke derision, so I doubled it. "My God, the boy lives in penury", he shouted, and departed to spread the glorious news.

My most cherished ambition was sternly frowned on by the Jesuits. They refused to allow me to act in the school play, saying that I spent too much of my time reading plays, producing them and press-ganging my classmates to act in them.

There was no sex education – not a scrap – just a looming certainty, never discussed, that sex destroyed the soul, and a chorus of squeaking bedsprings after lights out, as the tiny cubicles in which we slept sprang to life. I remember two slightly older boys telling me of the torments that awaited the soul of a boy who masturbated. I swore I'd never do it again. I lasted a good few hours.

The other boys' fathers were vast, remote figures, their mothers fashionable and semi-detached. Parents had parted from their off-spring with a sigh of relief, and seldom came to take them out.

My parents were completely different. They wanted, with every fibre of their being, to be real parents. They came to see me at Beaumont on the smallest excuse. A play I wasn't in, normally attended only by the relatives of the cast, brought my parents' car (increasingly an elderly and unreliable heap of junk, picked up for next to nothing at a local second-hand car lot) wheezing from Hertfordshire to Berkshire.

John could now laugh as old fascist comrades made asses of themselves. He noted that Mosley's powers of self-deception were undimmed: the Leader appears genuinely to have thought he was going to win North Kensington in the 1959 general election, when he lost his deposit.

That year Colin Jordan got in touch with John for the last time. "I was organising indoor, private meetings at the spacious home of a London supporter", Jordan told me.

> I wrote to him to ask if he would come and speak. He declined in words which, while I cannot precisely quote them, amounted to saying that he was thoroughly disillusioned with the British public and thought that activity designed to appeal to that public and solicit its support was a waste of time. He was not prepared, he intimated, to waste more of his time in this way, and urged me not to also; advice which obviously I ignored.

I am sure Jordan's account is accurate. But even John would have had more sense than to get involved with Jordan in 1959. Jordan had gone from John's BPP to A.K.'s Empire Loyalists, and left that to form the White Defence League in 1956. He had moved, as he put it to me, from British nationalism to pan-Aryan National Socialism, and held "Hitler Was Right" meetings. The next year he was to found the British National Party.

John felt sad for him, and angry when he heard that Jordan had been fired from his teaching post for his political activities in 1962. But he wanted nothing more to do with neo-Nazis. Slowly and painfully, he was starting to accept that the Holocaust was not an invention of British warmongers, or Jewish international capitalists, or anyone else; it had really happened.

The idea that he could afford Beaumont's enormous fees had always been absurd, even though he had made the appalling calculation that he could afford a splendid public school for one child so long as he economised on the other two. The very last time we went to Gows, the manager intimated politely that he wasn't keen on another signed bill, and a cheque would be appreciated. Mr Beckett didn't have his cheque book with him? No problem, they had a book of blank cheques.

Clare, now six, had her third change of school – from local primary, to home schooling, she now started at St Joan of Arc's Convent in Rickmansworth, where I had been. She would not be there long.

Advice and Information was going nowhere, and the family had to move out of the front of Thurlwood House, so that it could be let to Mr and Mrs Binkhorst. Mr Binkhorst was something senior in the Dutch embassy in London. The Binkhorsts had for some years rented the better of the two flats on the first floor, and Mrs Binkhorst rented the field to keep her horses. They wanted more space, and we needed more rent.

This time there was to be no gracious house in Chorleywood, not even a cottage in the grounds of Thurlwood, for that had been sold. We just crept round to the back of Thurlwood House, and put our things in the servants quarters at the back of the ground floor, which had once been the offices of the BPP. It made a small, cold, damp flat, with a scullery doing duty for kitchen and a family of five crammed into it, and there we camped, while our parents hoped for better times.

They tried to keep up a decent front, but saw almost no one, for they were ashamed of the circumstances in which they lived. My parents were resilient people; they could both still joke, and they both still had a talent for making me laugh, so I never really understood the situation. They were still my witty, amusing, loving parents.

If John did see anyone, he did so on one of his visits to town. "Beckett entertained me to tea at the Waldorf Hotel, Aldwych, where he seemed at home", Colin Cross, the author of the first book about the BUF, told Colin Holmes.

> He was a man with a considerable sense of humour and I enjoyed various anecdotes he told me, although suspecting that

perhaps he embroidered them for effect. He struck me as a man of strong and independent personality who had lived on his wits and had had a most interesting life. An excellent talker.

All true, but what Cross never knew was that it was all unravelling when they met in 1960.

One sports day, or something – an excuse for my parents to visit me at Beaumont, anyway – I trailed after them along the side of the cricket pitch and heard them mention Rickmansworth Grammar School.

"They seemed hurt", said Anne, and John said: "They thought we'd given the piano to them for good." And as they talked, not knowing I could hear, I realised with dawning horror why there were now two virtually unused pianos in the Beaumont school hall instead of one. They had taken the Duke of Bedford's magnificent grand piano away from Rickmansworth Grammar School and given it to Beaumont.

Sometimes we only know what we want when we can't have it. In that moment I knew what I wanted. I wanted to go back to the grammar school, and my foolish father had casually put a match to my boats. I couldn't face Mr Arch after that.

I was awoken from my misery by Father Ezekiel's hectoring public schoolmaster's voice. "Beckett, if you walk behind the sight screen again, a visit to Father Brogan will ensue." Then he saw my parents. "I'm sorry, Mr Beckett, but I have told this boy at least a dozen times." He was lying. Walking behind the sight screen on the cricket pitch was about the only sin in Beaumont's long list of sins that I hadn't committed before. It shocked me that a priest should lie.

It must have been on one of my first holidays from Beaumont that the electricity was cut off because the bill hadn't been paid. It was still off when I went back to school, but by then John had realised that our rooms had access to the cellar, where in happier times he had kept his wine, and its supply was charged to the Binkhorsts, not to us. Guiltily, we ran electric fires and lights from it for weeks.

That term, on one of the three days in the term when our parents could take us out, the elderly wreckage that passed for a car in the

Beckett household by then refused to start, and the parents of another Hertfordshire boy were asked to collect me and drop me at a cafe in Rickmansworth.

After lunch we took the bus to the flat in Thurlwood. My sister Clare turned on the lights in triumph. The repair man had been, she said. She had been told there was a fault.

Having been at a state school, I was naturally placed in the bottom stream, and in spite of coming regularly at the top of it, I stayed there while others leap-frogged, until after five terms I gave up trying, and did no work whatsoever.

Years later, when I left university, I taught for a couple of terms in a comprehensive school, where as the youngest and least experienced teacher in the History department, I was given the remedial classes to teach. I realised then that the bottom stream at Beaumont was a remedial class for rich kids. My classmates propped up the rugby scrum and acquired such simple skills as city gents and estate agents require.

This led to a tricky protocol problem. While all the other classrooms were on the main classroom corridor, the C stream in the second year were shoved into a grubby little room off the "second playroom". (Older boys were in the "higher line", the next oldest in "second playroom" and the youngest in the "third playroom.") You didn't get to "second playroom" until you reached a certain age. Most of my classmates had reached it, but I and a couple of others were young in the year, and were still in "third playroom". To reach our classroom, therefore, we had to pass through a room which we were not yet entitled to enter.

How could this dilemma be resolved? Perhaps we could be permitted entry so long as we marched, as in the higher line gallery? While the debate raged, getting to my classroom involved a hazardous journey. Eventually it was agreed that we might pass through without marching, so long as we looked neither to left nor right, and did not stop to speak to anyone.

The room, when we got to it, was the shabbiest classroom I have ever seen. There was a jagged hole on the dirty back wall which the geography master claimed to have caused when he threw a blackboard wiper at an inattentive boy. It was the only break in the bare walls.

Bullying was institutionalised. There were always one or two boys right at the bottom of the heap, who were teased and tormented and bullied from dawn til bedtime, when they must have cried themselves to sleep. How they were selected, no one knew, though a title would normally protect you, or being the scion of one of the old Beaumont families or being good at rugger and keen on it.

One of these victims managed to get himself expelled at the start of the second year, and after intensive psychotherapy he went on to be happy. Another was less lucky. His father was a Pole who had come to England, made money, and drove a pink Bentley Continental. So everyone muttered "nouveau riche" meaningfully whenever he was near.

He had been to Beaumont's prep school as well, and the little boy's life was irremediably destroyed one dreadful day at the age of seven, when the other boys discovered the shaming information that his Irish mother's first name was Pixie. He was tormented with this every day of his life until he left Beaumont at 17, and the Jesuits could think of nothing to do with him but have him regularly beaten for fighting and not working.

By the time I knew him, when we were both 13, the pattern was set. Each day, sometimes each hour, he would have to walk past groups of boys all hissing "Pixie, Pixie". Sometimes he pretended not to notice, other times he piled into the centre of the group in a fury, both fists flying, perhaps inflicting a bruise or two, often receiving bruises. He was always fighting, always hurting or being hurt, never for half a day at peace.

I met him once, a few years later. He wore a tweed jacket, white shirt and Beaumont old boys' tie – this in the 1960s – and muttered a few reactionary prejudices. He was still trying to earn the respect of Beaumont, subject to uncontrollable rages, and his despairing mother was taking him to a psychiatrist. He died in his fifties, apparently by his own hand.

Almost never seeing women, older boys became obsessively interested in younger boys, and kept lists of their favourites. Generally it stopped at that, but in my year there was a circle about whose activities in the woods we all sniggered. Eventually most of them were expelled.

Shortly afterwards my class was taken by coach to a museum in London, and we saw one of the expelled boys on the pavement as we climbed into the coach. My classmates set up a cry of "homo" and "Oscar" (two films about the life of Oscar Wilde had just been released). I sat unusually silent. I was thinking: when the coach has pulled out, that boy is free. I must return to prison.

I begged to be allowed out to audition for the National Youth Theatre, but the rector turned me down. My parents told a lie for me, and collected me and delivered me at the interview, but I couldn't act that day. I thought that Beaumont had destroyed my confidence.

Advice and Information was still coming out, but the number of subscribers was dwindling. There was a serious effort to talk about stock markets instead of politics, but its author's knowledge was decaying. My mother told me years later that it was making virtually no money.

One day my father picked me up at Beaumont, in a tiny, elderly, battered Fiat 500 which he nursed along the road with all the care that he had once taken driving racing cars round Brooklands. The engine stopped when we had to stop at traffic lights unless he revved it constantly.

He told me that he had a new job. He would, he said, be working for a big security firm, watching their investments overnight so that he could take instant action if their value looked likely to decrease.

It was not until the holiday, when I saw him set off from the house in the early evening wearing a uniform, that I realised the truth. He had by then, I imagine, a pretty shrewd idea of the sort of school he had sent me to, and the misery that would be visited on me if it were known that my father was a night security guard for Securicor.

After I left Beaumont the pretence was dropped. He told me how Securicor had demanded an account of his employment for the previous 25 years, and he had to invent something for the years 1940 to 1943 because they would never employ a man who had seen the inside of a prison. And he told me what he would do if his van were attacked. "I would put up the fiercest token resistance", he said, and laughed his loud, cracked, full-hearted laugh.

Anne brushed up her shorthand and found a secretarial job.

And none of it was enough. So John must have asked Beaumont to allow me to be a day boy, so as to pay lower fees. There were only about four day boys in the school, and all the others were the sons of masters. But the Rector must have said yes. And so the family wearily picked itself up and moved again, to a town none of us knew.

We rented a flat on the upper two floors of a riverside house in Staines, a bus ride from Beaumont. Clare, at eight, had her fourth change of school, to Staines Preparatory School, where she did not thrive since she had not been taught any of the things her classmates had been taught, so after a few months she had her fifth change, to a smaller school in Staines.

By now John and Anne were getting on very badly, and John's past kept coming back to haunt them. The first unit trusts were advertised, and John asked aloud, with quiet bitterness, how they differed from his scheme which he had been prevented from developing. They didn't.

The *Evening Standard* diarist got in touch for a "where are they now" piece and John said he had played no part in politics for 16 years and now ran a stock exchange advisory newsletter called *Advice and Information*. How much did it make? "No – well, I manage", he was quoted as saying. As for his old political associates, " 'I never see or hear from them, nor do I read their publications' Mr Beckett told me firmly."

After 30 years John had made peace with his younger brother, and Cecil started coming round – a tall and very thin man who kept a shop in East Ham. I learned later that he had been fired from several jobs during and after the war when his employer found out who his brother was; but he never told John. "It would just make him angry, and he couldn't do anything about it", he told Anne after John's death.

Even when we visited Anne's mother and her older sister Hilda in their Wandsworth flat, the shadow of the past fell over us, though we did not know it at the time. For there I met a boy called Peter Holford, the son of Anne's cousin. We got on well enough, but apparently his father, normally apparently a placid man, told him furiously afterwards: "He's Beckett's son. He was Mosley's right hand man." "To me he looked like a harmless old man hunched in a chair", says Peter Holford now.

I proceeded to fail most of my O-levels, and I suppose the Jesuits lied to my parents again, and said it would all have been different if I hadn't been a day boy. So the money had to be found to send me back to board for a year, and I managed to acquire a small but serviceable clutch of O-levels.

We moved out of the Staines flat and back to the servants' quarters in Thurlwood. My sister Clare's sixth school change took her back to St Joan of Arc's Convent in Rickmansworth, aged about ten.

And Clare remembers from that brief period a father who loved her, who turned up at the Convent all good cheer and whom everyone there seemed to like, and who, when she got into some sort of trouble, came into the school and sorted it out quietly, calmly and without drama.

But there was nothing else left to sell, so Thurlwood was put on the market.

Anne's mother and her sister Hilda lived in a Victorian block of flats in Wandsworth, south London, and they found us another small flat in the block to rent, so that we would be near to them. Clare, aged nine, had her seventh change of school, going this time to a crammer in Hammersmith; then, swiftly, her eighth, to the Arts Educational Trust in Piccadilly.

Notes on sources

Peter Holford (*Cockney Ancestor*, 142, Spring 2014).

25

STRUTS AND FRETS HIS HOUR UPON THE STAGE, AND THEN IS HEARD NO MORE

In 1962 I left school, Thurlwood House was sold, my parents were at last free to get married with the death of my father's second wife, and we moved home for the tenth time in my 17 years. The next year my parents got married, we moved home for the eleventh time and President Kennedy was assassinated.

In my last term at Beaumont I started dimly to realise the sacrifice my parents had made to send me there, and how poorly I had repaid them. Beaumont had kept me resolutely in the bottom stream, and I had made no effort to acquire sporting distinction, for I never mastered the trick of enjoying sports when they were compulsory. I had even managed to avoid any promotion at all in the CCF – most of my contemporaries were NCOs, but I was not, perhaps because I had never hidden from Major Roddy my contempt for the whole business. But it now occurred to me that I should try at least to do something that would make my father proud, and make him feel it had all been worthwhile.

The chance came when a small debating team was to be sent to speak at Eton. I had made a bit of a splash in the debating society, and was delighted when the Jesuit who ran it agreed that I could be in the team. But a deputation went up to the Jesuit charged with discipline asking that I be removed from the team, and he agreed to remove me. I never knew why. "It's because you smell, Beckett", a boy in the year above told me, but I don't think I did. At the time I thought perhaps they remembered the grammar school, or had found out how poor we were. The truth, I think, was that Beaumont was pathetically grateful to be invited to Eton, and feared I might say something out of place.

The sale of Thurlwood paid the debts and bought a small but new car, a Triumph Herald. We moved to a pleasant flat, the ground floor of a big house in Wimbledon. This flat seems to have been found for us by the West German embassy, and I think may even have been rented from them; and it was vacant because one of their top officials was going home. I don't know what story lies here, but John had been writing for help with growing desperation to every old contact who he thought might still feel kindly towards him. Did my father, 17 years after the war, still have friends, or friends of friends, at the West German embassy?

He still worked nights for Securicor, but took care not to be seen in the uniform. He feared meeting old friends, or, even worse, old Beaumont boys whom I might know. He left the flat in the Triumph Herald wearing a sports jacket over his uniform trousers, and put on the cap and jacket when he got to work.

Kyrle's 1962 death certificate for the first time told the truth about her age – she was 75 – and described her as "wife of John Beckett, journalist (retired)". But it left one final mystery. Notification of the death was given by someone called E.A. Beckett-Bourchier, described as Kyrle's daughter. Another half-sister I know nothing of? Almost certainly not, I'd say; no one in my father's family seemed to think you should tell the truth on these forms if you can possibly help it. A sister, describing herself as a daughter to avoid probate issues? Who knows?

Kyrle Bellew's death enabled my parents to get married at the register office in neighbouring Morden.

I don't think they wanted to particularly. They were sleeping in separate rooms – the Wimbledon flat was just big enough to allow this, though it meant that John's small bedroom had to double as his office, where he still wrote *Advice and Information* and answered letters from those clients still left to him.

Anne was now exasperated with John all the time. The noise his false teeth made chewing on his meat shredded her nerves, especially since he always talked loudly with his mouth full; and she no longer bothered to hide her feelings. Somewhere inside her, she knew what his foolishness had done to her.

She was desperately alone. She had never been comfortable with his Catholic friends from Rickmansworth, and anyway we never saw them. John and Anne ere not on speaking terms with any of their fascist friends.

She did, I think, have someone to talk to, but only in absolute secrecy. Sylvia Morris, William Joyce's old friend, Anne's comrade in arms in her campaign to get her husband released, had decisively broken with the anti-Semitic right and become fervently anti-racist. She had joined the Labour Party, and in the 1950s she was organising trade union holidays in Eastern Europe, until in 1962 she became secretary of the British Yugoslav Society.

She was also having an intense affair with a Jewish actor who had three children, and he was in the throes of a difficult separation from his wife.

Anne and Sylvia met for lunch from time to time, but it was awkward. Sylvia could not tell either her lover or her colleagues whom she was meeting; there had to be a cover story every time. She could never come to our home, or have Anne to hers. Anne and Sylvia took their troubles to each other over lunch in department stores.

I am not sure how much Anne could burden the younger woman with her troubles, though. Sylvia had her own troubles. Her actor turned out to be bipolar, married and occasionally violent. Just as Sylvia was ready to act on Anne's good advice and get out of this relationship quickly, the actor's wife killed herself, leaving him with three children whom he was clearly not capable of looking after.

Sylvia had grown close to the children, who faced a life in care. She stayed with them and their father, and brought them up. In Sylvia's lifetime, the three children she brought up never knew that she had been a fascist; and, of course, they never met Anne. But they are devoted to the memory of Sylvia.

I wonder how my parents managed to make sure that I and my brother and sister never found out about their wedding.

It probably wasn't hard. I was too busy enjoying myself to worry about what they did. I had come out of the stifling atmosphere of an English Catholic public school into London to find the 1960s waiting for me. It seemed to me as though I had come from a prison into a new world, cleaner, fairer, fresher, freer and infinitely more fun. I was filled with wild optimism – for me and for the world. It was as though the hopes of the generation of 1918 had been transferred to that of the 1960s: "Proud of having conquered our inherited inhibitions, in our innocence we believed there was little else to conquer", as my father had written of 1918.

I was able to join in the fun of the 1960s thanks to the last and best decision my parents made about my education. There was no money for the expensive crammers favoured by old Beaumont boys, so I went to the City of Westminster College, a state further education college off Victoria Street.

It was like being allowed back into Rickmansworth Grammar School. I rediscovered history. Instead of a dreary parade of long-dead martyrs and Catholic propaganda, Dr Warren taught us, methodically but with humour and passion, about Canning and Castlereagh, Napoleon III and Bismarck.

Dr Warren was short and plump and had an accent which I loved but could not place. Now I know it was that middle European accent which suggests that he was probably a Jewish refugee who had come to Britain in the 1930s, and had that passion for history which often engages intelligent Jews who have seen persecution. His original name, as my father might have said, was probably not Warren.

The English teacher was the playwright N.F. Simpson, who was just starting his theatrical success with *One Way Pendulum* and *A Resounding Tinkle*. He reminded me of the joy of reading poetry which my mother had given me as a child, and Beaumont had squeezed out of me.

Most of all, there were my fellow students. We had moved home so often that I had no social circle outside Beaumont. Now I was meeting people from comprehensive schools, people from Africa and India; people for whom my family's poverty was nothing unusual, to whom Beaumont's snobbery was another world. Most important of all, I was meeting girls.

Since I had left the grammar school a lifetime ago, my experience of girls was limited to gazing with hopeless longing at the chorus line on television. I still remember with appalling clarity the legs of a teenage girl I once glimpsed from the car window as she swung upside down from the branch of a tree when I was maybe 14 or 15. My father was talking, and talking, and he continued to drive, and to talk. For all I know, that day he chose to unburden himself of all his secrets.

Dr Warren taught a shortened course to the one-year students, stopping in 1914 though the syllabus went on to 1939. I imagine that European history in the years between the world wars might have been very close to home for him. He knew he had taught us enough to find questions on our A-level papers which we could answer.

But I asked my father to give me the inter-war years, and, impromptu, he gave me the most accomplished lecture I had ever heard, better even than those thoughtful, precise, illuminating lectures of Dr Warren's.

He could do that sort of thing. He could also do the most excruciatingly stupid things. Even the embarrassment I had felt about the Duke of Bedford's grand piano following me from school to school paled into insignificance when he told me proudly that he had written to his old friend Clem Attlee asking if the former Prime Minister would please put in a good word to get his son Francis into Clem's old Oxford College. I didn't even want to go there.

Attlee wrote back – a kind and chatty letter about his health and similar matters. He said, reasonably enough, that he didn't think he could write to University College on behalf of a young man he had not met. I remember my father showing it to me, and being surprised that a former Prime Minister should type his own letters, inaccurately, on a typewriter whose margins were clearly not working.

Years later I wrote a biography of Attlee and found that this was his way. I also found that one of his many political strengths was that he could remember names and faces from years ago. "I posted you in Spent Trench in 1915", Prime Minister Attlee told an old soldier whom he met as Prime Minister more than 30 years after 1915. John did not have this precious gift, but he had a trick. If a man over 50 approached him and said, "Hallo, John, don't you remember me", he would say: "Of course I do. How's the old complaint?" on the grounds that every person of late middle age has got one.

"There may have been good grounds why Napoleon and Hitler should have been liquidated", John told his few, no doubt bemused, subscribers in March 1963. "They were not, however, destroyed because they were bloodthirsty dictators or immoral men. They were destroyed because they sought to organise a united European economy which would make Europe independent of the money magnates." General de Gaulle, he said, was now doing that, and this meant that the general was courting danger.

He seemed to be trying belatedly to adopt a set of safe, conventional opinions. When *Private Eye* attacked Winston Churchill, calling him the Greatest Dying Englishman, John was incandescent with Blimpish rage, which surprised me. Surely, I protested, we don't approve of Churchill. What about warmongering, what about Tonypandy? What about Baruch and the Jews? No, no, he said, this is an elderly man who has done his country some service, harrumph. He was shocked by the behaviour of John Profumo, the War Minister who lied to Prime Minister Macmillan about his relationship with Christine Keeler. Dreadful, he intoned, for the man to place his wife in that danger by returning to her after consorting with a prostitute. He seemed to be striving belatedly after respectability. But it was too late. There was no one to hear but me.

He was still dragging himself to Securicor most nights, until the husband of an old friend of Anne's, Reggie Keenan, who owned a Savile Row tailor, had a heart attack. Reggie and Ida Keenan had travelled back on the boat with Anne from New Zealand, and, unlike John, Anne kept relationships in good repair.

Anne must have told Ida that John knew the industry. So John was drafted in as temporary manager, nearly half a century after he had left his job as a draper's manager in Sheffield for the bright lights and glittering politics of London.

He had come full circle. He was back in the trade into which his father had apprenticed him, before the First World War. It was strange to see him welcoming customers with a passable effort at the proper obsequiousness. He doubled the wages of the elderly cutter and had him make me by far the finest suit I have ever possessed.

At last he was "living small". He had an "ordinary job" just as Anne had wanted ever since 1945, or even earlier.

But it was too late. By the end of 1963, his sixty-ninth year, John was in constant pain with what turned out to be stomach cancer.

It didn't stop our eleventh move. The last of the money from Thurlwood was sunk into buying a ten-year lease on an unused set of attic rooms on the top floor of a huge and splendid building in Kensington, right beside the Albert Hall, and putting in a kitchen and bathroom. Clare, aged 12, moved schools for the ninth time to a convent in Kensington called More House.

I am not quite sure why we made the move. The lease was going cheap, and it took us into an area which, even then, was fabulously rich – we were going to be the poor neighbours of everyone we met. It must have seemed a good idea at the time.

There was something else, though. John and Anne thought the Wimbledon flat was haunted.

It was a ground floor flat, and the first floor was occupied by a pair of elderly ladies who told my parents why the West German embassy official was going home. His wife had killed herself in the flat.

John had believed in Mosley, in William Joyce, in papal infallibility, in Doris Chesterton's power to see the future, in a Hell with no one in it, in spirits and table-rapping. It was not so hard to imagine that his cancer might have something to do with a malign and unhappy ghost.

By the time we moved, John was taking herbal remedies and could eat nothing more than Complan, a revolting sort of mush for invalids. For a hearty carnivore, never happier than when he had a steak and a glass of red wine or a pint of ale in front of him, it was torment.

The doctors told him he must have an operation. He never trusted doctors and never liked the idea of operations, but he wrote to Bob Forgan for advice. "If I am ever able to eat a decent lunch again it would give me great pleasure to buy you one", he added wretchedly. Forgan wrote back: yes, he should have the operation.

John carried on trying to get *Advice and Information* out, but it is clear from their style that great chunks were now being written by Anne. He was growingly appalled by the idea of a Labour government led by Harold Wilson, for whom he had conceived a distant loathing so intense that I think Wilson must somehow have reminded him of Ramsay MacDonald.

At the start of October 1964, now dictating his newsletter to Anne from a hospital bed, he was predicting a Conservative victory. Harold Wilson narrowly won the general election that month.

He had the operation. Two incoherent *Advice and Information* newsletters appeared in November, dictated from a hospital bed.

He told me he was dying, and tolerated with patience and kindness my squirming, stilted 19-year-old response, which was to look longingly through the hospital window at the traffic and say tonelessly that I would miss him. He answered, without a hint of irony, that it was kind of me to say so.

But there was one day when, against medical orders, he was sitting bolt upright in his bed when my mother and I arrived. He almost shouted to us: you could hear, for the last time, the dim echoes of the huge voice which had quelled hundreds of great meetings in that Indian summer of political oratory between the two world wars. "They've seen it at last, they've admitted I was right all along." I knew what he meant. He meant: right about Ramsay MacDonald, right about Mussolini and Hitler, right about war and peace.

My mother tried to say something soothing, but he was not a man to be soothed. "It's all over the papers."

I walked swiftly out, leaving the full burden of his unhappiness to fall on my mother, which was where I usually dumped unwanted burdens. I knew now what went on during those long, solitary walks in the countryside. As I left I heard him ask where I was going, and my mother told him I was going to get the papers. The next time I saw him, he was lucid again, and for the few weeks of life remaining to him, he never again allowed himself the indulgence of dreaming in public.

Just before Christmas we brought him home to Queensgate to die. On Christmas Day we gave him a drop of brandy drowned in a glass of water. He was looking forward to it, but he choked on it. Early on the morning of 28 December my mother woke me quietly to say that he was dead. The only useful thing I could think of to do was to ring Father Brendan, though we had not seen him for years. He burst into tears. I listened, impassive, while the priest sobbed.

John had asked to be cremated. He said it was because he dreaded the thought of being buried alive, and partly it was. But he had never forgotten Arthur Bourchier's funeral pyre in South Africa, where the mourners were ushered away as the flames roared towards the sky and consumed his friend. He would quote G.K. Chesterton:

> If I had been a heathen
> I'd have piled my pyre high
> And in a great red whirlwind
> Gone roaring to the sky.
> But Higgins is a heathen
> And a richer man than I
> And they put him in an oven
> Just as if he were a pie.

I am afraid that putting him in an oven was the best we could manage. We took him to the crematorium after Father Brendan had said a Requiem Mass.

Bob Forgan wrote to Anne:

> Perhaps you don't know that some months ago John wrote asking my advice, and from his letter I was certain that – short of a miracle – his time on earth was nearly over. Should I have told him so? He wished to save you worry, and his question was whether he should seek (and act on) orthodox advice...
>
> Of course he depended on you in so many ways; and he talked of you a lot on the occasions when he and I met for lunch – three times, I think, in the last six years.

It was still Anne, not John, who held Forgan's loyalty. "I'm sorry I lost touch with him", Forgan wrote to Colin Holmes. "His wife Anne was my secretary and I regret losing touch with her even more."

26
LEGACY OF A JEWISH ANTI-SEMITE

After John Beckett's death the far right continued its unlovely progress, showing a growing tendency to split into ever tinier fragments.

Two years after he died, in 1966, Mosley returned to England from his home in France to contest a by-election in Shoreditch, but lost his deposit. John would have loved his explanation – it was exactly the same one that he gave when the BUF was humiliated in east London in 1937: he had done better than Hitler in his first election.

Mosley, writes Graham Macklin, "never faltered in his belief that he was a man of destiny, even if it was increasingly obvious to all and sundry that his time had passed".

Robert Skidelsky's 1975 biography, which seemed uncritically to accept Mosley's spin on events, provided temporary rehabilitation for the old monster, but Macklin writes that, especially when he had been drinking, his urbane and cultured veneer started to slip, his eyes flared and he was the fascist leader again, screaming hate. He died in 1980, aged 84.

In 1967, three years after John died, A.K. Chesterton merged the far right groups to form the National Front, becoming its first chairman. By then, new racial minorities, immigrants from Africa and Asia, had largely replaced Jews as the necessary fascist enemy.

Chesterton seems to have thought the merger would give his rather ridiculous League of Empire Loyalists a working-class base, writing to British National Party leader John Bean: "You also have, what we do not have to any extent, an appeal to the working classes, which seemed to us another good reason for a merger."

The LEL had sufficient respectability to be acceptable on the far right of the Conservative Party, especially as Chesterton had renounced fascism. Going in with the likes of Bean lost him that, and involved him in bitter internecine battles with people half his age. Doris Chesterton thought it was the worst mistake of his life, though I would argue that it has some strong competition. He died in 1973, aged 74, having, like the Bourbons in 1815, learned nothing and forgotten nothing.

Chesterton's new National Front was too moderate for Colin Jordan, who had co-founded the BNP with John Bean. Jordan was elected "world Führer" with American Nazi Lincoln Rockwell as his designated successor, and married Christian Dior's niece Francoise Dior in a blood-mingling ceremony, using an SS dagger to spill their blood over a copy of Hitler's *Mein Kampf*.

When he was 82, in 2005, Jordan became a kind of father figure to a new incarnation of John Beckett's British People's Party, this time avowedly pro-Nazi. Jordan died in 2009, and his new BPP outlived him by four years. Its Wikipedia entry made me jump: "it was largely dedicated to the legacies of British Nazis who pre-date the party, such as Arnold Leese, John Beckett and Colin Jordan". Is that the company that the shades of my entertaining, very human Jewish socialist father now keeps?

The year that A.K. Chesterton founded the National Front, 1967, the Jesuits closed Beaumont. It had outlived my father by three years. Today almost no one has heard of the Catholic Eton, but a few elderly men still gather every year at the East India and Public Schools Club, without their wives (for women are not admitted), to reminisce about the glory days when they rowed or boxed against Eton, and congratulate each other on the award of papal knighthoods.

That year, Clem Attlee died. He was John's best political mentor, and gave John his best job in politics. Did Attlee, I wonder, remember those evenings in Limehouse, talking politics and literature and compiling a full genealogy of the Forsytes?

Anne tried to pick up the wreckage of her life. Finding the coffers bare and with children to support, she went to work as secretary to a distinguished Harley Street psychiatrist, Dr William Sargent. Then she got a job as librarian at the crammers Davies Laing and Dick, and in 1976 she at last found a job in the theatre, as general secretary at London's Mermaid Theatre. The director, Bernard Miles, realised that she was a cut above the normal administrator and gave her play-scripts to read, and she wrote him brief but elegant summaries and appreciations of them.

She lived at Queensgate until the ten-year lease ran out in the early 1970s. She then begged the Commissioners for the Exhibition of 1851, who owned the freehold, not to evict her, but they had smelled money, and out she had to go. The London County Council rehoused her in a small flat in the East End and eventually she went to live with her sister Hilda in Wandsworth.

She stayed fiercely loyal to the man whose foolishness had caused her to waste her talents. I told her that I wanted to write about my father. She was pleased until I showed her a draft of an introduction. She told me angrily, "We don't wish to be apologised for", and I knew it could not be done in her lifetime. A young academic, Colin Holmes, was commissioned to write an entry for the *Dictionary for National Biography*. He interviewed her, and sent her his draft, and she wrote a long, hurt response, pages and pages of it, seeing attacks at the simplest statements. Why did Holmes make it sound as though the cottage in Chenies was ducal charity? she wanted to know – they paid three shillings and sixpence a week for it.

Her children found her increasingly hard work, and I am afraid she knew it. In the late 1980s, her last years were clouded with the onset of dementia. Though she was still fluent and graceful, she did not rec-ognise a photograph of her late husband when a doctor showed it to her. She died in 1989, aged 80, and I do not think she died happy.

For her youngest child, my sister Clare, who was 12 when her much loved father died, there were still two more eccentric changes of school.

Anne, who was heartily sick of the Catholic Church, took her out of More House, saying she could not afford it, which was perfectly true, although the nuns were signalling that they might be prepared to waive fees if Anne's husband had not left her enough money to pay them.

Anne thought that Clare could be taught at home by her mother and her two older brothers, believing that exam success was sufficient. Over the next two years Clare amassed an eccentric and not entirely useful clutch of examination passes. Finally, Anne got her daughter admitted to Godolphin and Latymer school in Hammersmith. Here the teachers concentrated on trying to provide her with qualifications that would give access to university should she ever want it.

Clare was 15, it was her eleventh change of school, and it was too late. All these worries had left Anne difficult and irrational, and one day when she was 16, Clare collected her wages from Saturday and evening work, took a train to Leeds, a city she had never visited before in her life, and never came back. It was, she now says nearly half a century later, not only the best decision she ever made, but the only one she could have made.

There she worked in cafés and factories for years, and eventually started to fill in the vast gaps in her education, to such good effect that she is now Dr Clare Beckett, senior lecturer in social policy at Bradford University.

Of all the deeply unpleasant people who populate this book – Mosley, Leese, A.K. Chesterton, W.E.D. Allen – the nastiest and creepiest is the one whose name my father never knew.

John knew there was someone there, watching and controlling him, and it helped make him mad. I have had the chance John never had to read some of Graham Mitchell's correspondence.

The slavering satisfaction at being able secretly to read another man's love letters; the malicious amusement when you falsely make him believe that one of his friends is spying on him; the pleasure at knowing that you can, without any risk to yourself, take another man's frail living from him, and the casual use of that power to make sure John never got out of the pit he had dug for himself; the delight in playing to the vanity of ministers to keep a man locked up; the love of being able to watch and manipulate his smallest activities; it is all there, in the secret memoranda of Graham Mitchell.

They are as revolting as anything I have ever read; and not a jot less so because the object of these attentions held and propagated deeply unpleasant opinions.

So I would love to have been able to tell my father the disaster that engulfed Graham Mitchell of MI5. John liked a laugh, especially at the expense of an enemy.

In the early 1960s Roger Hollis, the head of MI5, and his deputy, Graham Mitchell, were accused of being Soviet spies. One of them, it was alleged, was the "fifth man" who had protected the quartet of spies, Burgess, Maclean, Philby and Blunt. Suspicion of Mitchell was fed by the fact that he was known to have drafted the white paper which mendaciously whitewashed MI5 after Burgess and Maclean's departure for Moscow.

The investigation lasted from 1961 to 1974 and came to no firm conclusion, but Mitchell was forced to take early retirement in 1963, aged only 58.

They were probably not Soviet spies, any more than John Beckett was a traitor who talked of joining the Home Guard so that he could turn his guns on his own officers. But we will never know for certain, and a little suspicion, probably unjustified, will always linger over the name of Graham Mitchell. This strikes me as the nearest to justice we can get in this imperfect world.

For what it's worth, I don't think Mitchell was up to being a Soviet spy. Burgess, Maclean, Philby and Blunt lived on the edge every day, taking fearful risks in order to do something which, however perversely, they passionately believed in. Mitchell lived in a safe, sheltered world of bureaucracy and memoranda, first working for Conservative Central Office and spying for Neville Chamberlain, then for MI5. He sent others out to do the dirty work.

He lived for the secret power he wielded. He was the ultimate apparatchik. He was the sort of man who would benefit from communism, not the sort of man who fights for it. He died in 1982, aged 77.

A man like Mitchell needs a minister with a taste for the sort of power that does not sit well with democratic government and does not mind using it to pay off old scores, and Heaven sent him Herbert Morrison. Lord Morrison of Lambeth died the year after John, in 1965, aged 77.

Grubby though the politicians and spies were, they were right to lock John up in 1940.

He argued that habeus corpus – the right not to be locked up in secret and without trial – is a key guarantee of our liberty. He protested that his only crime was to say what he believed and advocate policies he thought were right; and if we cannot do that with impunity, we are not free.

He was right about that. But in the summer of 1940 Britain was in hourly danger of invasion; and if Hitler had launched a successful invasion, we would have said goodbye to all our liberties. A plot to send messages to our enemies had been uncovered, albeit a disastrously amateurish one which John had nothing to do with. If ever there was a moment when it could be right to suspend our liberties, that was the moment.

So if I had been Home Secretary in the summer of 1940, I too would have rounded up the Oswald Mosleys, John Becketts, Maule Ramsays, Barry Domviles, Ben Greenes and the rest of them, and put them where they could do no harm.

I would go further than the government did. Their titles would not protect the Marquis of Tavistock and Lord Lymington, and Mosley would share the privations of his followers.

I would do this even though I believe detention without trial is, as Winston Churchill himself said later in the war, "in the highest degree odious". But I would do it with the proviso that normal liberties should be resumed as soon as possible.

And by early 1941 things were very different. The invasion hadn't happened; the blitz had failed to bring Britain to her knees; and it was perfectly clear that there wasn't a fifth column.

What the security services' papers show, unmistakably, is that by then a few key people had acquired a taste for unaccountable power over people's lives.

Men like Graham Mitchell and Herbert Morrison grew to enjoy that power, and to use it long after the justification for it had disappeared; they were still enjoying it well after the war had finished, preventing travel abroad and keeping people under what amounted to house arrest, and quietly scuppering their chances of getting work.

John Beckett wasn't a traitor, or a fifth columnist. He was an anti-Semite, but he was not kept locked up for that, for the very good reason that, if anti-Semitism had been an offence in 1942, the prisons would have overflowed with many of the greatest in the land.

I have heard it argued that since these men were fascists, and their friends in Germany were doing incomparably worse things than what was being done to them, it hardly matters how they were treated. But once you accept that argument, you say goodbye to your liberties. When Tony Blair's government invaded Iraq and I was among the million people who demonstrated against the war, government ministers told us insinuatingly that we would not be allowed to demonstrate in Saddam Hussein's Iraq – as though somehow that meant we should not demonstrate here. "Go back to Russia" was what really stupid people shouted at the Aldermaston marchers in the 1950s.

When Rose Cohen was in Moscow in the 1930s, in danger of arrest and execution on suspicion of being a Trotskyite, the Foreign Office could not be bothered to make more than a token effort for her, because she was a communist. "We always knew of course that she was a thoroughly undesirable person", minuted one official. "Her case was only taken up with the Soviet government ... despite her undesirability." The *Daily Sketch* gloated: "A woman who was an apostle of this anti-democratic creed must now rely upon the protests of a 'capitalist' state." It was not much to rely on: the Soviet Union executed Cohen.

There will always be an enemy who behaves worse than us.

Everyone whose parents are dead thinks wistfully of conversations they wish they had had. I do this more than most, because of the sort of lives my parents led, because I was only 19 when my father died and because he told me so much about his life when I was too young to understand.

But if there was one conversation I want to have with him more than any other, it's the one that begins with me looking him in the eye and saying: "You're a Jew, aren't you?"

What would he say? I think he would be amused and perhaps relieved that he had been found out, and he might say: "Don't tell your mother." Because I think it is possible that Anne didn't know, and she had suffered far too much for an anti-Semitism she didn't share.

Then he would tell me that he was never an anti-Semite; he just disliked financial power, and Jews exercise a lot of it. He had nothing against the ordinary Jewish man or woman in the East End of London, he would tell me.

It would not be a conscious lie. He was the least self-aware of men, and could persuade himself of the most unlikely things. He was clever but intellectually lazy. "The study of human nature," he wrote, "is an evil drug which brings much unnecessary unhappiness. 80 per cent of people are slightly varying replicas of types one knows by heart; but in the other 20 per cent there is incalculable interest, repulsiveness or charm."

Then I think he'd tell me that that the Jews and the communists attacked him, so he attacked them back. And somewhere along the road, I think he'd tell me that the point came where he might as well be hanged for a sheep as a lamb.

So what's the truth? Here's the best I can do.

His father William was an active Conservative in the glory days of empire, and named his second son, born in 1899, Cecil Rhodes Beckett; so William's views on racial matters are pretty clear. His mother was a Jew, declared dead by her family for marrying out.

Children absorb ideas from their parents by a sort of osmosis, and often those ideas are more fiercely felt and more simplistic than their parents intended. I know this because I grew up certain, in some way that I cannot now pin down, that the Jews falsely pretended they had been persecuted in Nazi Germany.

John's childhood home contained the instinctive racism of his flag-waving father, chairman of the election committee for his local Conservative MP. It also contained his mother, whose relatives he never saw, and at some stage in his childhood he learned why. My guess is that he learned it quite early.

His father disliked Jews; his mother had been cruelly abandoned by her Jewish family. The little boy, his head filled with G.A. Henty's clean-cut Englishmen saving the world and defeating Johnny Foreigner, would have thought proudly that he knew where he stood, and what he would fight for.

My education helped me to discard some of the rubbish in my head. Great teachers like Dr Warren and, later, the philosopher Professor Anthony Flew taught me to think. My father didn't have that chance. His education finished abruptly and unexpectedly at 14, apart from some training at evening classes.

After the First World War John thought his mind was cleared of the detritus of childhood. But racism is adaptable. It can attach itself to right-wing opinions, and to left-wing ones too. The hard-faced men who did well out of the war existed, and some of them, like Sir Alfred Mond, were Jewish. John tried to nail Mond; he failed. H.H. Beamish tried too, and he failed far more spectacularly. Nick Toczek argues convincingly that John must already have known the obsessive anti-Semite Beamish, probably quite well.

All the same, in the mid 1920s I do not think John Beckett was noticeably more anti-Semitic than many other socialists of the time. His mother's Jewishness was not yet a dark secret, though I don't suppose he talked of it much. I imagine his friends Attlee, Dalton and Maxton did not know about her.

Fenner Brockway told me exactly what John was then: a rebel, without a thought-out political philosophy but outraged by poverty. He was instinctively uneasy if he found himself, by some mischance, swimming with the current. I know this feeling: I have it too.

Then came Labour's 1929–31 government. Its failure filled him with such blind rage that he could not see clearly. I can see how that could happen. I had far less invested in politics than he did, but I felt growing anger in the Blair years. Tony Blair, I think, was Ramsay Macdonald on steroids. I recognise the rage I felt: I read about it in my father's unpublished autobiography written in 1938. The far right often benefits when the left is perceived to have failed.

John's personal and professional life disintegrated in the early 1930s, and I think it was then that he completely lost the plot. He went to Mosley partly because he needed paid work fast. Within weeks of his arrival, the BUF became formally anti-Semitic. John was told that the Jews had attacked the fascists first. It wasn't true, but he wanted to believe it, and he was very, very good at believing things he wanted to believe.

I think that then he absorbed the anti-Semitism around him, and grafted it on to the anti-Semitism within him.

Because he had never taken the trouble to think through his politics, he seems to have thought he could call himself a fascist and still make jokes at the expense of the Leader. Under a fascist government, he would have been the first to be executed.

And that, I think, is why, despite everything, those of his old socialist friends whom I could talk to – Fenner Brockway, the members of the Peckham Labour Party – spoke of him with a sort of puzzled, wistful affection; but for the old BUF people, he had betrayed the Leader, and there could be no forgiveness.

When he left Mosley, he could either get out of politics – perhaps look for work in journalism, which he had a talent for – or move into the obsessively anti-Semitic laager in which even Mosley was not sufficiently extreme. The latter was easier.

He emerged from prison in 1943 far more anti-Semitic than he had been in 1940, partly because he spent his time there with people like Arnold Leese, and partly because his impotent rage at what was being done to him left him just a little mad.

Shami Chakrabati, when she resigned as director of Liberty in January 2016, told a BBC interviewer: "When you lock people up without trial … whether it is in Belmarsh or Guantanamo Bay, you recruit more terrorists than you contain." What is true of terrorists is also true of fascists, racists and anti-Semites.

John was proud of holding himself together in prison when others went to pieces, but this came at the cost of internalising rage, bitterness and loneliness. These, I think, stayed with him during the years after the war when he knew they were watching him. He may have been paranoid, but he was also persecuted.

That is why I think the man I knew was a shadow of the man Clem Attlee knew. He was noisy and entertaining, he could tell a good anecdote. But there was something strange about him. He talked to himself a lot. He told small, unnecessary lies over trivial matters. There was a void where a faith had once been, and the Catholic Church could not quite fill it. Just sometimes, he would say something about a race – about Jews, or about black people – so gross and offensive that, even in the 1950s, it made me start and stare.

After the Duke of Bedford died in 1952, John was desperate to sustain the standard of living the duke had subsidised. He no longer cared what he did, or whom he worked with. Did he ever ask himself why Colonel Ulius Louis Amoss of Maryland wanted political gossip from London? Perhaps he knew, but didn't care. All that mattered was that Amoss was, or seemed to be, willing to pay for it.

Everything he said contradicted everything he was. A Jew who denounced Jews, a socialist who denounced socialists, a working-class champion with snobbish disdain for the working class, an opponent of the "money power" who spent the last 20 years of his life looking for moneyed patrons and admiring wealth. He had forgotten who he was.

The phrase "self-hating Jew" is often dreadfully misused, but I think somewhere inside him John must have been full of self-loathing. He knew he had damaged those he cared about most, and Anne, whom he loved most, he damaged most.

My father seemed to me as a small child to be a rock. In fact he was not reliable or truthful or sensible, but he was talented and loveable and passionate and larger than life and humorous, with a sort of honesty at his core, and though he is identified with hate, he was capable of more love than he knew how to handle.

Notes on sources

Ideology of Obsession: A.K. Chesterton and British Fascism by David Baker (I.B. Tauris, 1996).

Stalin's British Victims (for Rose Cohen's story) by Francis Beckett (Sutton, 2004).

Very Deeply Dyed in Black by Graham Macklin (I.B. Tauris, 2007).

White Racial Nationalism in Britain by Graham Macklin (Routledge, 2017).

FOR FURTHER READING

On fascism and the fascists

Baker, D. *Ideology of Obsession: A.K. Chesterton and British Fascism* (London: I.B. Tauris, 1996).

Beckman, M. *The 43 Group: Battling with Mosley's Blackshirts* (London: Centerprise, 1993).

Clough, B. *State Secrets: The Kent Wolkoff Affair* (Hove: Hideaway Publications, 2005).

Cole, J.A. *Lord Haw-Haw: The Full Story of William Joyce* (London: Faber & Faber, 1987).

Cross, C. *The Fascists in Britain* (London: Barrie & Rockliffe, 1961).

Crowson, N.J. ed. *Fleet Street, Press Barons and Politics: The Journals of Collin Brooks 1932–40* (Cambridge: Cambridge University Press, 1998).

Day, P. *Franco's Friends* (London: Biteback, 2011).

Dorril, S. *Blackshirt: Sir Oswald Mosley and British Fascism* (London: Viking, 2006).

Griffiths, R. *Patriotism Perverted* (London: Constable, 1998).

Griffiths, R. *What Did You Do During the War? The Last Throes of the British Pro-Nazi Right 1940–45* (Abingdon: Routledge, forthcoming 2017).

Grundy, T. *Memoir of a Fascist Childhood* (London: Heinemann, 1998).

Hodgson, K. *Fighting Fascism: The British Left and the Rise of Fascism, 1919–39* (Manchester: Manchester University Press, 2010).

Holmes, C. *Anti-Semitism in British Society 1876–1939* (London: Edward Arnold, 1979; republished Abingdon: Routledge, 2015).

Holmes, C. *Searching for Lord Haw-Haw: The Political Lives of William Joyce* (Abingdon: Routledge, forthcoming 2016).

Kenny, M. *Germany Calling: A Personal Biography of William Joyce, "Lord Haw-Haw"* (Dublin: New Island, 2003).

Lewis, J. *Shades of Greene* (London: Jonathan Cape, 2010).

Linehan, T.P. *East London for Mosley: The British Union of Fascists in East London and South West Essex* (London: Frank Cass, 1996).

Macklin, G. *Very Deeply Dyed in Black: Sir Oswald Mosley and the Postwar Reconstruction of British Fascism* (London: I.B. Tauris, 2007).

Macklin, G. *White Racial Nationalism in Britain* (Abingdon: Routledge, forthcoming 2017).

Mosley, N. *Beyond the Pale* (London: Secker & Warburg, 1983).

Mosley, N. *Time at War* (London: Orion, 2006).

Pugh, M. *"Hurrah for the Blackshirts!" Fascists and Fascism in England between the Wars* (London: Jonathan Cape, 2005).

Simpson, A.W.B. *In the Highest Degree Odious: Detention without Trial in Wartime Britain* (Oxford: Oxford University Press, 1994).

Skidelsky, R. *Oswald Mosley* (London: Papermac, 1975).

Thurlow, R. *Fascism in Britain: A History 1918–1985* (Oxford: Blackwell, 1998).

Tilles, D. *British Fascist Anti-Semitism and Jewish Responses 1932–40* (London: Bloomsbury, 2015).

Toczek, N. *Haters, Baiters and Would-be Dictators: Anti-Semitism and the UK Far Right* (Abingdon: Routledge, 2016).

Todd, N. *In Excited Times: The People Against The Blackshirts* (Newcastle: Bewick Press, 1995).

On socialism and socialists

Attlee, C. *As It Happened* (London: Heinemann, 1954).

Beckett, F. *Enemy Within: The Rise and Fall of the British Communist Party* (London: John Murray, 1998).

Beckett, F. *Stalin's British Victims: The Story of Rosa Rust* (Stroud: Sutton, 2004; republished Abingdon: Routledge, 2015).

Beckett, F. *Clem Attlee* (London: Haus, 2015).

Brockway, F. *Towards Tomorrow* (London: Hart-Davis MacGibbon, 1977).

Brown, G. *James Maxton* (Edinburgh: Mainstream, 1986).

Dalton, H. *Call Back Yesterday* (London: Frederick Muller, 1953).

Dalton, H. and Pimlott, B. eds. *The Political Diary, 1918–40, 1945–60* (London: Jonathan Cape, 1987).

Howell. D. *A Lost Left: Three Studies in Socialism and Nationalism* (Manchester: Manchester University Press, 1986).

Hyde, D. *I Believed: The Autobiography of a Former British Communist* (London: Heinemann, 1952).

McGovern, J. *Neither Fear nor Favour* (London: Blandford, 1960).

Marquand, D. *Ramsay MacDonald* (London: Jonathan Cape, 1977).

Perkins, A. *A Very British Strike* (Basingstoke: Macmillan, 2006).

Pimlott, B. *Hugh Dalton: A Life* (London: Harper Collins, 1995).

Scanlon, J. *The Decline and Fall of the Labour Party* (London: Peter Davies, 1932).

Skidelsky, R. *Politicians and the Slump* (London: Papermac, 1994).

Vernon, B. *Ellen Wilkinson: A Biography* (London: Croom Helm, 1982).

Webb, B. and Mackenzie, J. ed. *The Diaries of Beatrice Webb* (London: Virago, 2002).

Wheen, F. *Tom Driberg: His Life and Indiscretions* (London: Pan, 1992).

On spies and spying

Dorril, S. *MI6: Fifty Years of Special Operations* (London: Fourth Estate, 2000).

Lownie, A. *Stalin's Englishman: The Lives of Guy Burgess* (London: Hodder, 2015).

On actors and the theatre

Kenshaw, B. ed. *The Cambridge History of British Theatre Volume 3* (Cambridge: Cambridge University Press, 2015).

Merkin, R. "The Theatre of the Organised Working Class" (Unpublished PhD Thesis, University of Warwick, 1993).

Tanitch, R. *The London Stage in the Twentieth Century* (London: Haus, 2007).

INDEX

941·082 BEC.